HAL•LEONARD ESSENTIAL

FOR ORGANS, PIANOS & ELECTRONIC KEYBOARDS

E-Z PLAY® TODAY

53

The 1970s

ISBN 0-634-09242-1

HAL•LEONARD® CORPORATION

7777 W. BLUEMOUND RD. P.O. BOX 13819 MILWAUKEE, WI 53213

Visit Hal Leonard Online at
www.halleonard.com

CONTENTS

ABC

Registration 8
Rhythm: Rock or 8 Beat

Words and Music by Alphonso Mizell, Frederick Perren,
Deke Richards and Berry Gordy

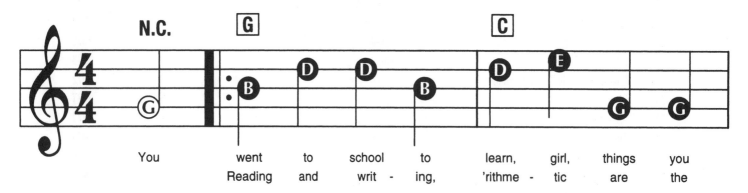

You went to school to learn, girl, things you
Reading and writ - ing, 'rithme - tic are the

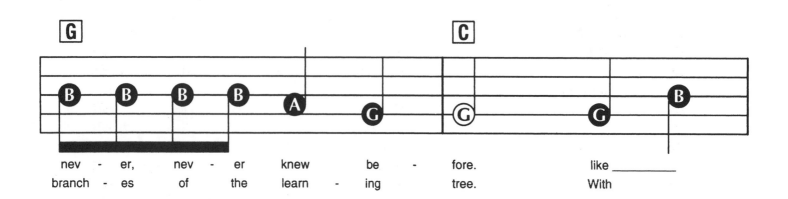

nev - er, nev - er knew be - fore. like _____
branch - es of the learn - ing tree. With

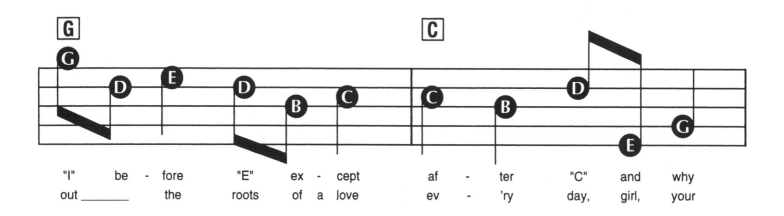

"I" be - fore "E" ex - cept af - ter "C" and why
out _____ the roots of a love ev - 'ry day, girl, why your

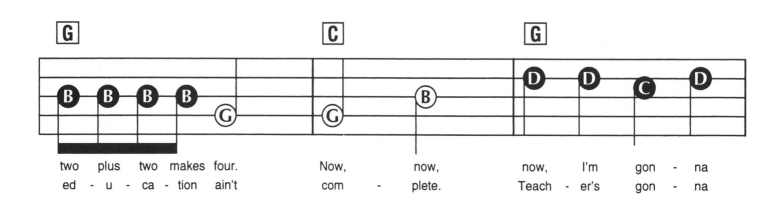

two plus two makes four. Now, now, now, I'm gon - na
ed - u - ca - tion ain't com - plete. Teach - er's gon - na

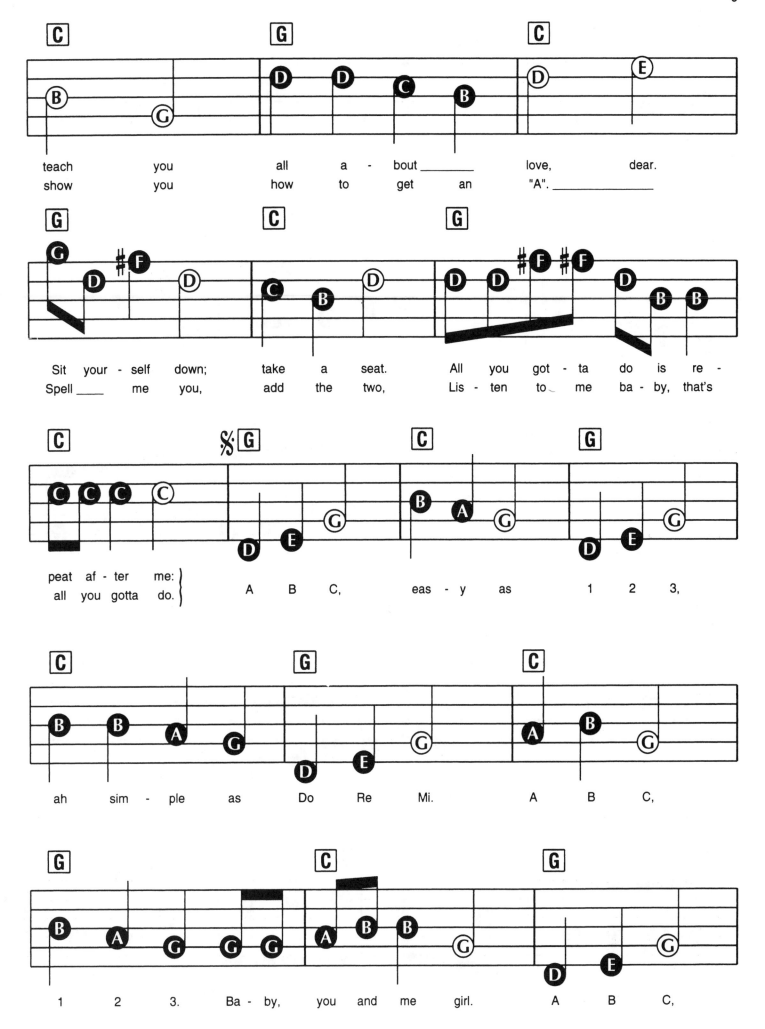

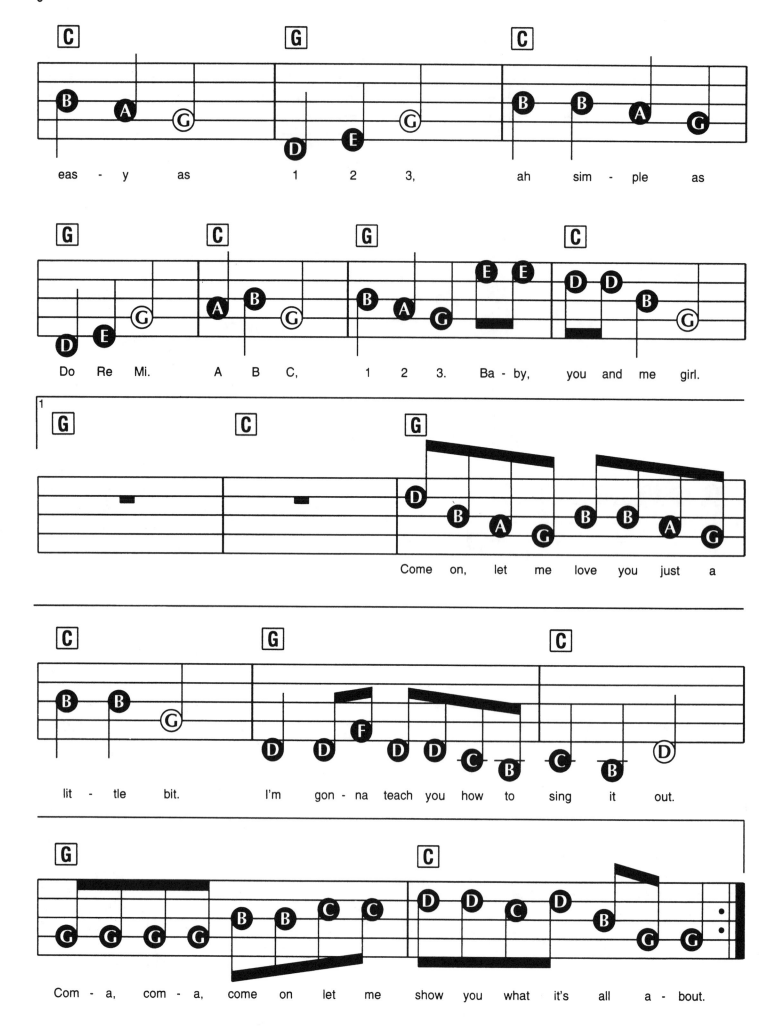

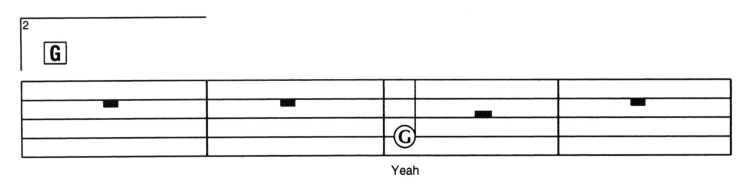

Yeah

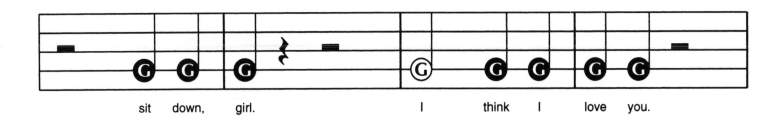

sit down, girl. I think I love you.

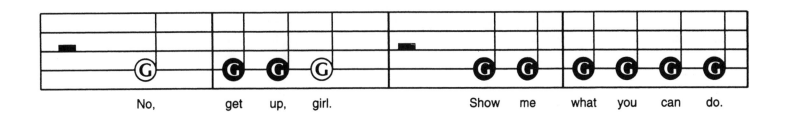

No, get up, girl. Show me what you can do.

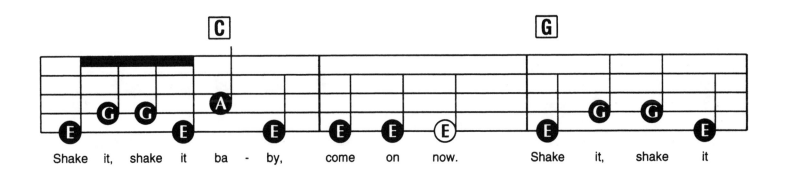

Shake it, shake it ba - by, come on now. Shake it, shake it

D.S. and Fade
(Return to 𝄋
and Fade)

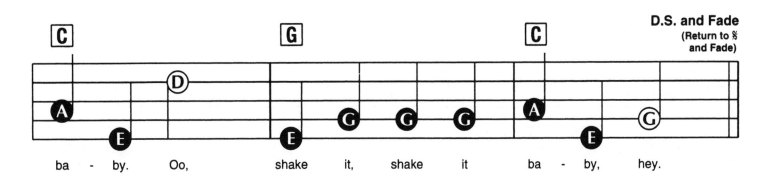

ba - by. Oo, shake it, shake it ba - by, hey.

Afternoon Delight

Registration 1
Rhythm: Rock or 8 beat

Words and Music by
Bill Danoff

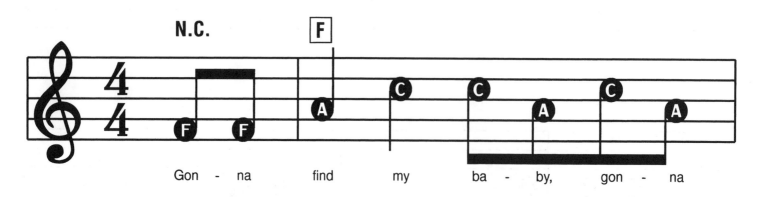

Gon - na   find   my   ba - by,   gon - na

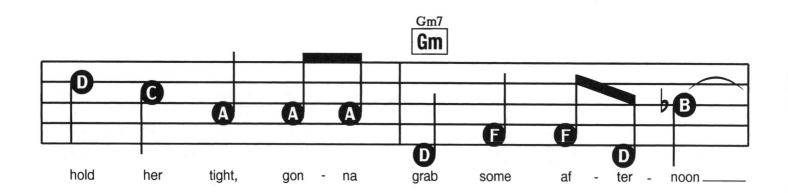

hold   her   tight,   gon - na   grab   some   af - ter - noon _____

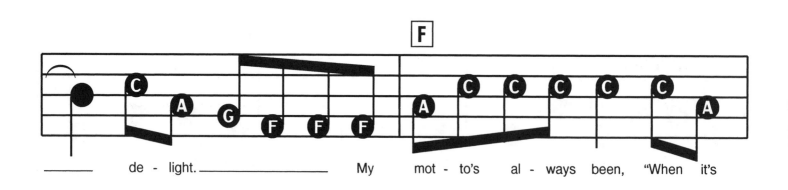

_____   de - light. _____   My   mot - to's   al - ways   been,   "When   it's

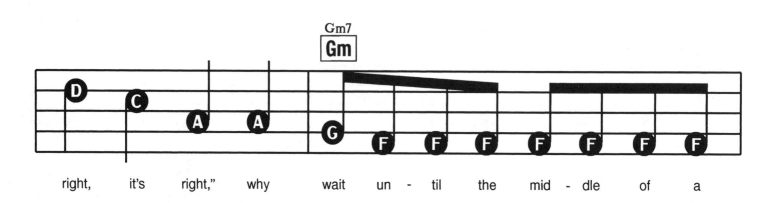

right,   it's   right,"   why   wait   un - til   the   mid - dle   of   a

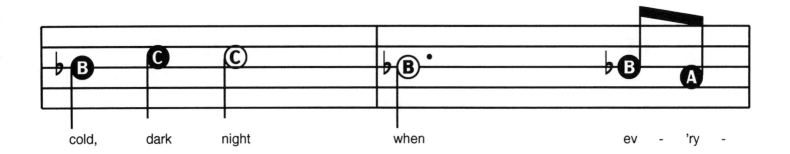

cold,   dark   night   when   ev - 'ry -

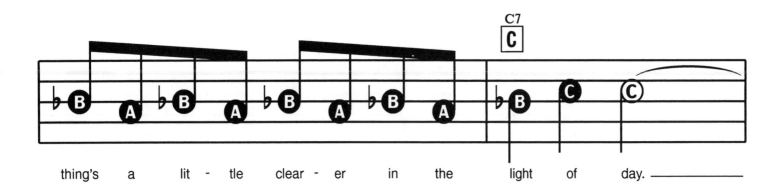

thing's   a   lit - tle   clear - er   in   the   light   of   day. _____

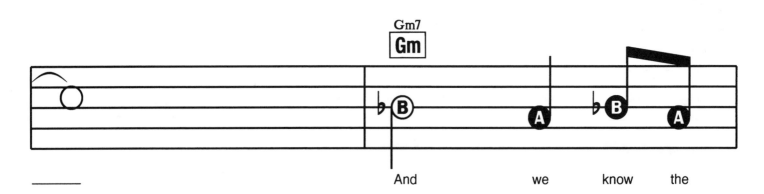

_____   And   we   know   the

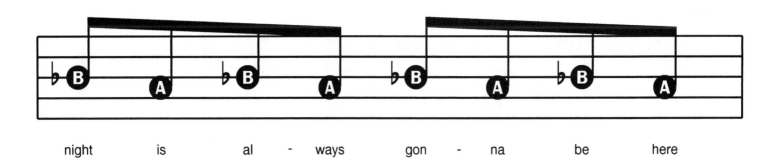

night   is   al - ways   gon - na   be   here

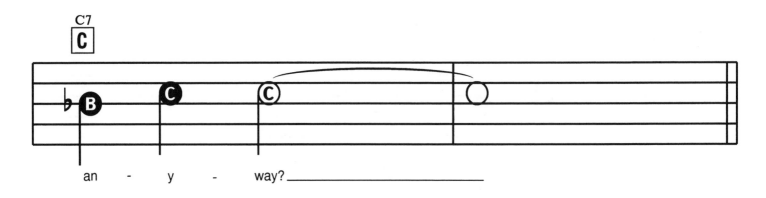

an - y - way? _____

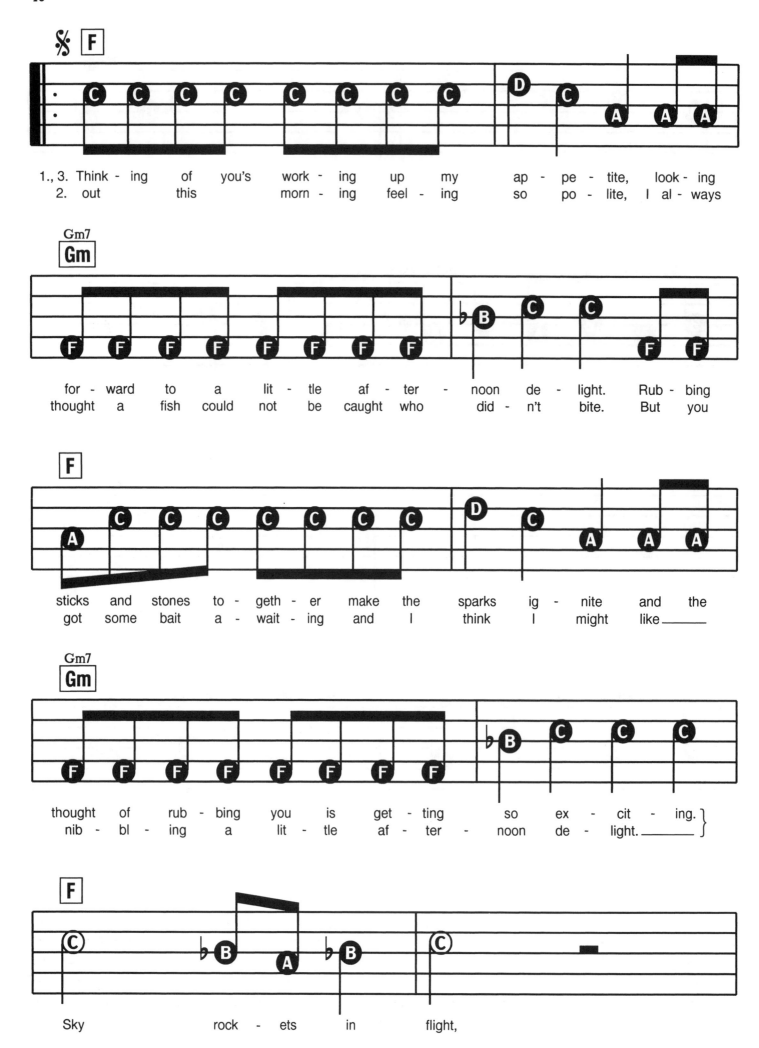

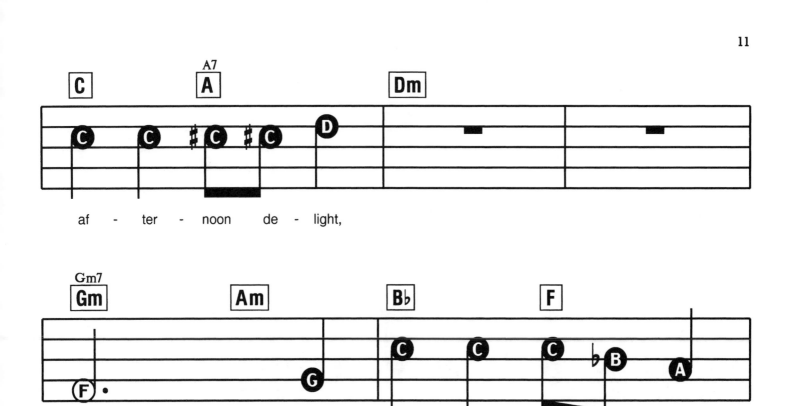

af - ter - noon de - light,

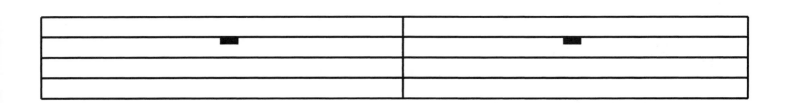

af - ter - noon de - light,

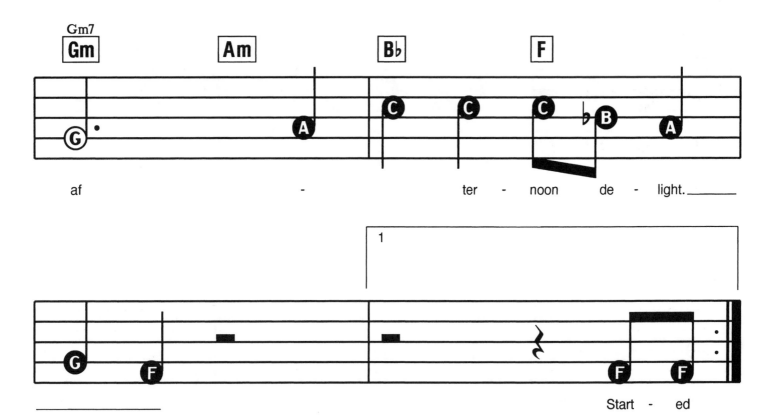

af - ter - noon de - light.____

Start - ed

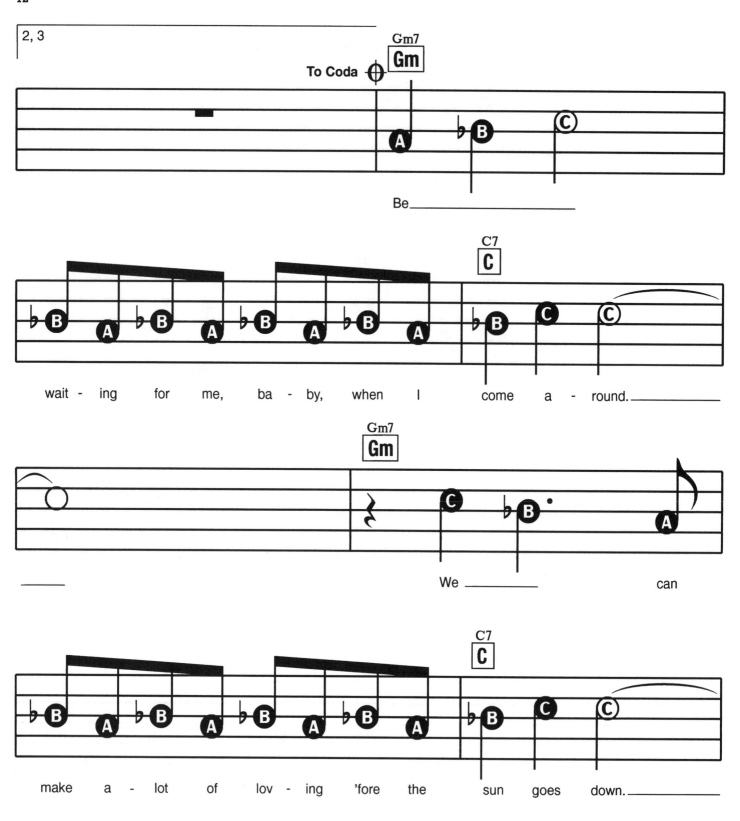

2, 3

To Coda ⊕ | **Gm** Gm7

Be

waiting for me, baby, when I come a-round.

We can

make a lot of loving 'fore the sun goes down.

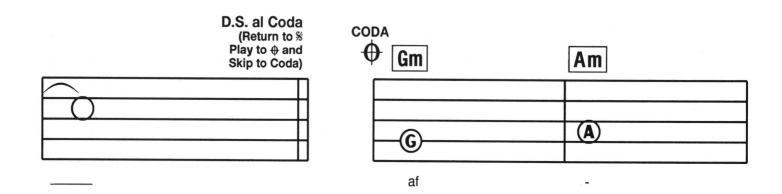

D.S. al Coda
(Return to %
Play to ⊕ and
Skip to Coda)

CODA

⊕ | **Gm** | **Am**

af -

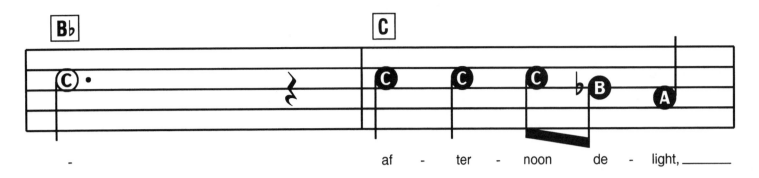

af - ter - noon de - light, _____

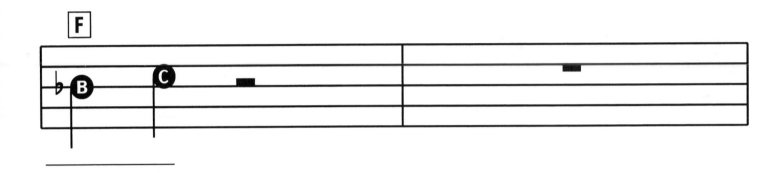

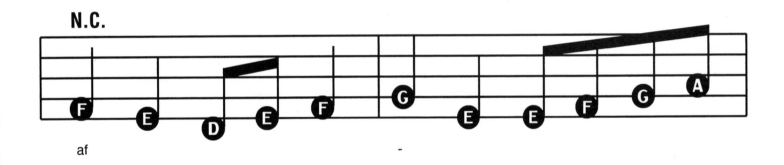

af

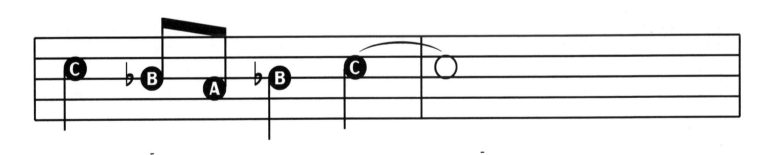

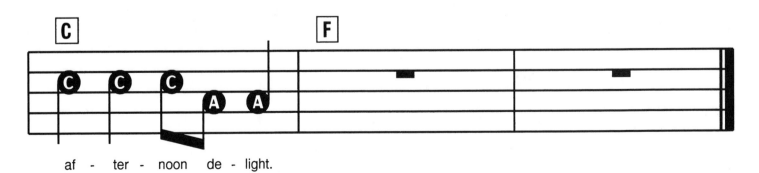

af - ter - noon de - light.

The Air That I Breathe

Registration 2
Rhythm: Rock

Words and Music by Albert Hammond
and Michael Hazelwood

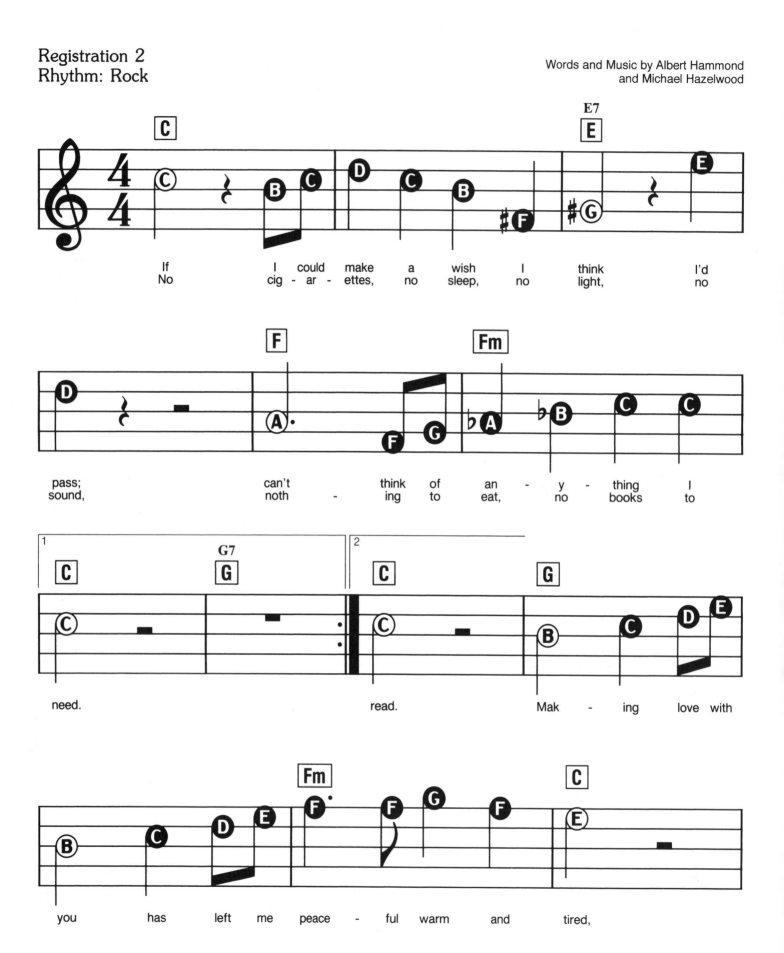

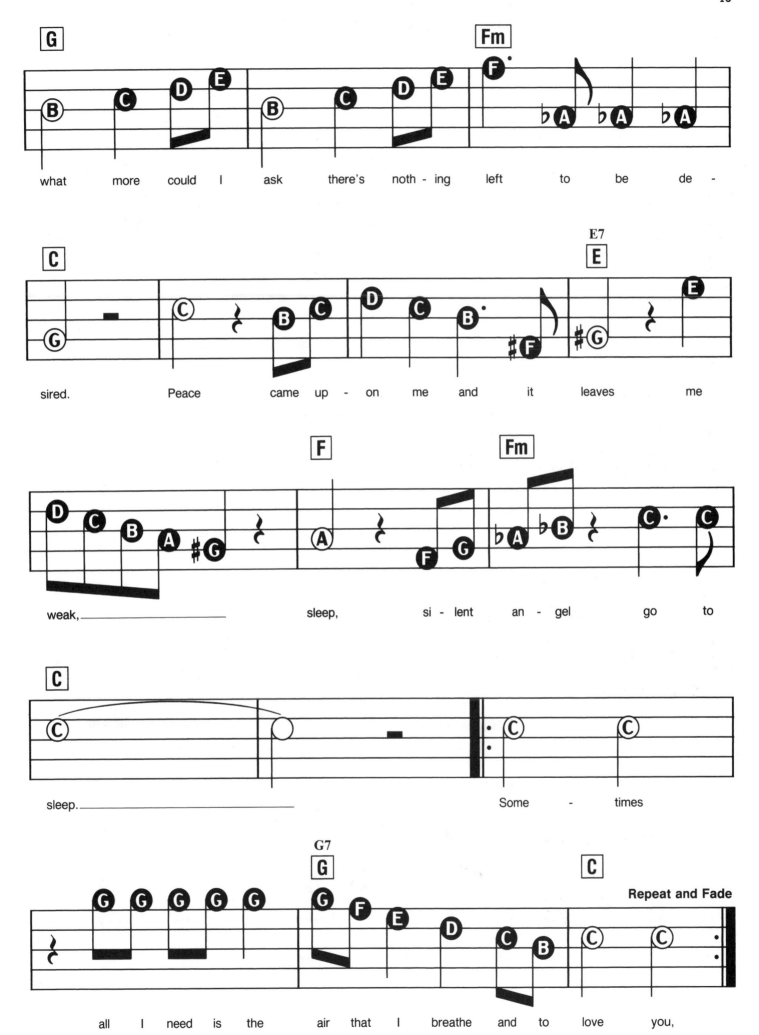

American Pie

Registration 2
Rhythm: Rock

Words and Music by
Don McLean

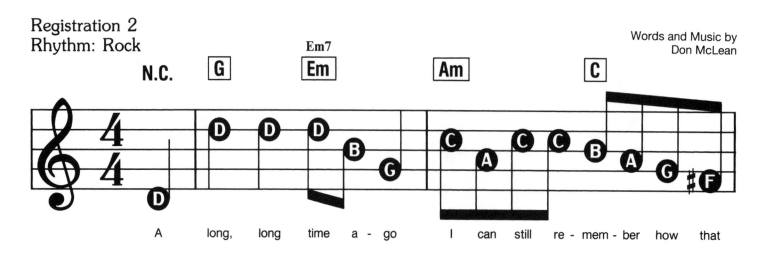

A long, long time a-go I can still re-mem-ber how that

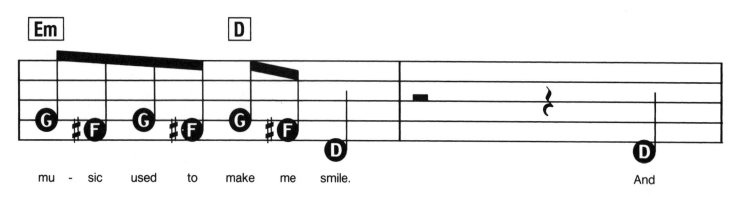

mu - sic used to make me smile. And

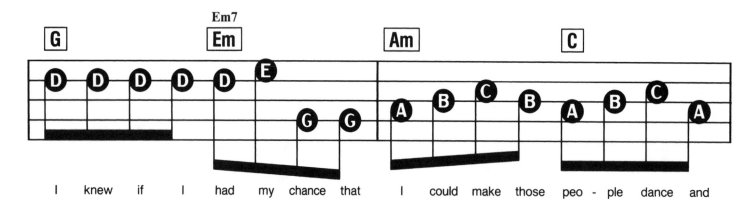

I knew if I had my chance that I could make those peo - ple dance and

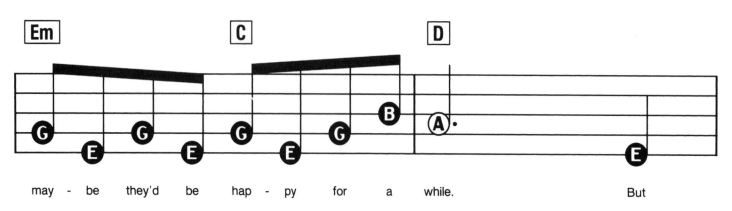

may - be they'd be hap - py for a while. But

17

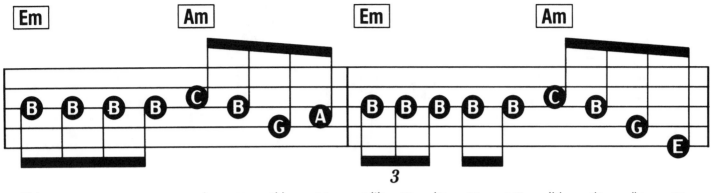

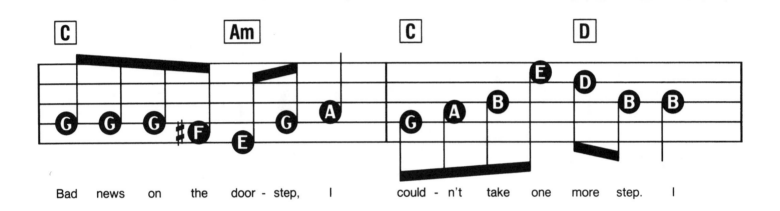

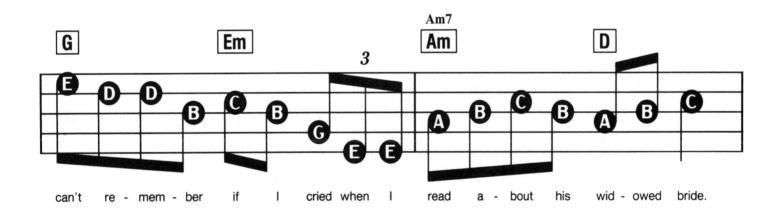

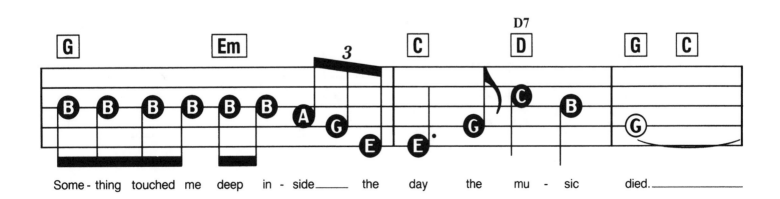

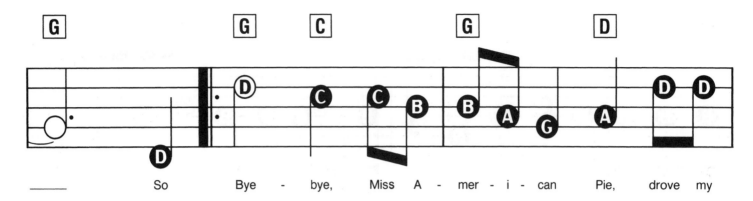

So Bye - bye, Miss A - mer - i - can Pie, drove my

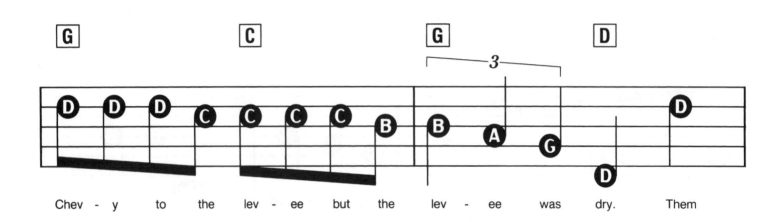

Chev - y to the lev - ee but the lev - ee was dry. Them

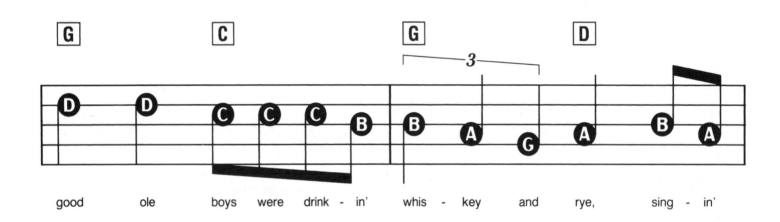

good ole boys were drink - in' whis - key and rye, sing - in'

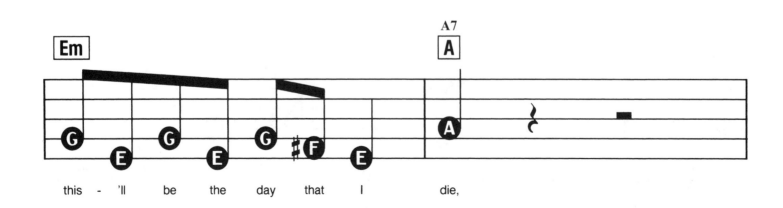

this - 'll be the day that I die,

19

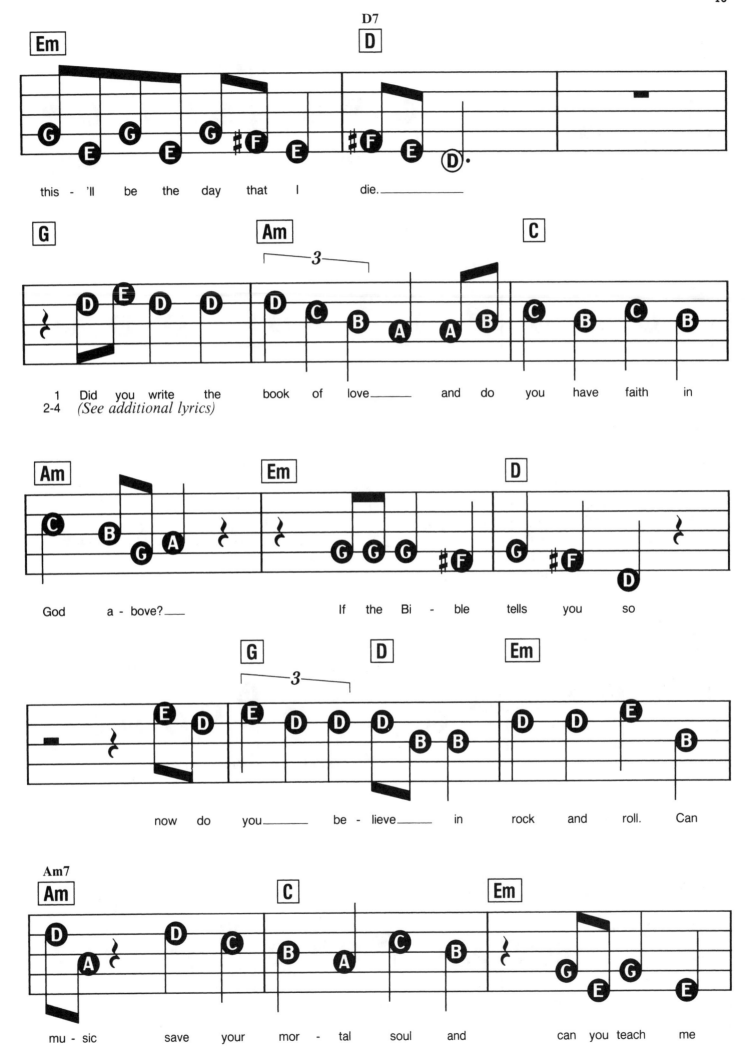

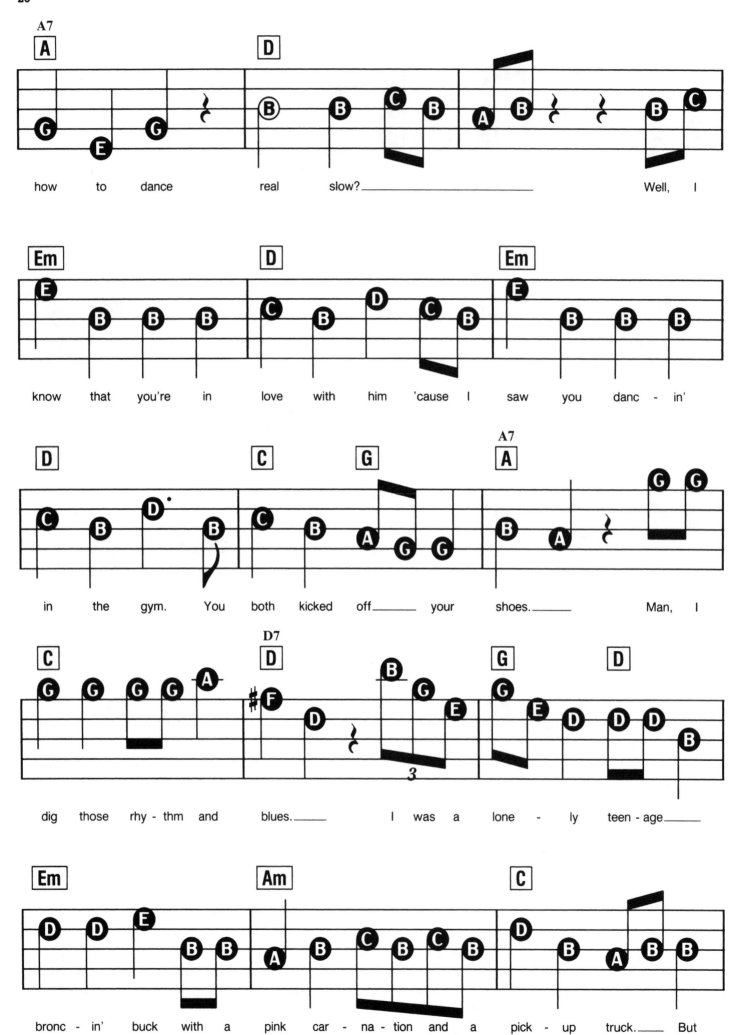

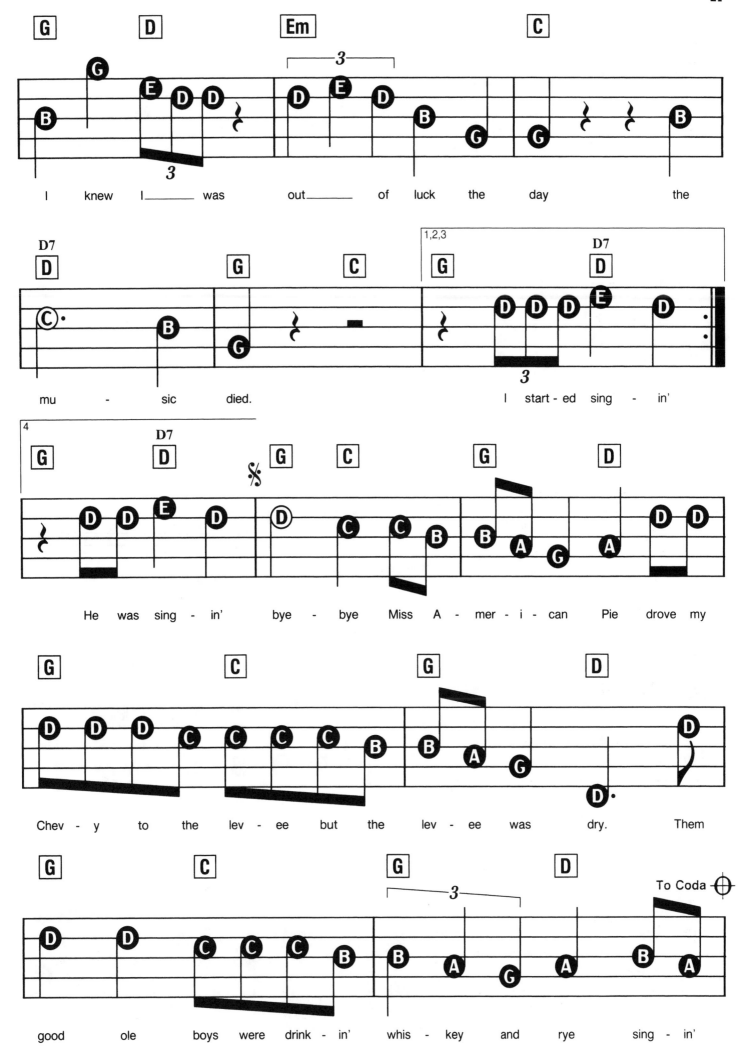

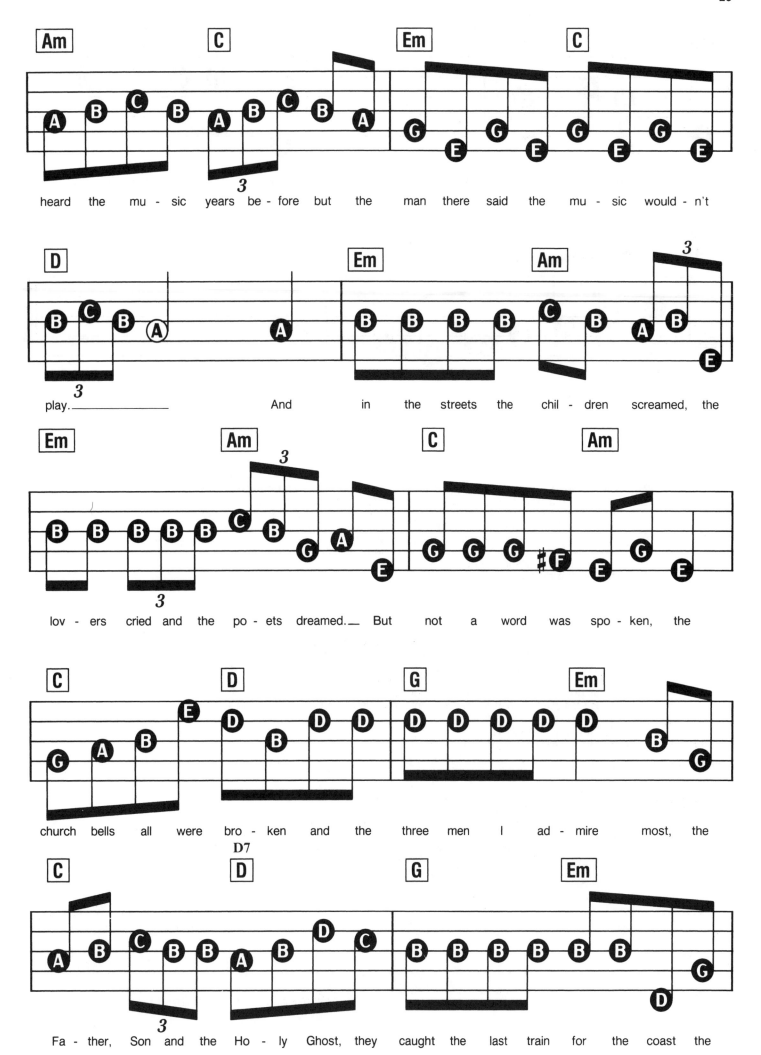

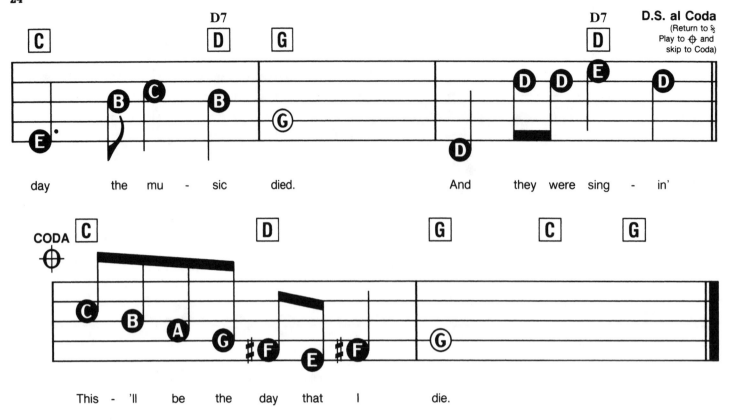

day   the mu - sic died.   And   they were sing - in'

This - 'll   be   the   day   that   I   die.

Additional Lyrics

2.   Now for ten years we've been on our own, and moss grows fat on a rollin' stone
      But that's not how it used to be when the jester sang for the king and queen
      In a coat he borrowed from James Dean and a voice that came from you and me
      Oh and while the king was looking down, the jester stole his thorny crown
      The courtroom was adjourned, no verdict was returned
      And while Lenin read a book on Marx the quartet practiced in the park
      And we sang dirges in the dark
      The day the music died
      We were singin'. . . bye-bye. . .,etc.

3.   Helter-skelter in the summer swelter the birds flew off with a fallout shelter
      Eight miles high and fallin' fast, it landed foul on the grass
      The players tried for a forward pass, with the jester on the sidelines in a cast
      Now the half-time air was sweet perfume while the sergeants played a marching tune
      We all got up to dance but we never got the chance
      'Cause the players tried to take the field, the marching band refused to yield
      Do you recall what was revealed
      The day the music died
      We started singin'. . . bye-bye. . .,etc.

4.   And there we were all in one place, a generation lost in space
      With no time left to start again
      So come on, Jack be nimble, Jack be quick, Jack Flash sat on a candlestick
      'Cause fire is the devil's only friend
      And as I watched him on the stage my hands were clenched in fists of rage
      No angel born in hell could break that Satan's spell
      And as the flames climbed high into the night to light the sacrificial rite
      I saw Satan laughing with delight the day the music died.
      He was singin'. . . bye-bye. . .,etc.

Baby, I Love Your Way

Registration 8
Rhythm: Rock or 4/4 Ballad

Words and Music by
Peter Frampton

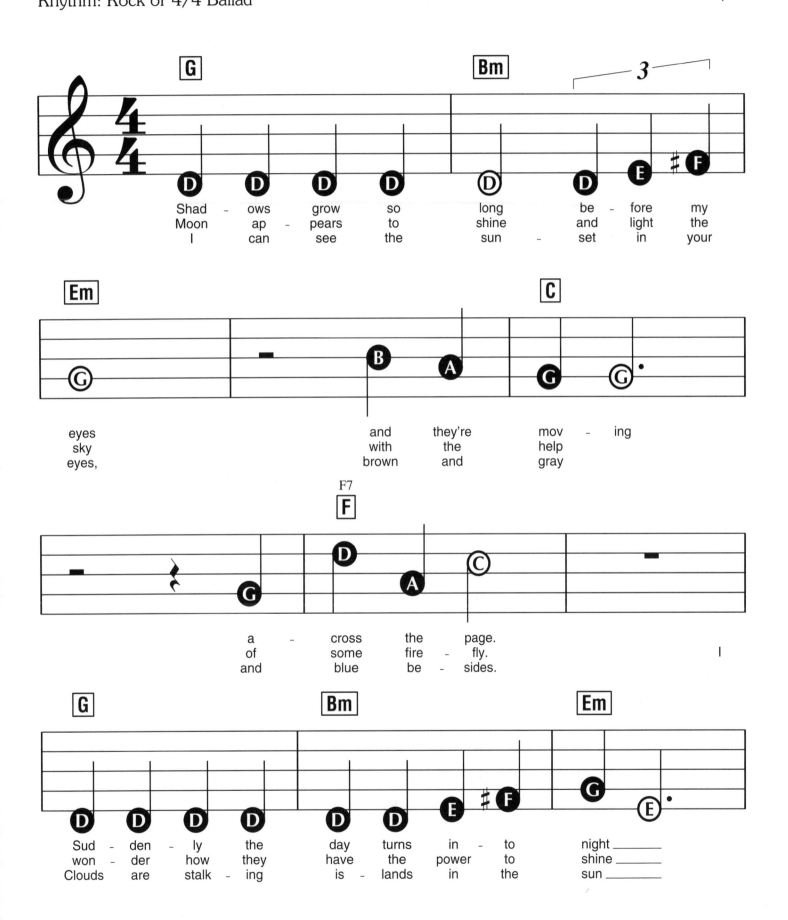

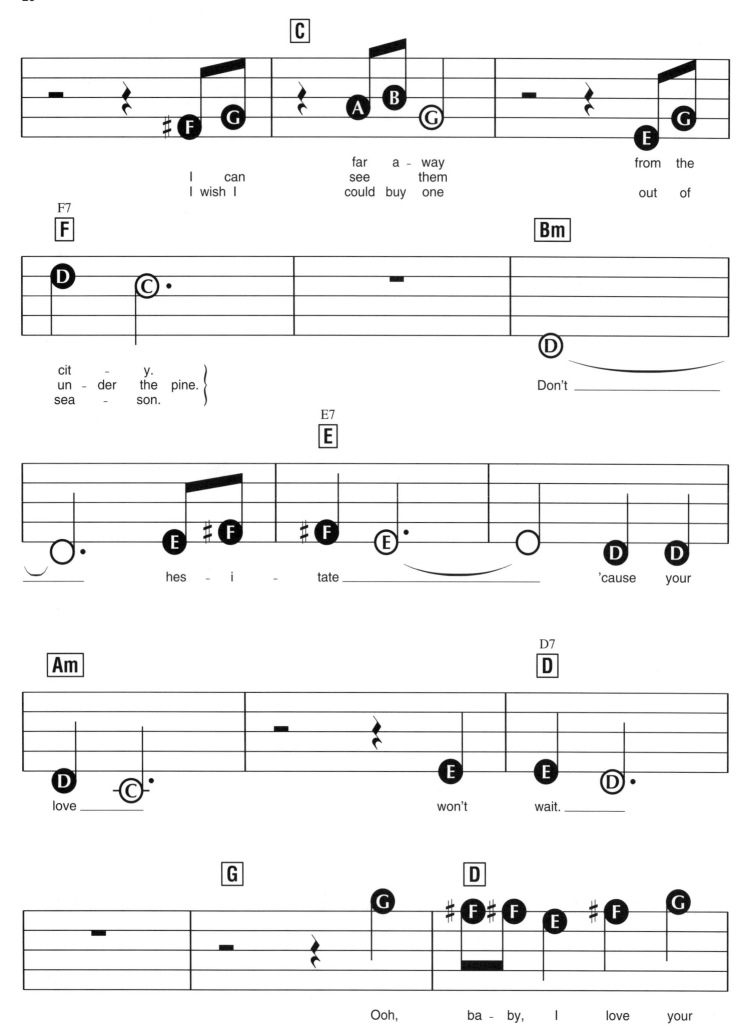

27

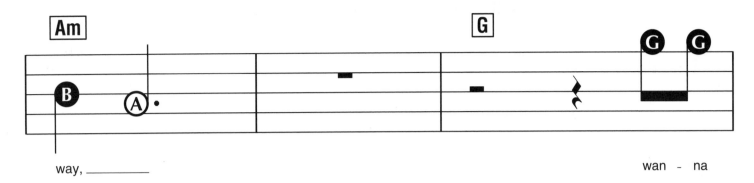

way, _____ wan - na

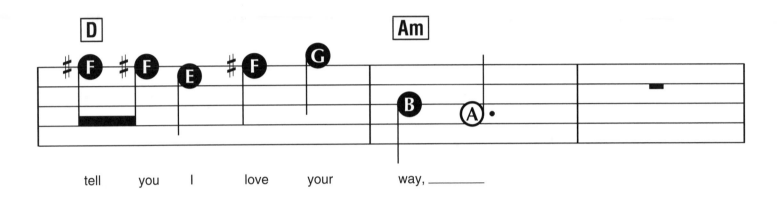

tell you I love your way, _____

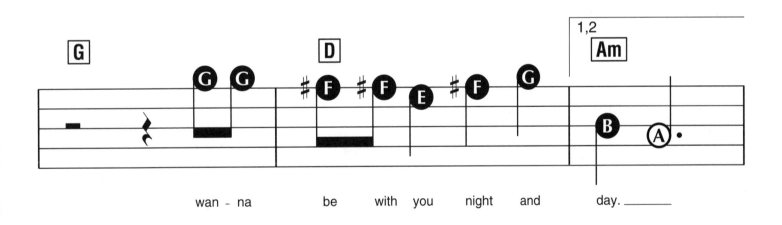

wan - na be with you night and day. _____

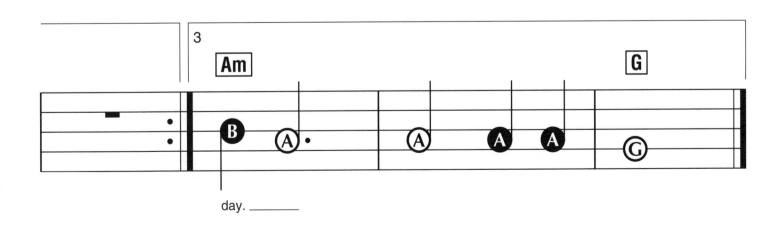

day. _____

At Seventeen

Registration 4
Rhythm: Rock or 8 Beat

Words and Music by
Janis Ian

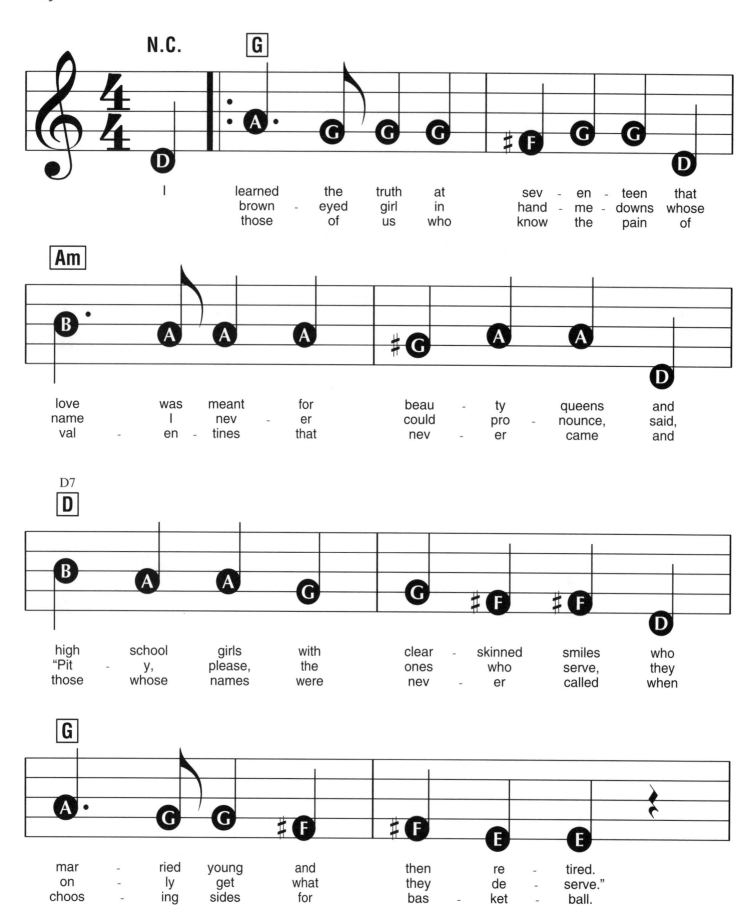

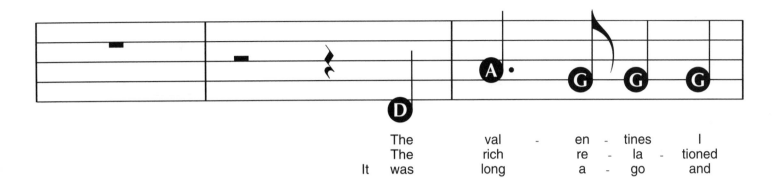

The | val - en - tines | I
The | rich | re - la - tioned
It was | long | a - go | and

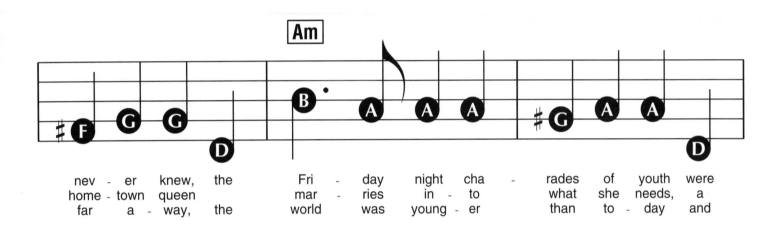

nev - er knew, the | Fri - day night cha - rades of youth were
home - town queen the | mar - ries in - to what she needs, a
far a - way, the | world was young - er than to - day and

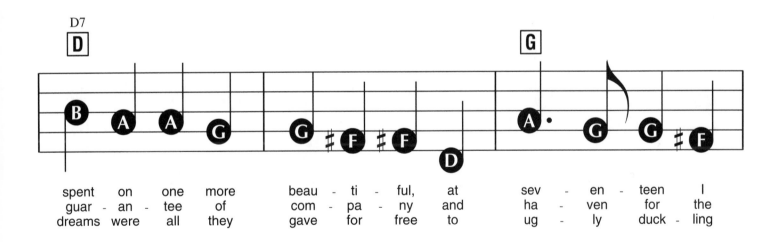

spent on one more | beau - ti - ful, at | sev - en - teen | I
guar - an - tee of | com - pa - ny and | ha - ven for the
dreams were all they | gave for free to | ug - ly duck - ling

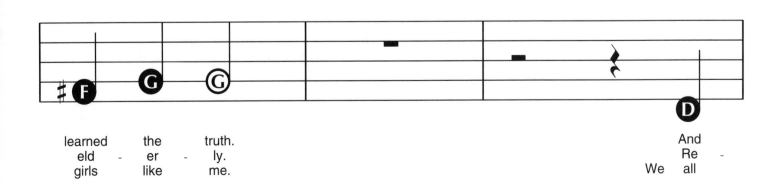

learned the truth. | | And
eld - er - ly. | | Re -
girls like me. | | We all

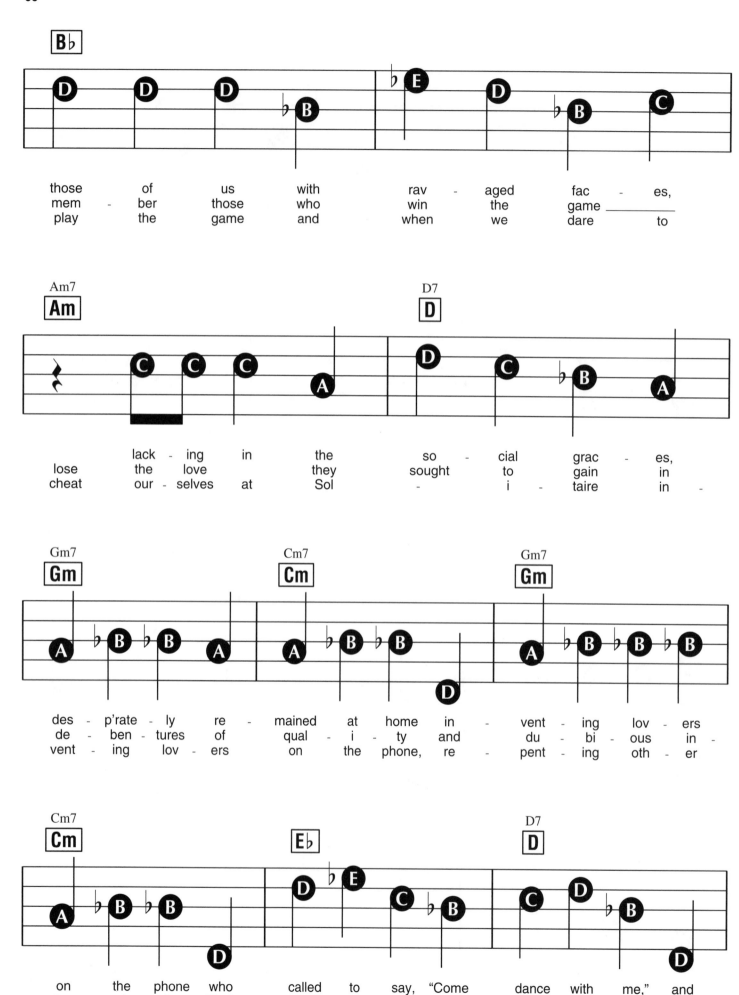

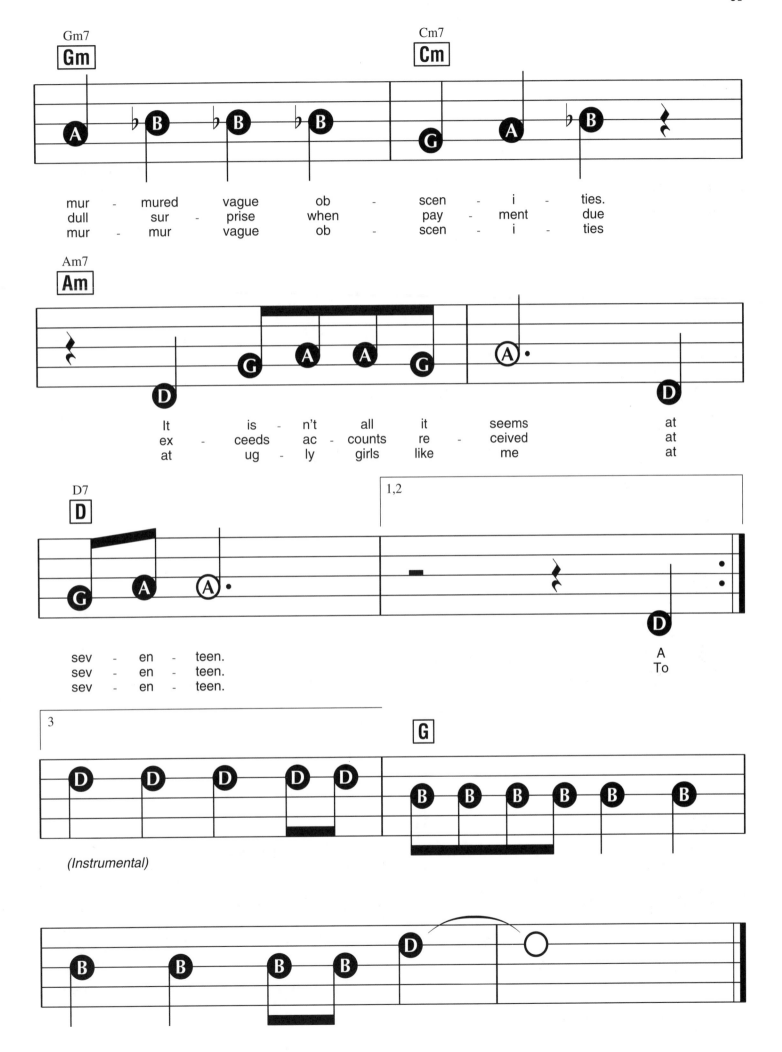

murmured vague obscenities.
dull surprise when payment due
murmur vague obscenities

It isn't all it seems at
exceeds accounts received at
at ugly girls like me at

seventeen.
seventeen.
seventeen.

A
To

(Instrumental)

Baby Come Back

Registration 7
Rhythm: 8 Beat or Rock

Words and Music by John C. Crowley
and Peter Becken

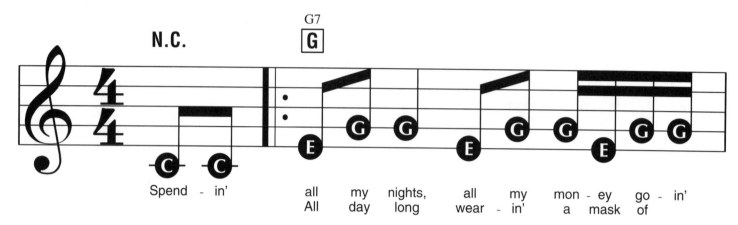

Spend - in' all my nights, all my mon - ey go - in'
All my day long wear - in' a mask of

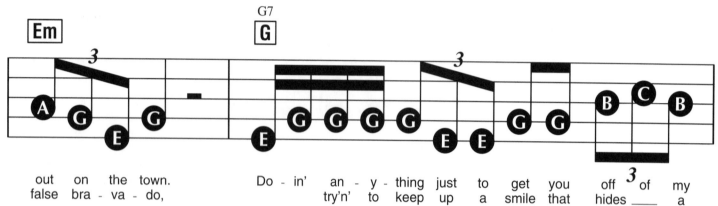

out on the town. Do - in' an - y - thing just to get you off of my
false bra - va - do, try'n' to keep up a smile that hides ___ a

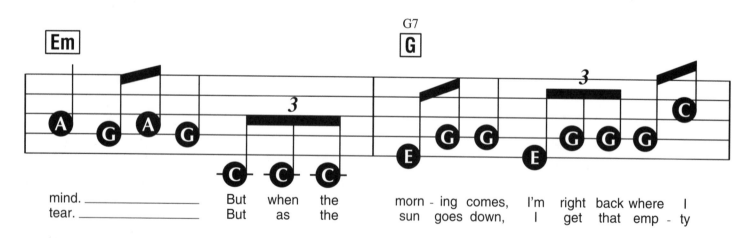

mind. ___ But when the morn - ing comes, I'm right back where I
tear. ___ But as the sun goes down, I get that emp - ty

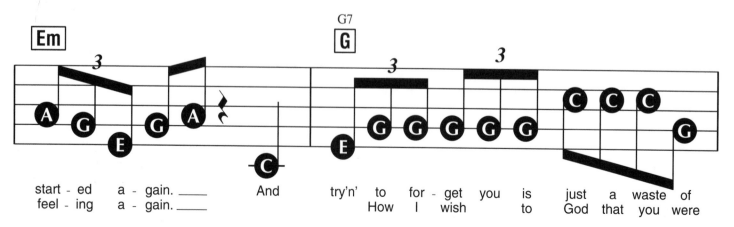

start - ed a - gain. ___ And try'n' to for - get you is just a waste of
feel - ing a - gain. ___ How I wish to God that you were

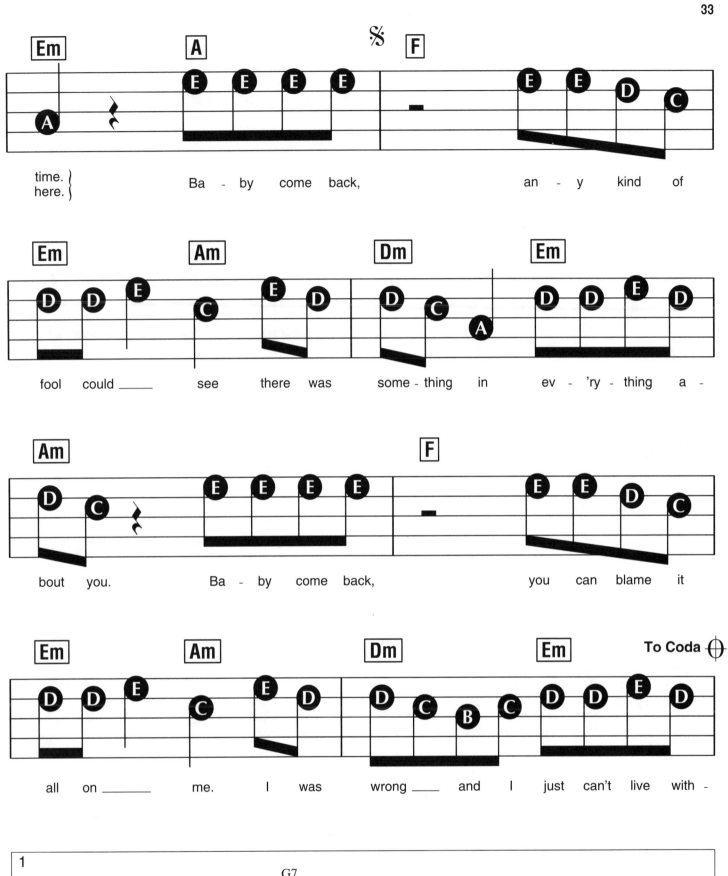

time.
here.
Ba - by come back, an - y kind of

fool could _____ see there was some - thing in ev - 'ry - thing a -

bout you. Ba - by come back, you can blame it

To Coda ⊕

all on _____ me. I was wrong _____ and I just can't live with -

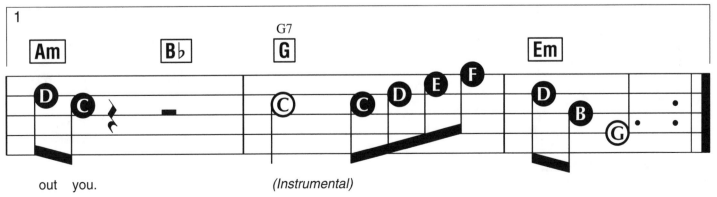

out you. (Instrumental)

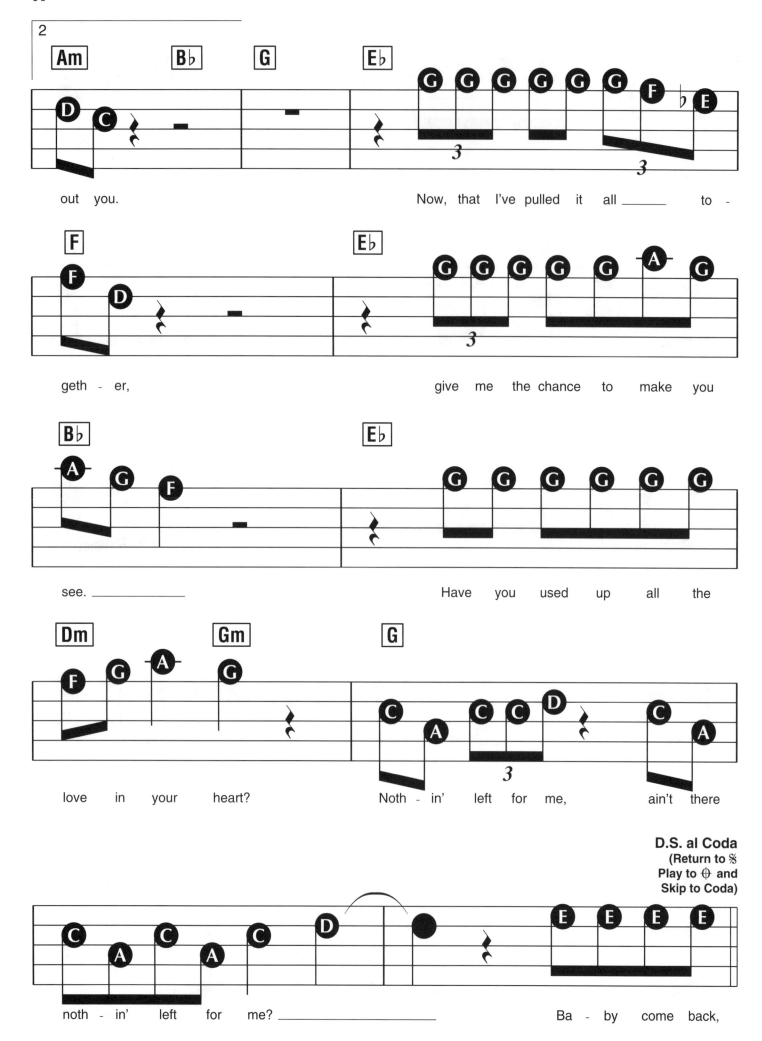

35

CODA

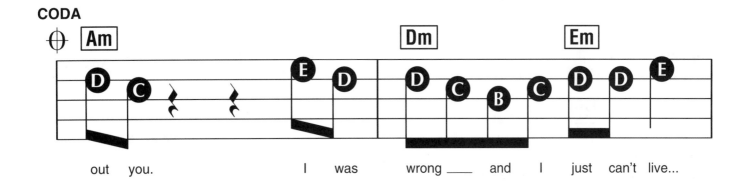

out you. I was wrong ___ and I just can't live...

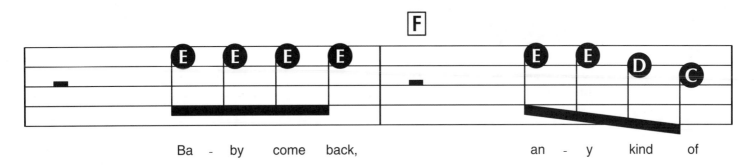

Ba - by come back, an - y kind of

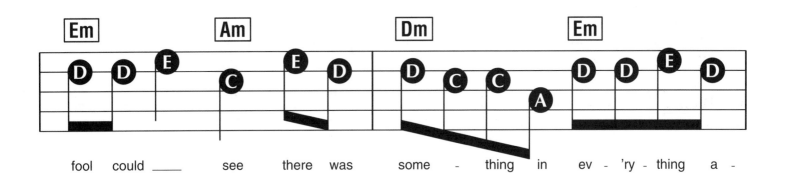

fool could ___ see there was some - thing in ev - 'ry - thing a -

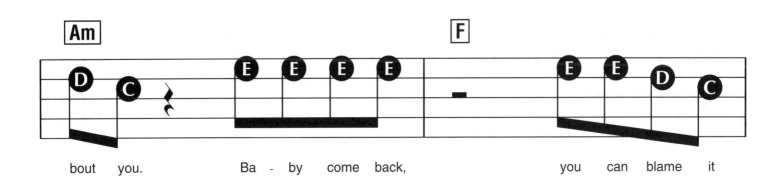

bout you. Ba - by come back, you can blame it

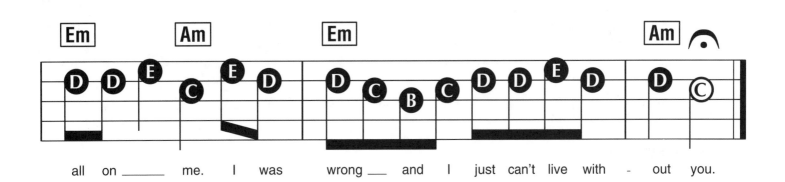

all on ___ me. I was wrong ___ and I just can't live with - out you.

Baby, I'm-A Want You

Registration 4
Rhythm: Slow Rock or Ballad

Words and Music by
David Gates

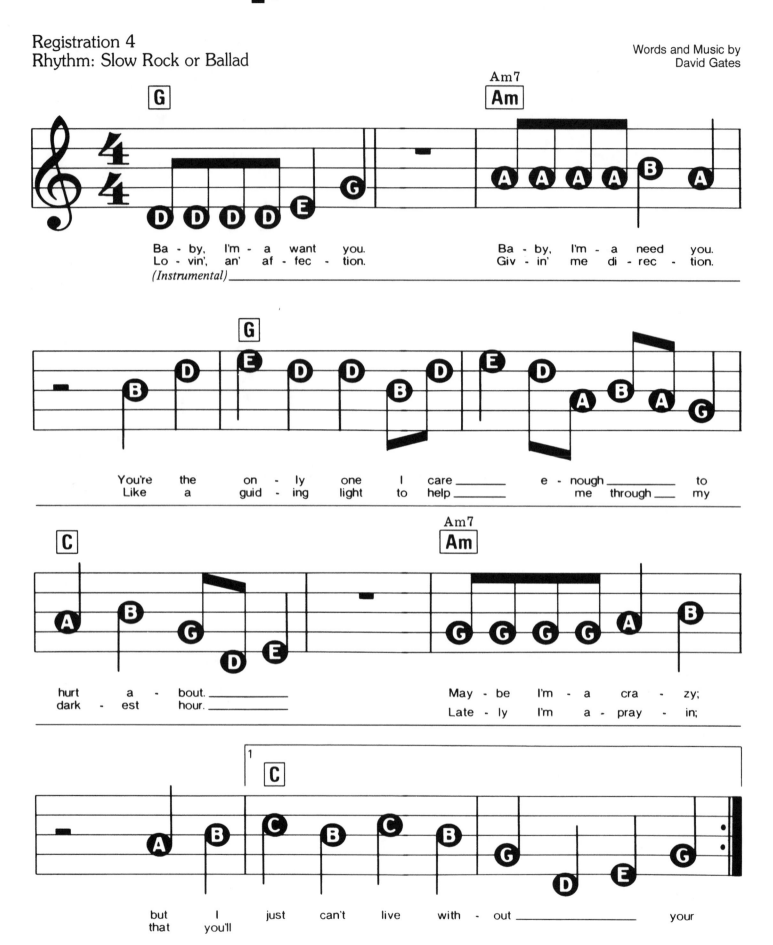

37

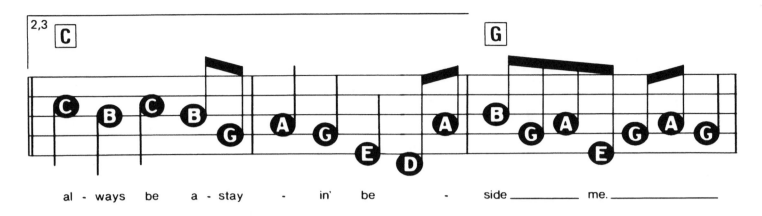

al - ways be a - stay - in' be - side _____ me. _____

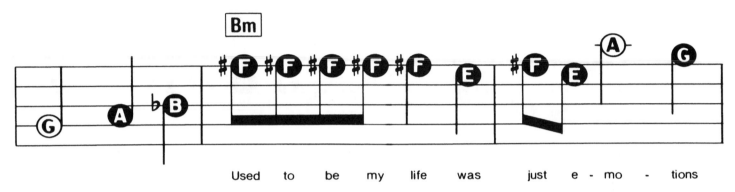

Used to be my life was just e - mo - tions

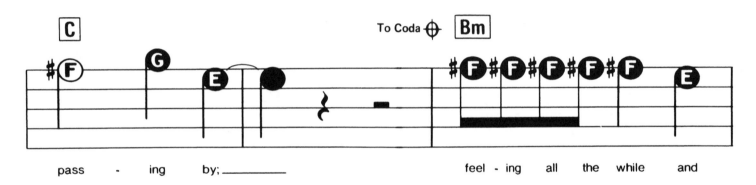

pass - ing by; _____ feel - ing all the while and

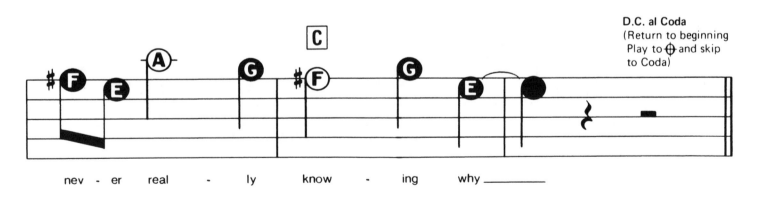

nev - er real - ly know - ing why _____

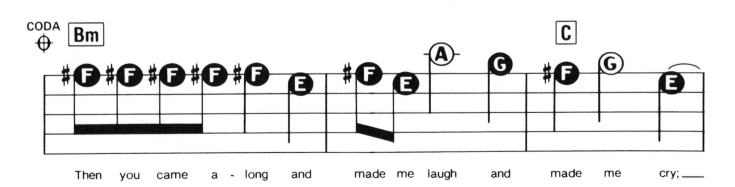

Then you came a - long and made me laugh and made me cry; ___

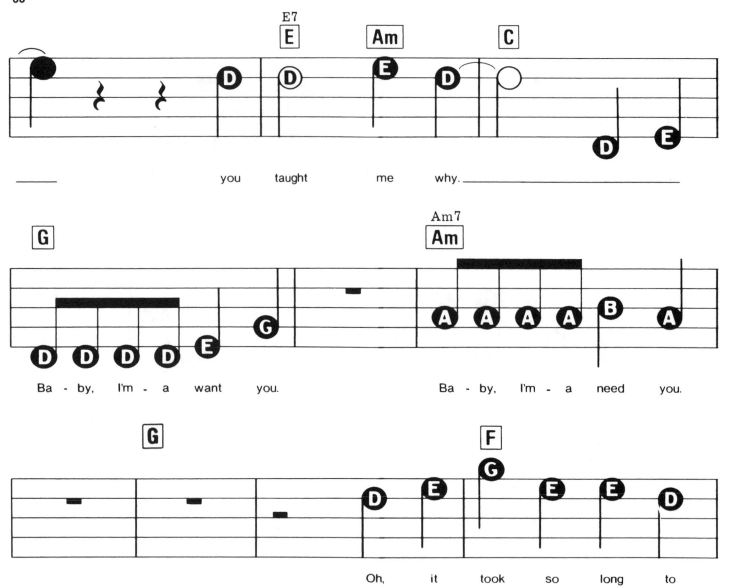

you taught me why. _____

Ba - by, I'm - a want you.   Ba - by, I'm - a need you.

Oh, it took so long to

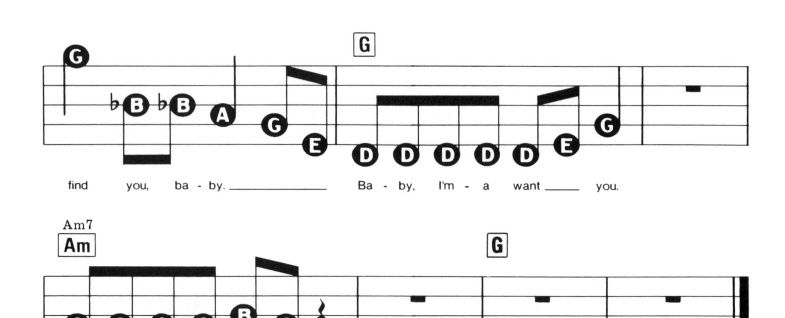

find you, ba - by. _____ Ba - by, I'm - a want ____ you.

Ba - by, I'm - a need you.

Bad Girls

Registration 8
Rhythm: Rock

Words and Music by Joe "Beans" Esposito,
Edward Hokenson, Bruce Sudano
and Donna Summer

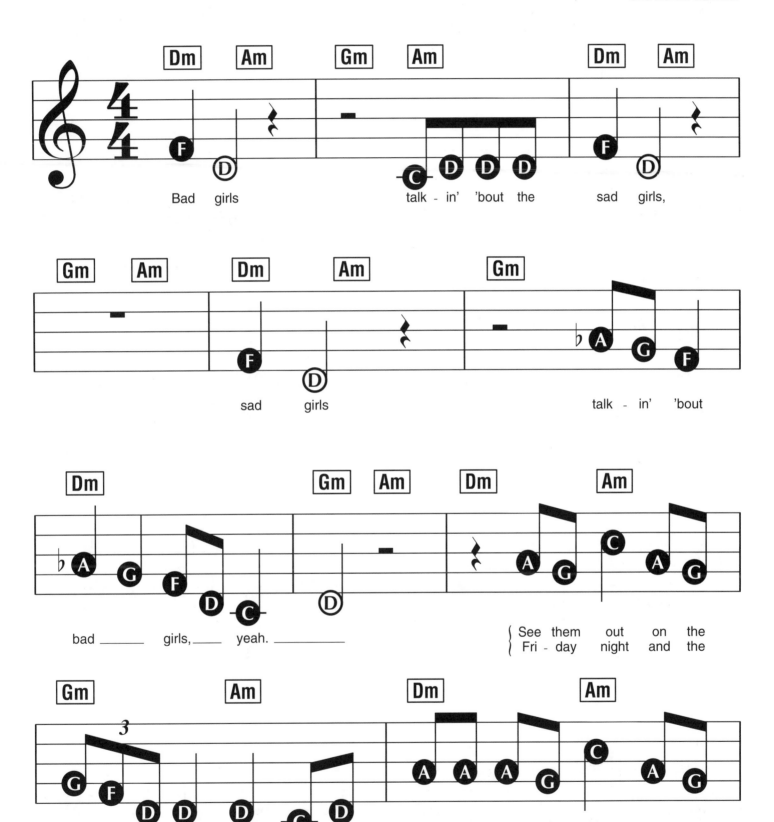

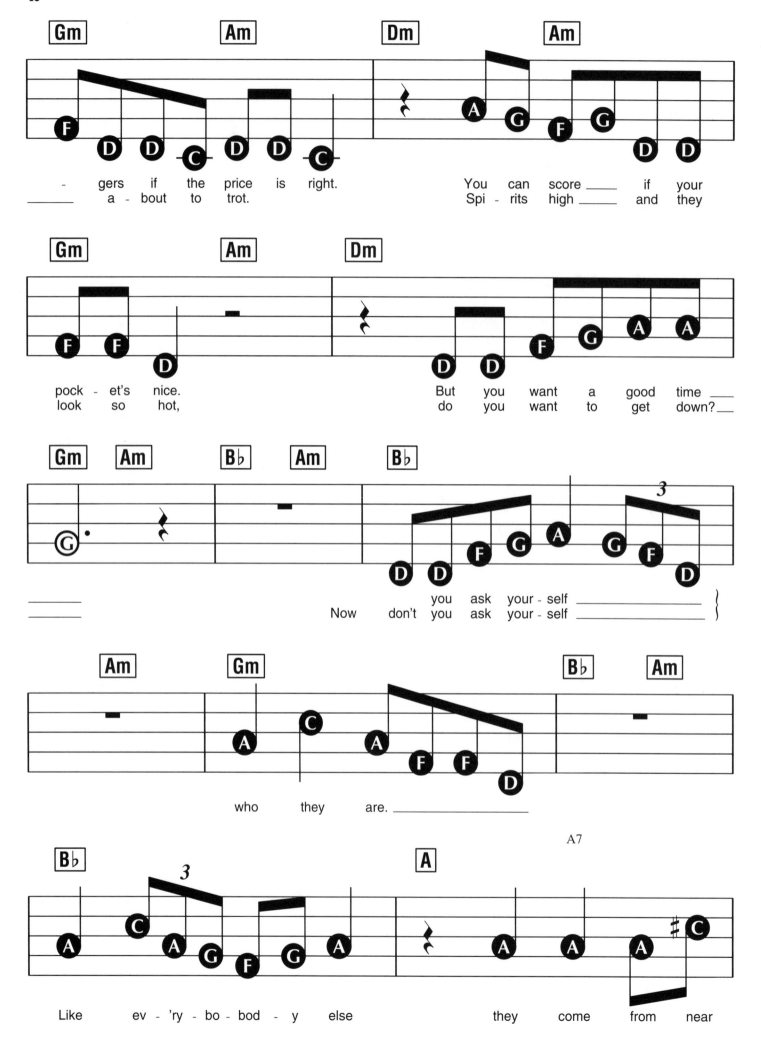

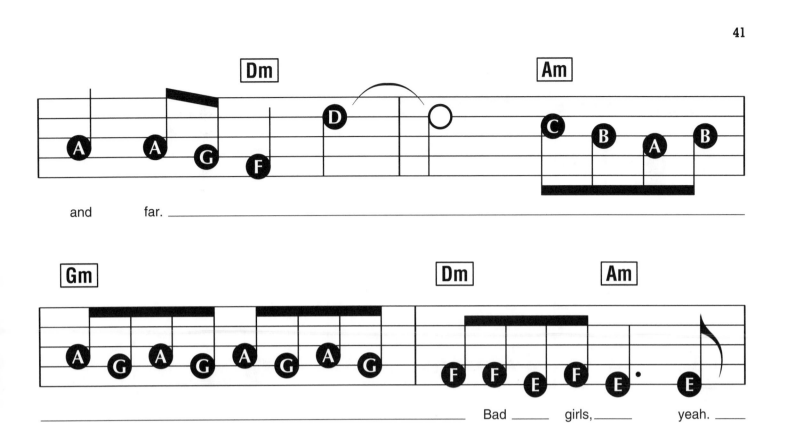

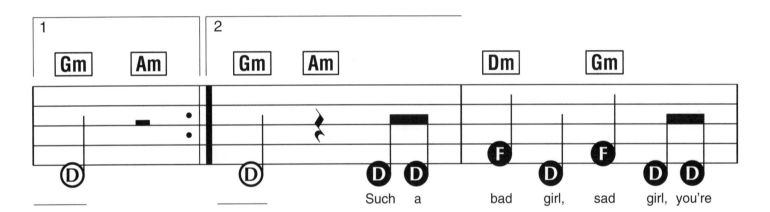

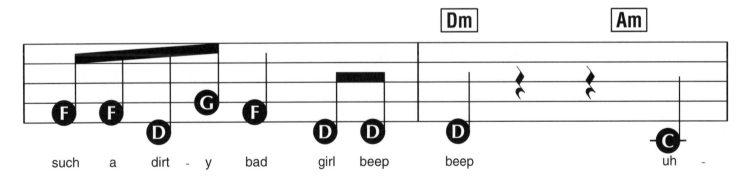

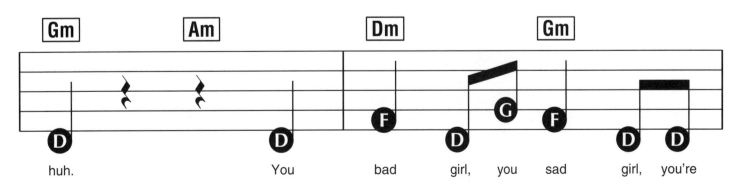

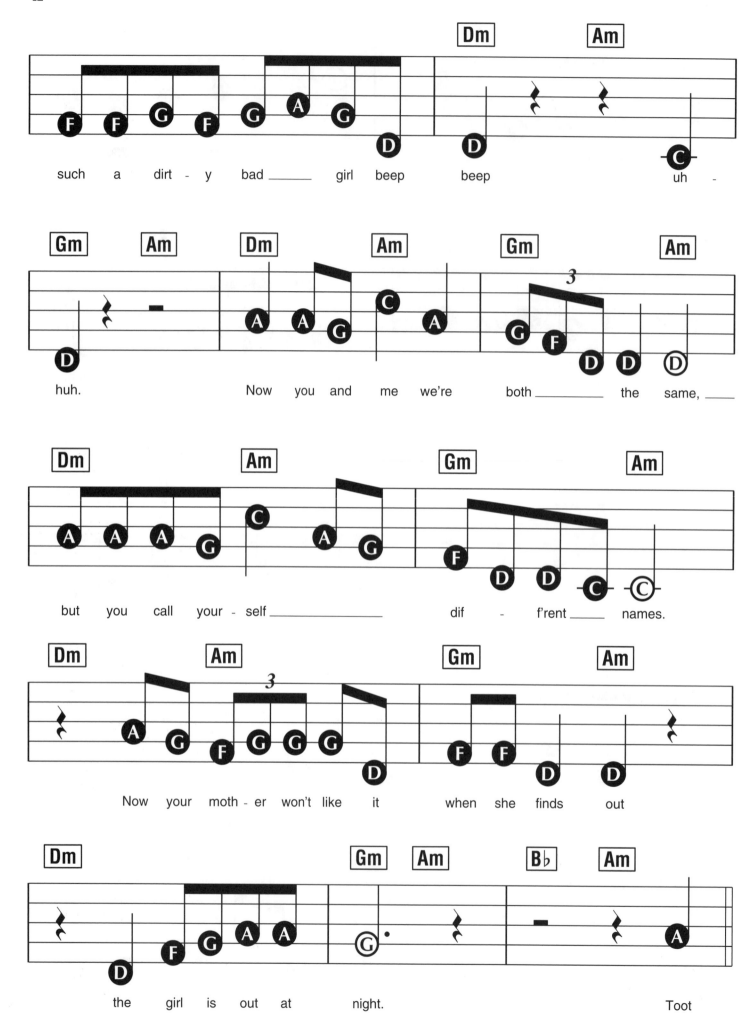

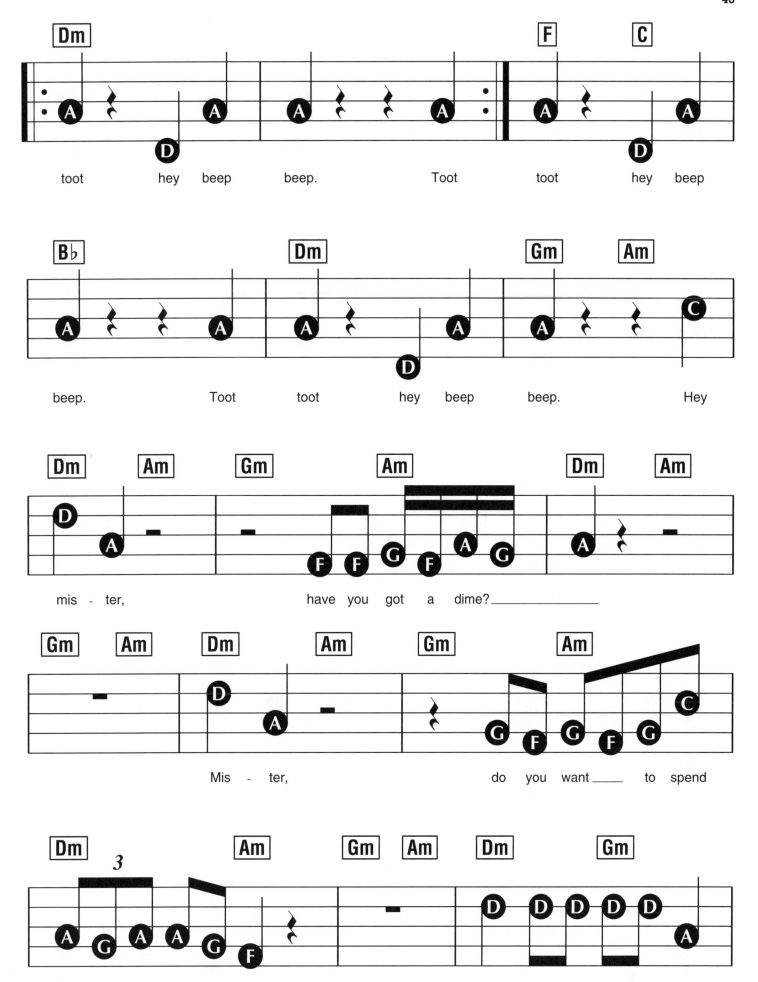

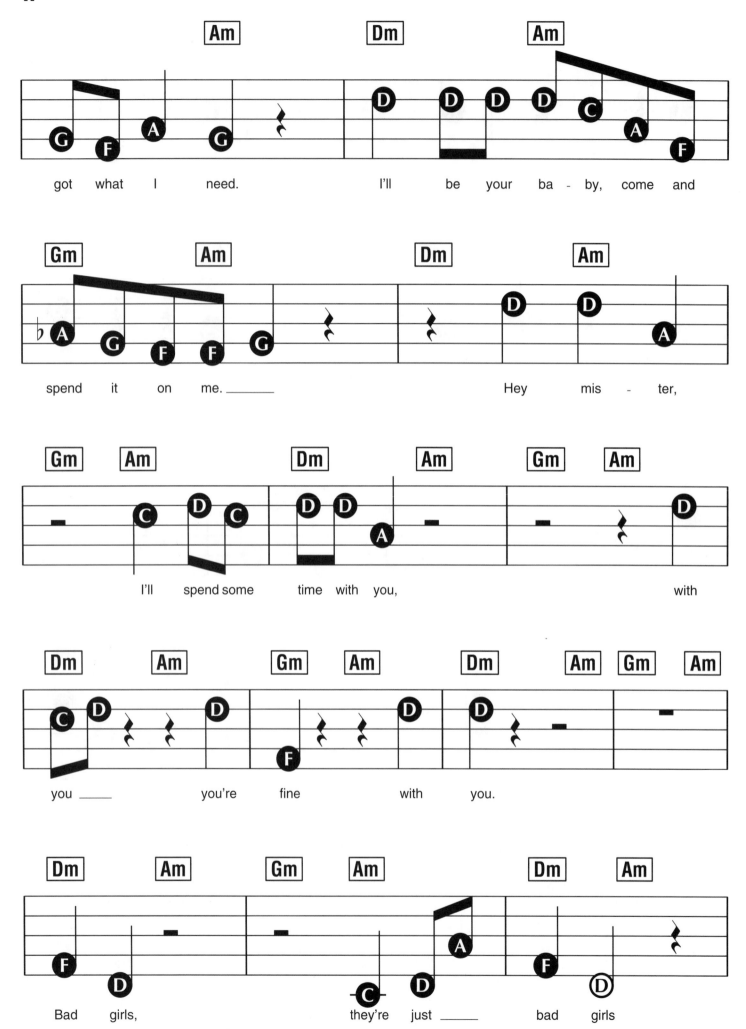

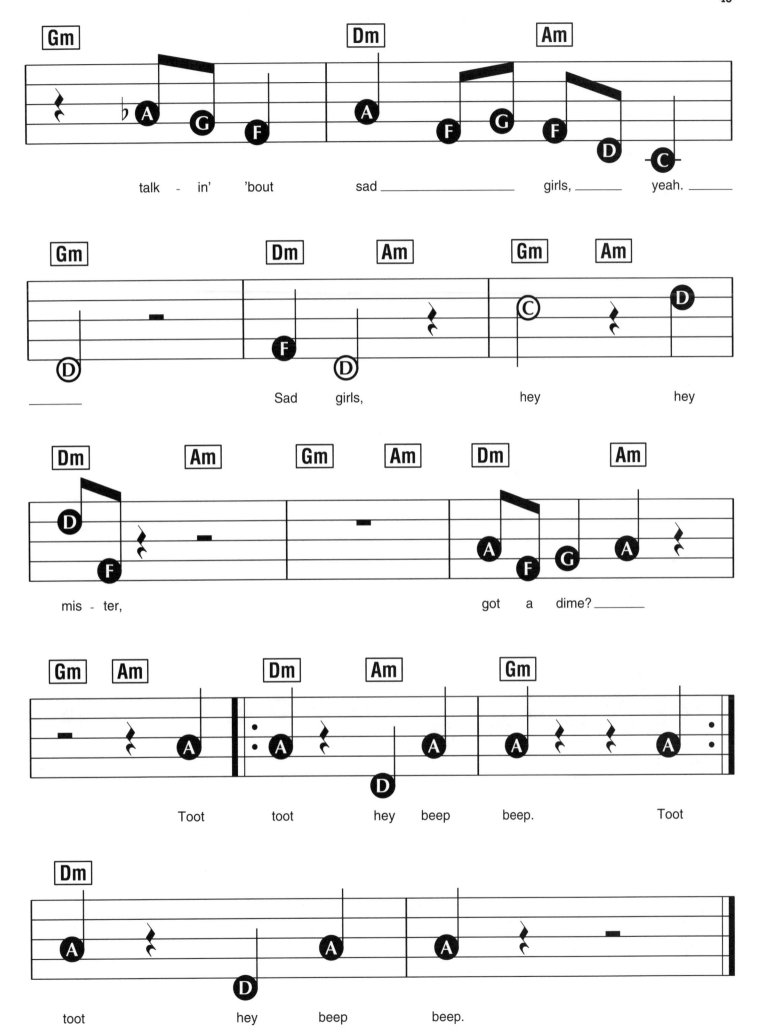

Baker Street

Registration 8
Rhythm: 8 Beat or Rock

Words and Music by
Gerry Rafferty

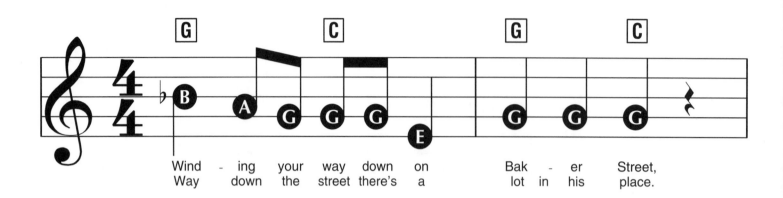

Wind - ing your way down on Bak - er Street,
Way down the street there's a lot in his place.

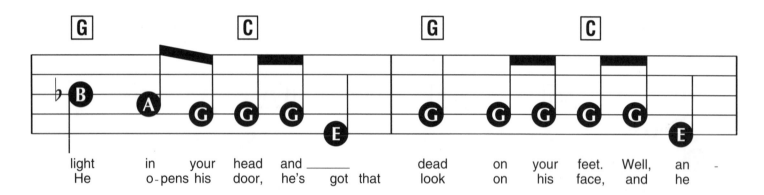

light in your head and _____ dead on your feet. Well, an -
He o-pens his door, he's got that look on his face, and he

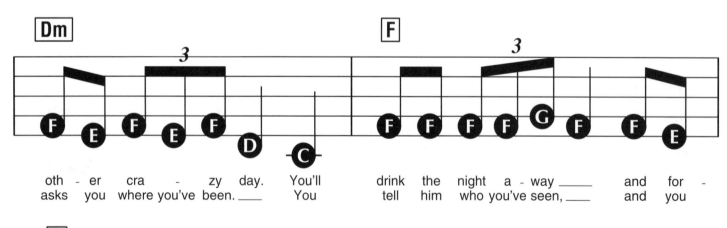

oth - er cra - zy day. You'll drink the night a - way _____ and for -
asks you where you've been. ____ You tell him who you've seen, ____ and you

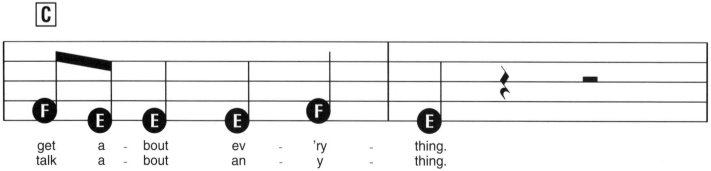

get a - bout ev - 'ry - thing.
talk a - bout an - y - thing.

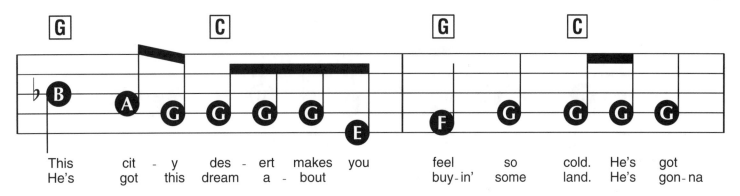

This cit - y des - ert makes you feel so cold. He's got
He's got this dream a - bout buy - in' some land. He's gon - na

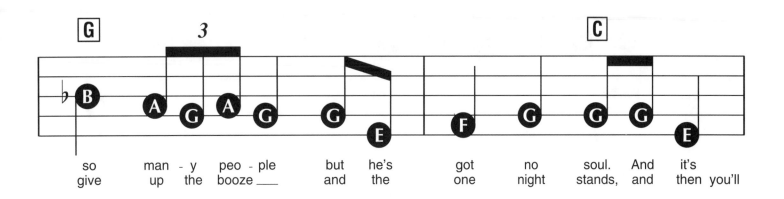

so man - y peo - ple but he's got no soul. And it's
give up the booze ____ and the one night stands, and then you'll

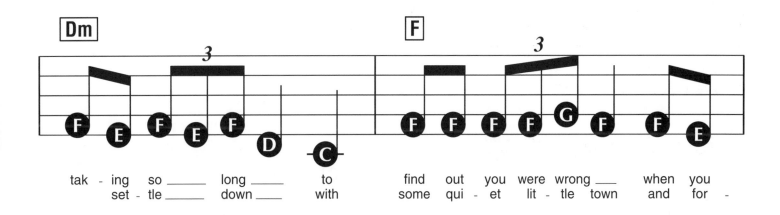

tak - ing so ____ long ____ to find out you were wrong ____ when you
set - tle ____ down ____ to with some qui - et lit - tle town and for -

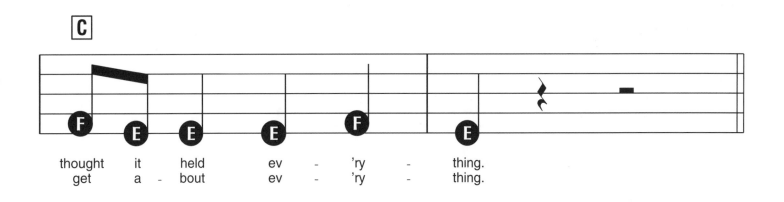

thought it held ev - 'ry - thing.
get a - bout ev - 'ry - thing.

48

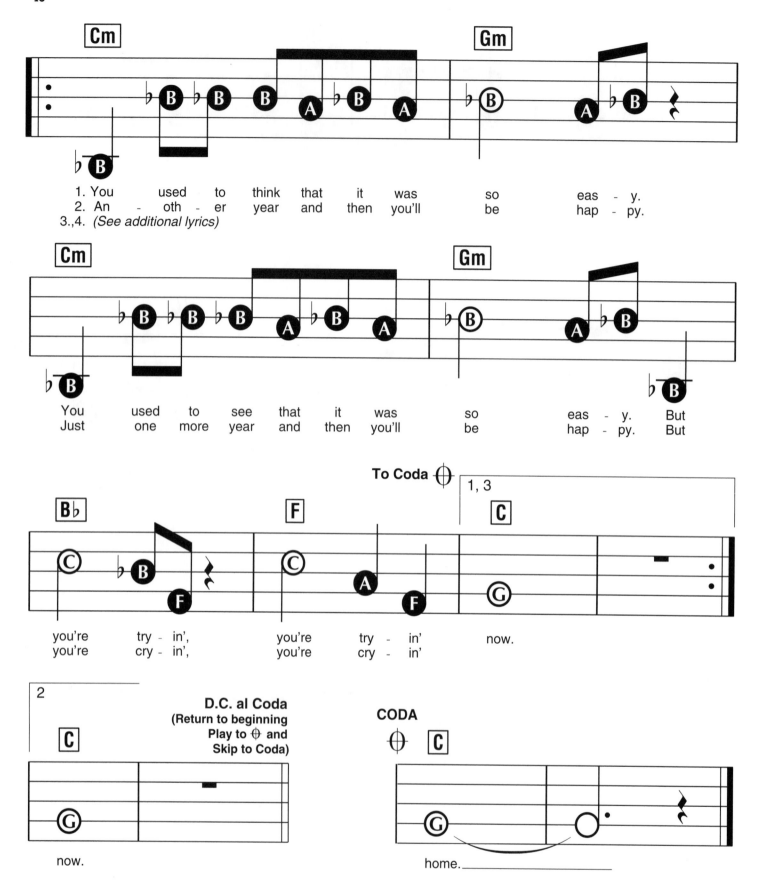

1. You used to think that it was so eas - y.
2. An - oth - er year and then you'll be hap - py.
3.,4. *(See additional lyrics)*

You used to see that it was so eas - y. But
Just one more year and then was you'll be hap - py. But

To Coda ⊕

1, 3

you're try - in', you're try - in' now.
you're cry - in', you're cry - in'

2

D.C. al Coda
(Return to beginning
Play to ⊕ and
Skip to Coda)

now.

CODA
⊕

home. _____

Additional Lyrics

3. But you know you'll always keep movin'
You know he's never gonna stop movin'
'Cause he's rollin', he's the rollin' stone.

4. When you wake up it's a new mornin'
The sun is shinin', it's a new mornin'
And you're goin', you're goin' home.

Band on the Run

Registration 4
Rhythm: Rock

Words and Music by
Paul and Linda McCartney

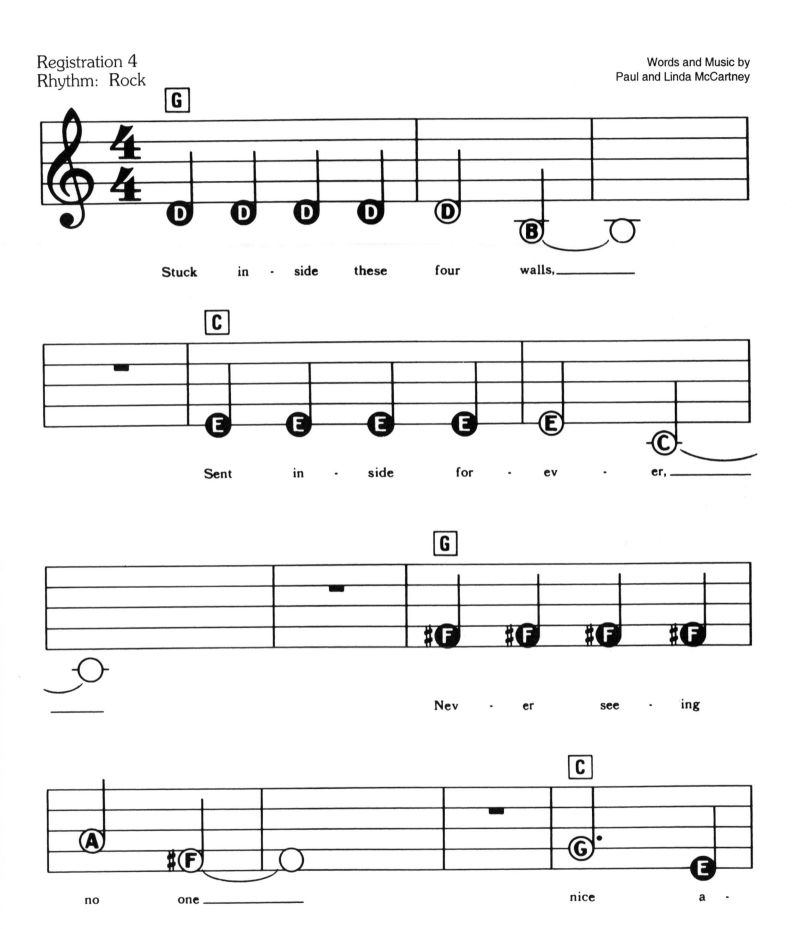

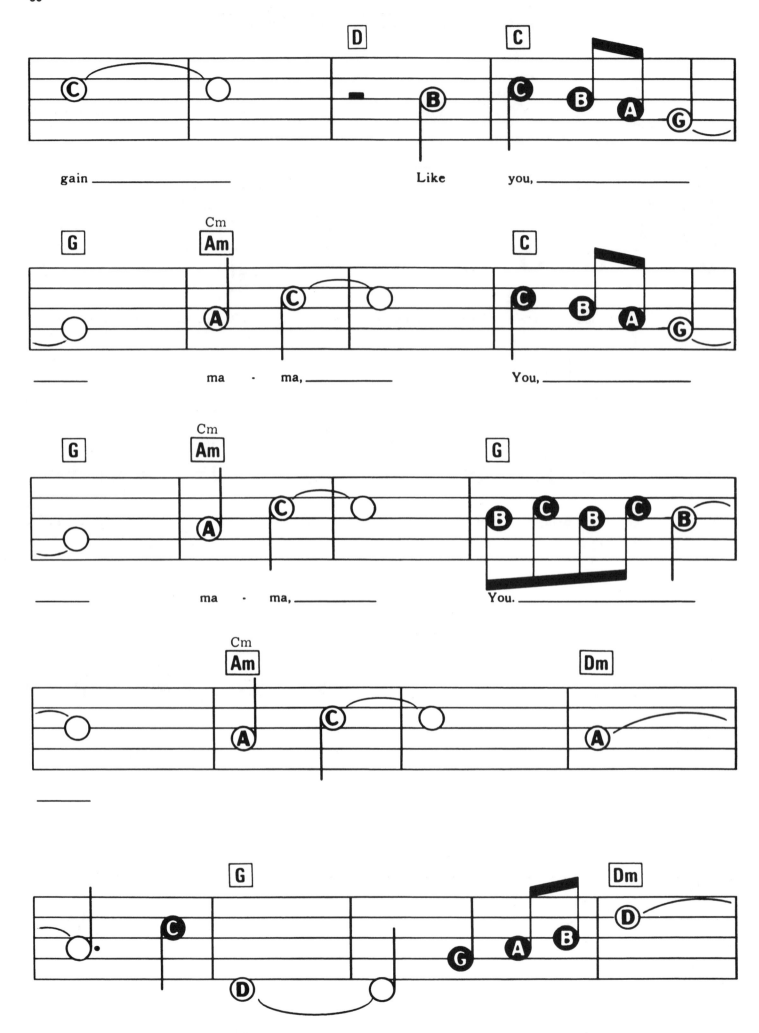

51

If I ev-er get out of here

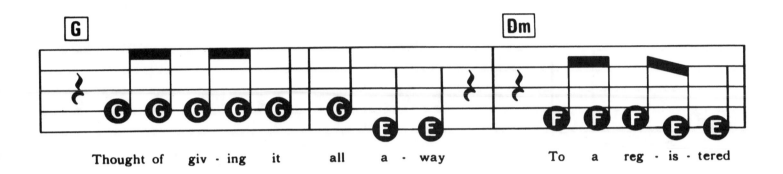

Thought of giv-ing it all a-way   To a reg-is-tered

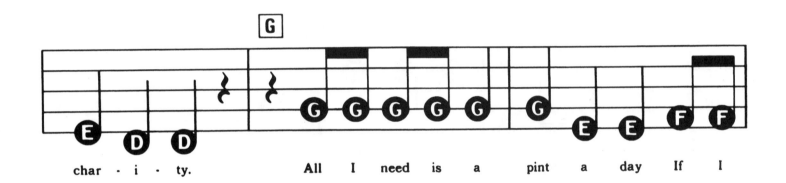

char-i-ty.   All I need is a pint a day If I

ev-er get out of here,   (If we ev-er get out of

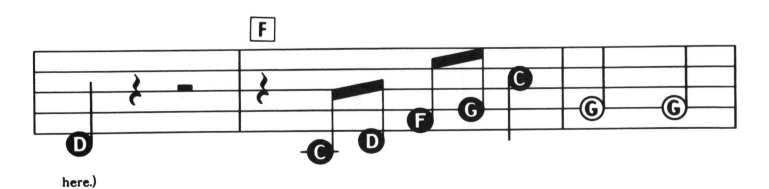

here.)

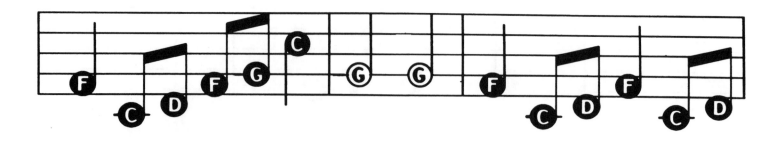

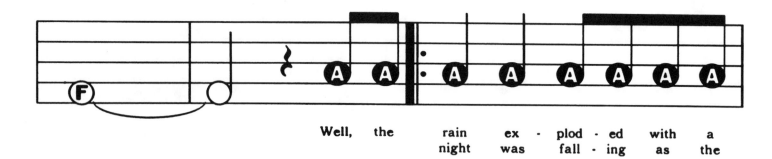

Well, the rain ex - plod - ed with a
night was fall - ing as the

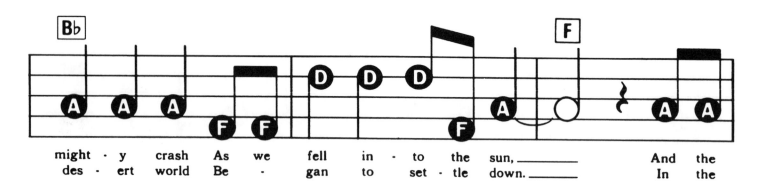

might - y crash As we fell in - to the sun, _____ And the
des - ert world Be - gan to set - tle down. _____ In the

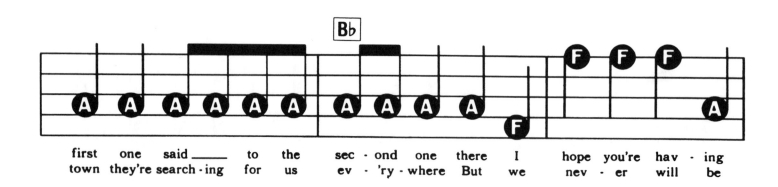

first one said _____ to the sec - ond one there I hope you're hav - ing
town they're search - ing for us ev - 'ry - where But we nev - er will be

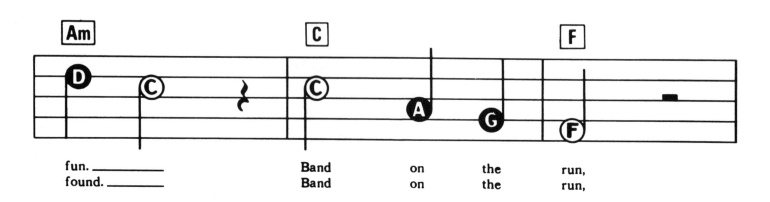

fun. _____ Band on the run,
found. _____ Band on the run,

53

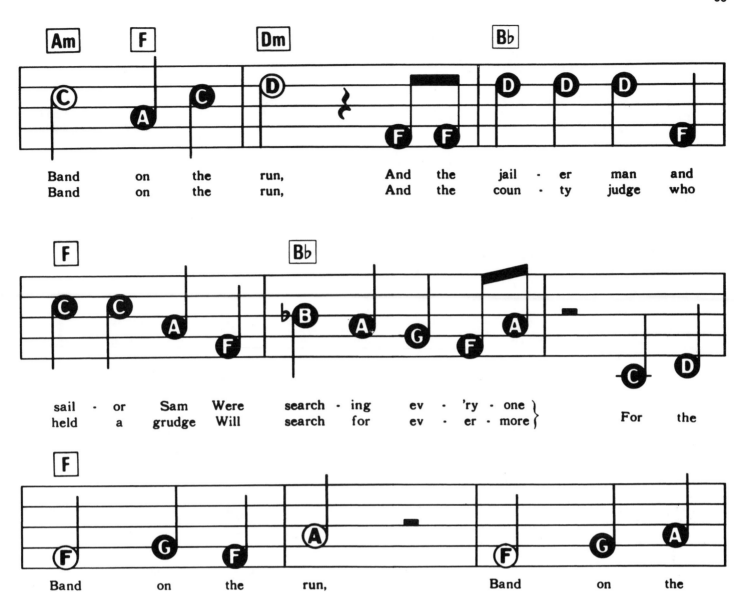

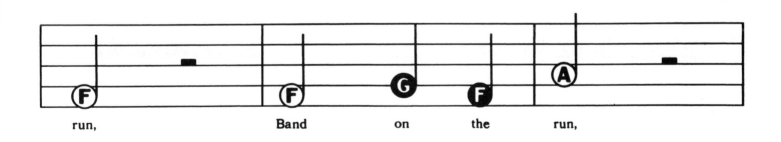

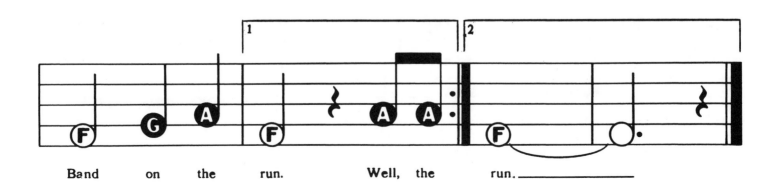

Ben

Registration 1
Rhythm: Pops or 8 Beat

Words by Don Black
Music by Walter Scharf

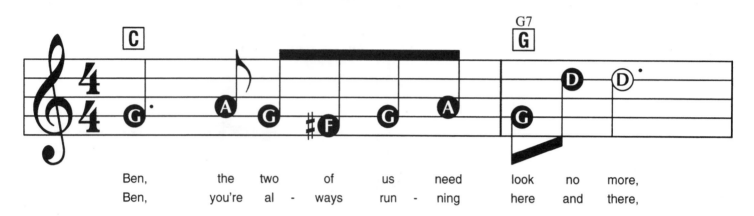

Ben, the two of us need look no more,
Ben, you're al - ways run - ning here and there,

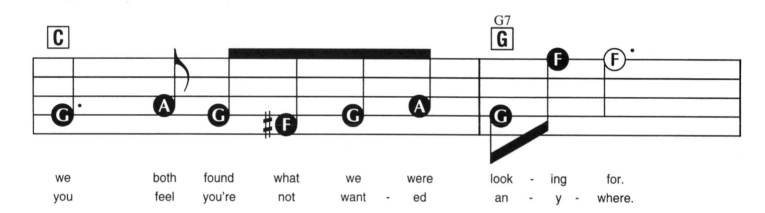

we both found what we were look - ing for.
you feel you're not want - ed an - y - where.

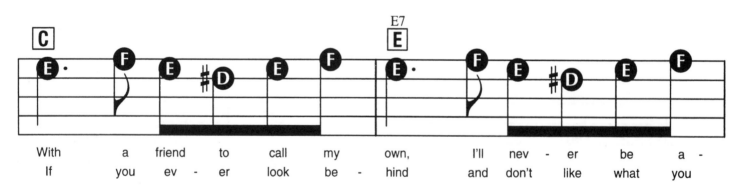

With a friend to call my own, I'll nev - er be a -
If you ev - er look be - hind and don't like what you

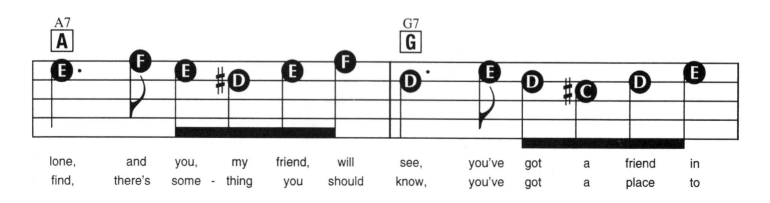

lone, and you, my friend, will see, you've got a friend in
find, there's some - thing you will should know, you've got a place to

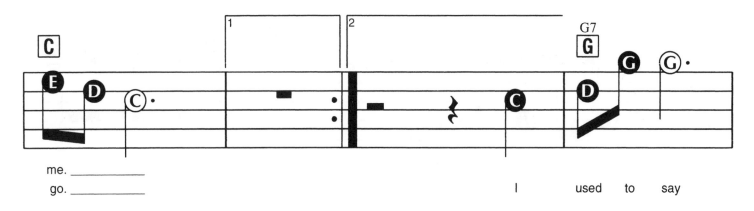

me. _____
go. _____   I   used   to   say

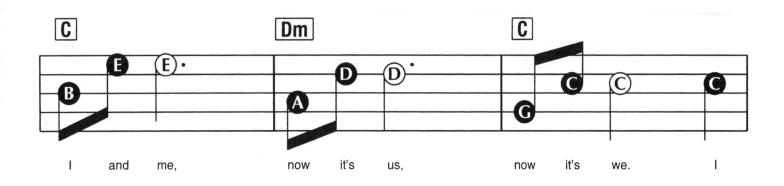

I   and   me,   now   it's   us,   now   it's   we.   I

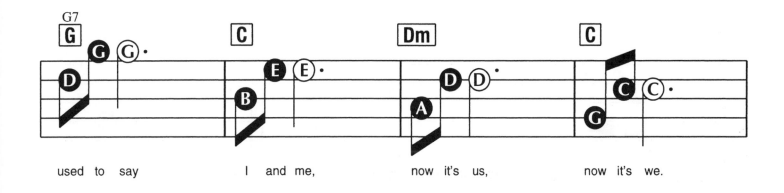

used   to   say   I   and   me,   now   it's   us,   now   it's   we.

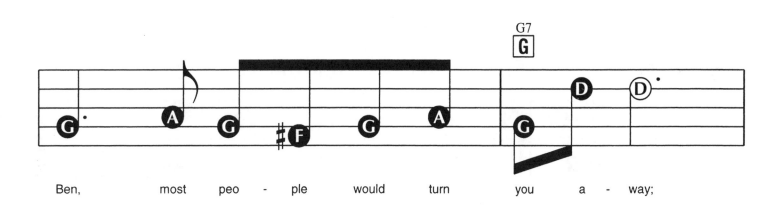

Ben,   most   peo   -   ple   would   turn   you   a   -   way;

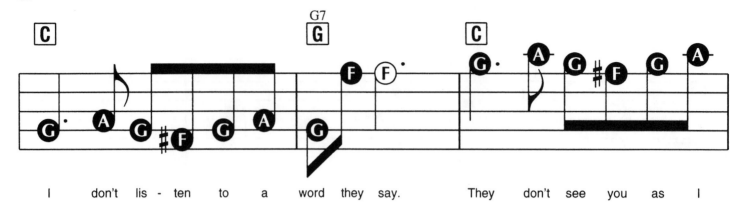

I don't lis - ten to a word they say. They don't see you as I

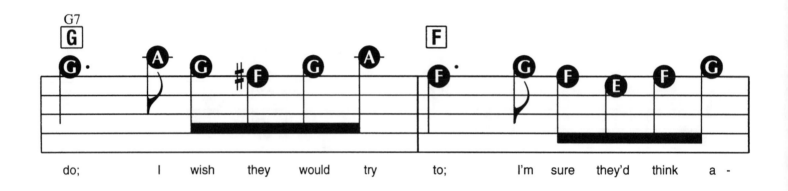

do; I wish they would try to; I'm sure they'd think a -

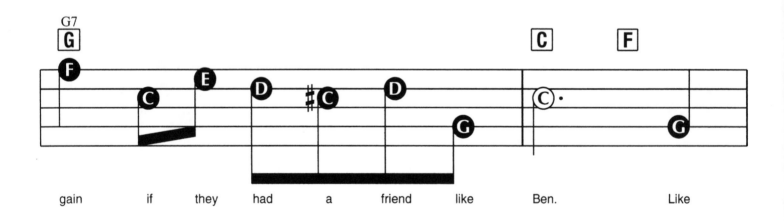

gain if they had a friend like Ben. Like

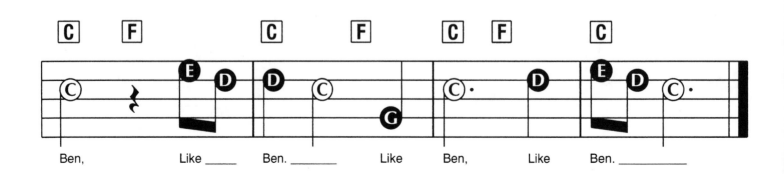

Ben, Like _____ Ben. _____ Like Ben, Like Ben. _____

Bohemian Rhapsody

Registration 8
Rhythm: Ballad

Words and Music by
Freddie Mercury

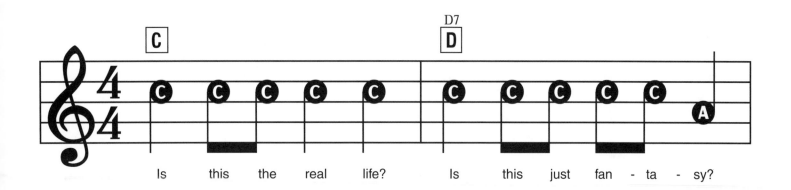

Is this the real life? Is this just fan - ta - sy?

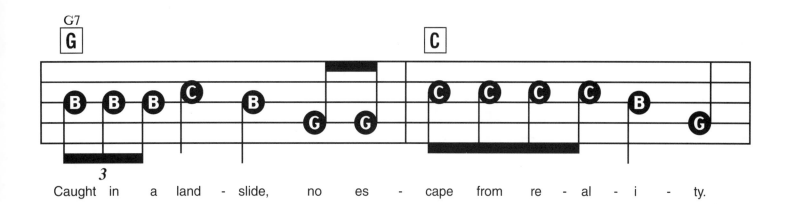

Caught in a land - slide, no es - cape from re - al - i - ty.

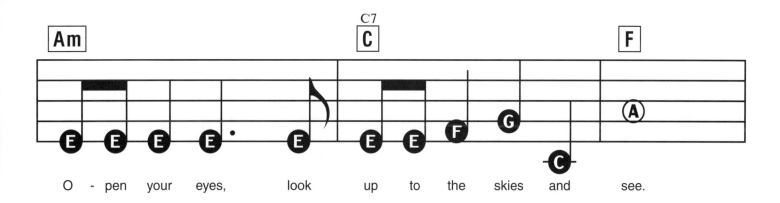

O - pen your eyes, look up to the skies and see.

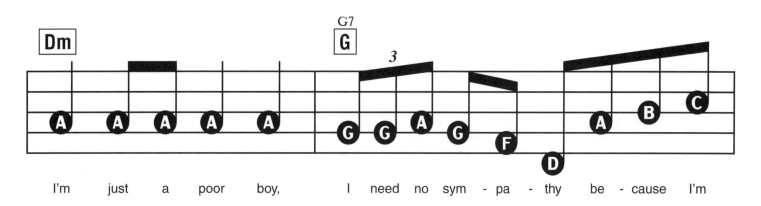

I'm just a poor boy, I need no sym - pa - thy be - cause I'm

58

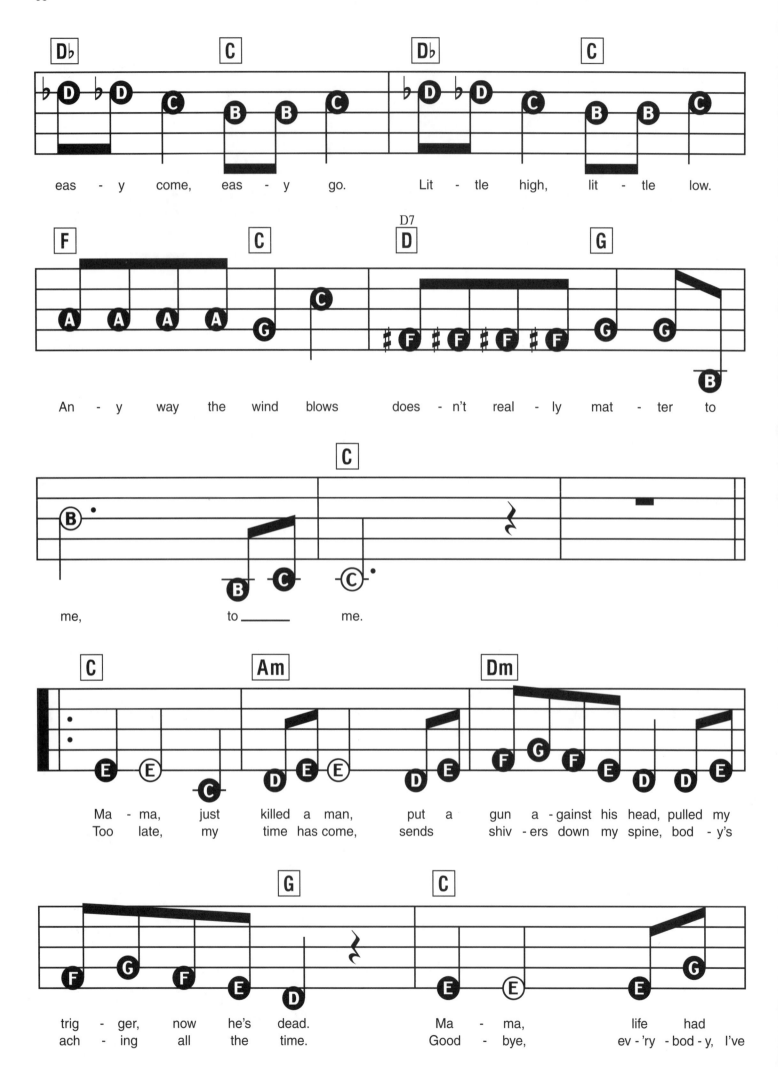

59

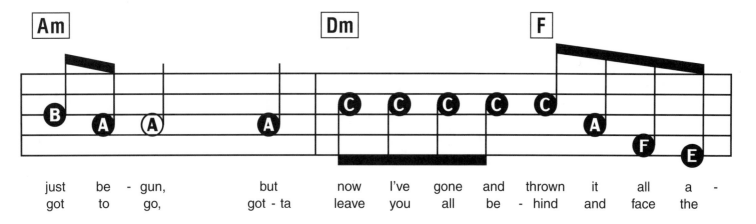

just be - gun, but now I've gone and thrown it all a -
got to go, got - ta leave you all be - hind and face the

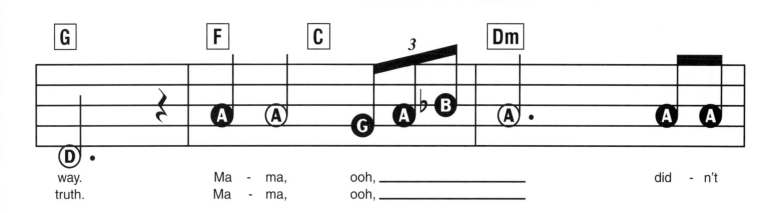

way. Ma - ma, ooh, _____ did - n't
truth. Ma - ma, ooh, _____

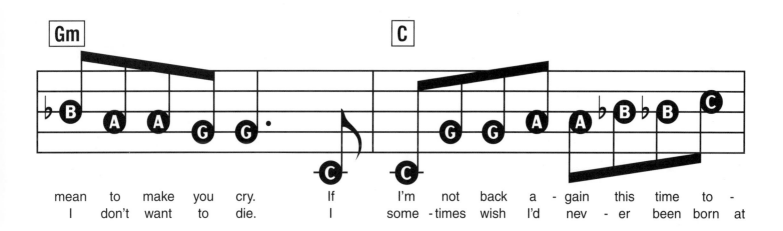

mean to make you cry. If I'm not back a - gain this time to -
I don't want to die. I some - times wish I'd nev - er been born at

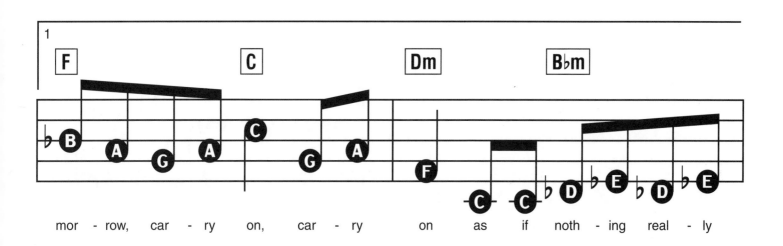

mor - row, car - ry on, car - ry on as if noth - ing real - ly

60

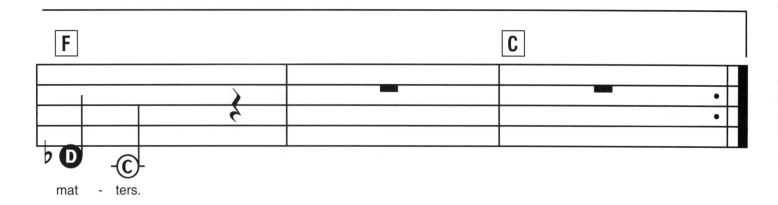

mat - ters.

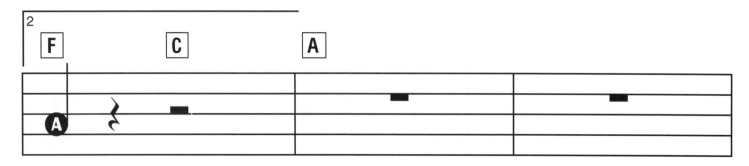

all.

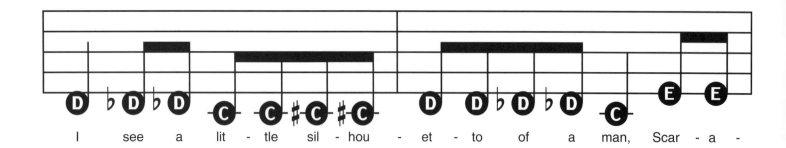

I see a lit - tle sil - hou - et - to of a man, Scar - a -

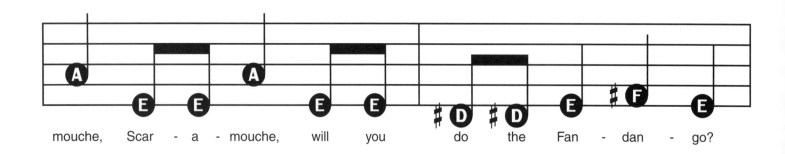

mouche, Scar - a - mouche, will you do the Fan - dan - go?

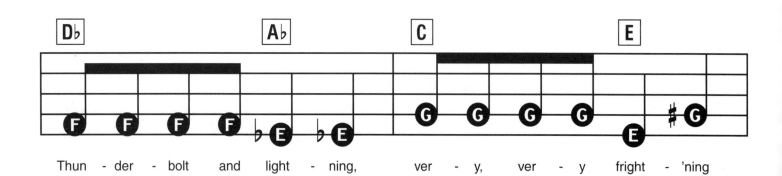

Thun - der - bolt and light - ning, ver - y, ver - y fright - 'ning

61

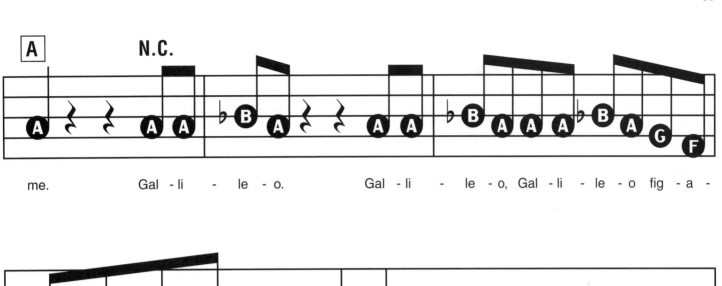

me. Gal - li - le - o. Gal - li - le - o, Gal - li - le - o fig - a -

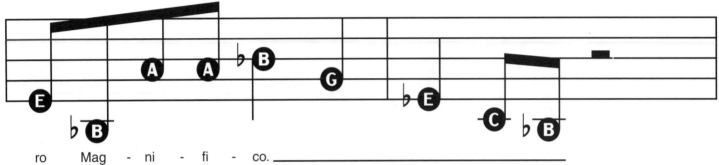

ro Mag - ni - fi - co. _____

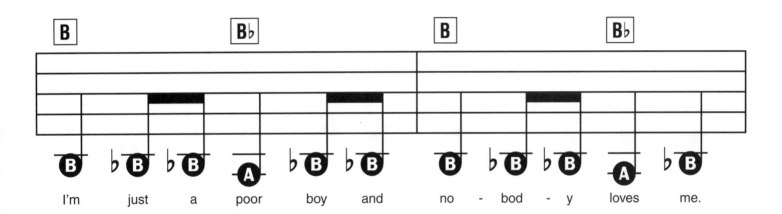

I'm just a poor boy and no - bod - y loves me.

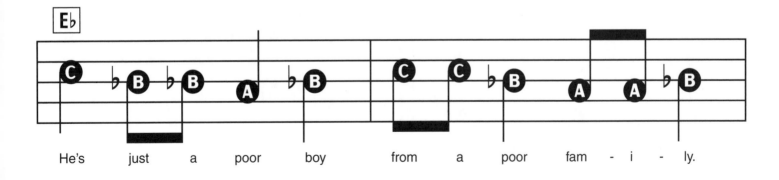

He's just a poor boy from a poor fam - i - ly.

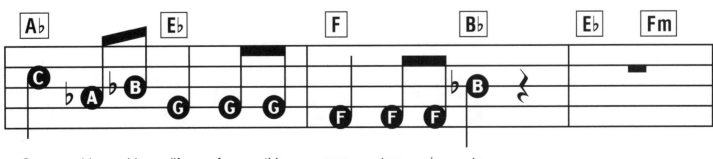

Spare him his life from this mon - stros - i - ty.

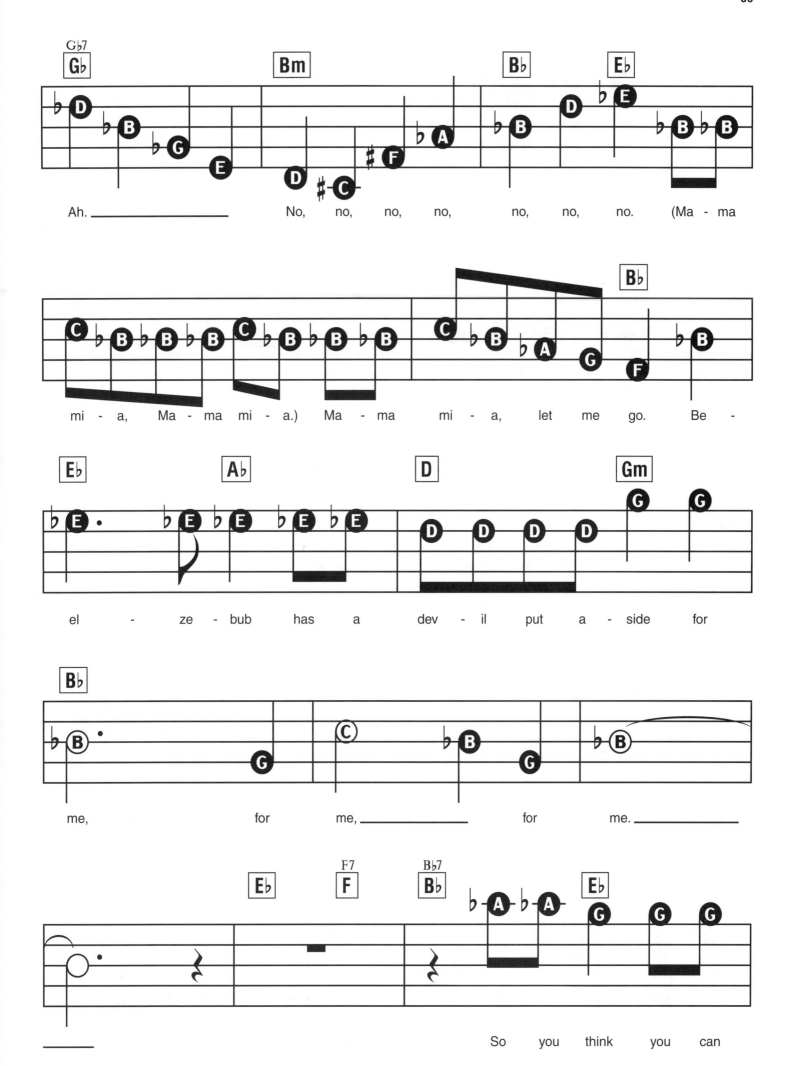

64

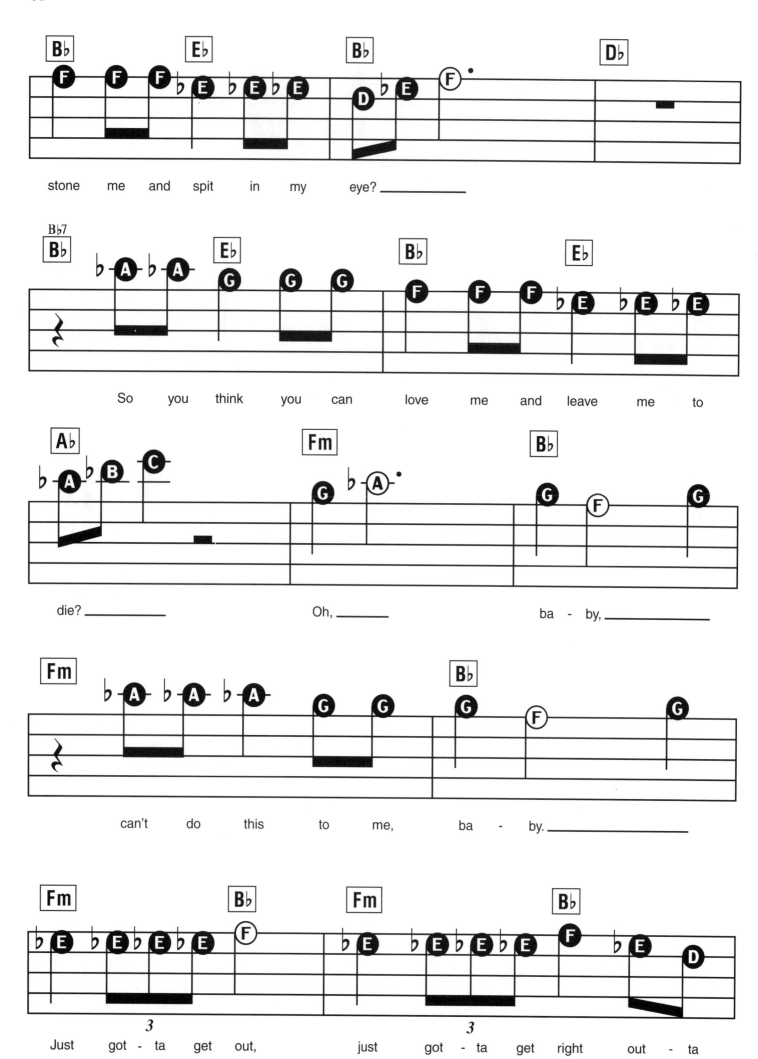

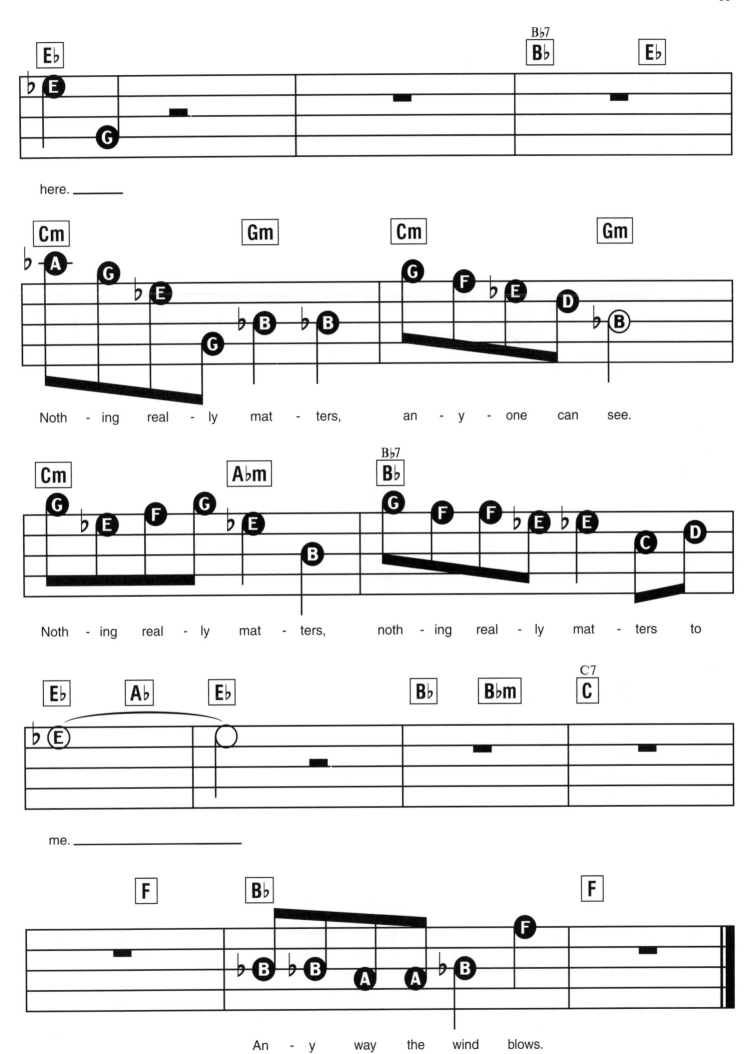

Best of My Love

Registration 8
Rhythm: Rock or Disco

Words and Music by John David Souther,
Don Henley and Glenn Frey

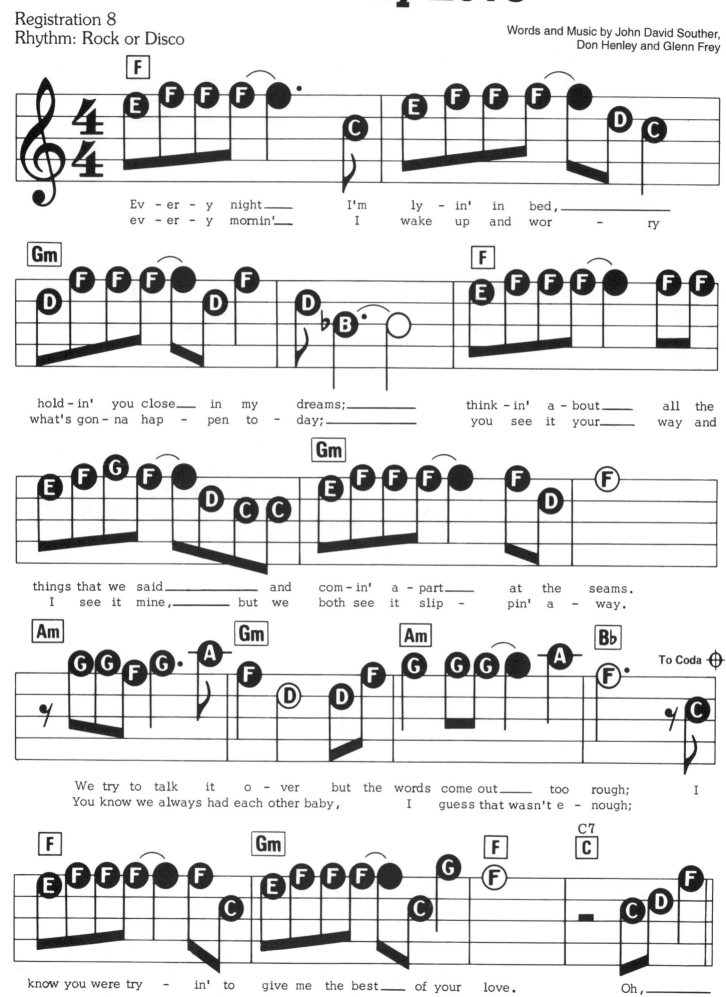

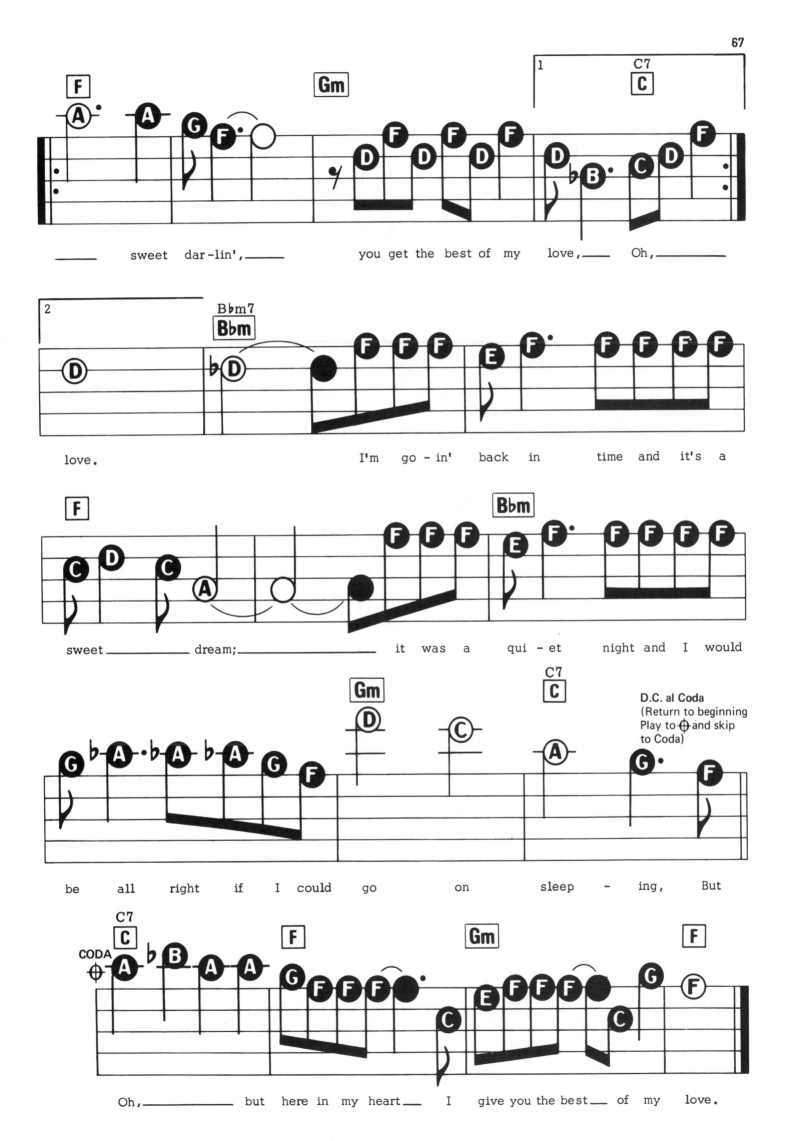

Billy, Don't Be a Hero

Registration 2
Rhythm: March

Words and Music by Peter Callender
and Mitch Murray

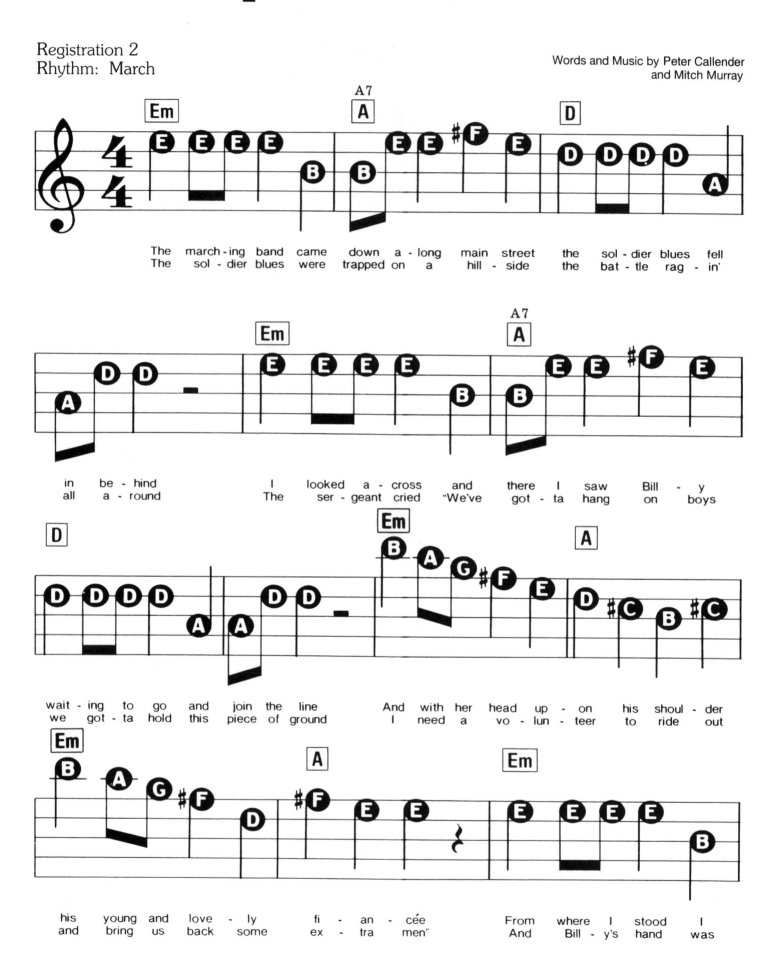

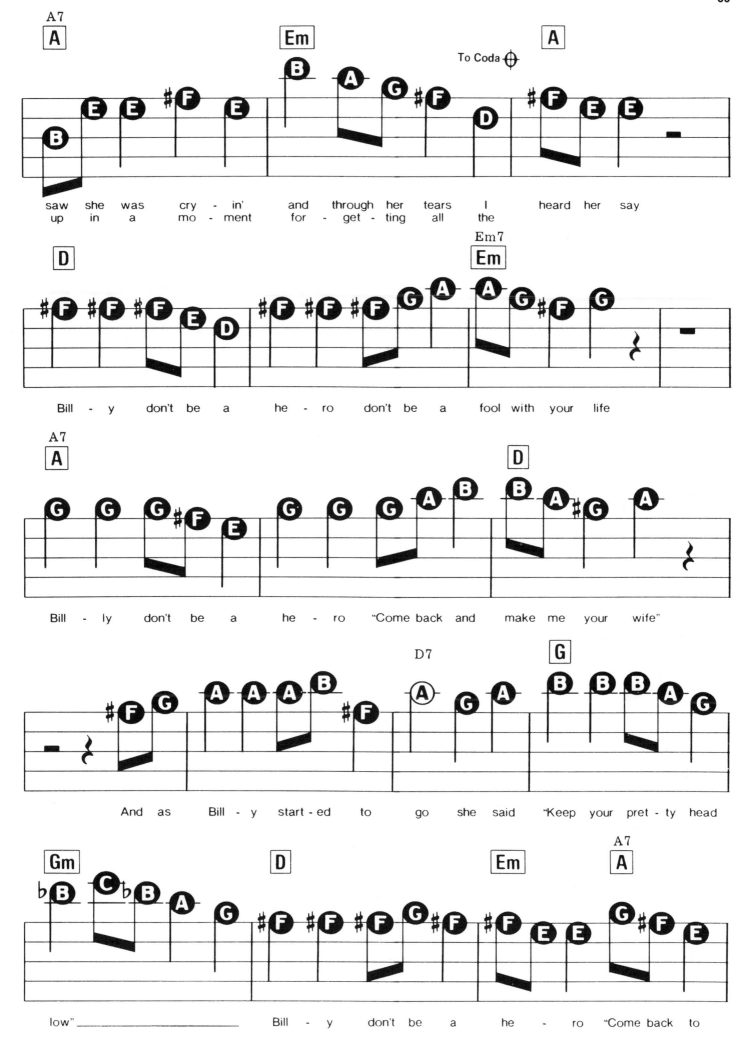

D.C. al Coda
(Return to Beginning
Play to ⊕ and
skip to Coda)

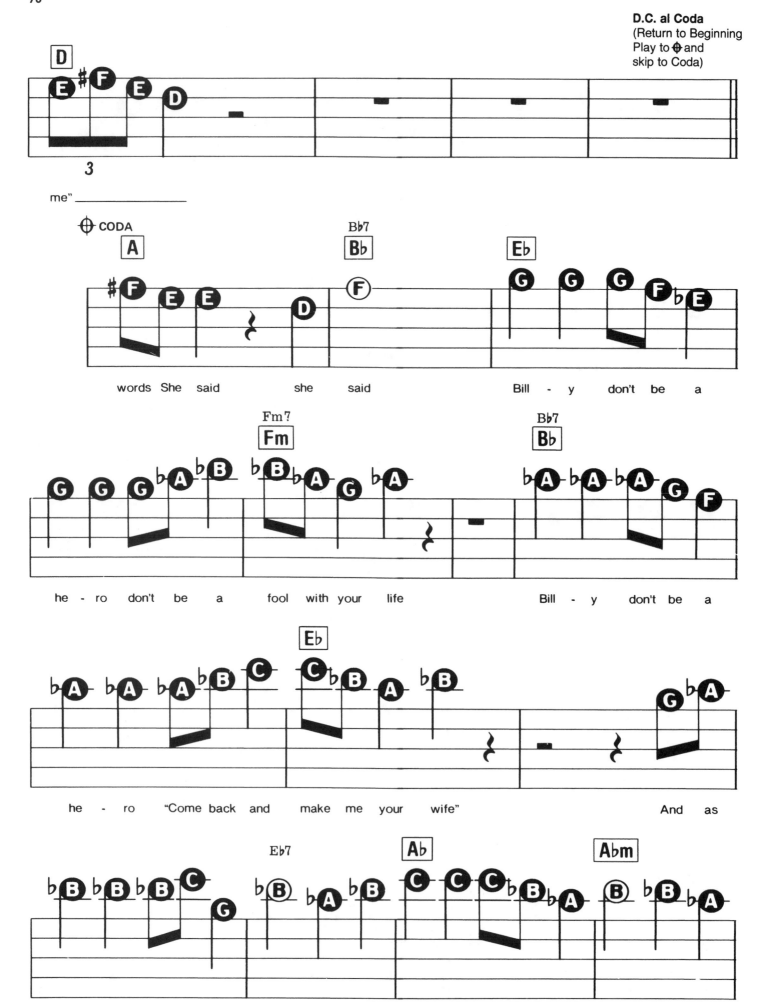

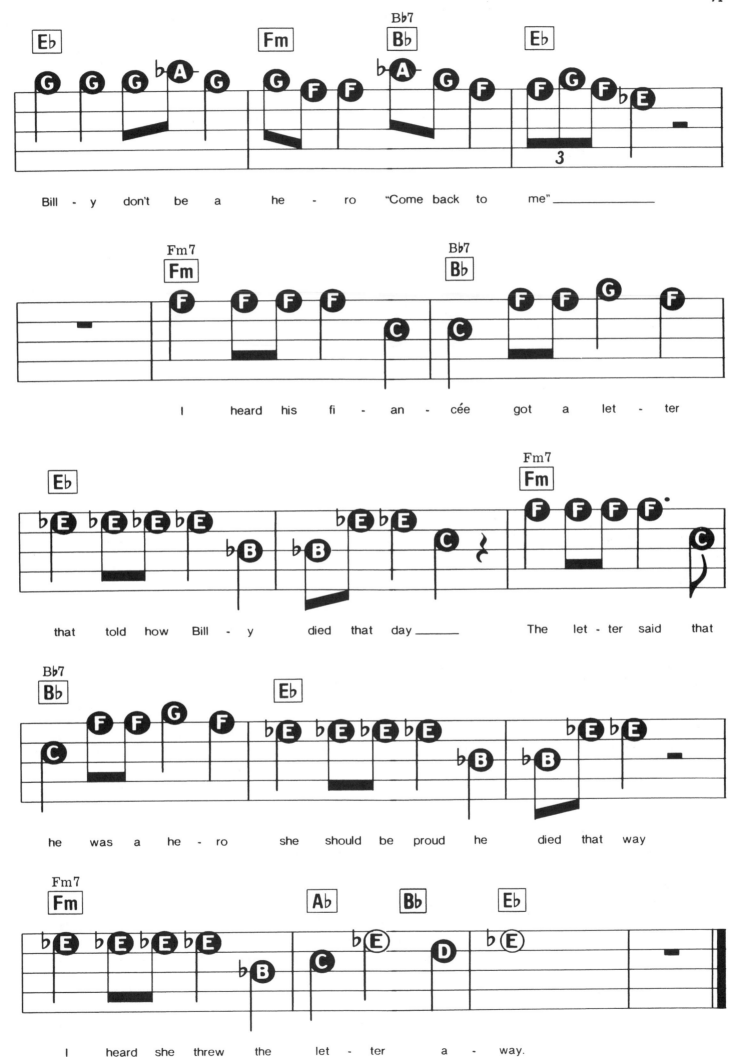

Boogie Nights

Registration 4
Rhythm: Dance or Rock

Words and Music by
Rod Temperton

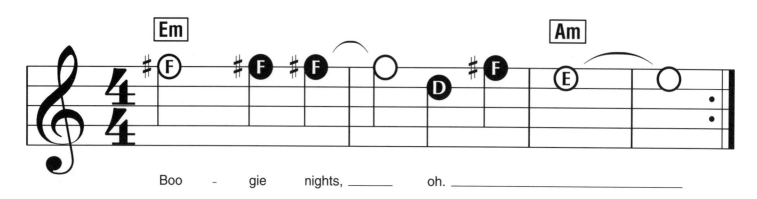

Boo - gie nights, _____ oh. _____

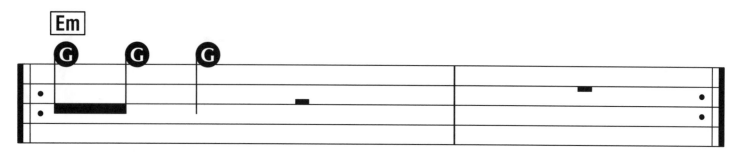

Boo - gie nights.

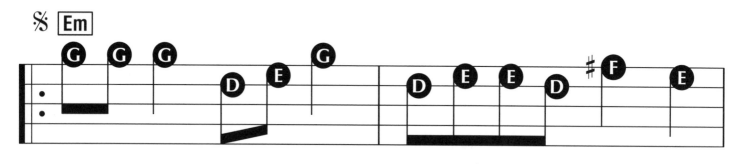

Boo - gie nights,	ain't	no	doubt	we	are	here	to	par	- ty.
Boo - gie nights,	get	that	groove;	we	let	it	take	you	high	- er.
Boo - gie nights,	it's	so	right	when	you	got	the	feel	- ing.

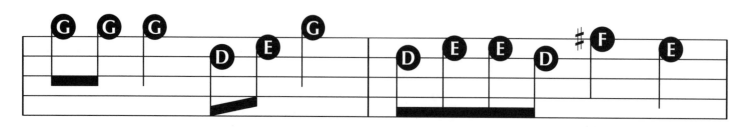

Boo - gie nights,	come	on	out.	Got	to	get	it	start	- ed.
Boo - gie nights,	make	it	move.	Set	this	place	on	fire. _____
Boo - gie nights,	hold	it	tight.	Got	to	keep	on	deal	- ing.

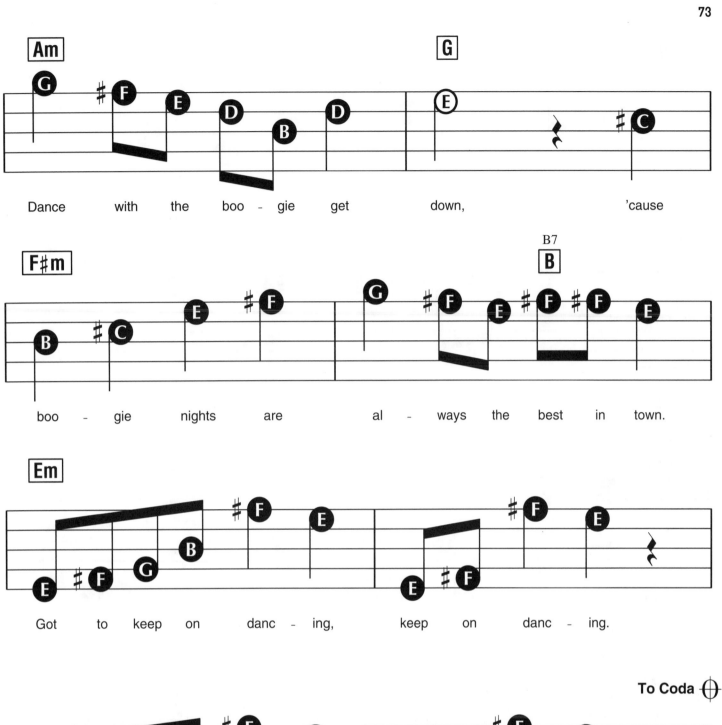

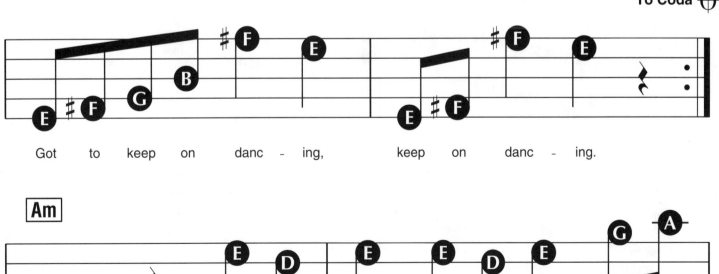

74

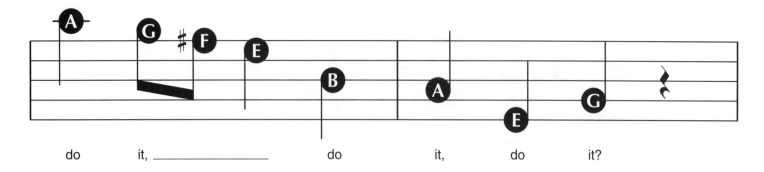

do it, _____ do it, do it?

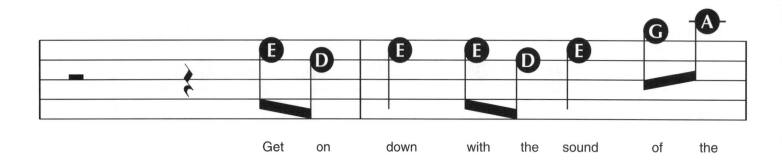

Get on down with the sound of the

D.S. al Coda
(Return to 𝄋
Play to ⊕ and
Skip to Coda)

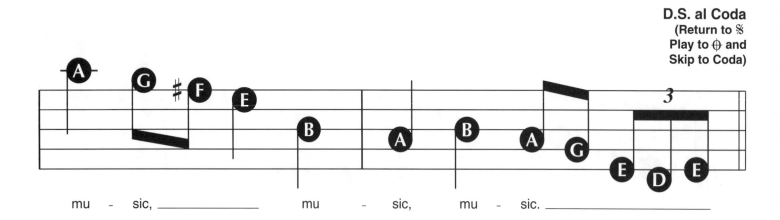

mu - sic, _____ mu - sic, mu - sic. _____

CODA

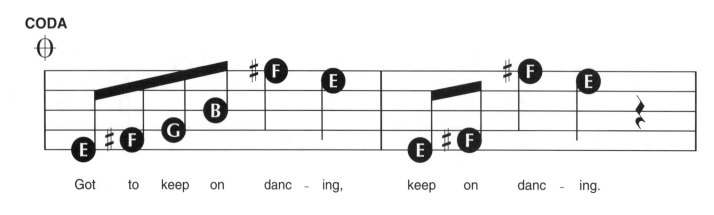

Got to keep on danc - ing, keep on danc - ing.

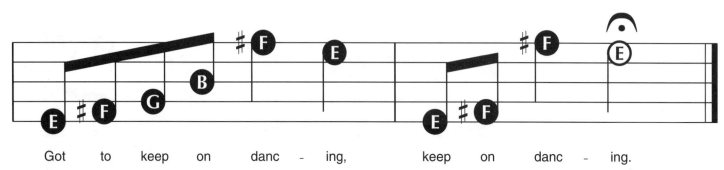

Got to keep on danc - ing, keep on danc - ing.

Can't Get Enough of Your Love, Babe

Registration 8
Rhythm: Rock or 8 Beat

Words and Music by
Barry White

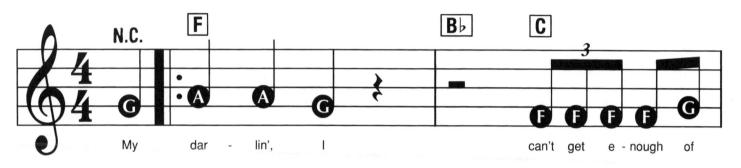

My dar - lin', I   can't get e - nough of

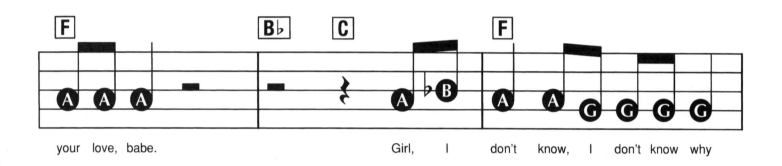

your love, babe.   Girl, I don't know, I don't know why

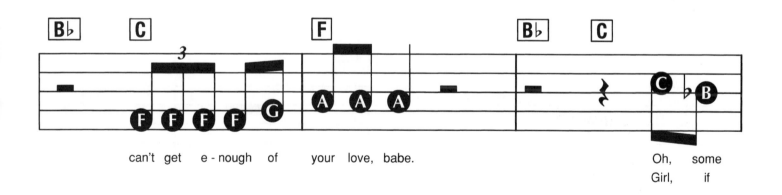

can't get e - nough of your love, babe.   Oh, some
Girl, if

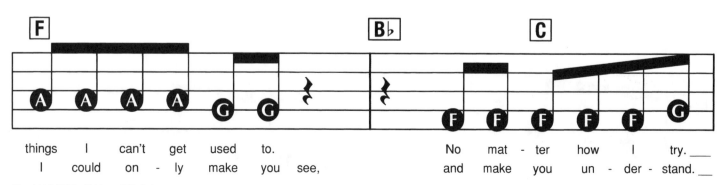

things I can't get used to.   No mat - ter how I try. ___
I could on - ly make you see,   and make you un - der - stand. ___

The Boys Are Back in Town

Registration 9
Rhythm: Rock or 8 Beat

Words and Music by
Philip Parris Lynott

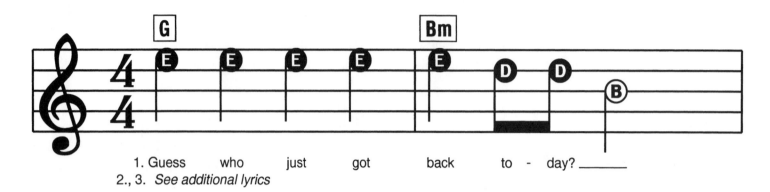

1. Guess who just got back to - day? _____
2., 3. *See additional lyrics*

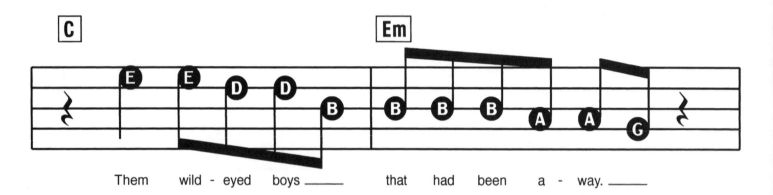

Them wild - eyed boys _____ that had been a - way. _____

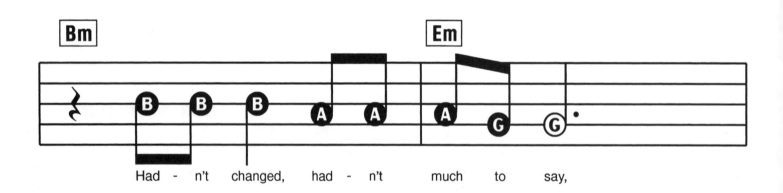

Had - n't changed, had - n't much to say,

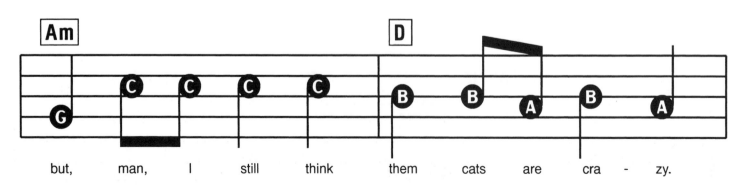

but, man, I still think them cats are cra - zy.

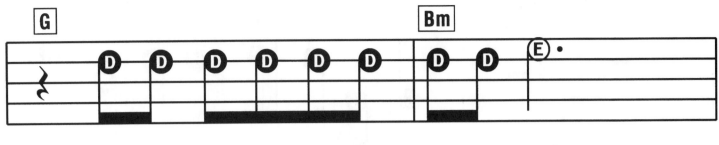

They were ask - ing if you were a - round,

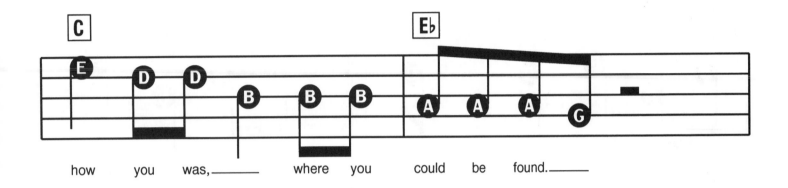

how you was,_____ where you could be found._____

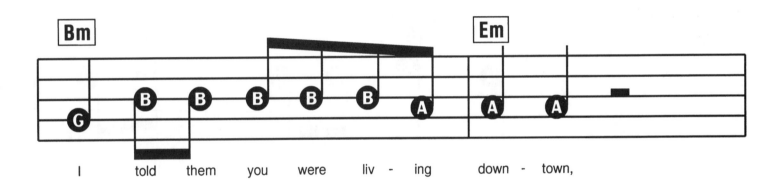

I told them you were liv - ing down - town,

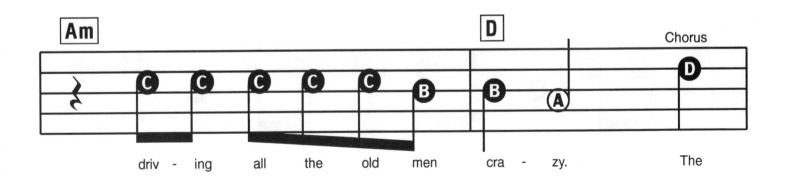

driv - ing all the old men cra - zy. The

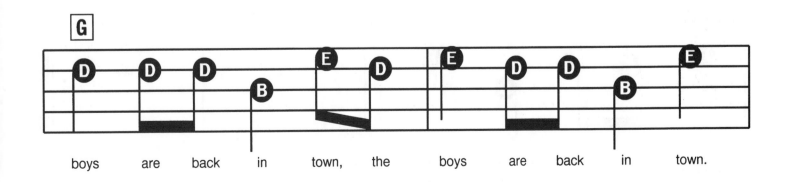

boys are back in town, the boys are back in town.

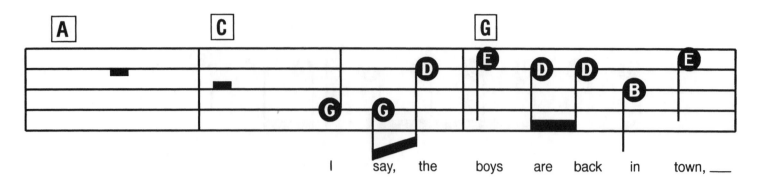

I say, the boys are back in town, ___

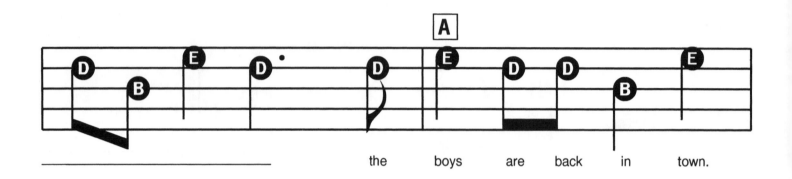

the boys are back in town.

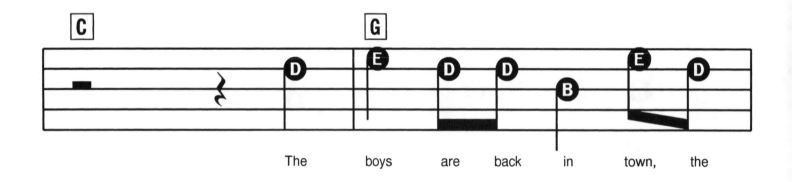

The boys are back in town, the

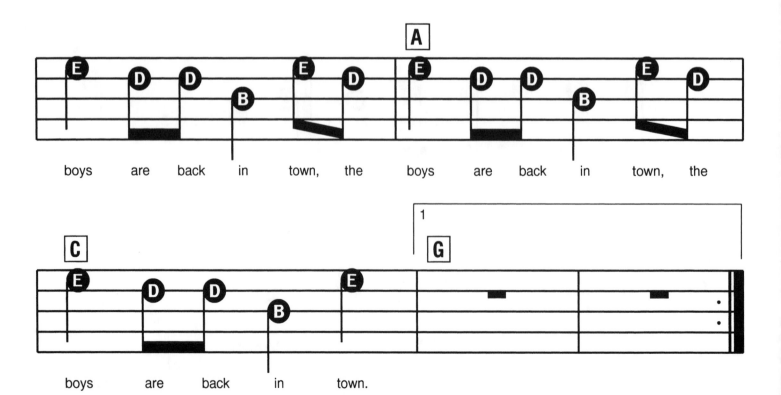

boys are back in town, the boys are back in town, the

boys are back in town.

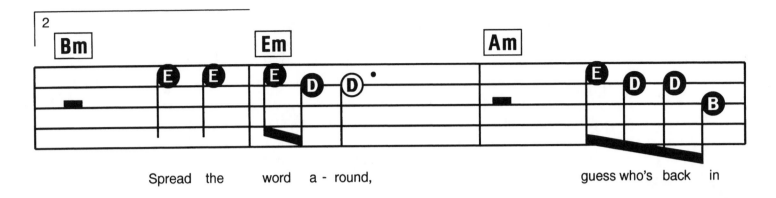

Spread the word a - round, guess who's back in

D.C. and Fade
(Return to beginning
and Fade after Chorus)

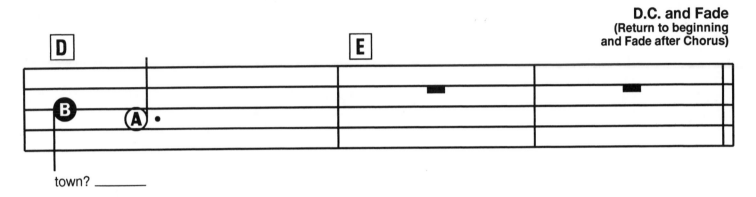

town? _____

Additional Lyrics

2. You know that chick that used to dance a lot,
   Every night she'd be on the floor shaking what she'd got;
   Man, when I tell you she was cool, she was hot,
   I mean she was steaming.

   And that time over at Johnny's place,
   Well, this chick got up and she slapped Johnny's face.
   Man, we just fell about the place;
   If that chick don't wanna know, forget her.
   To Chorus:

3. Friday night they'll be dressed to kill
   Down at Dino's Bar and Grill;
   The drink will flow and blood will spill
   And if the boys want to fight, you better let 'em.

   That jukebox in the corner blasting out my favorite song
   The nights are getting warmer, it won't be long.
   It won't be long till summer comes,
   Now that the boys are here again.
   To Chorus:

Brandy
(You're a Fine Girl)

Registration 1
Rhythm: Soft Rock or Ballad

Words and Music by
Elliot Lurie

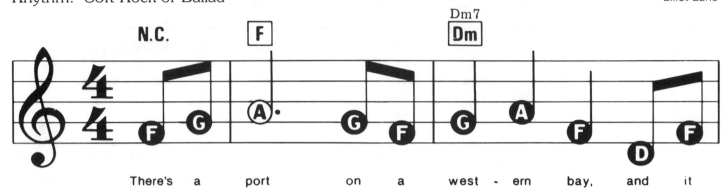

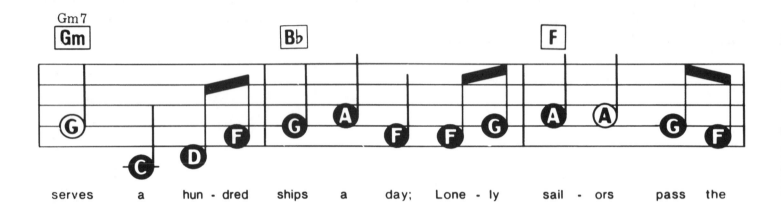

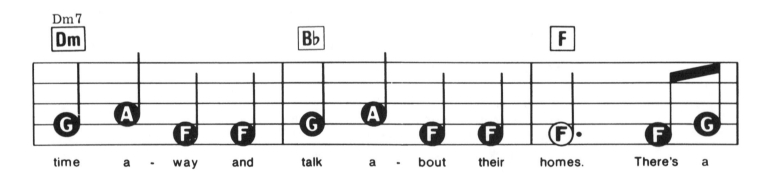

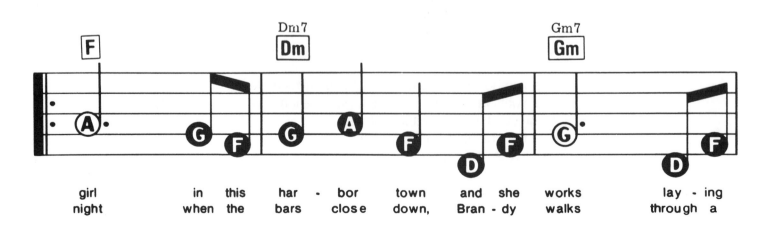

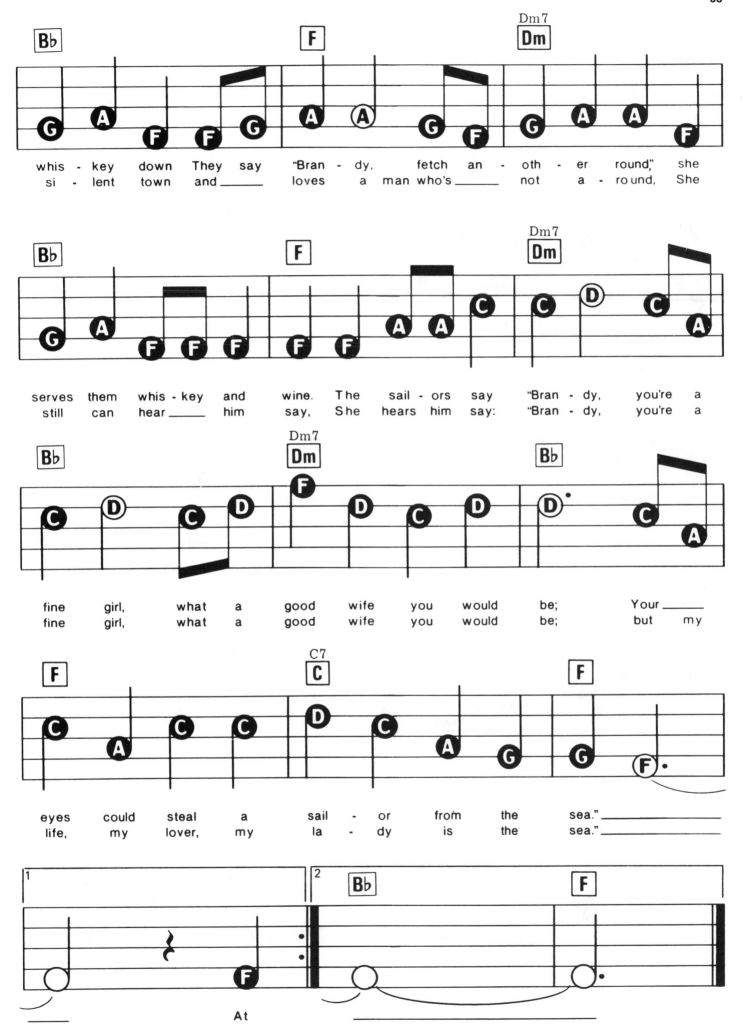

Car Wash

Registration 7
Rhythm: 16 Beat or Rock

Words and Music by
Norman Whitfield

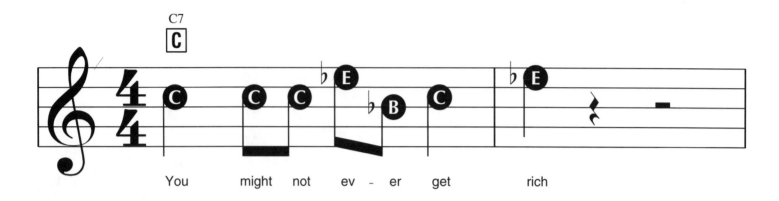

You might not ev – er get rich

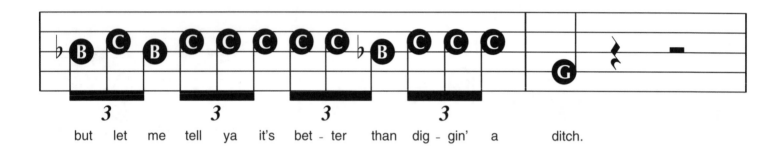

but let me tell ya it's bet – ter than dig – gin' a ditch.

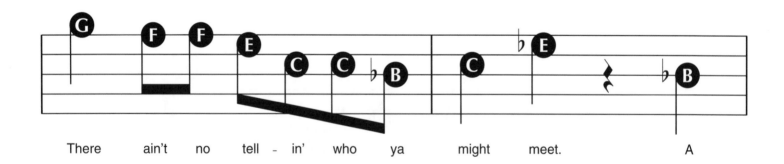

There ain't no tell – in' who ya might meet. A

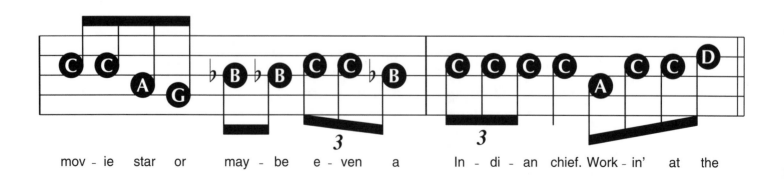

mov – ie star or may – be e – ven a In – di – an chief. Work – in' at the

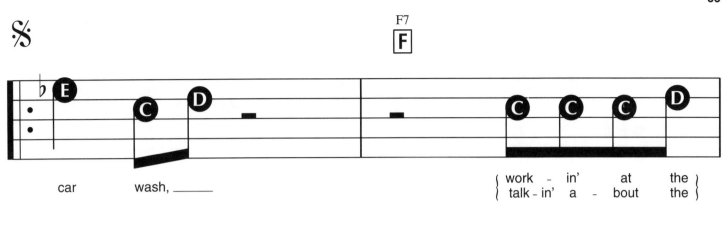

car wash, _____

{ work - in' at the }
{ talk - in' a - bout the }

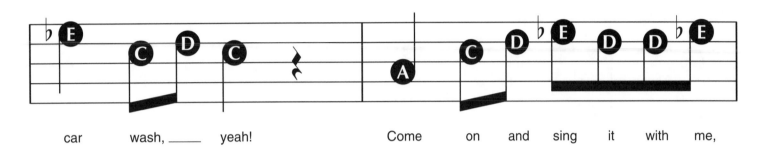

car wash, ____ yeah!   Come on and sing it with me,

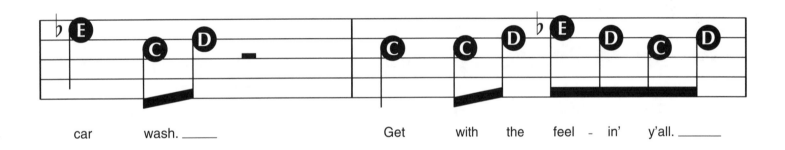

car wash. ____   Get with the feel - in' y'all. ____

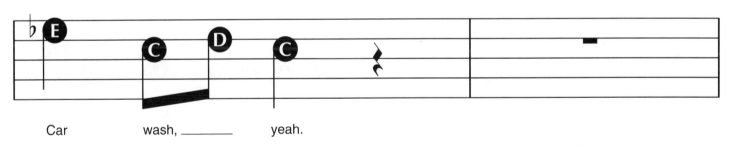

Car wash, _____ yeah.

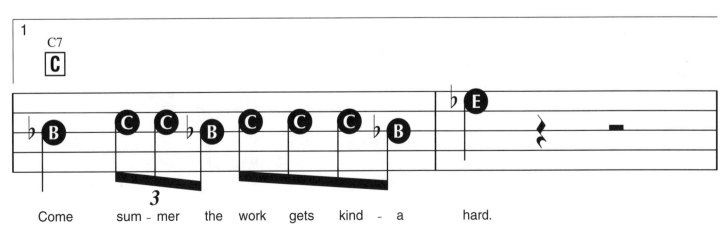

Come sum - mer the work gets kind - a hard.

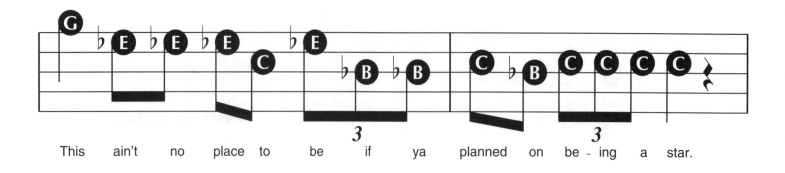

This ain't no place to be if ya planned on be - ing a star.

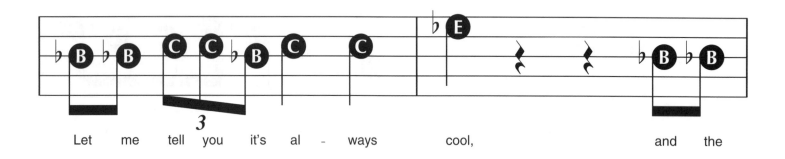

Let me tell you it's al - ways cool, and the

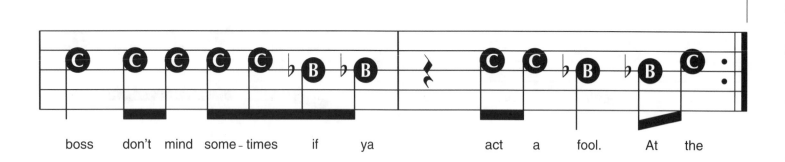

boss don't mind some - times if ya act a fool. At the

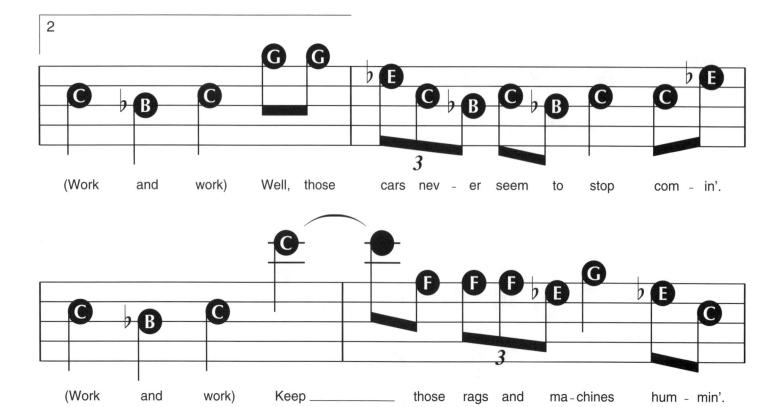

(Work and work) Well, those cars nev - er seem to stop com - in'.

(Work and work) Keep _____ those rags and ma - chines hum - min'.

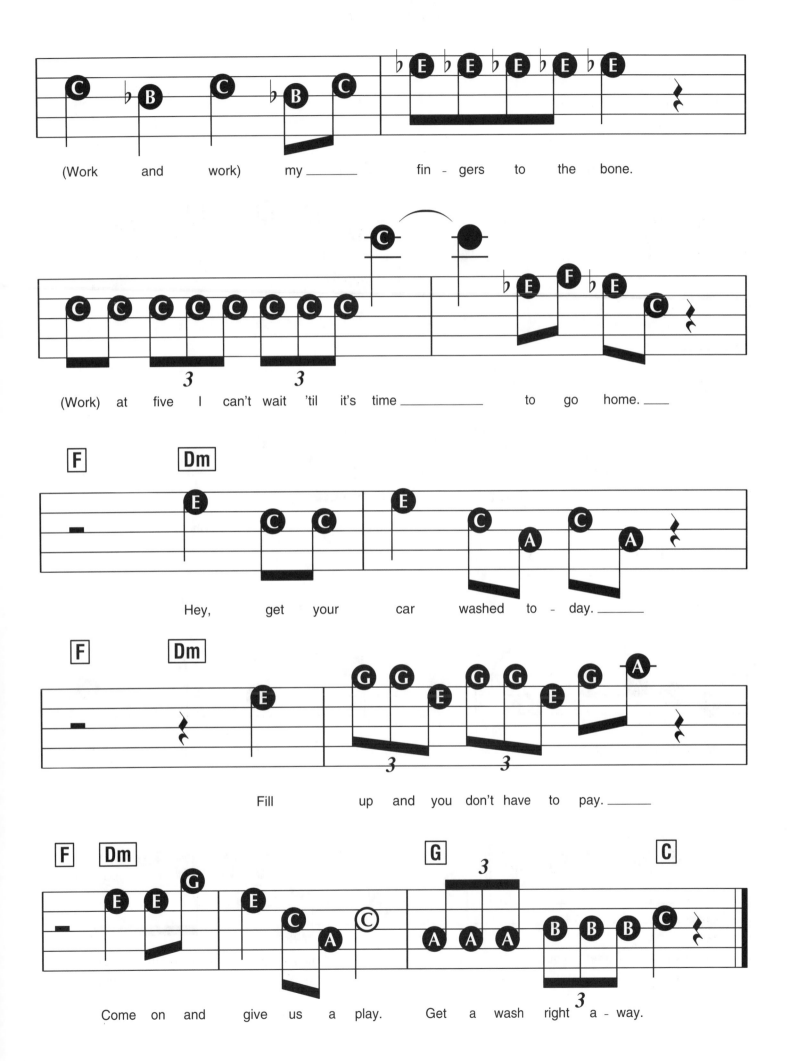

Clair

Registration 5
Rhythm: Ballad or 8 Beat

Words and Music by
Gilbert O'Sullivan

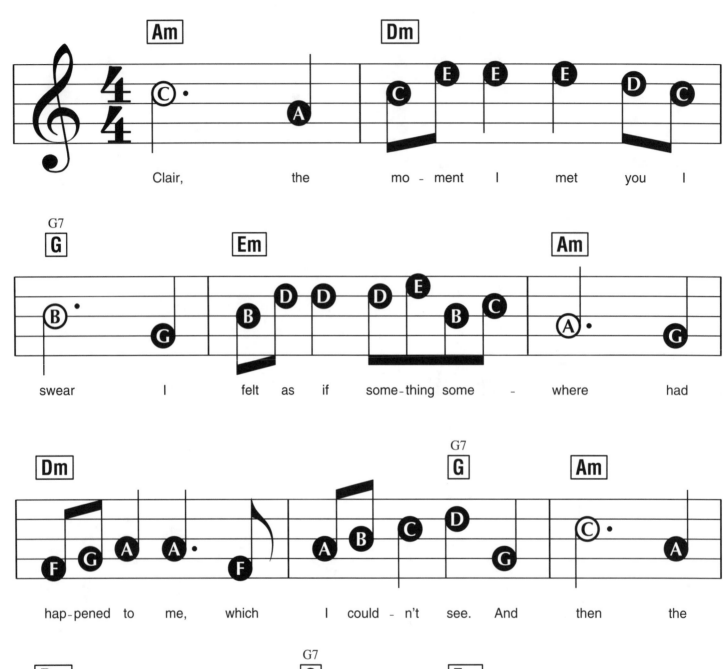

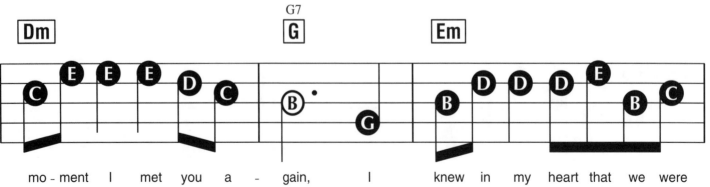

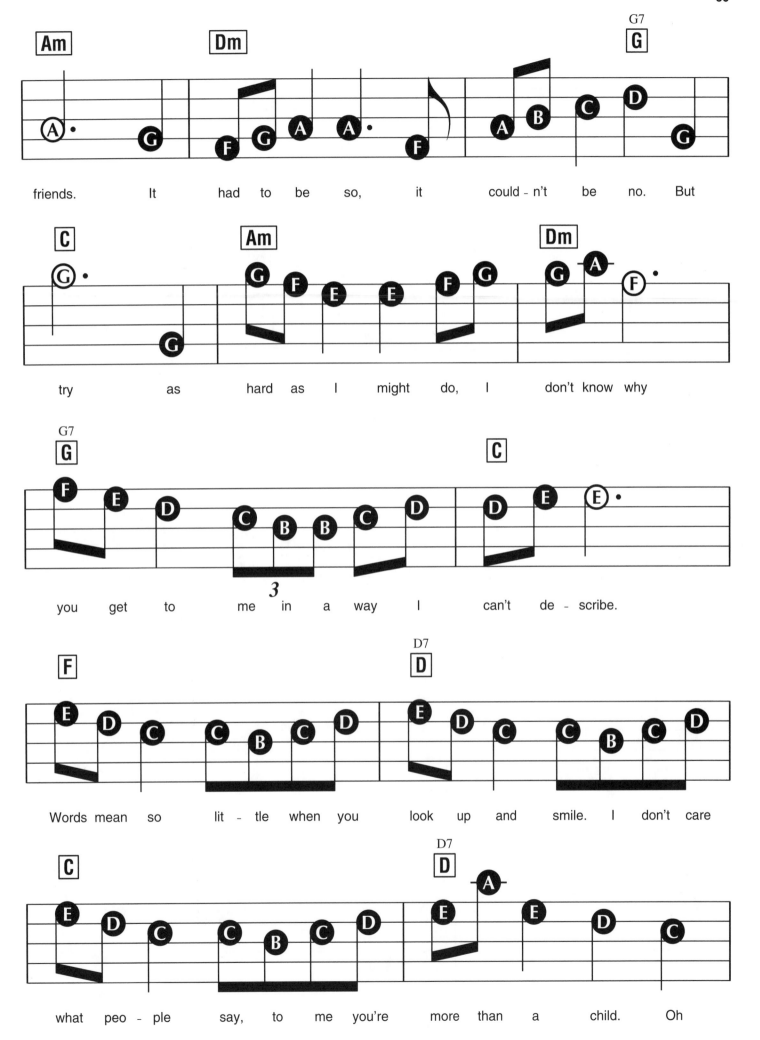

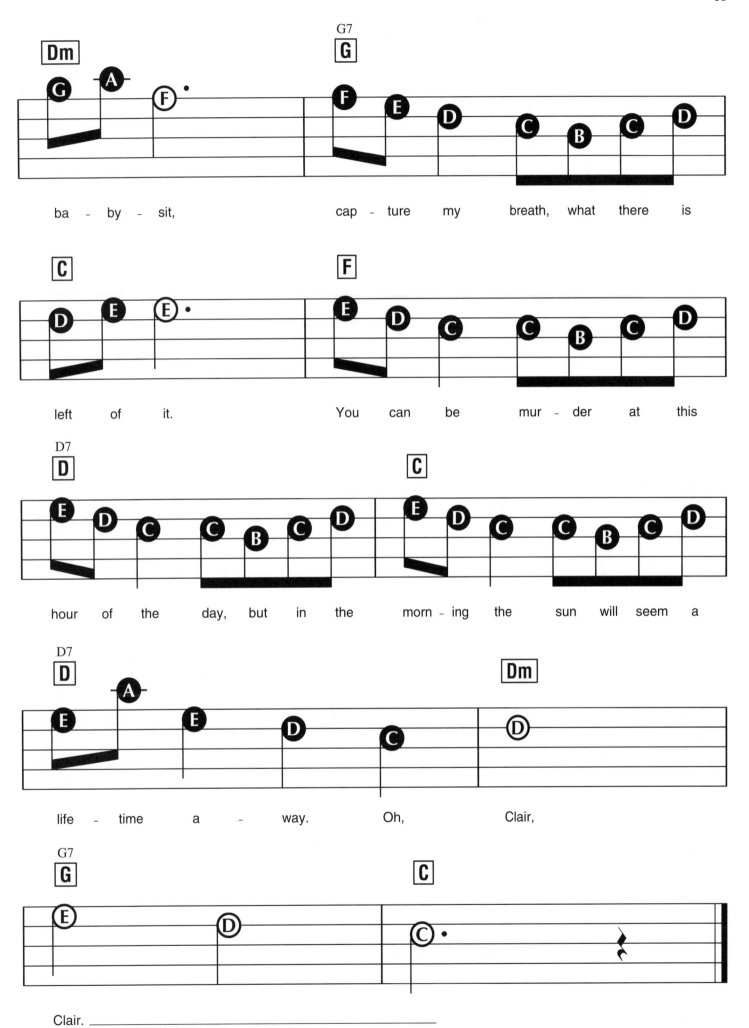

The Closer I Get to You

Registration 8
Rhythm: Ballad or 8 Beat

Words and Music by James Mtume
and Reggie Lucas

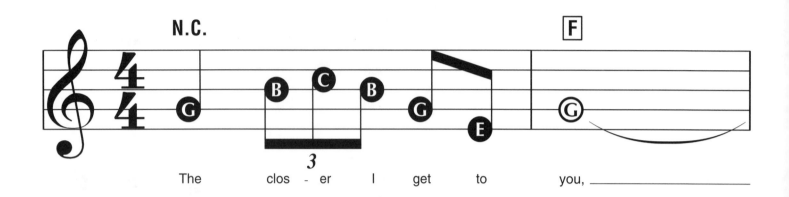

The clos - er I get to you, _____

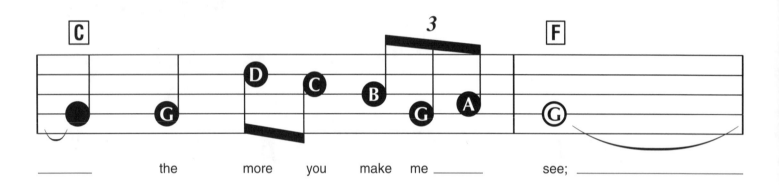

_____ the more you make me _____ see;

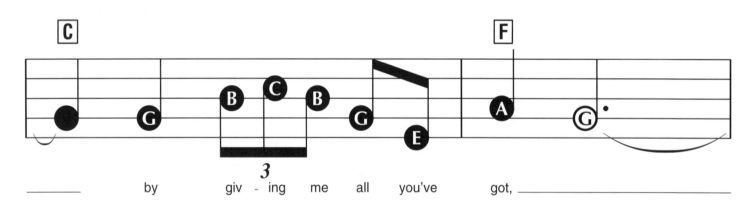

_____ by giv - ing me all you've got, _____

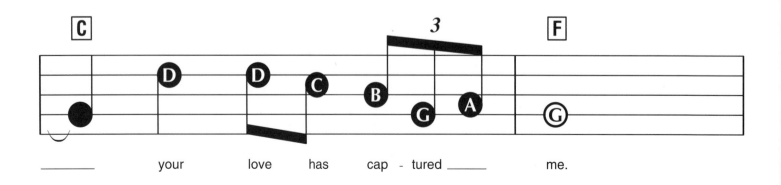

_____ your love has cap - tured _____ me.

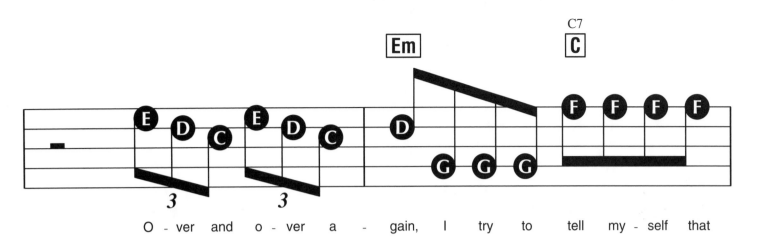

O – ver and o – ver a – gain, I try to tell my – self that

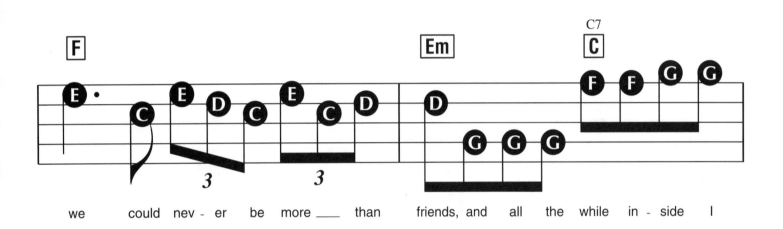

we could nev – er be more ____ than friends, and all the while in – side I

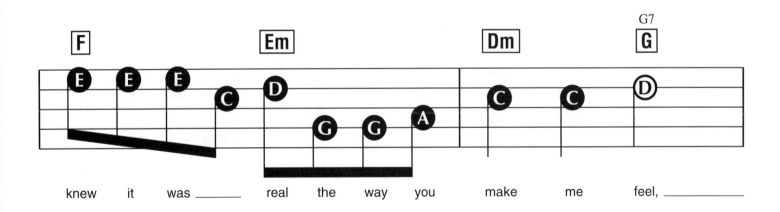

knew it was ____ real the way you make me feel, ____

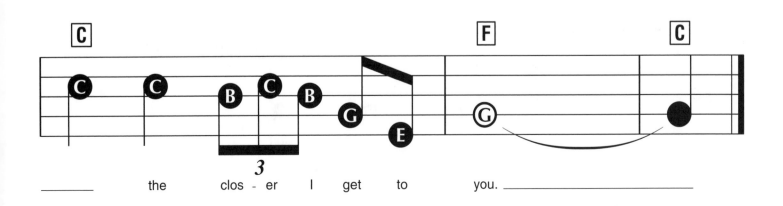

____ the clos – er I get to you. ____

Come and Get It

Registration 3
Rhythm: 8 Beat or Rock

Words and Music by
Paul McCartney

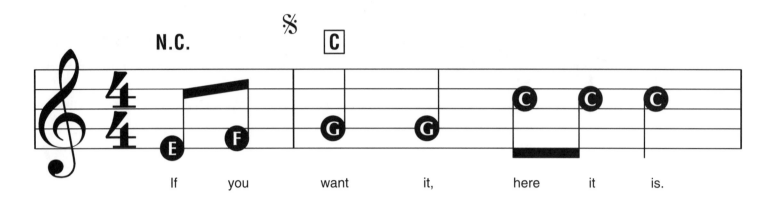

If you want it, here it is.

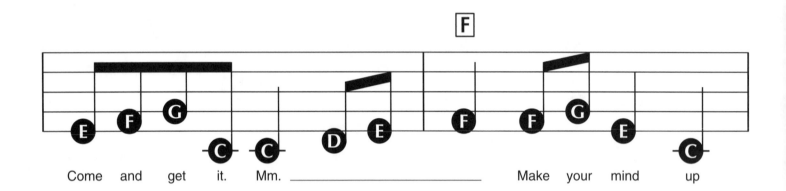

Come and get it. Mm. _____ Make your mind up

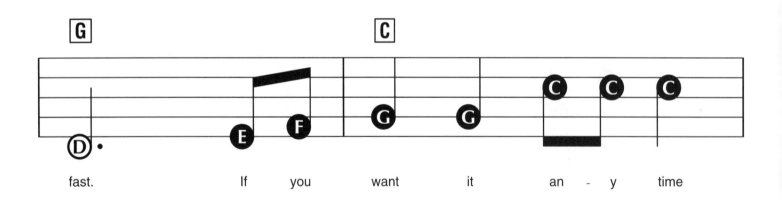

fast. If you want it an - y time

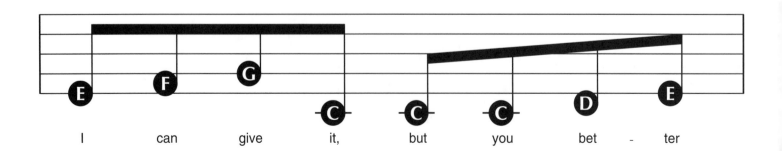

I can give it, but you bet - ter

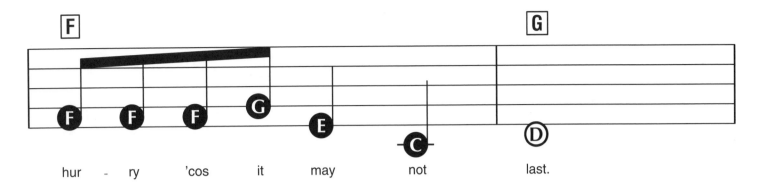

hur - ry 'cos it may not last.

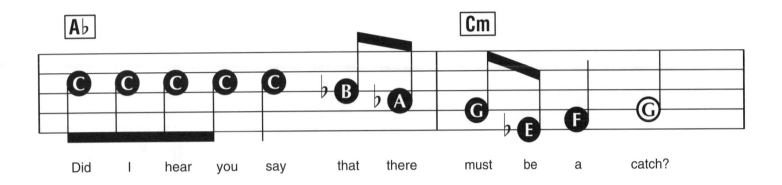

Did I hear you say that there must be a catch?

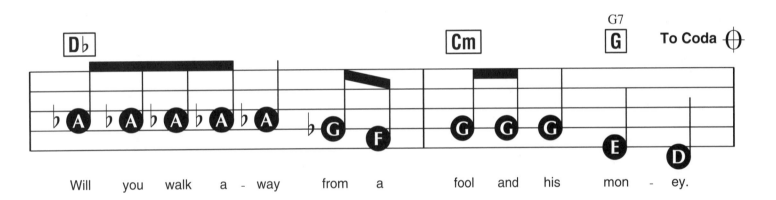

Will you walk a - way from a fool and his mon - ey.

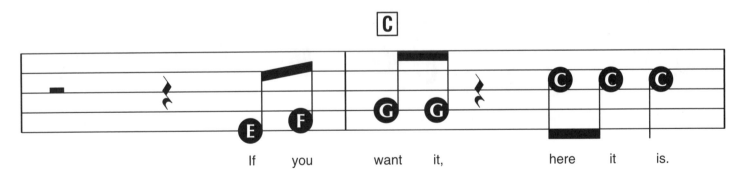

If you want it, here it is.

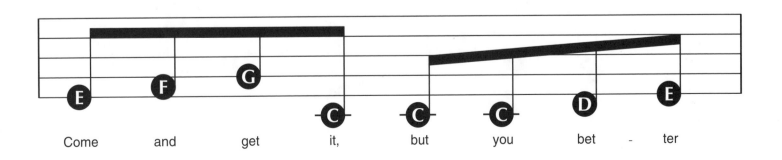

Come and get it, but you bet - ter

96

D.S. al Coda
(Return to %
Play to ⊕ and
Skip to Coda)

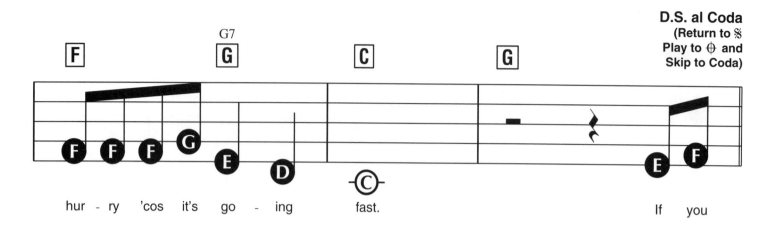

hur – ry 'cos it's go – ing   fast.   If   you

CODA

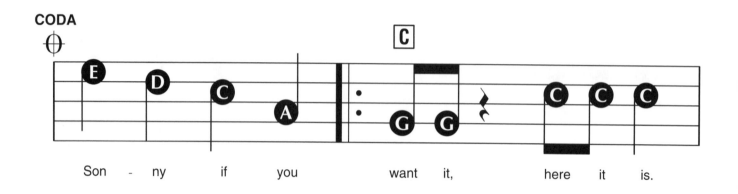

Son – ny   if   you   want it,   here it is.

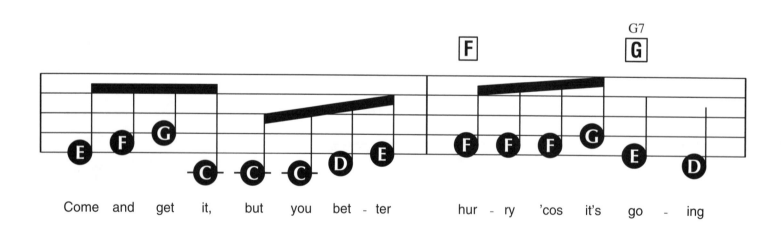

Come and get it, but you bet – ter   hur – ry 'cos it's go – ing

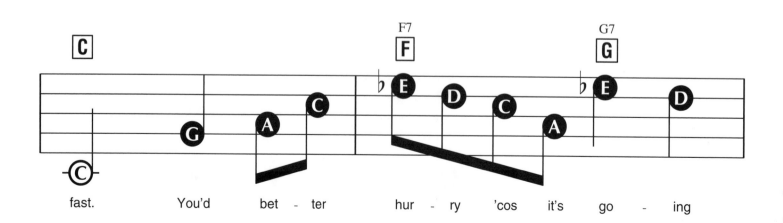

fast.   You'd   bet – ter   hur – ry 'cos   it's   go – ing

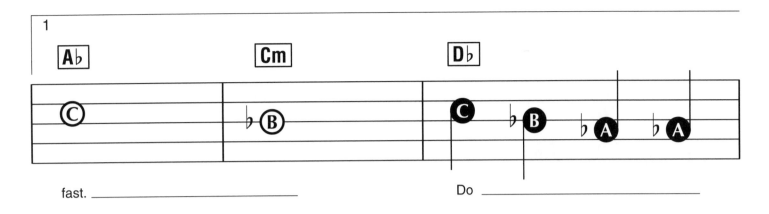

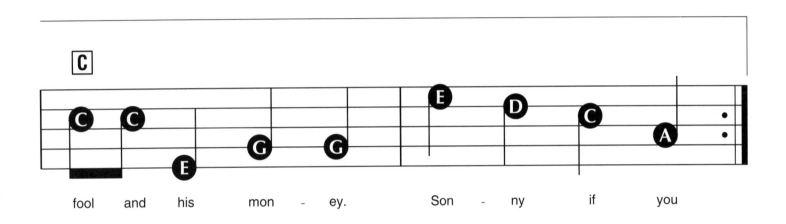

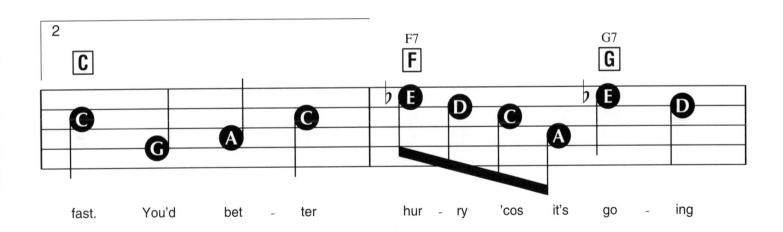

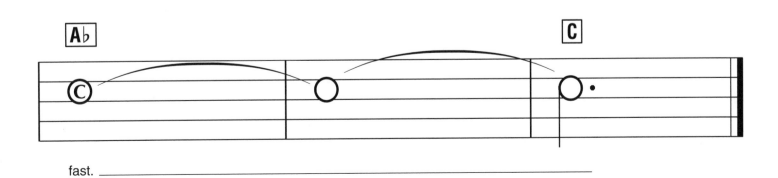

Come Sail Away

Registration 4
Rhythm: 8 Beat or Rock

Words and Music by
Dennis DeYoung

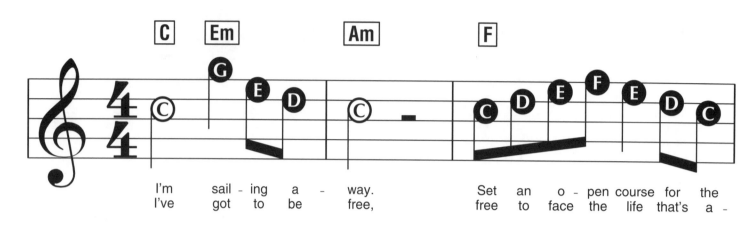

I'm sail - ing a - way.   Set an o - pen course for the
I've got to be free,   free to face the life that's a -

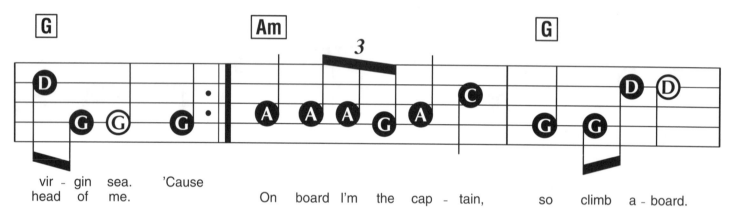

vir - gin sea. 'Cause   On board I'm the cap - tain,   so climb a - board.
head of me.

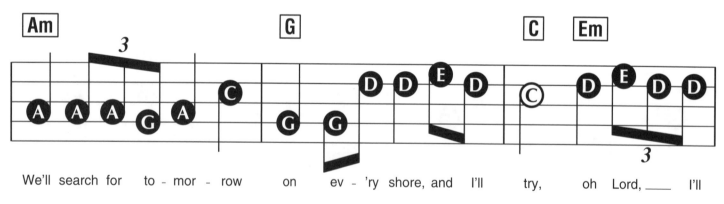

We'll search for to - mor - row   on ev - 'ry shore, and I'll   try,   oh Lord, ___ I'll

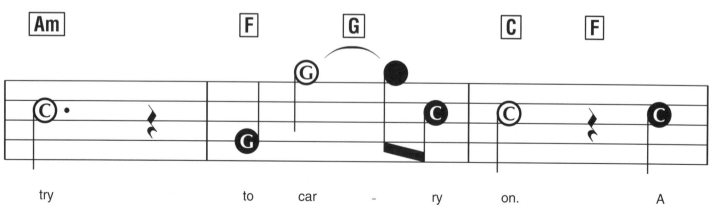

try   to car - ry on.   A

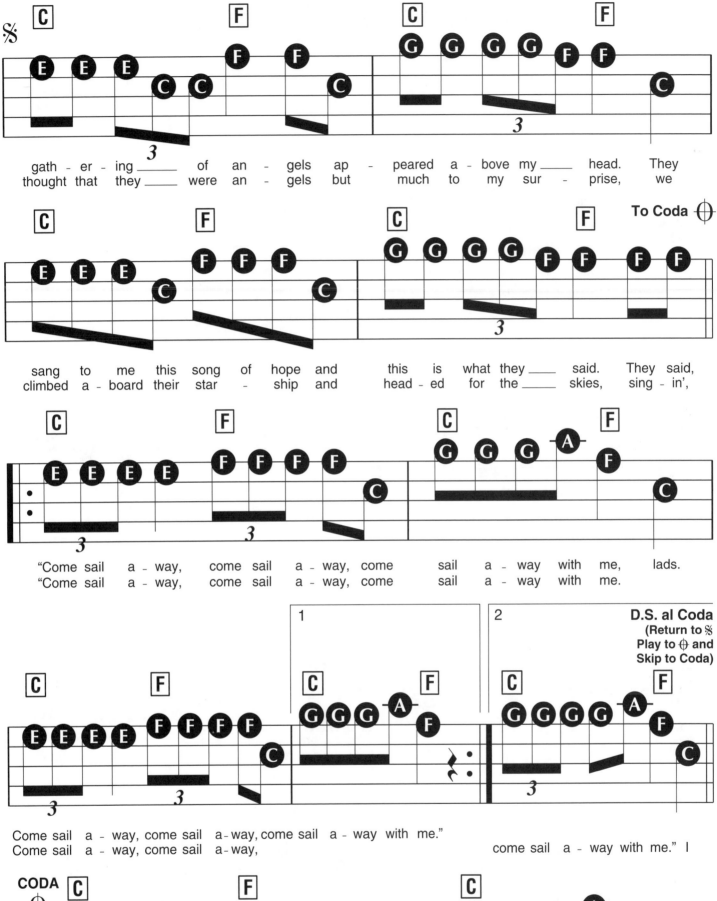

gath - er - ing _____ of an - gels ap - peared a - bove my _____ head. They
thought that they _____ were an - gels but much to my sur - prise, we

sang to me this song of hope and this is what they _____ said. They said,
climbed a - board their star - ship and head - ed for the _____ skies, sing - in',

"Come sail a - way, come sail a - way, come sail a - way with me, lads.
"Come sail a - way, come sail a - way, come sail a - way with me.

Come sail a - way, come sail a - way, come sail a - way with me."
Come sail a - way, come sail a - way, come sail a - way with me." I

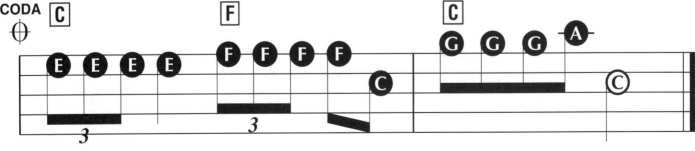

"Come sail a - way, come sail a - way, come sail a - way with me."

Cracklin' Rosie

Registration 5
Rhythm: Fox Trot or Ballad

Words and Music by
Neil Diamond

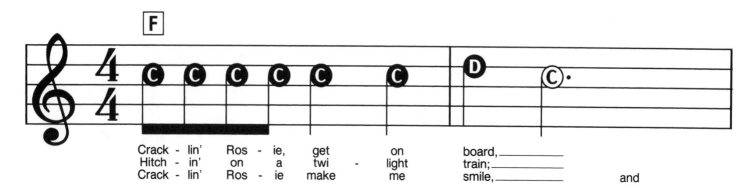

Crack - lin' Ros - ie, get on board,_____
Hitch - in' on a twi - light train;_____
Crack - lin' Ros - ie make me smile,_____ and

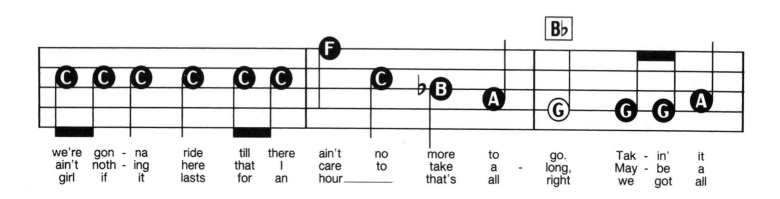

we're gon - na ride till there ain't no more to go. Tak - in' it
ain't noth - ing here that I care no to take a - long, May - be it a
girl if it lasts for an hour_____ that's all right we got all

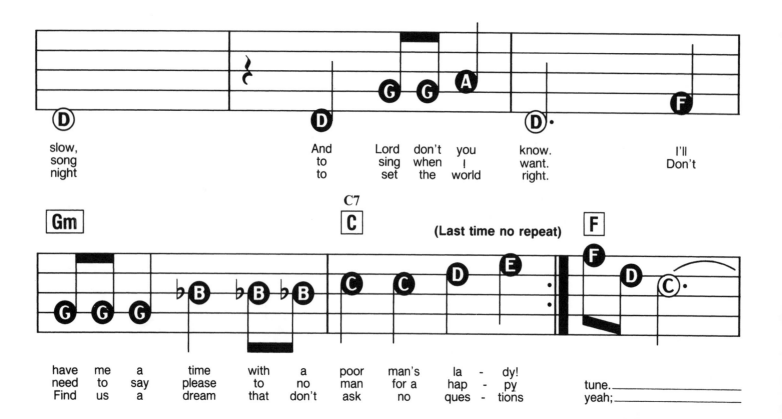

slow, And Lord don't you know. I'll
song to sing when I want. Don't
night to set the world right.

have me a time with a poor man's la - dy!
need to say please to no man for a hap - py
Find us a dream that don't ask no ques - tions

(Last time no repeat)

tune._____
yeah;_____

101

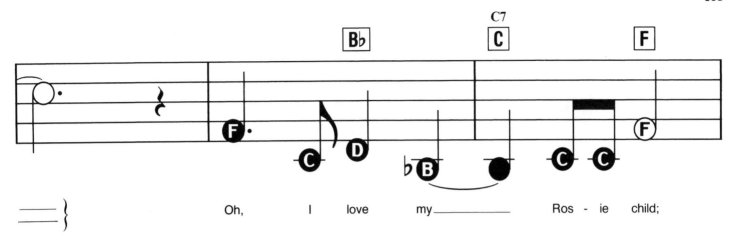

Oh, I love my_____ Ros - ie child;

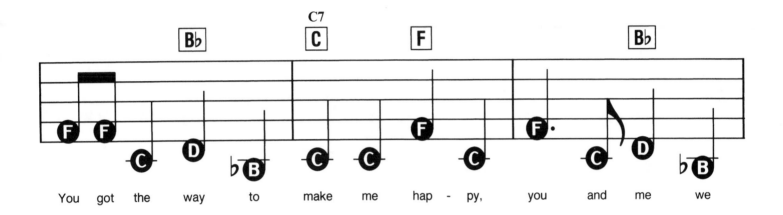

You got the way to make me hap - py, you and me we

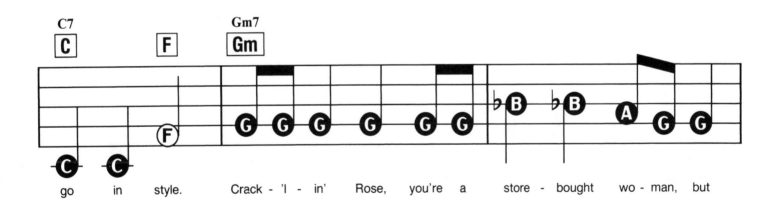

go in style. Crack - 'l - in' Rose, you're a store - bought wo - man, but

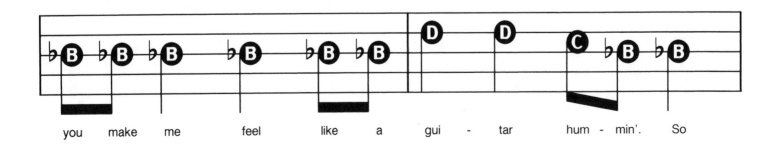

you make me feel like a gui - tar hum - min'. So

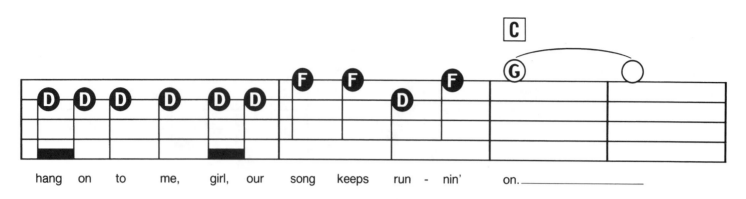

hang on to me, girl, our song keeps run - nin' on._____

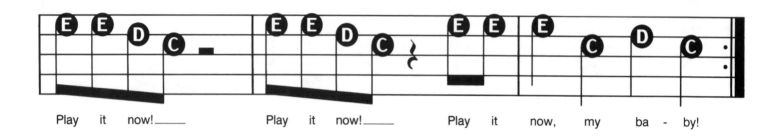

Play it now!_____ Play it now!_____ Play it now, my ba - by!

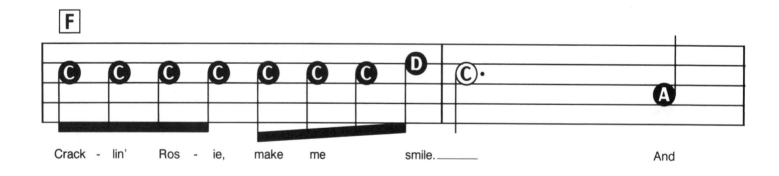

Crack - lin' Ros - ie, make me smile._____ And

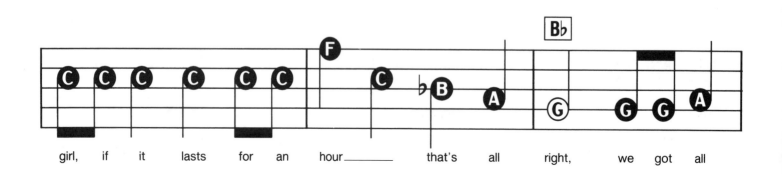

girl, if it lasts for an hour_____ that's all right, we got all

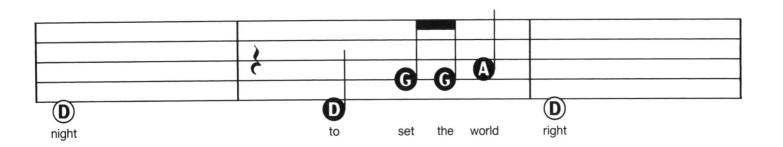

night ... to set the world right

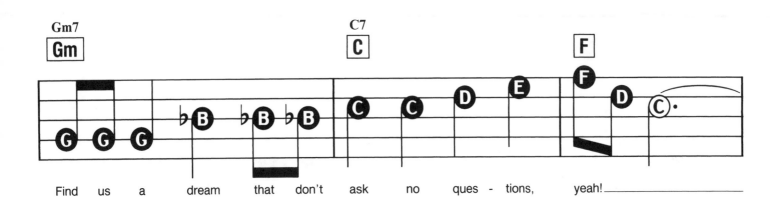

Find us a dream that don't ask no ques - tions, yeah!

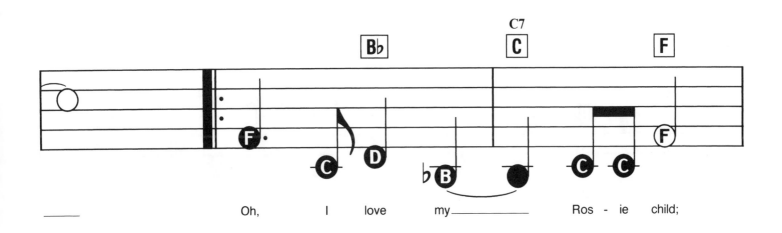

Oh, I love my Ros - ie child;

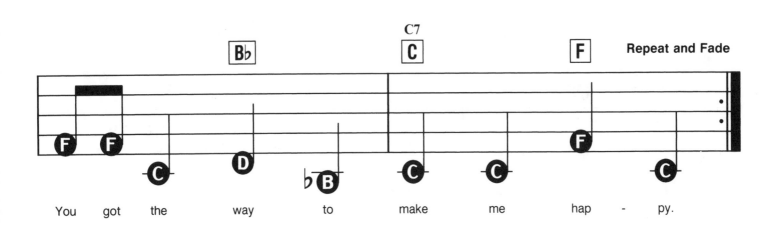

You got the way to make me hap - py.

Da Ya Think I'm Sexy

Registration 4
Rhythm: Disco or Rock

Words and Music by Rod Stewart
and Carmine Appice

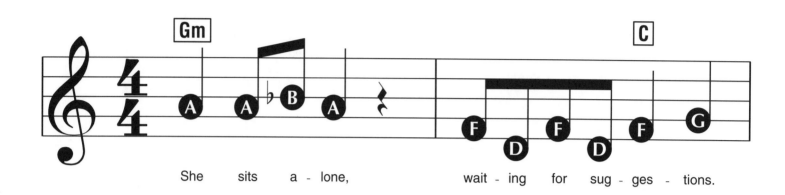

She sits a - lone, waiting for sug - ges - tions.

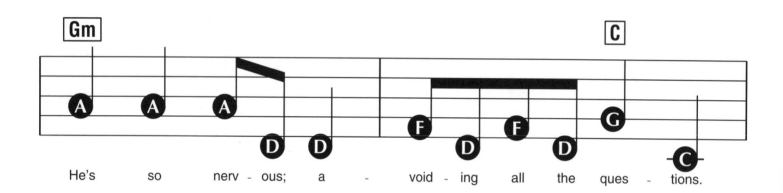

He's so nerv - ous; a - void - ing all the ques - tions.

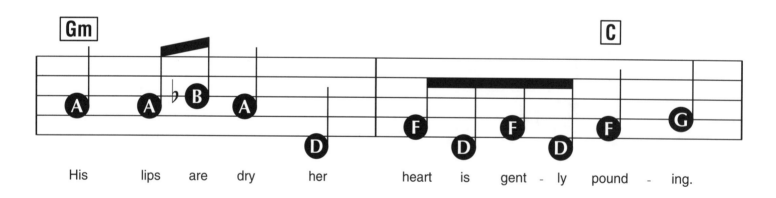

His lips are dry her heart is gent - ly pound - ing.

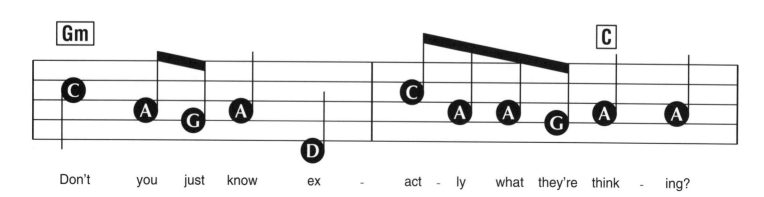

Don't you just know ex - act - ly what they're think - ing?

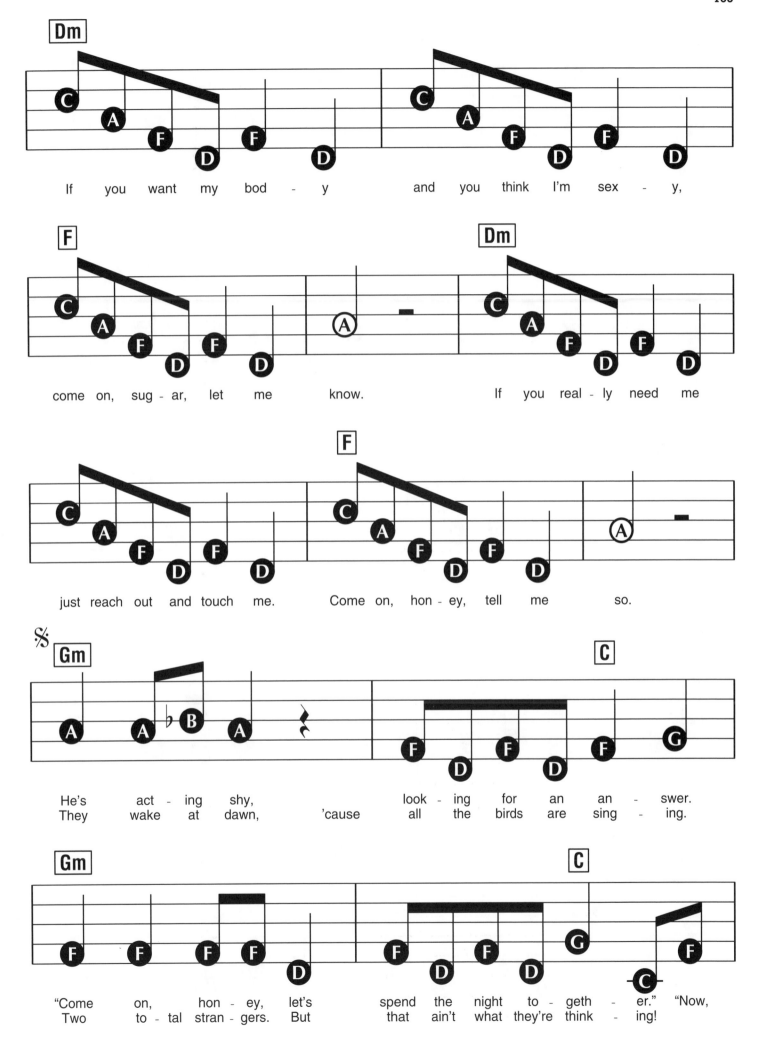

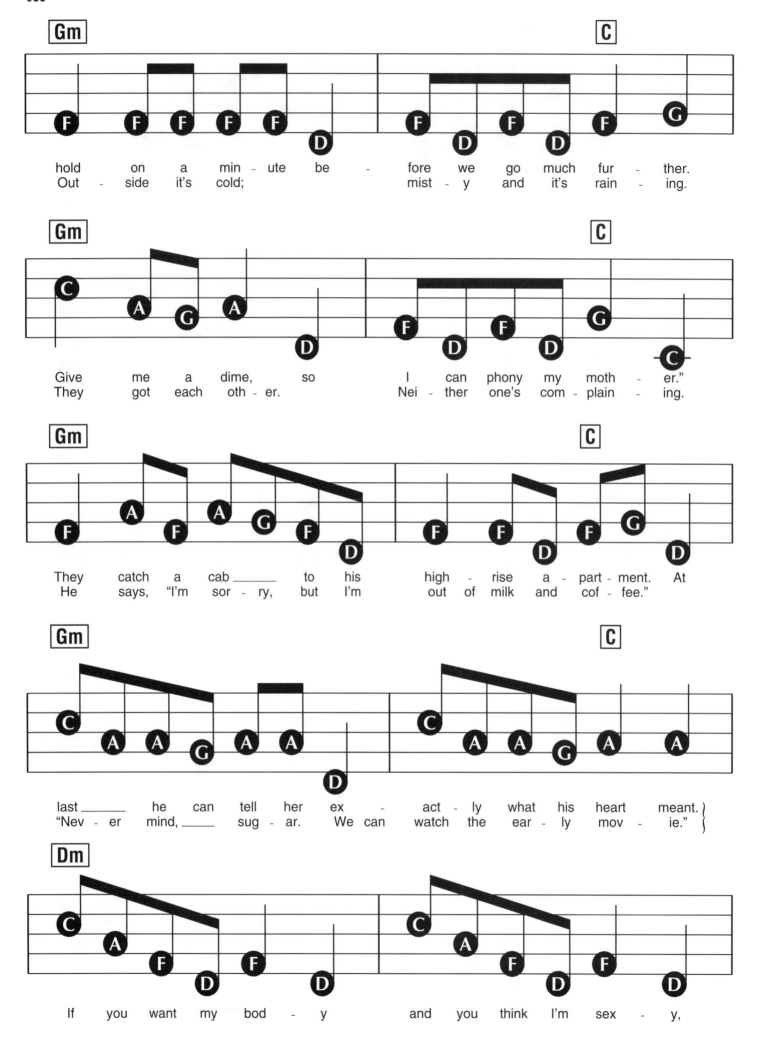

Daniel

Registration 2
Rhythm: Latin or Rock

Words and Music by Elton John
and Bernie Taupin

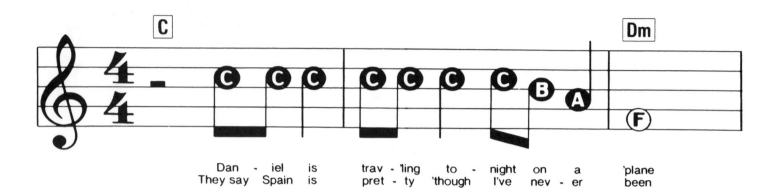

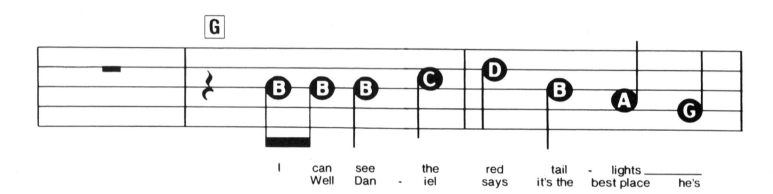

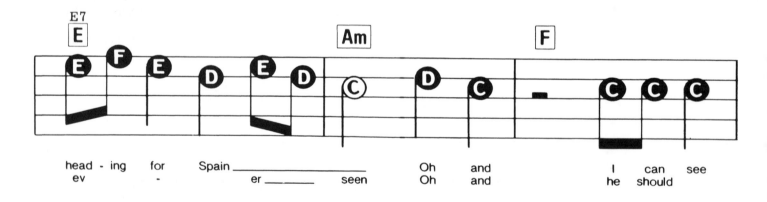

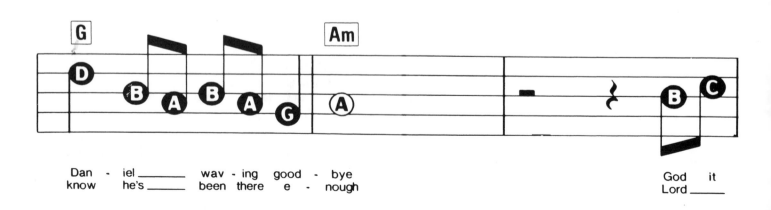

109

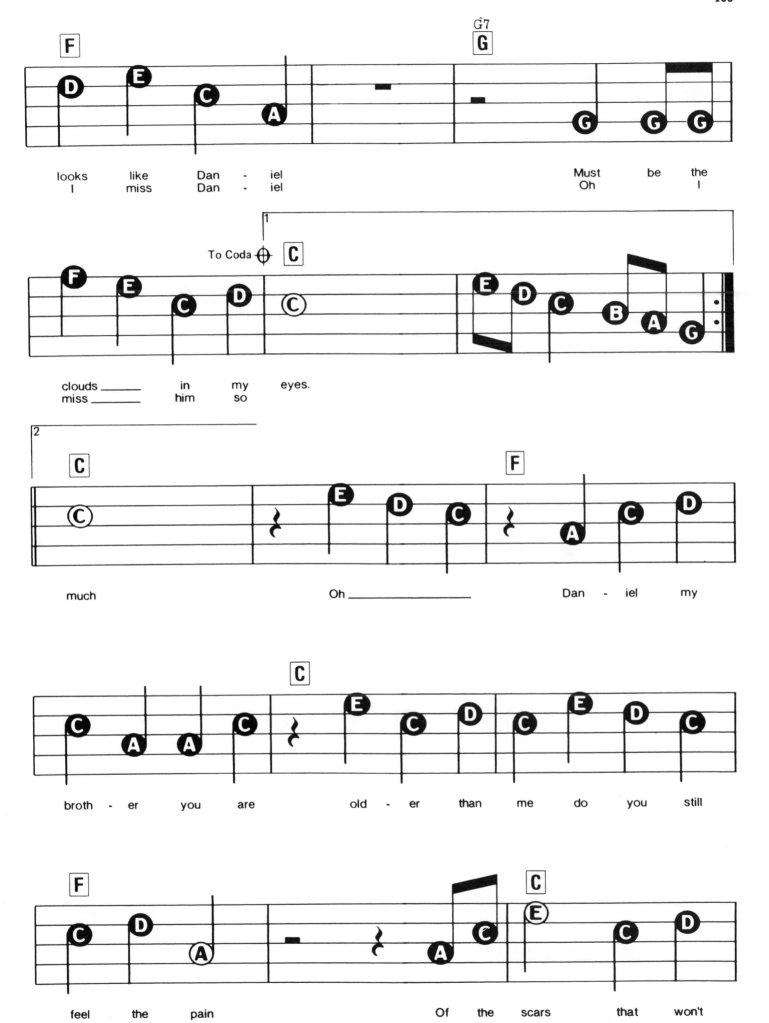

110

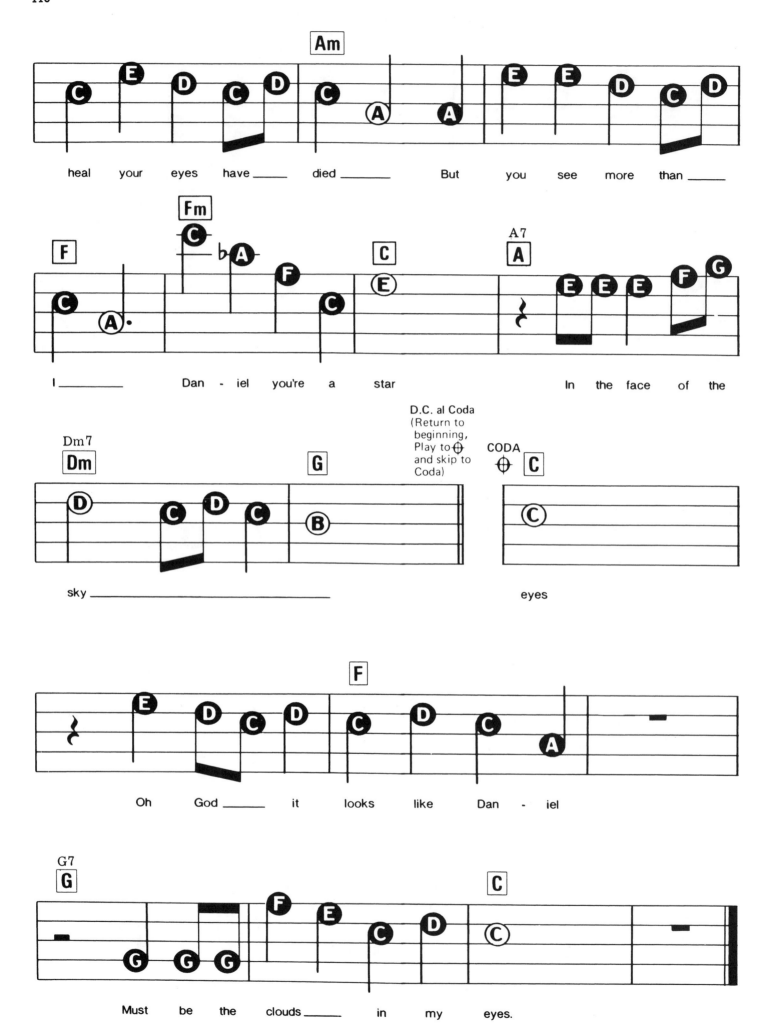

Disco Lady

Registration 7
Rhythm: Disco or Rock

Words and Music by Don Davis,
Harvey Scales and Al Vance

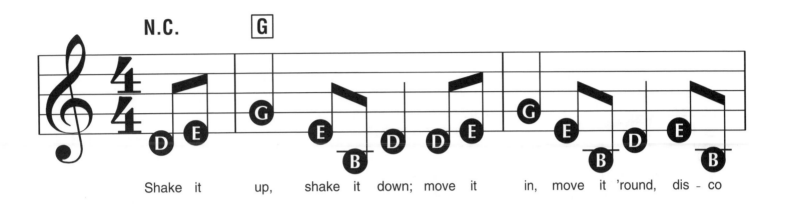

Shake it up, shake it down; move it in, move it 'round, dis - co

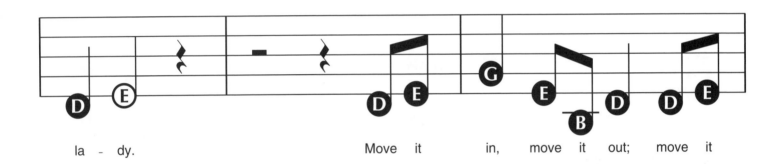

la - dy. Move it in, move it out; move it

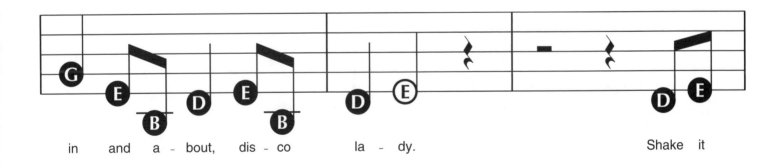

in and a - bout, dis - co la - dy. Shake it

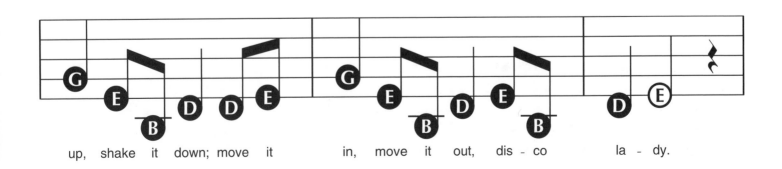

up, shake it down; move it in, move it out, dis - co la - dy.

112

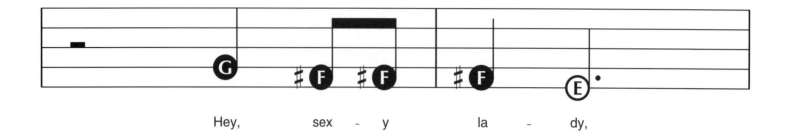

Hey, sex – y la – dy,

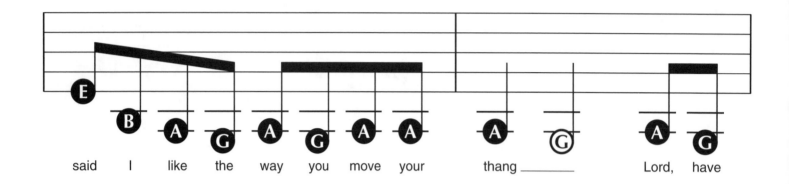

said I like the way you move your thang _____ Lord, have

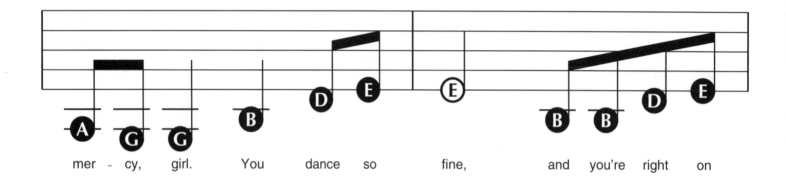

mer – cy, girl. You dance so fine, and you're right on

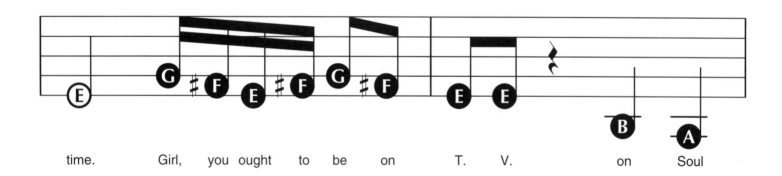

time. Girl, you ought to be on T. V. on Soul

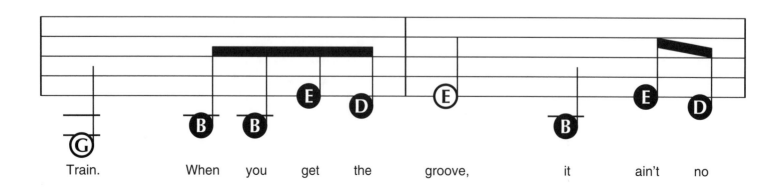

Train. When you get the groove, it ain't no

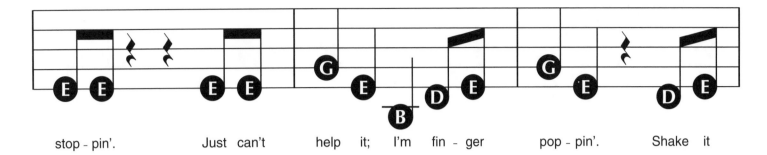

stop - pin'.   Just can't   help it; I'm fin - ger   pop - pin'.   Shake it

% G

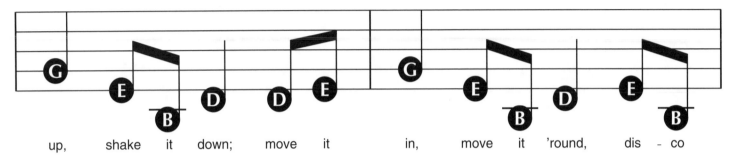

up, shake   it down; move   it   in,   move   it 'round,   dis - co

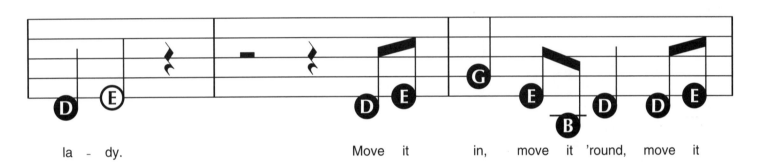

la - dy.   Move it   in,   move it 'round, move it

To Coda ⊕

in   and a - bout, dis - co   la - dy.

F#7

F#

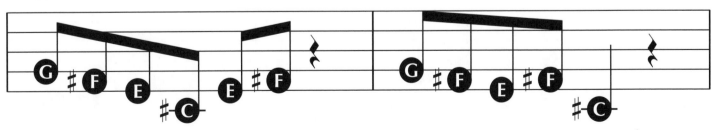

Shake it,   ba - by, shake it.   Ba - by, shake your thang.

114

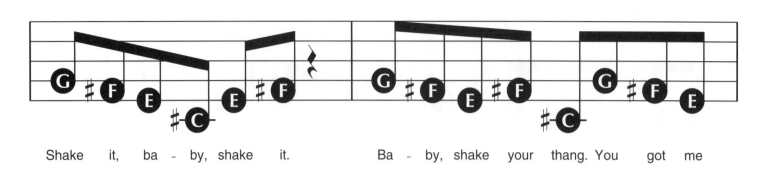

Shake it, ba - by, shake it. Ba - by, shake your thang. You got me

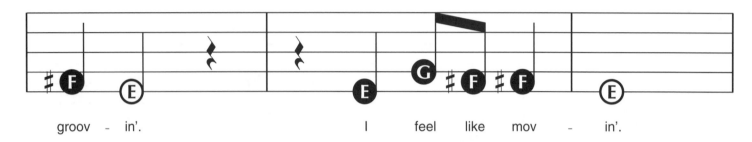

groov - in'. I feel like mov - in'.

A7
[A]

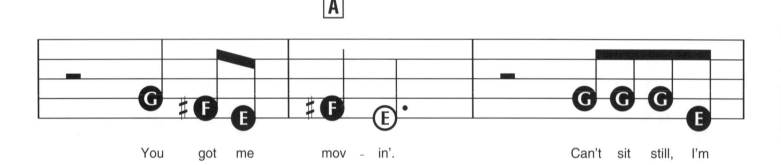

You got me mov - in'. Can't sit still, I'm

F#7
[F#]

D.S. al Coda
(Return to 𝄋
Play to ⨁ and
Skip to Coda)

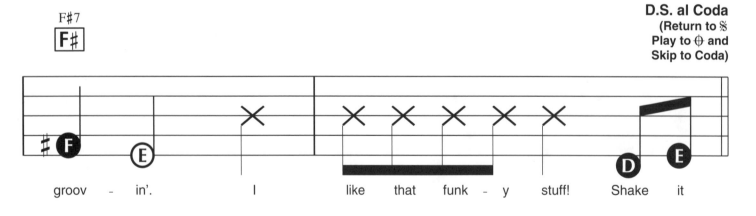

groov - in'. I like that funk - y stuff! Shake it

CODA
⨁

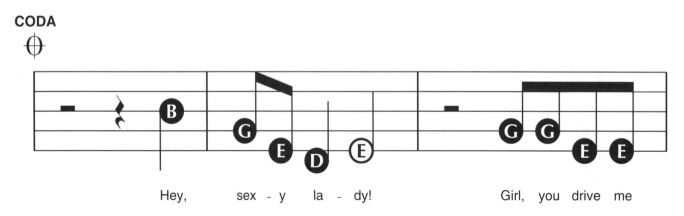

Hey, sex - y la - dy! Girl, you drive me

115

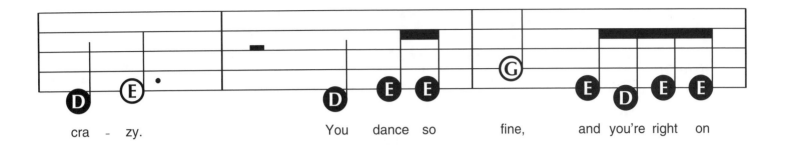

cra - zy.　　　You dance so fine, and you're right on

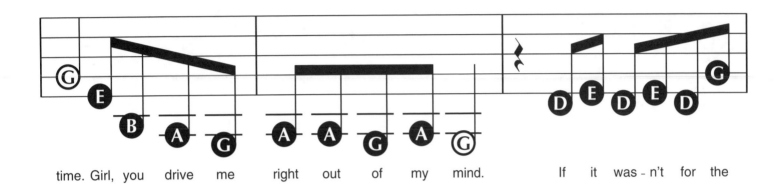

time. Girl, you drive me right out of my mind. If it was-n't for the

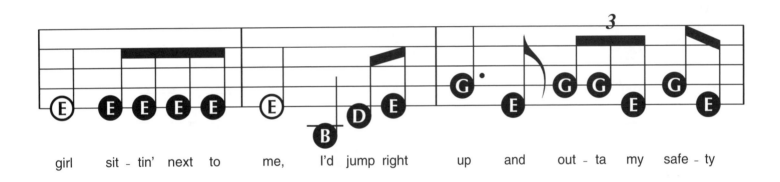

girl sit - tin' next to me, I'd jump right up and out - ta my safe - ty

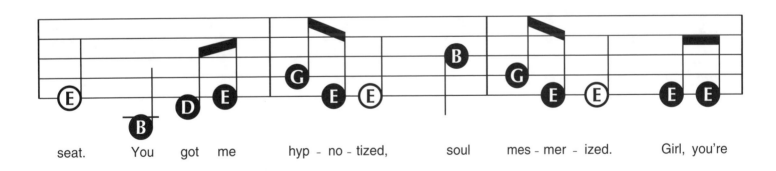

seat. You got me hyp - no - tized, soul mes - mer - ized. Girl, you're

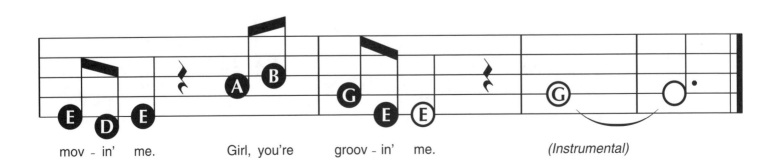

mov - in' me. Girl, you're groov - in' me. *(Instrumental)*

Do You Know Where You're Going To?

Theme from MAHOGANY

Words by Gerry Goffin
Music by Mike Masser

Registration 5
Rhythm: Slow Rock or Ballad

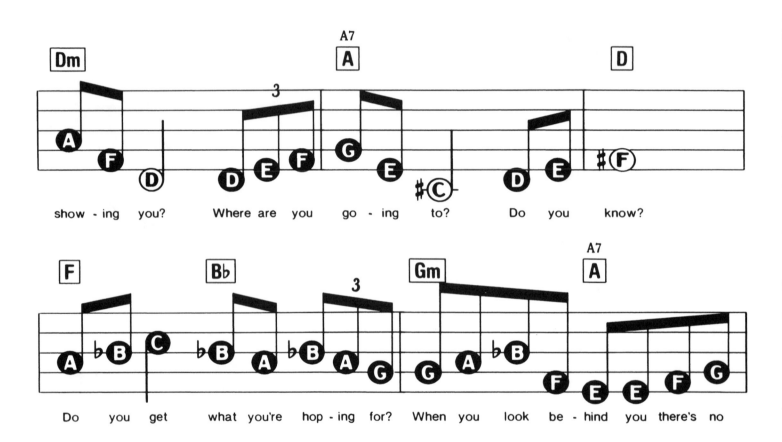

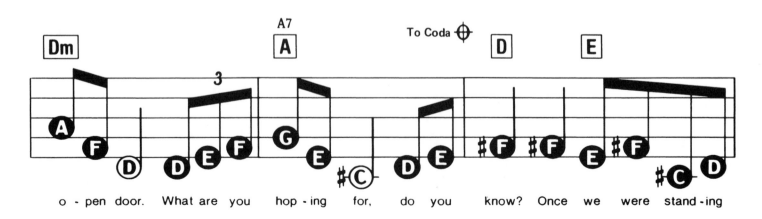

117

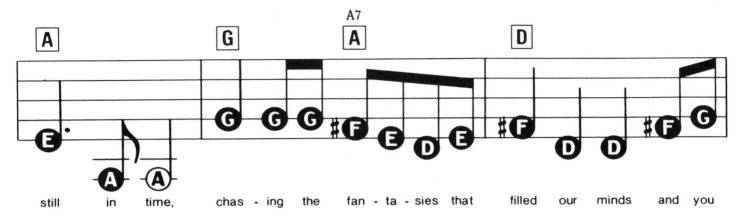

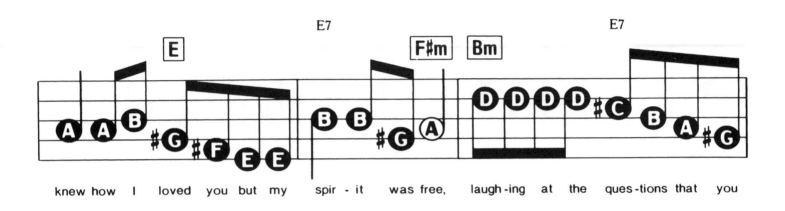

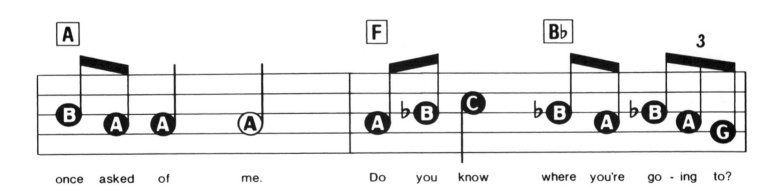

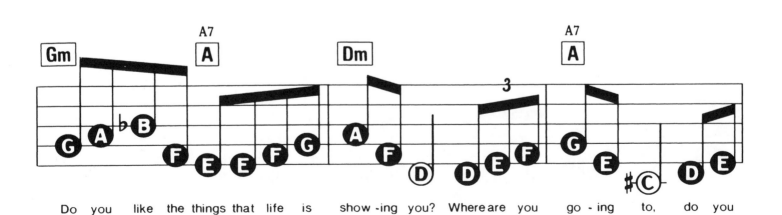

118

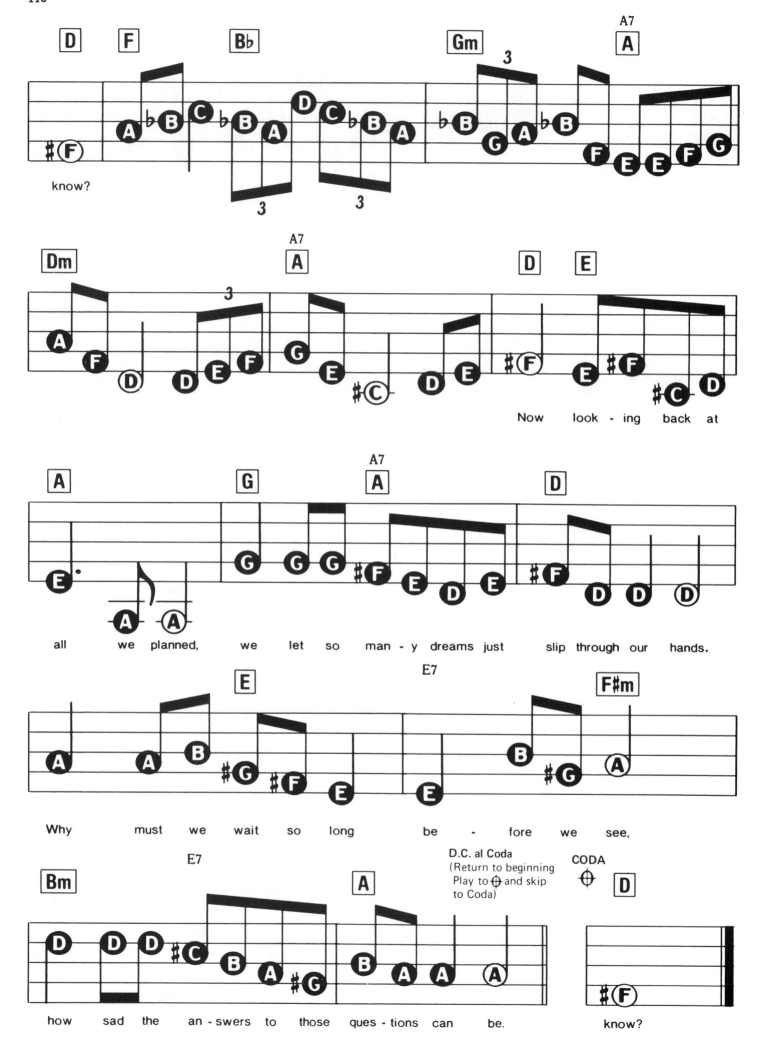

Don't Give Up on Us

Registration 7
Rhythm: 8 Beat or Pops

Words and Music by
Tony Macaulay

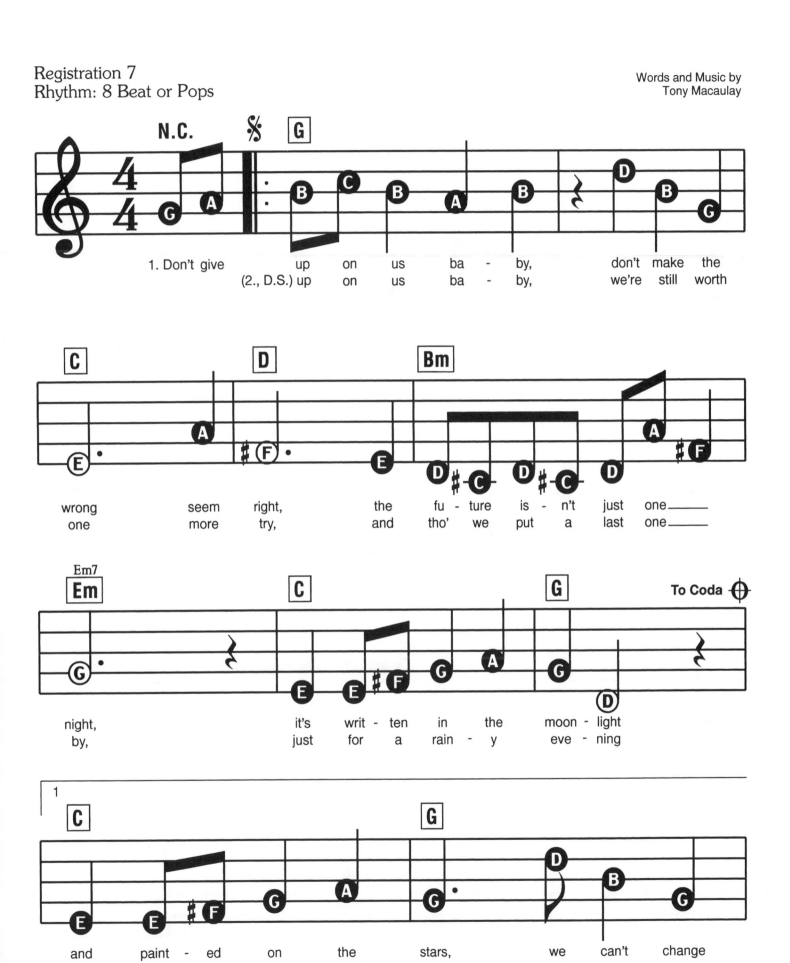

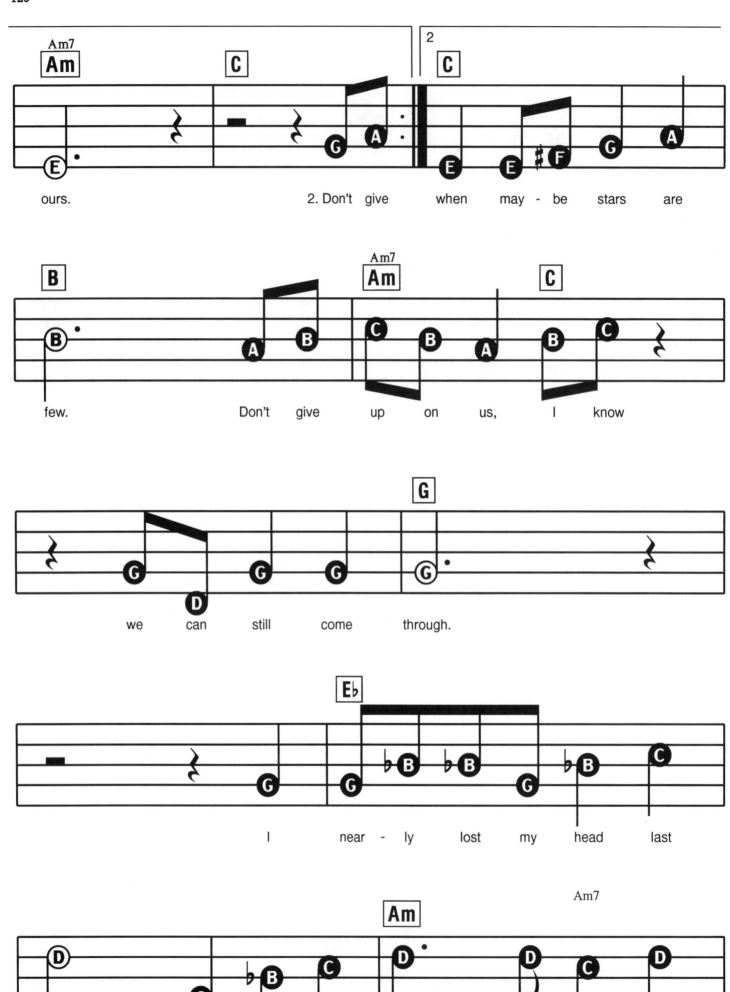

120

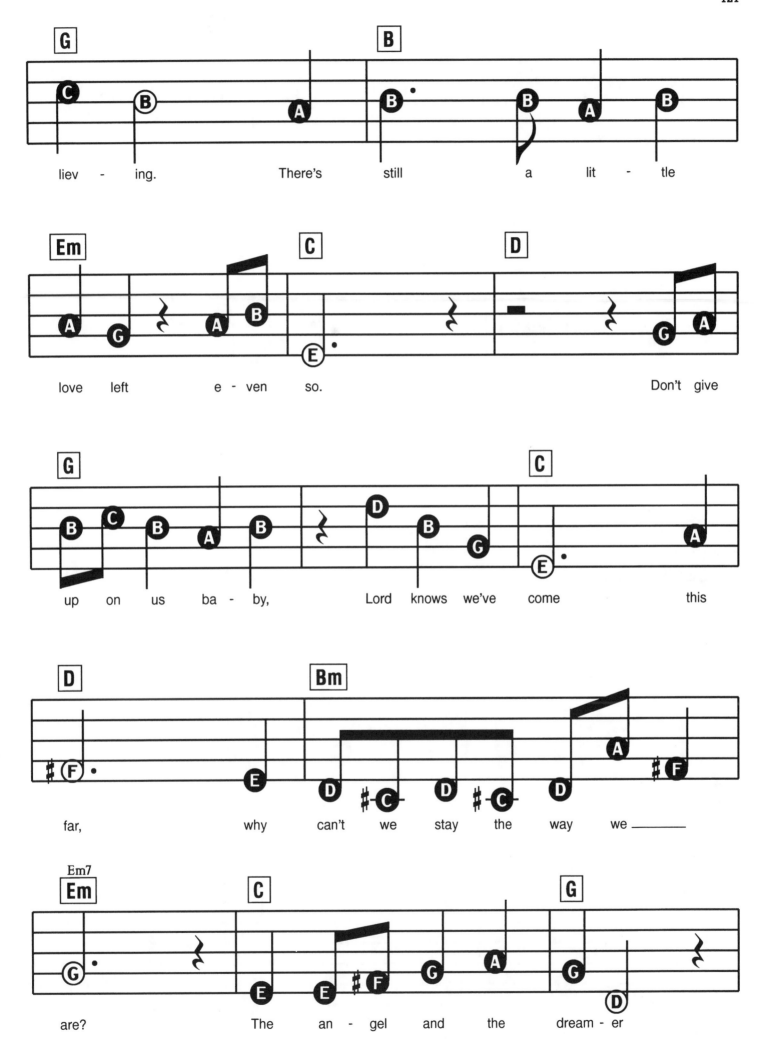

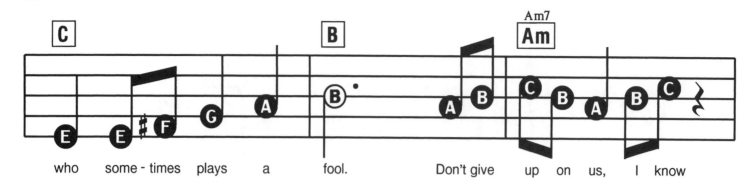

who some-times plays a fool. Don't give up on us, I know

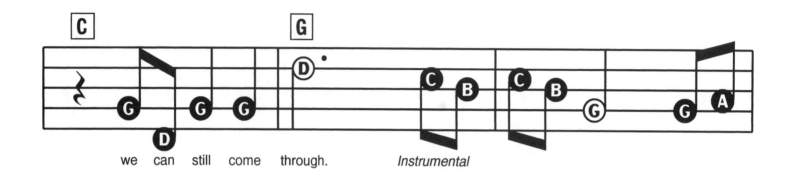

we can still come through. *Instrumental*

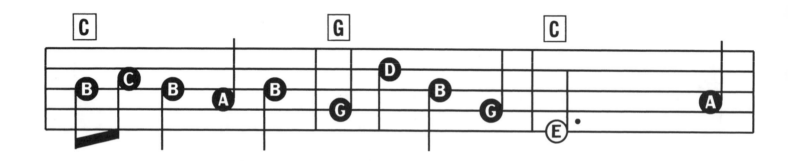

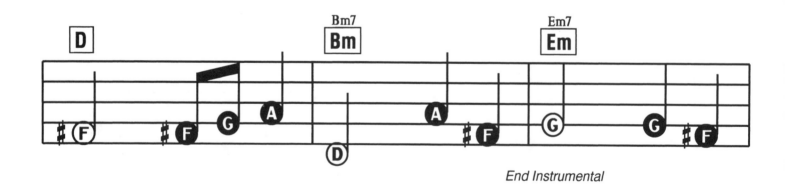

End Instrumental

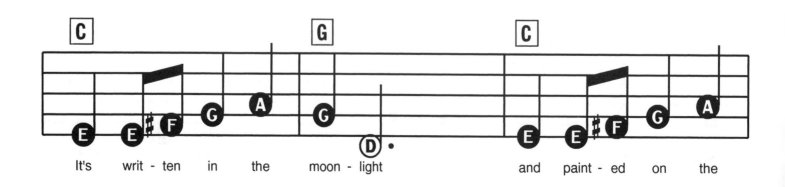

It's writ-ten in the moon-light and paint-ed on the

D.S. al Coda
(Return to 𝄉
Play to ⊕ and
Skip to Coda)

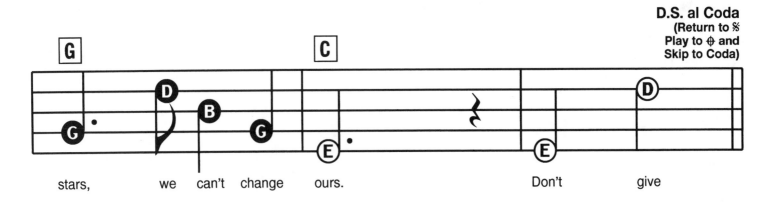

stars,   we can't change ours.   Don't give

CODA

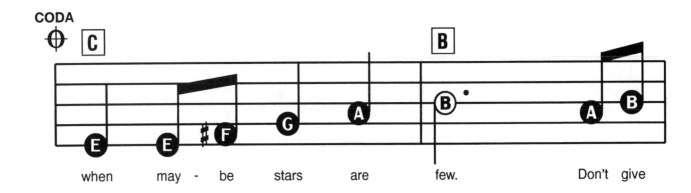

when   may - be   stars   are   few.   Don't give

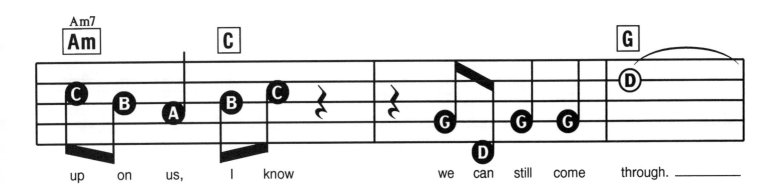

up   on   us,   I   know   we   can   still   come   through. _____

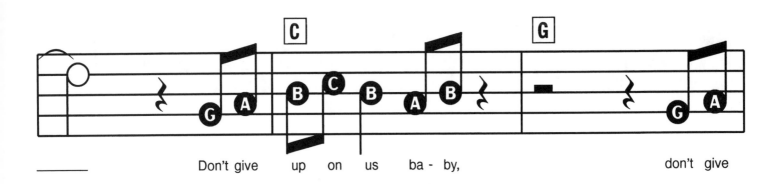

_____   Don't give   up   on   us   ba - by,   don't give

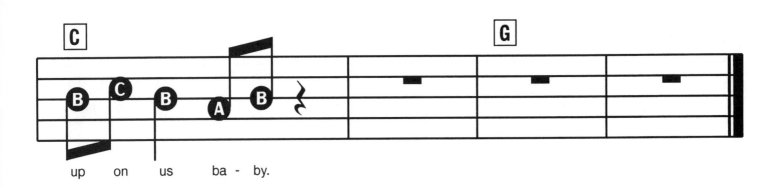

up   on   us   ba - by.

Don't Let the Sun Go Down on Me

Registration 4
Rhythm: Rock or Pops

Words and Music by Elton John
and Bernie Taupin

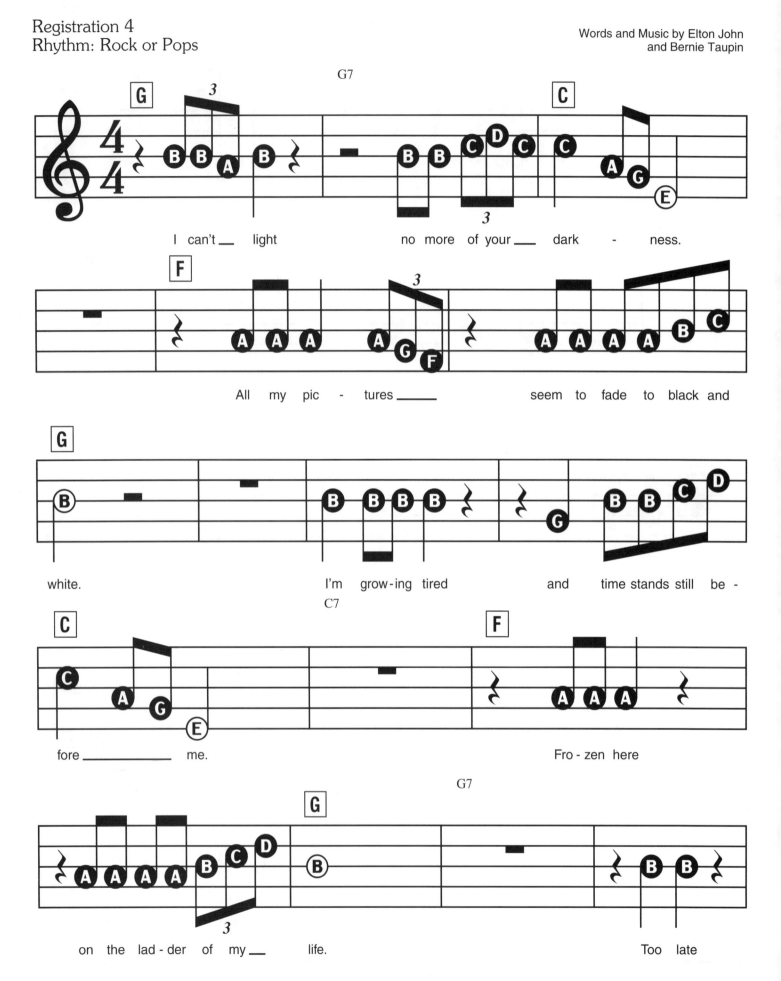

125

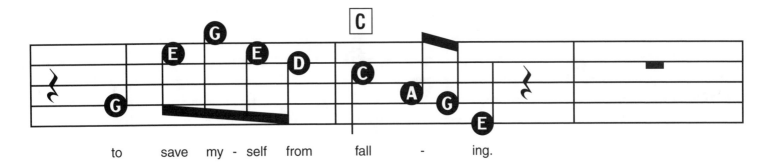

to save my-self from fall - ing.

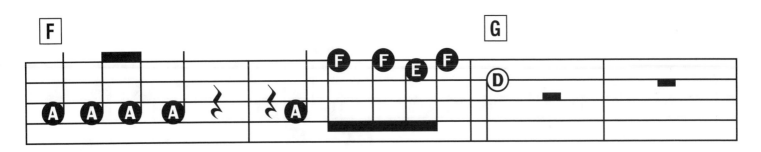

I took a chance and changed your way of life.

G7

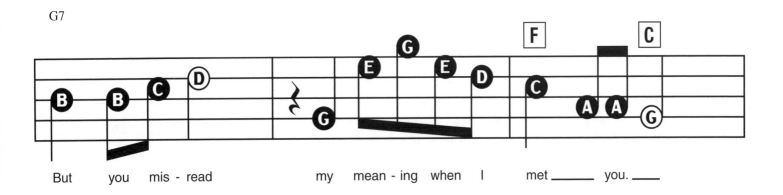

But you mis - read my mean - ing when I met _____ you. _____

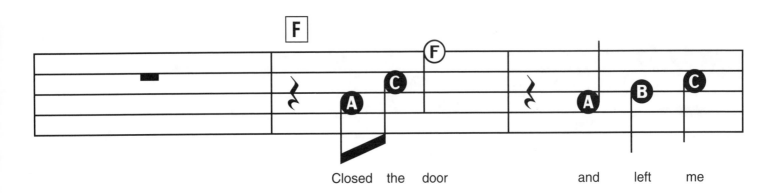

Closed the door and left me

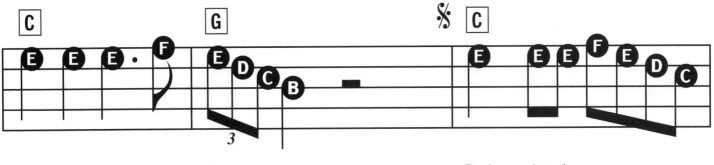

blind - ed by the light. _____ Don't let the sun _____ go

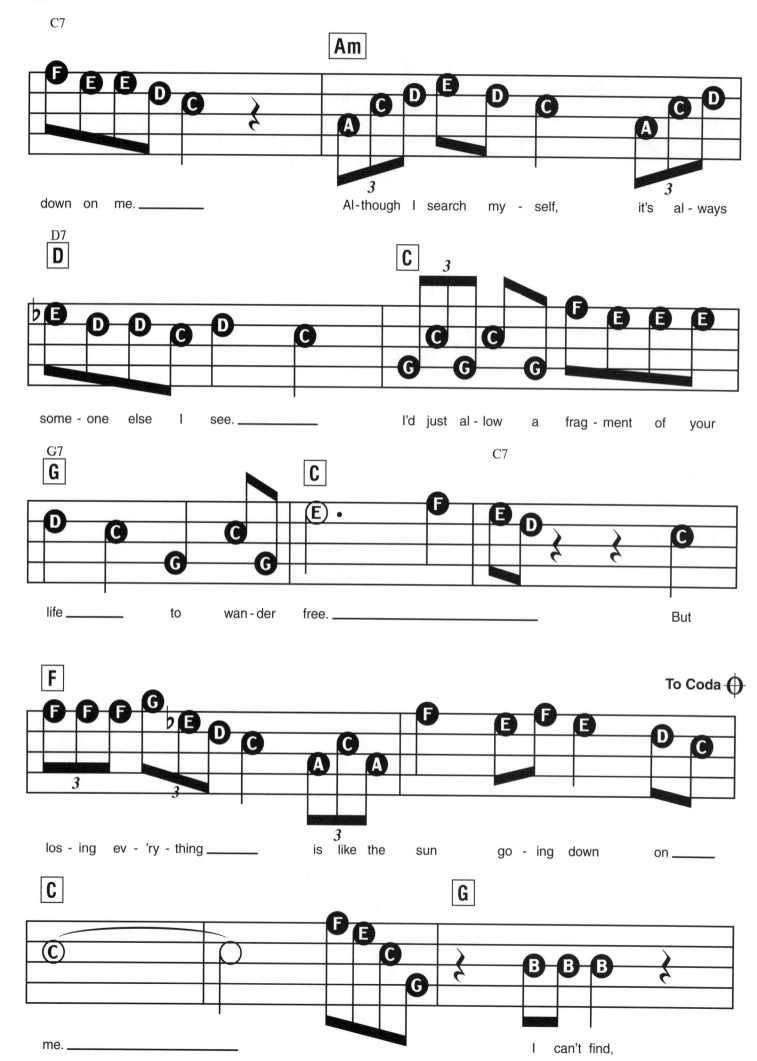

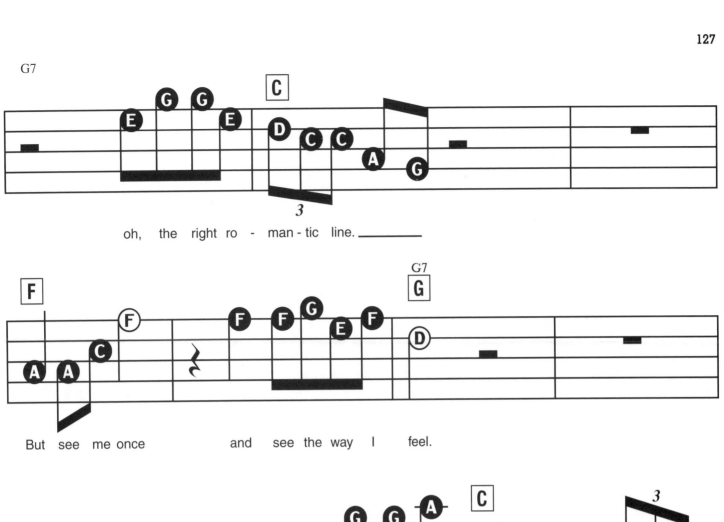

oh, the right ro - man - tic line. _____

But see me once and see the way I feel.

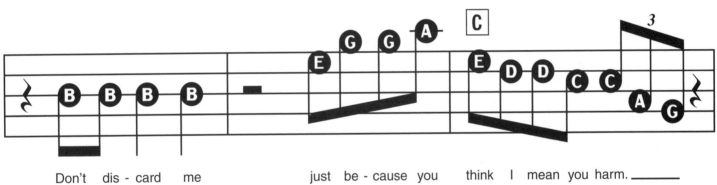

Don't dis - card me just be - cause you think I mean you harm. _____

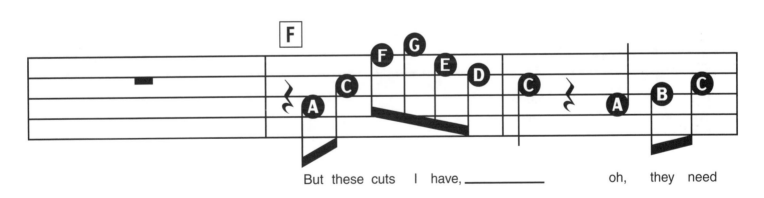

But these cuts I have, _____ oh, they need

D.S. al Coda
(Return to 𝄋
Play to ⊕ and
Skip to Coda)

CODA
⊕

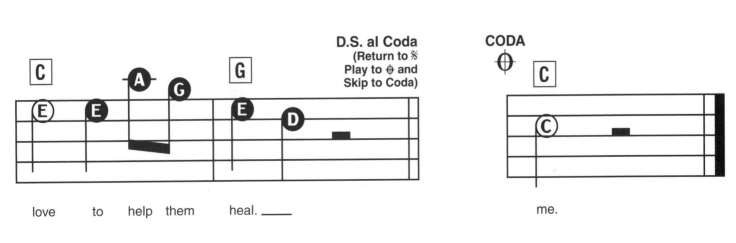

love to help them heal. ___

me.

Dreams

Registration 7
Rhythm: Rock

Words and Music by
Stevie Nicks

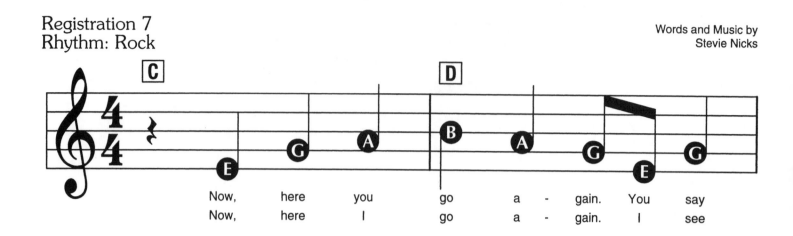

Now, here you go a - gain. You say
Now, here I go a - gain. I see

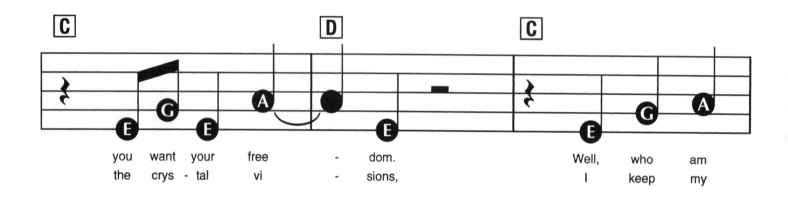

you want your free - dom. Well, who am
the crys - tal vi - sions, I keep my

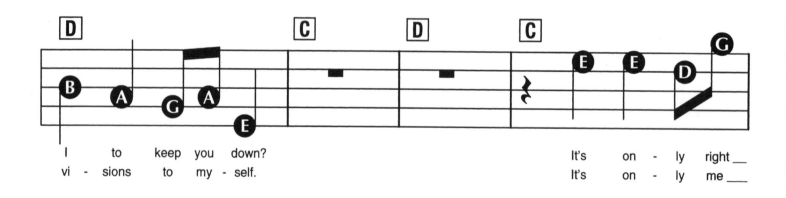

I to keep you down? It's on - ly right __
vi - sions to my - self. It's on - ly me __

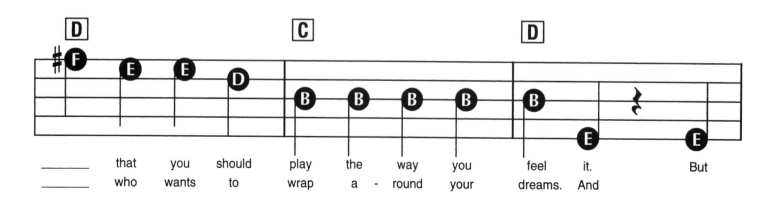

_____ that you should play the way you feel it. But
_____ who wants to wrap a - round your dreams. And

130

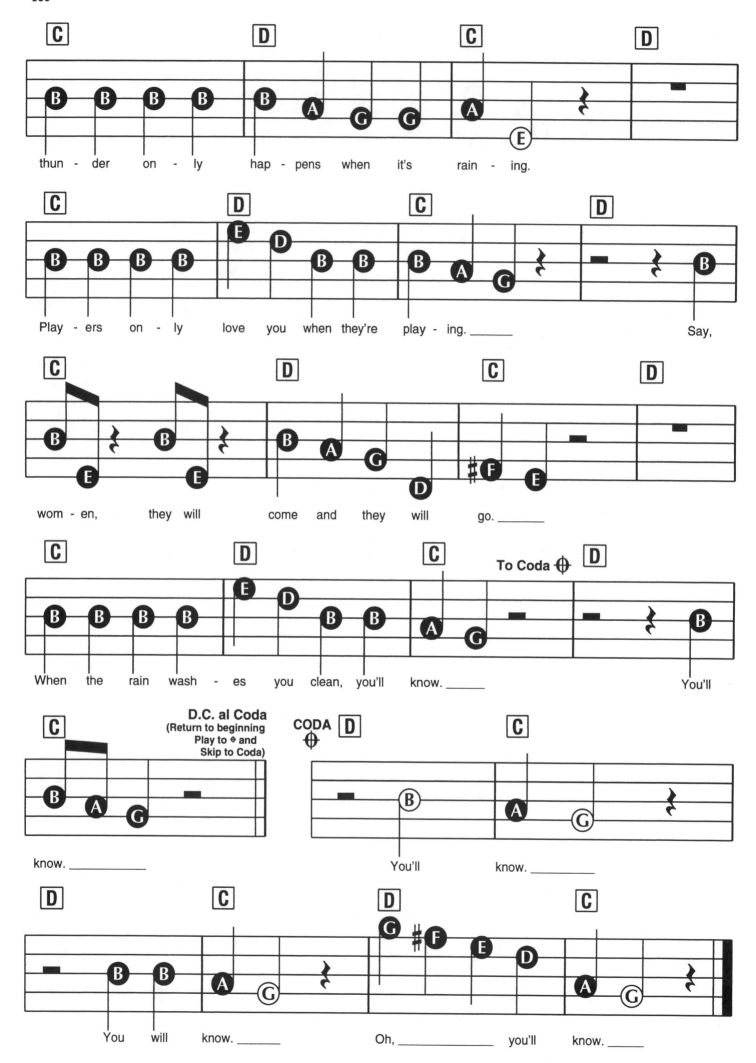

Fame

Registration 8
Rhythm: 8 Beat or Rock

Words and Music by John Lennon,
David Bowie and Carlos Alomar

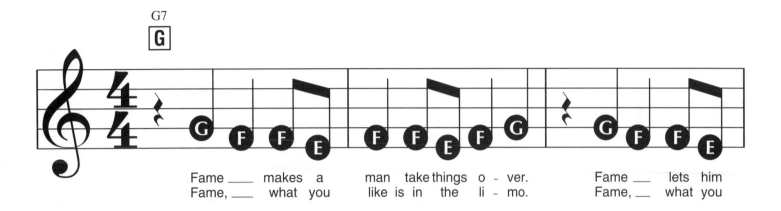

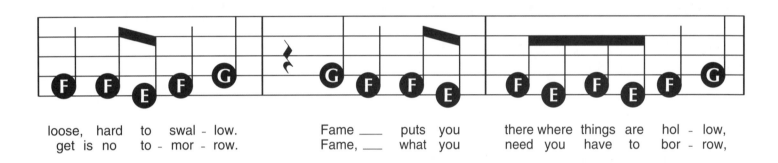

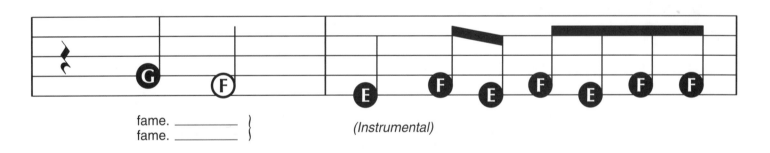

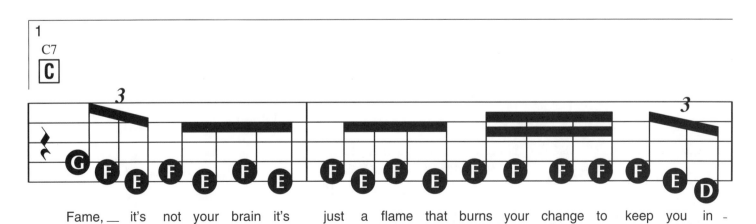

132

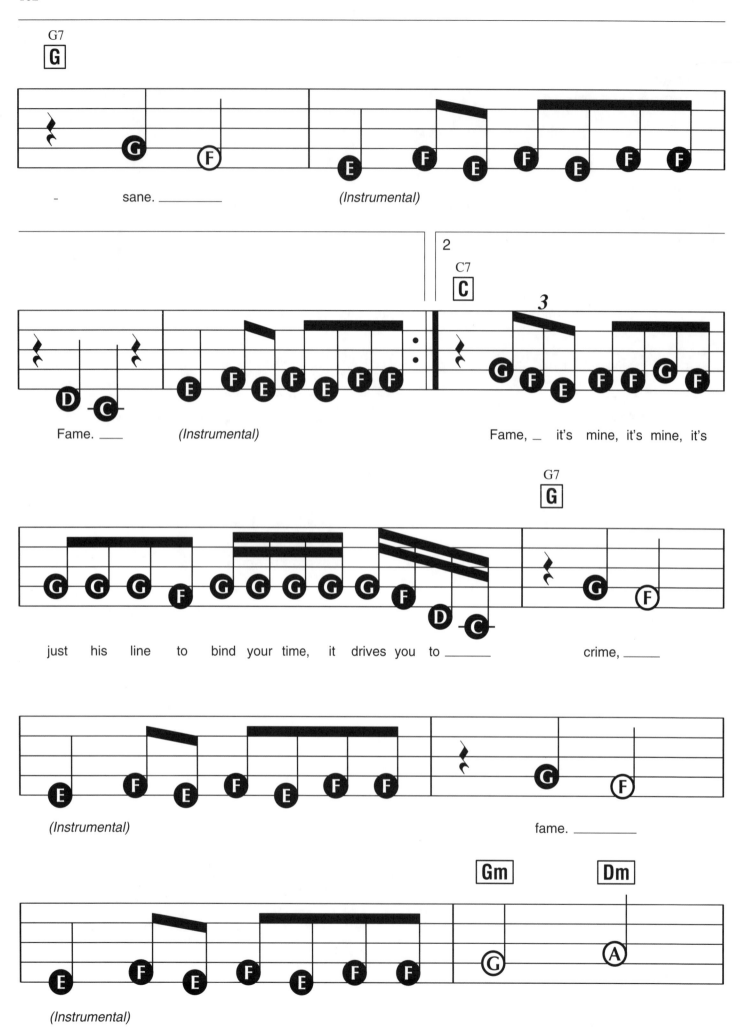

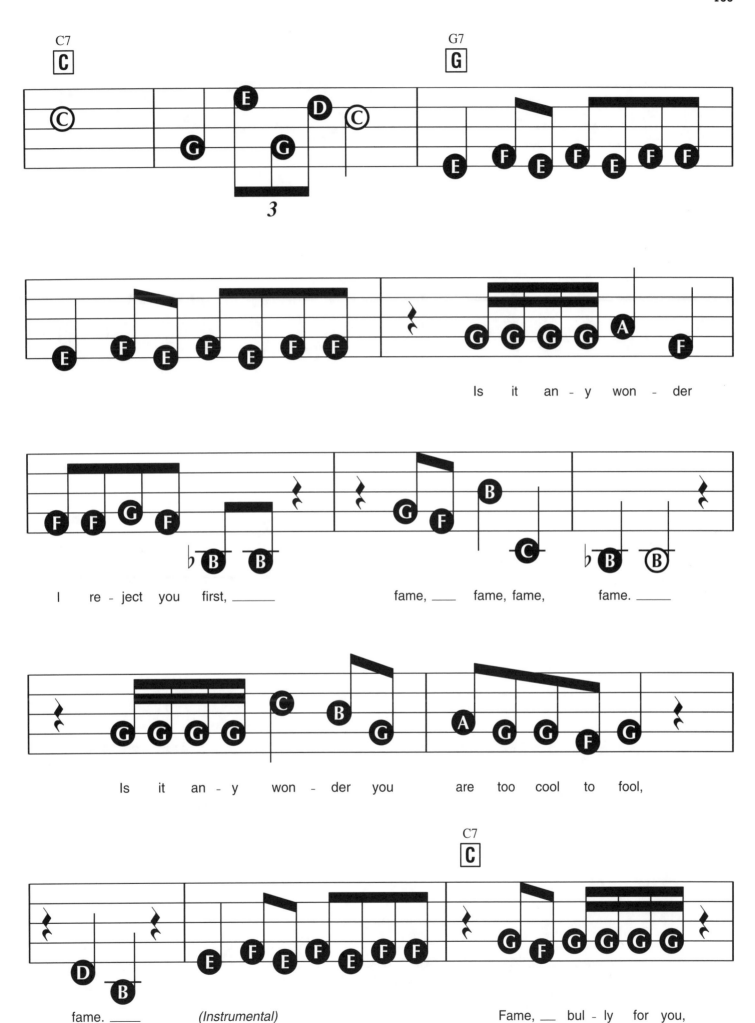

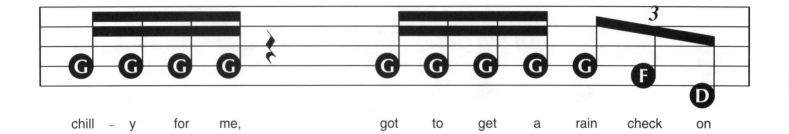

chill - y for me,   got to get a rain check on

G7

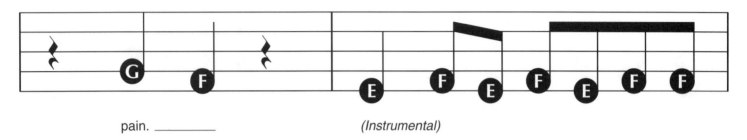

pain. _____   *(Instrumental)*

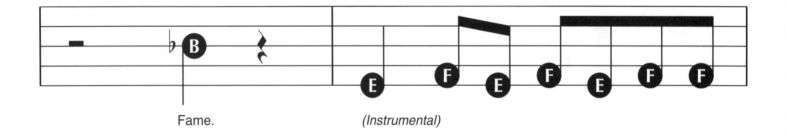

Fame.   *(Instrumental)*

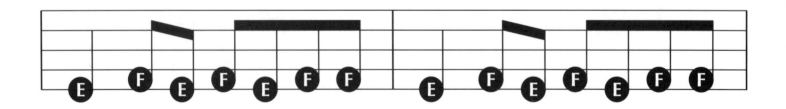

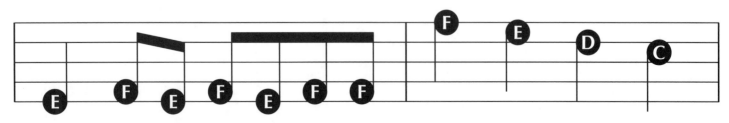

Fame, _____   fame, _____

135

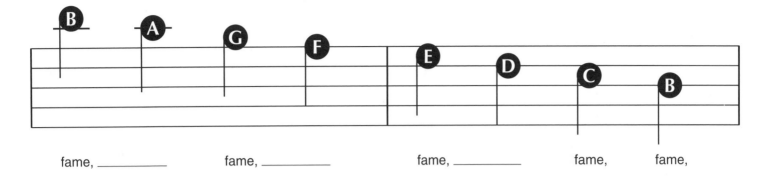

fame, _____ fame, _____ fame, _____ fame, fame,

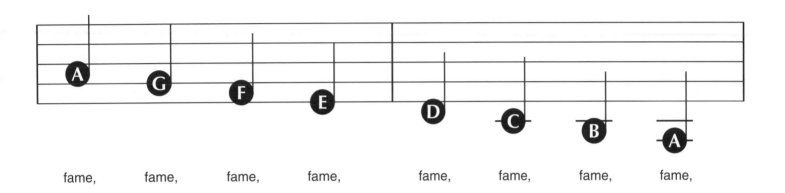

fame, fame, fame, fame, fame, fame, fame, fame,

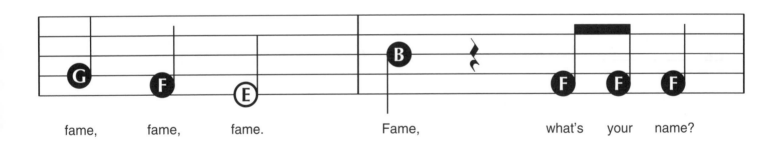

fame, fame, fame. Fame, what's your name?

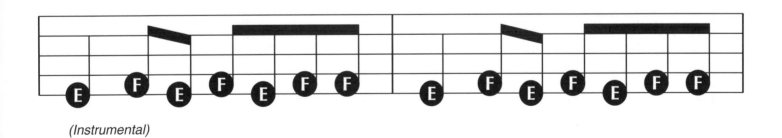

(Instrumental)

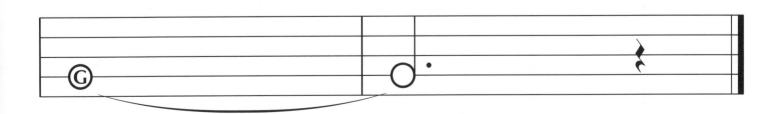

Dust in the Wind

Registration 10
Rhythm: Rock

Words and Music by
Kerry Livgren

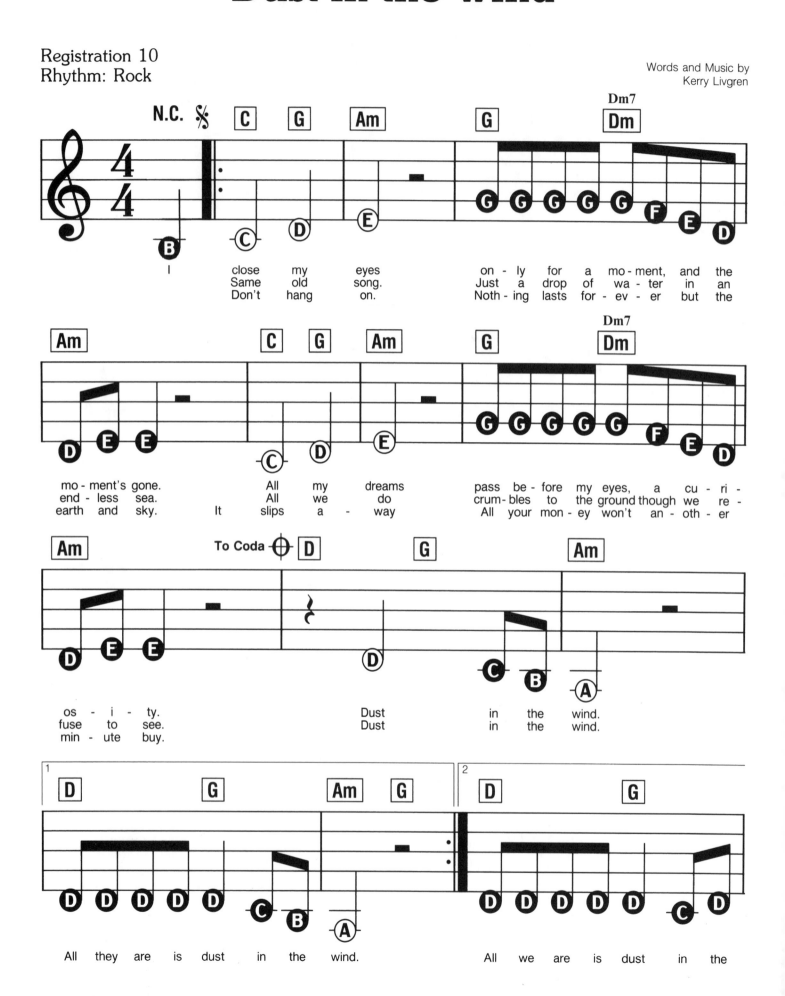

D.S. al Coda
(Return to 𝄋
Play to ⊕ and
skip to Coda)

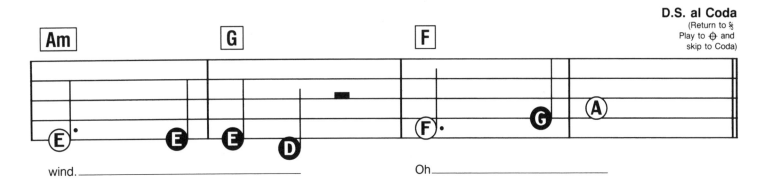

wind. Oh

CODA

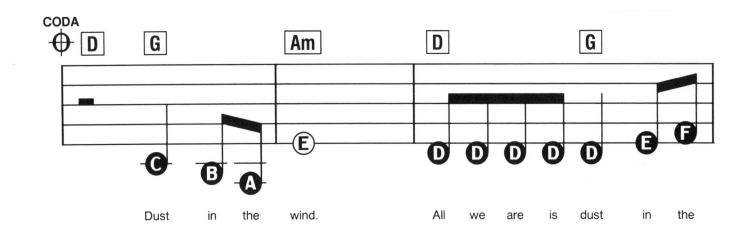

Dust in the wind. All we are is dust in the

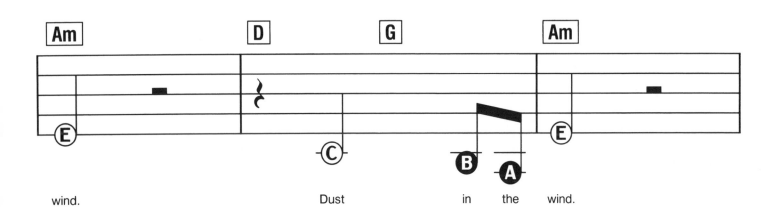

wind. Dust in the wind.

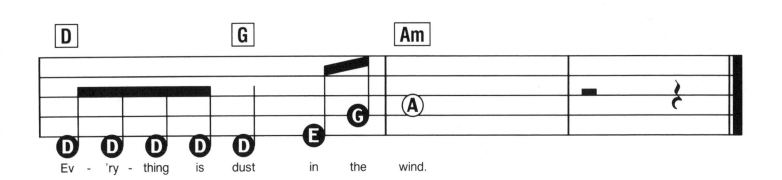

Ev - 'ry - thing is dust in the wind.

Everything Is Beautiful

Registration 8
Rhythm: Rock or Jazz Rock

Words and Music by
Ray Stevens

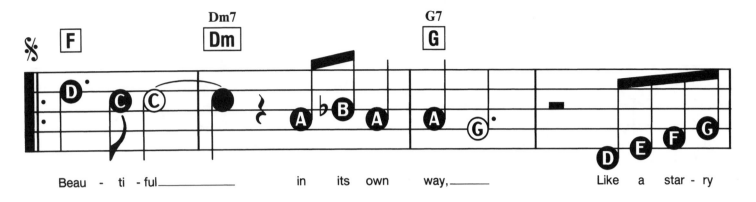

Beau - ti - ful_____ in its own way,_____ Like a star - ry

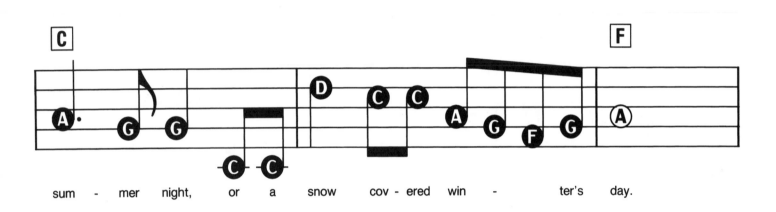

sum - mer night, or a snow cov - ered win - ter's day.

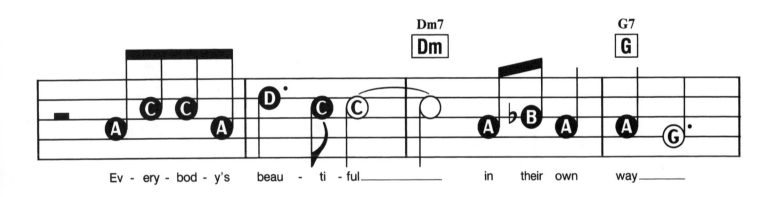

Ev - ery - bod - y's beau - ti - ful_____ in their own way_____

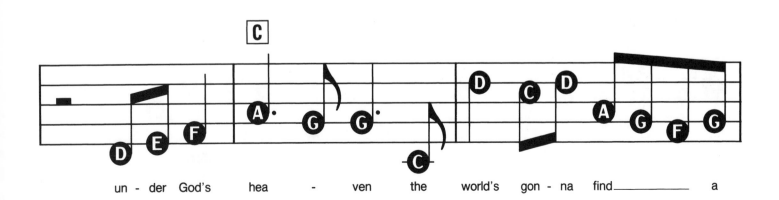

un - der God's hea - ven the world's gon - na find_____ a

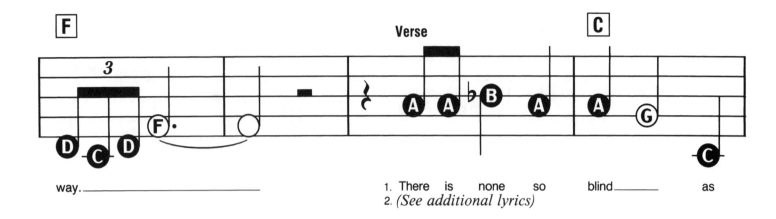

way.

Verse

1. There is none so blind_____ as
2. *(See additional lyrics)*

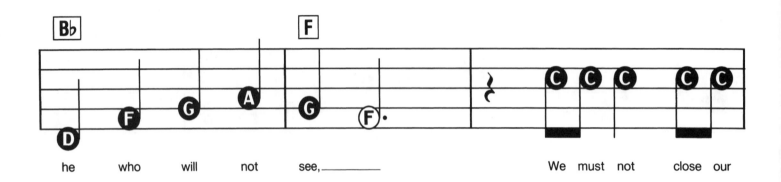

he who will not see,_____ We must not close our

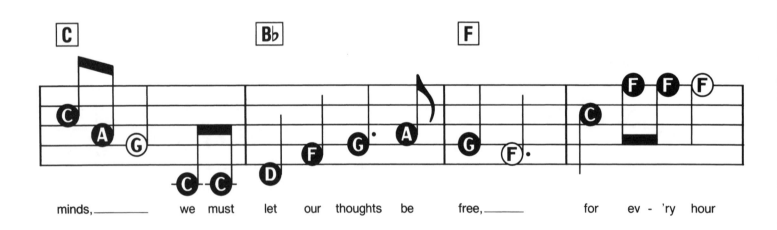

minds,_____ we must let our thoughts be free,_____ for ev - 'ry hour

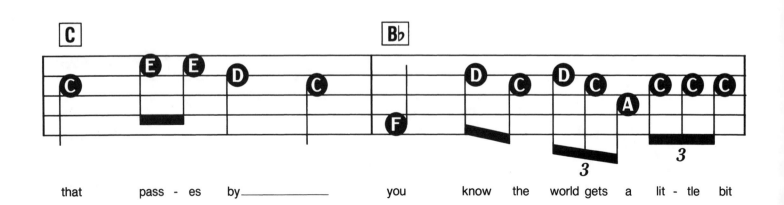

that pass - es by_____ you know the world gets a lit - tle bit

141

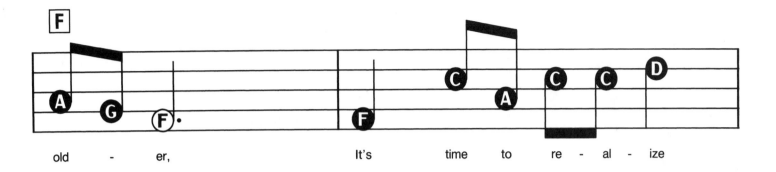

old - er,   It's   time   to   re - al - ize

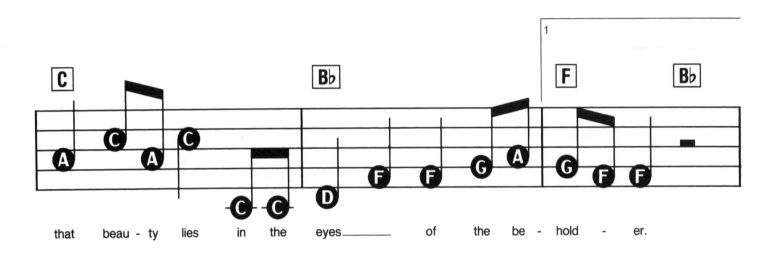

that   beau - ty   lies   in   the   eyes_____   of   the   be - hold - er.

D.S. and Fade
(Return to 𝄋 and Fade)

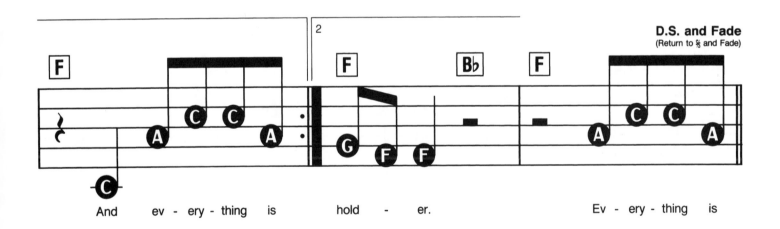

And   ev - ery - thing   is   hold - er.   Ev - ery - thing   is

Additional Lyrics

2. We shouldn't care about the length of his hair or the color of his skin,
Don't worry about what shows from without but the love that lives within,
We gonna get it all together now and everything gonna work out fine,
Just take a little time to look on the good side my friend and straighten it out in your mind.

Feelings
(¿Dime?)

Registration 5
Rhythm: Slow Rock

English Words and Music by Morris Albert and Louis Gaste
Spanish Words by Thomas Fundora

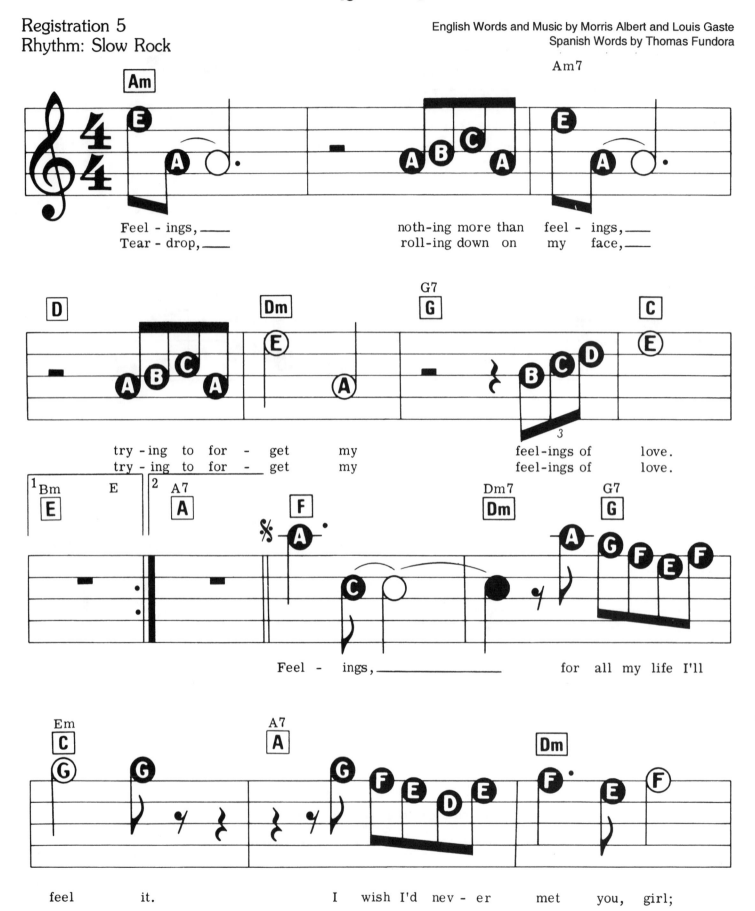

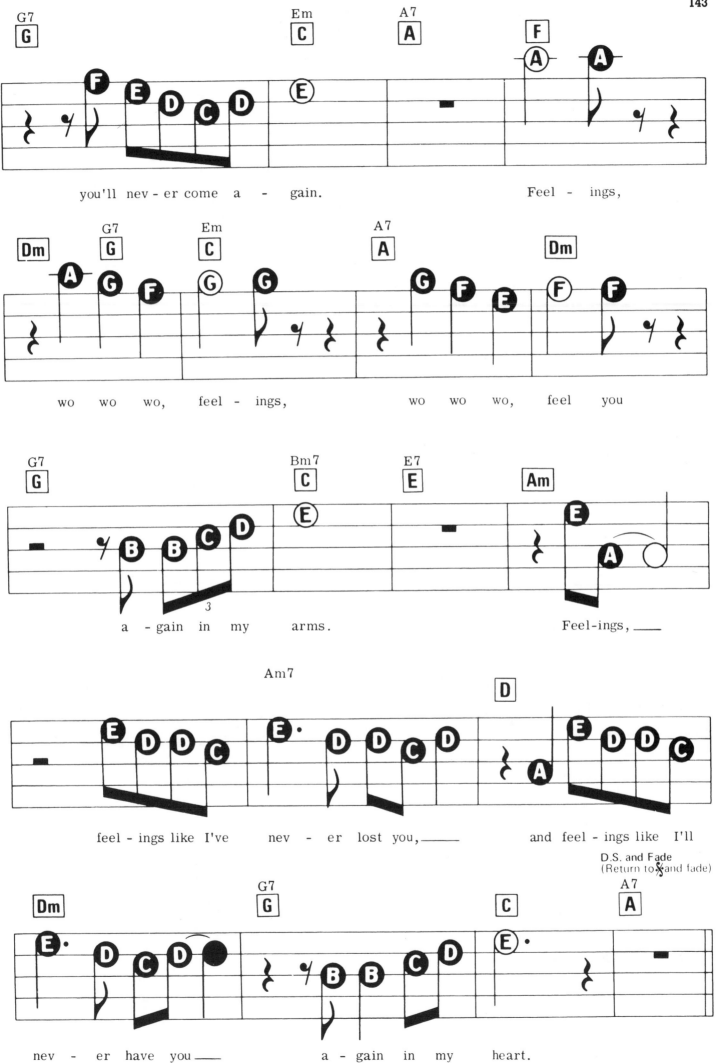

you'll nev - er come a - gain.   Feel - ings,

wo wo wo, feel - ings,   wo wo wo, feel you

a - gain in my arms.   Feel-ings, ___

feel - ings like I've nev - er lost you, ___   and feel - ings like I'll

D.S. and Fade
(Return to 𝄋 and fade)

nev - er have you ___   a - gain in my heart.

The First Cut Is the Deepest

Registration 2
Rhythm: 8 Beat, Pops or Rock

Words and Music by
Cat Stevens

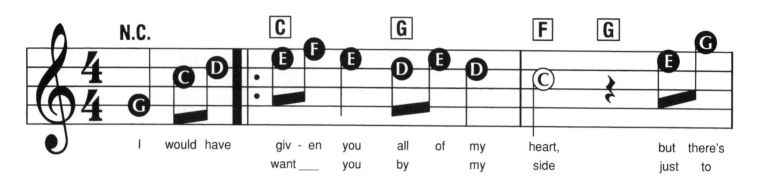

I would have giv - en you all of my heart, but there's
want ___ you by my side just to

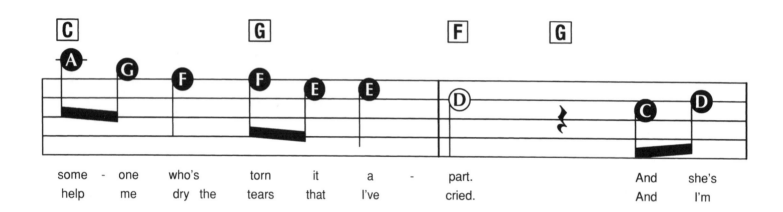

some - one who's torn it a - part. And she's
help me dry the tears that I've cried. And I'm

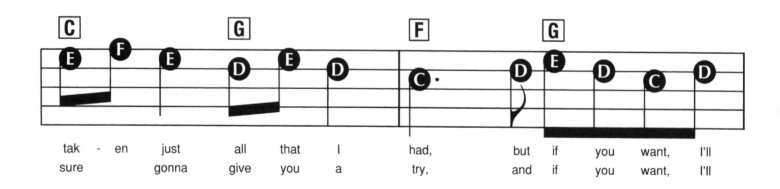

tak - en just all that I had, but if you want, I'll
sure gonna give you a try, and if you want, I'll

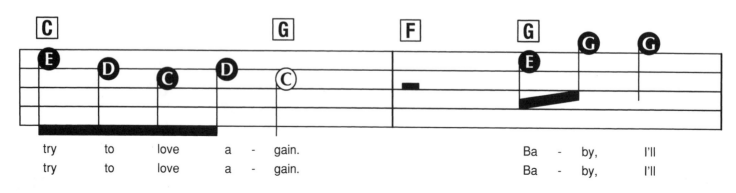

try to love a - gain. Ba - by, I'll
try to love a - gain. Ba - by, I'll

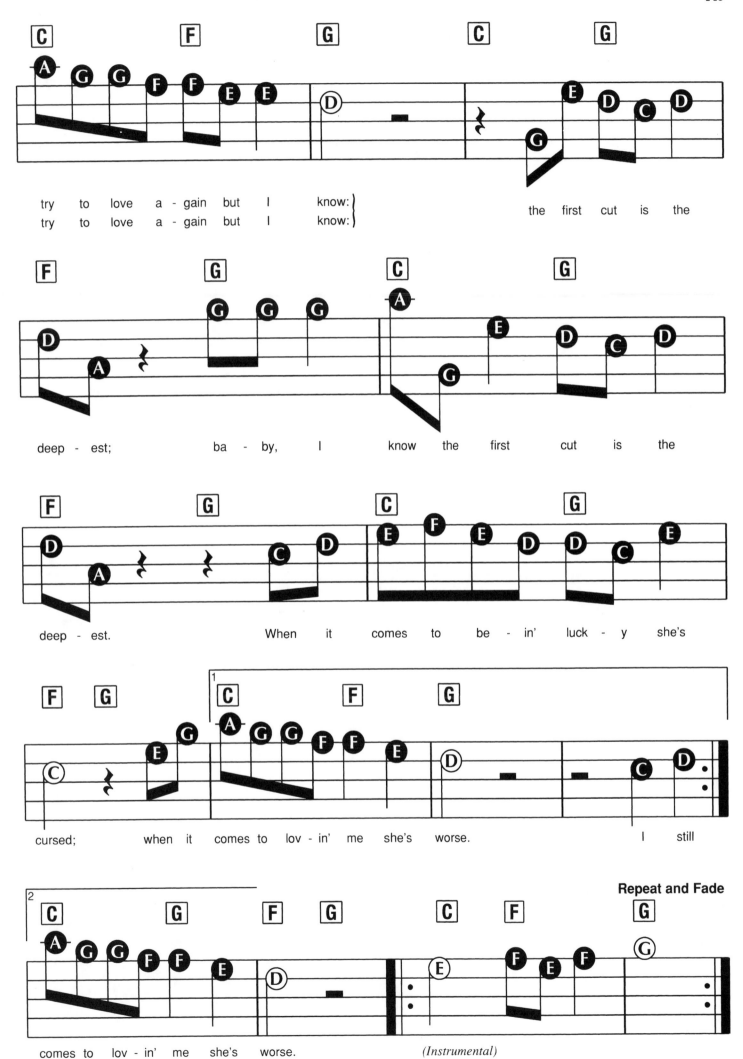

Fly Like an Eagle

Registration 9
Rhythm: Rock

Words and Music by
Steve Miller

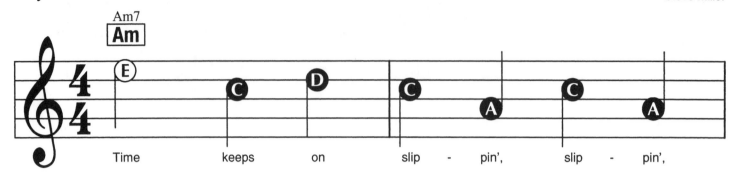

Time   keeps   on   slip - pin',   slip - pin',

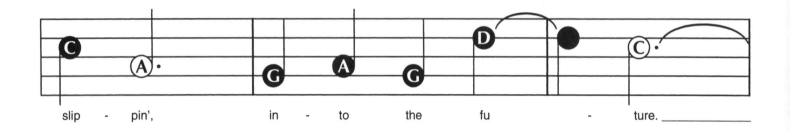

slip - pin',   in - to   the   fu   -   ture. _____

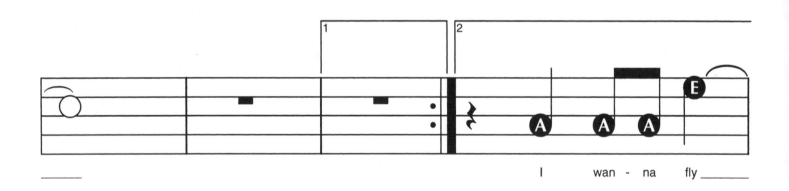

_____   I   wan - na   fly _____

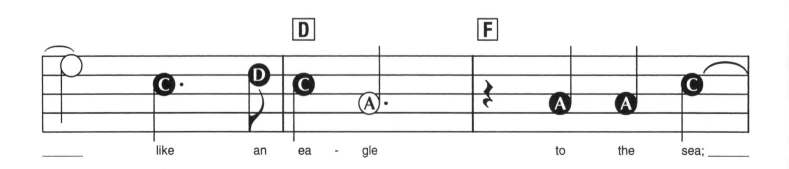

_____   like   an   ea - gle   to   the   sea; _____

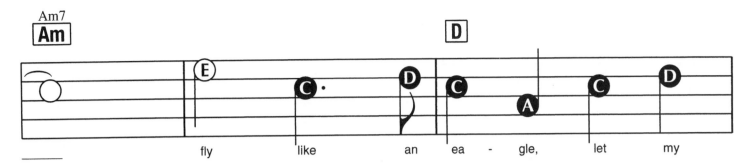

fly like an ea - gle, let my

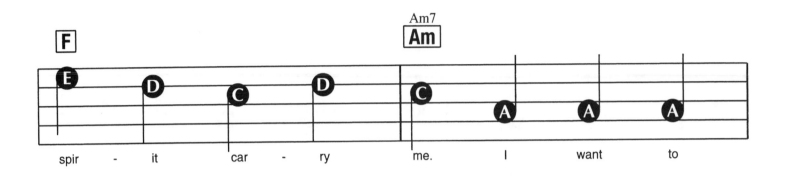

spir - it car - ry me. I want to

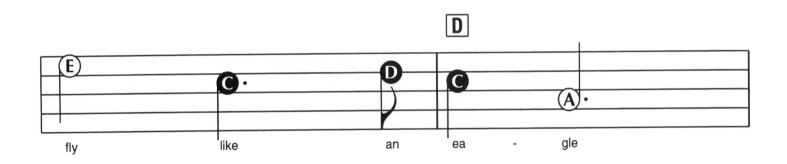

fly like an ea - gle

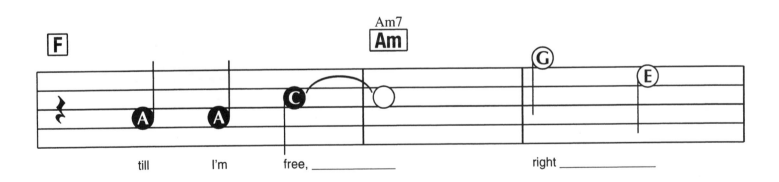

till I'm free, _____ right _____

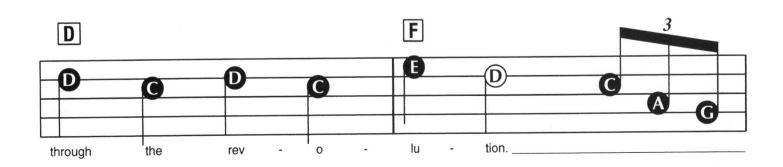

through the rev - o - lu - tion. _____

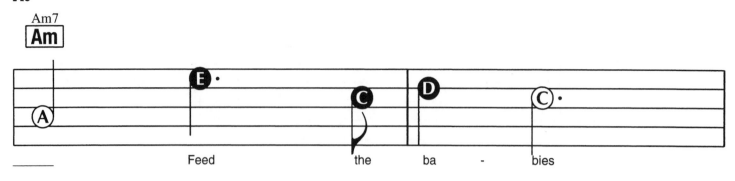

Feed the ba - bies

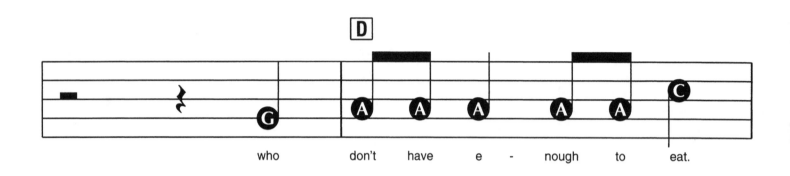

who don't have e - nough to eat.

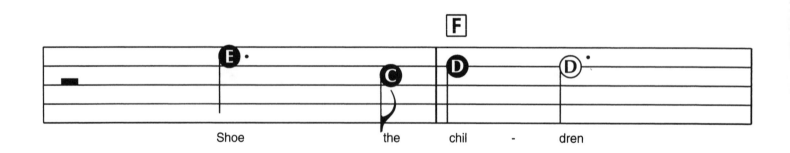

Shoe the chil - dren

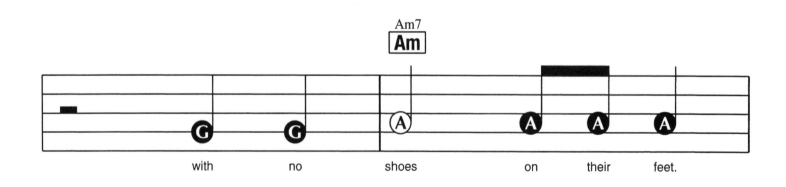

with no shoes on their feet.

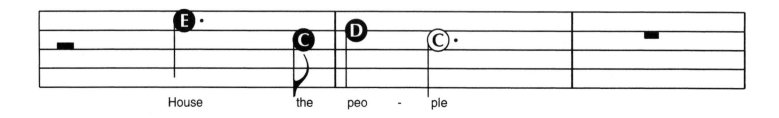

House the peo - ple

149

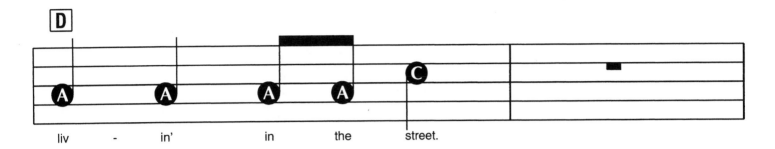

liv - in' in the street.

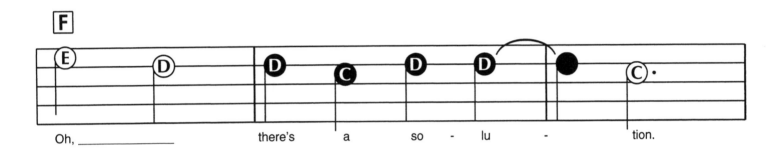

Oh, _____ there's a so - lu - tion.

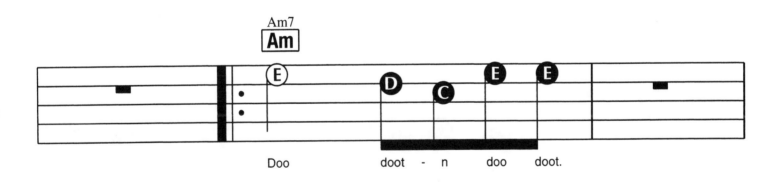

Doo doot - n doo doot.

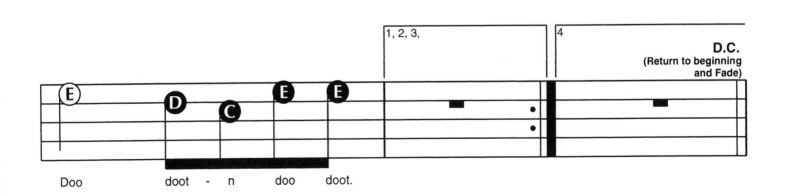

Doo doot - n doo doot.

Garden Party

Registration 1
Rhythm: Rock 'n' Roll or Shuffle

Words and Music by
Rick Nelson

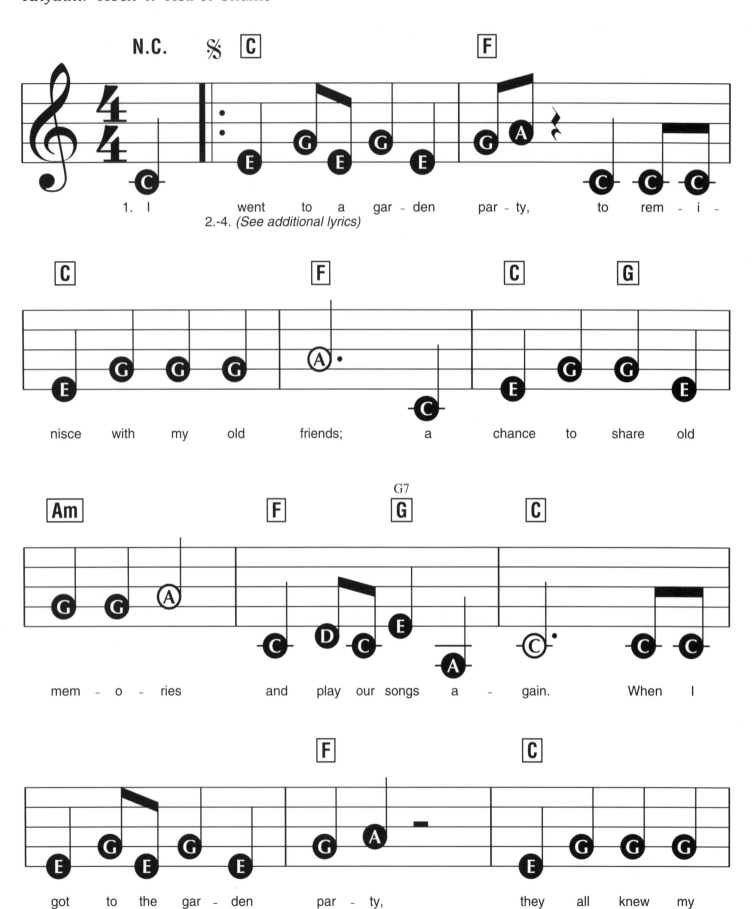

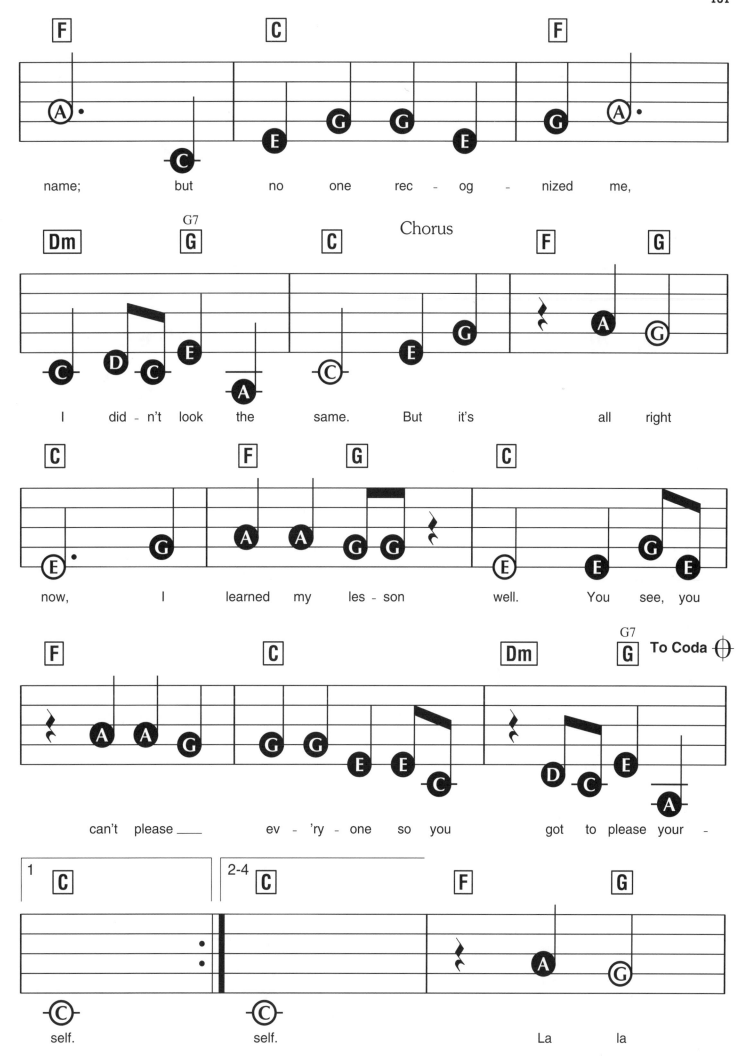

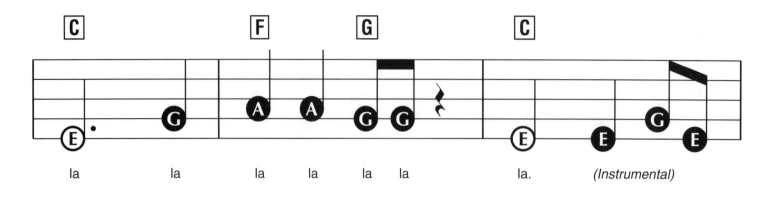

la   la   la   la   la   la   la.   *(Instrumental)*

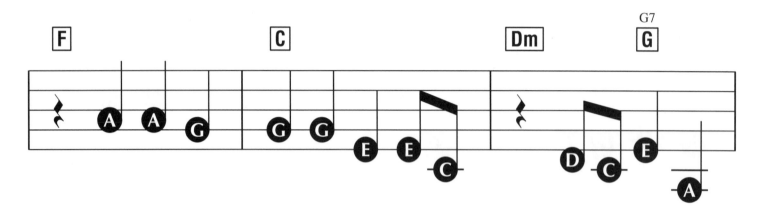

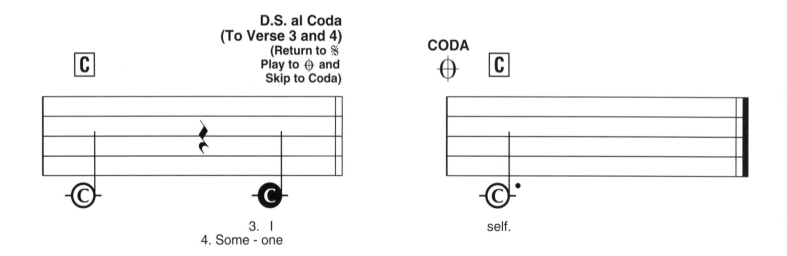

3. I
4. Some - one

self.

Additional Lyrics

2. People came from miles around, everyone was there;
   Yoko brought her walrus, there was magic in the air.
   And over in the corner, much to my surprise,
   Mr. Hughes hid in Dylan's shoes, wearing his disguise. *(Chorus)*

3. I played them all the old songs, I thought that's why they came;
   No one heard the music, we didn't look the same.
   I said hello to Mary Lou, she belongs to me;
   When I sang a song about a honky-tonk, it was time to leave. *(Chorus)*

4. Someone opened up a closet door and out stepped Johnny B. Goode;
   Playing guitar like a ring an' a bell, and lookin' like he should.
   If you gotta play at garden parties, I wish you a lot o' luck;
   But if memories were all I sang, I'd rather drive a truck. *(Chorus)*

Gypsys, Tramps and Thieves

Registration 9
Rhythm: Rock

Words and Music by
Robert Stone

154

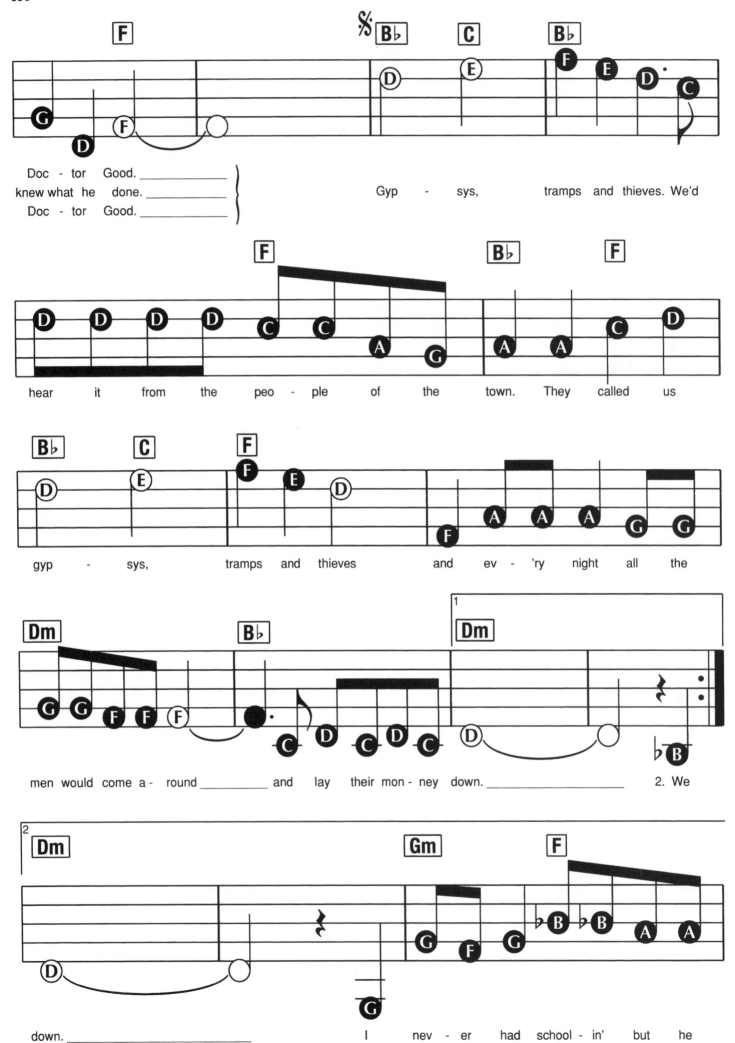

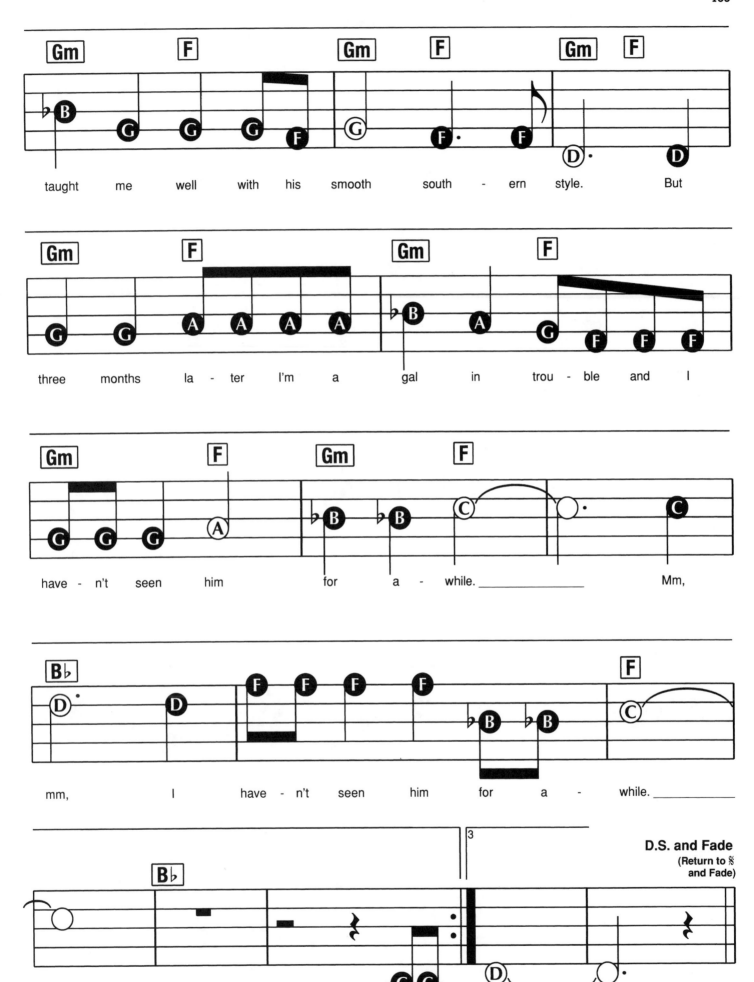

Hey There Lonely Girl
(Hey There Lonely Boy)

Registration 4
Rhythm: 8 Beat or Rock

Words and Music by Earl Shuman
and Leon Carr

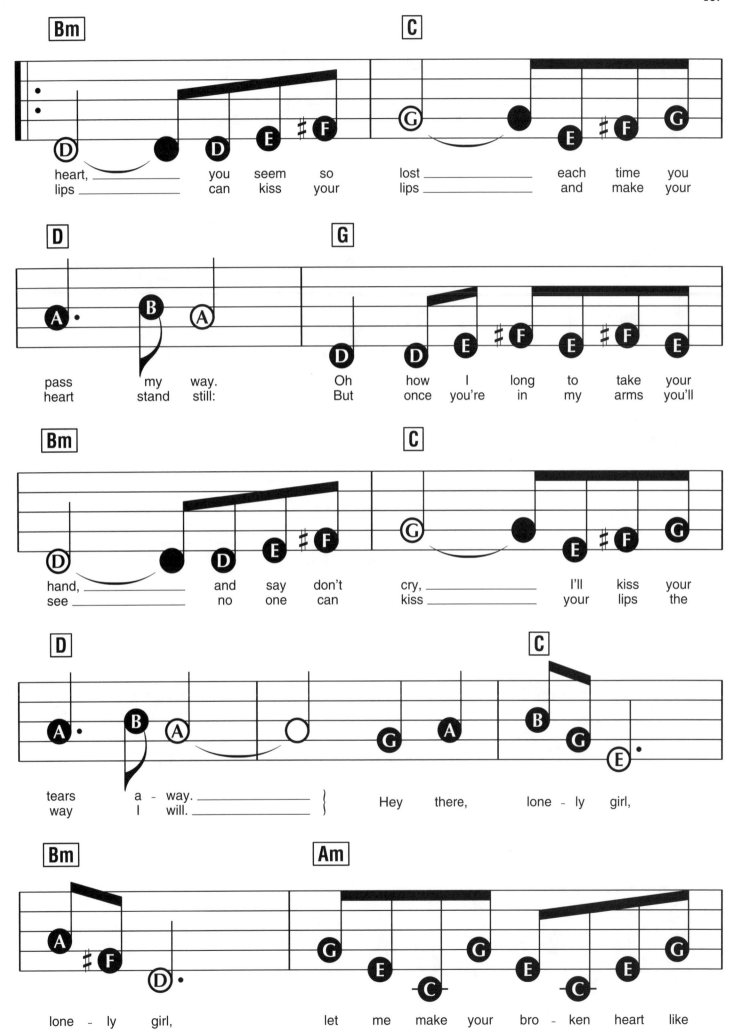

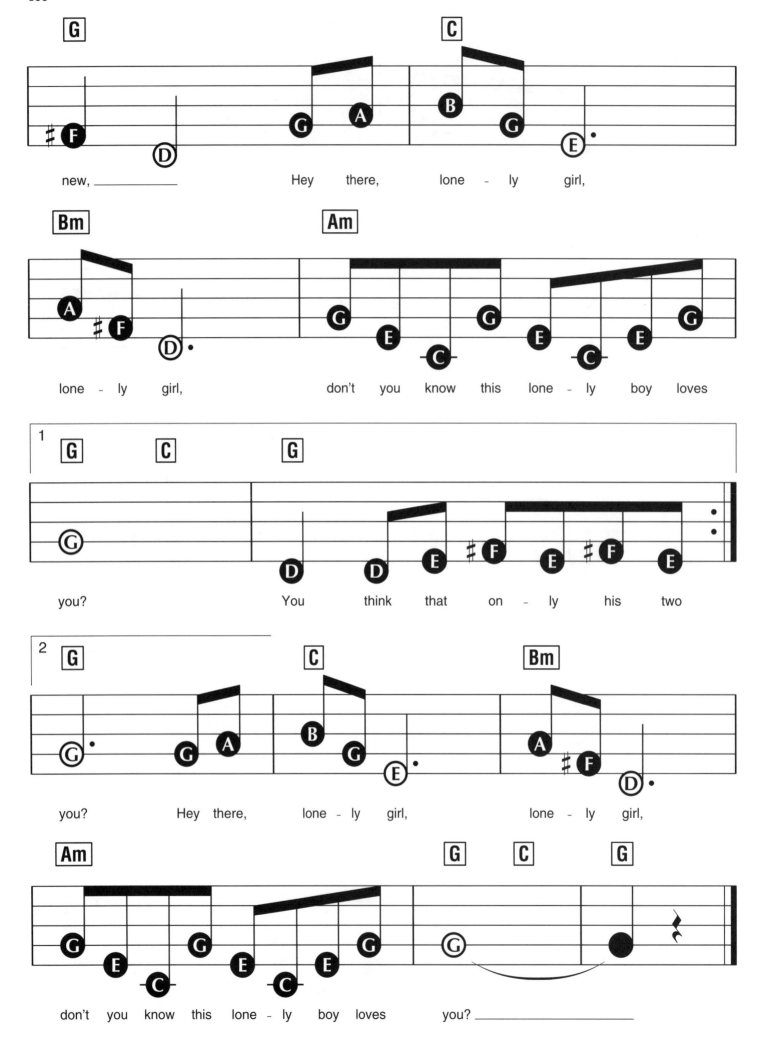

How Long

Registration 2
Rhythm: Ballad

Words and Music by
Paul Carrack

Dm   **Am**

G·   F   D   A   C   D

How   long _____   has   this   been

Gm   **Am**

G   F   F

go - ing   on?

Dm   **Am**

G·   F   D   A   C   D

How   long _____   has   this   been

Gm   **Am**

G   F   F   C   D

go - ing   on?   Well,   your

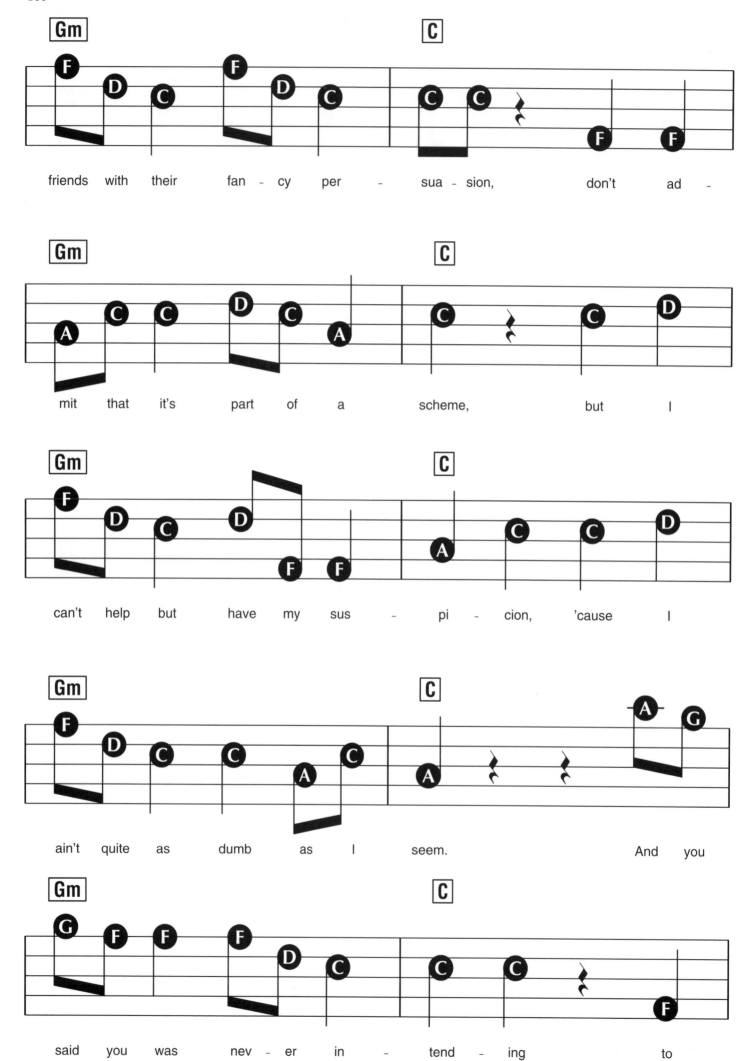

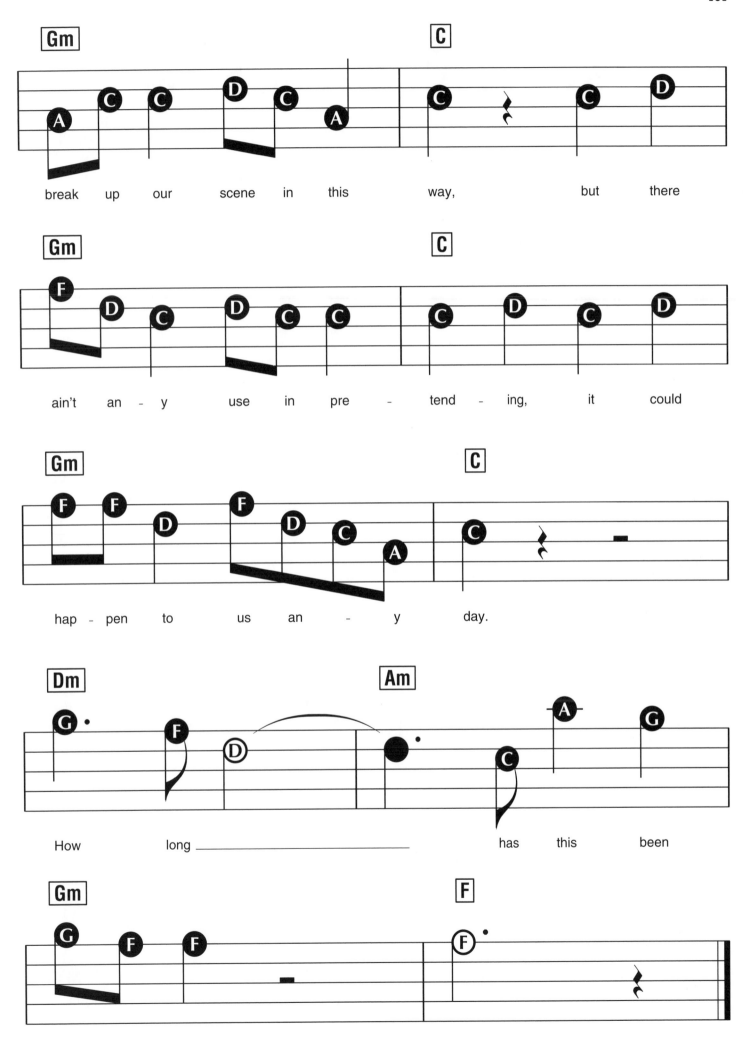

break up our scene in this way, but there

ain't an - y use in pre - tend - ing, it could

hap - pen to us an - y day.

How long _____ has this been

go - ing on?

(Hey, Won't You Play)
Another Somebody Done Somebody Wrong Song

Registration 1
Rhythm: Country or Shuffle

Words and Music by Larry Butler
and Chips Moman

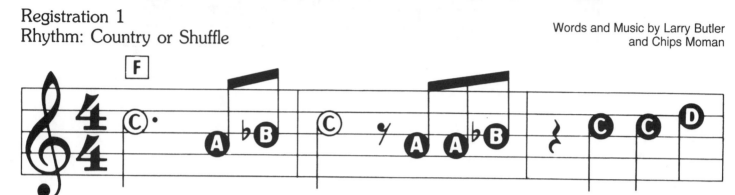

Hey won't you play an - oth - er some - bod - y

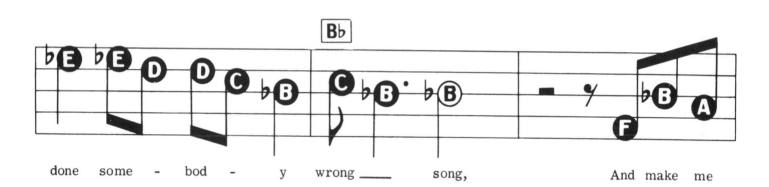

done some - bod - y wrong song, And make me

feel at home while I miss my ba - by,

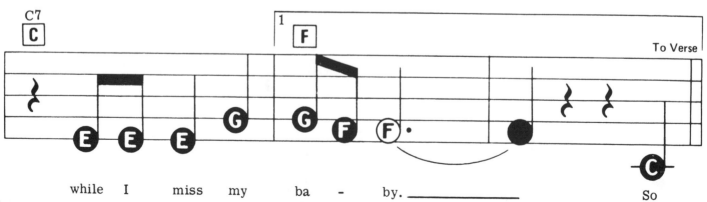

while I miss my ba - by. So

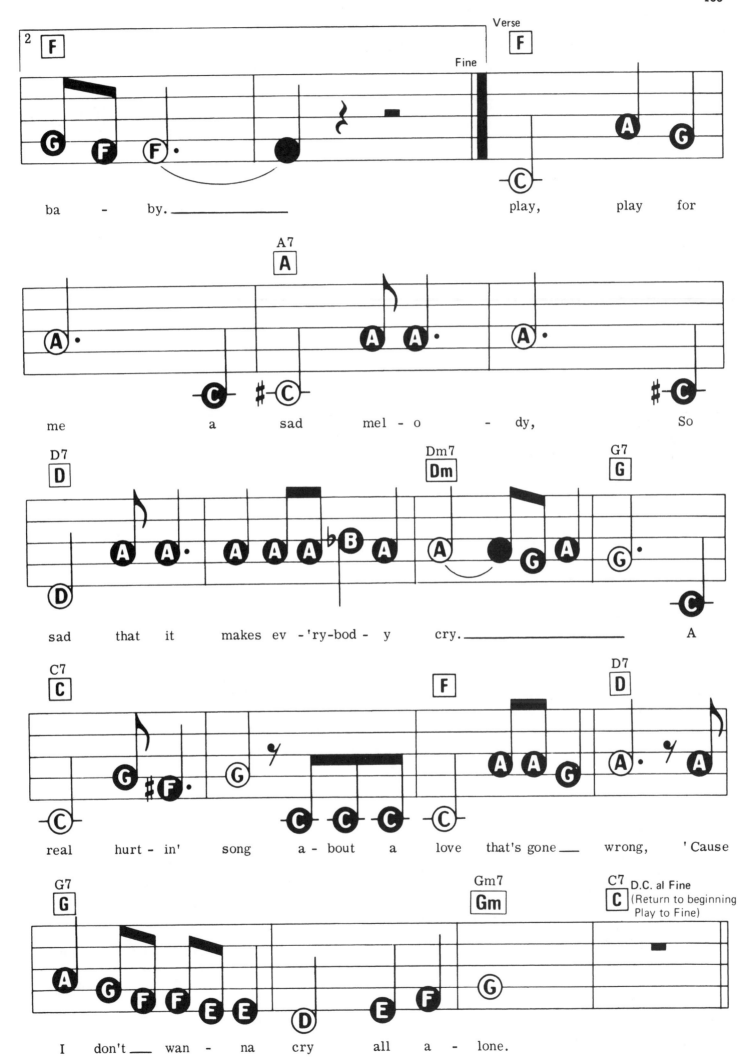

Honky Cat

Registration 8
Rhythm: Rock or Jazz Rock

Words and Music by Elton John
and Bernie Taupin

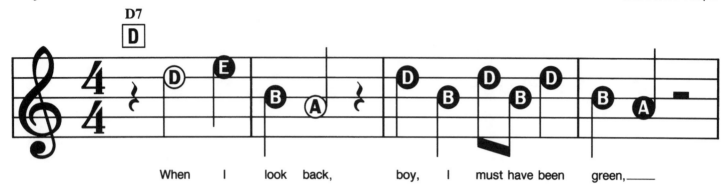

When I look back, boy, I must have been green,____

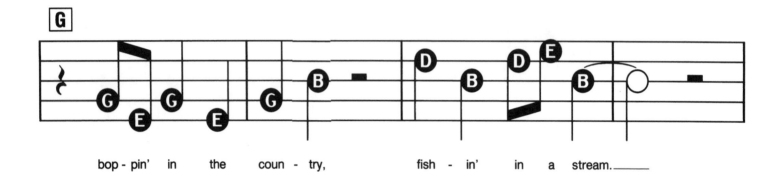

bop-pin' in the coun-try, fish-in' in a stream.____

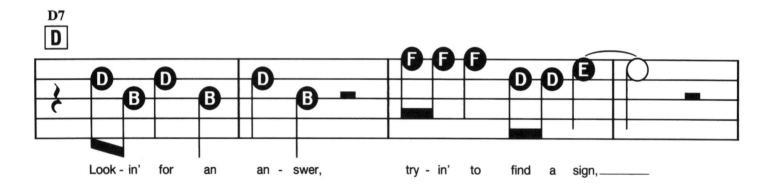

Look-in' for an an-swer, try-in' to find a sign,____

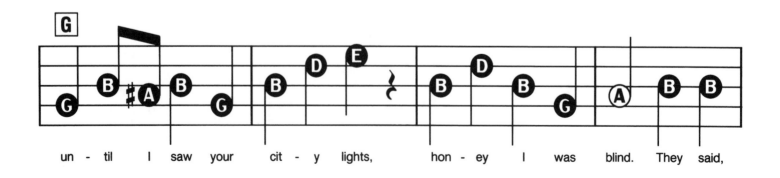

un-til I saw your cit-y lights, hon-ey I was blind. They said,

165

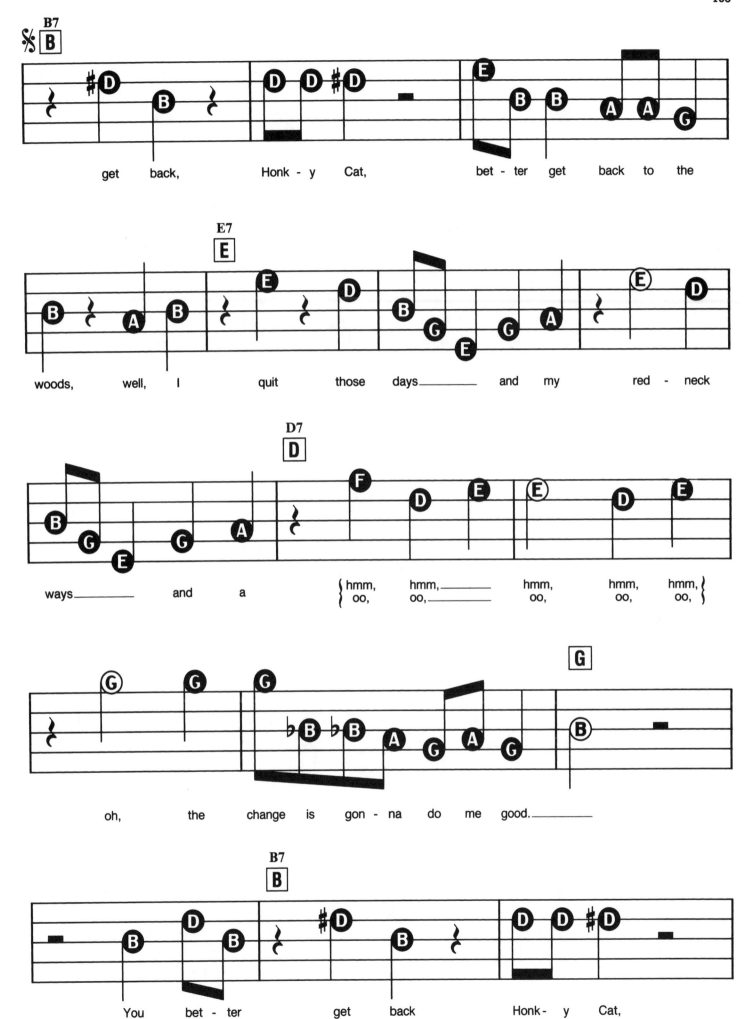

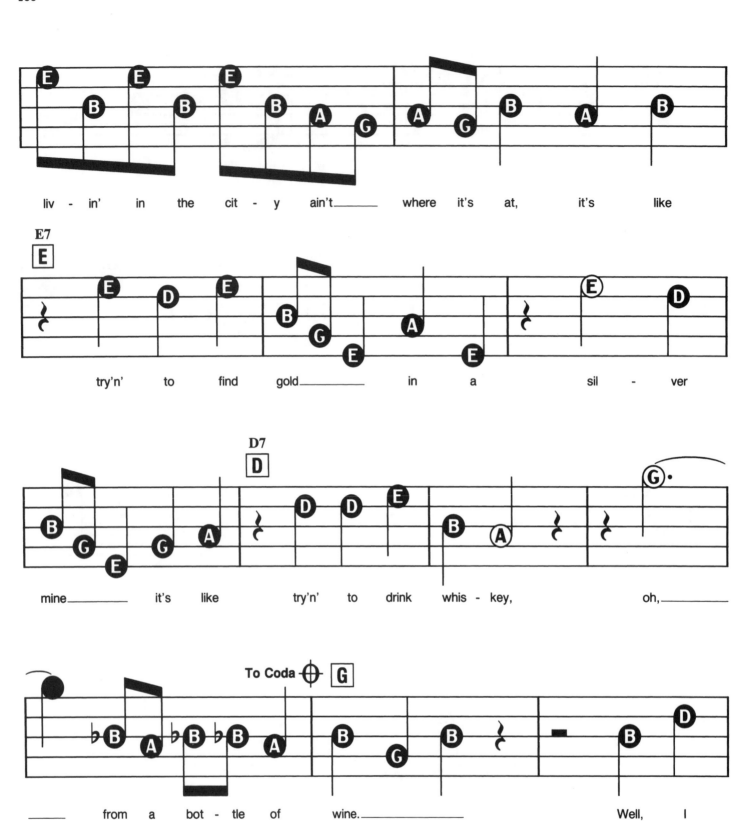

liv - in' in the cit - y ain't_____ where it's at, it's like

E7

try'n' to find gold_____ in a sil - ver

D7

mine_____ it's like try'n' to drink whis - key, oh,_____

To Coda **G**

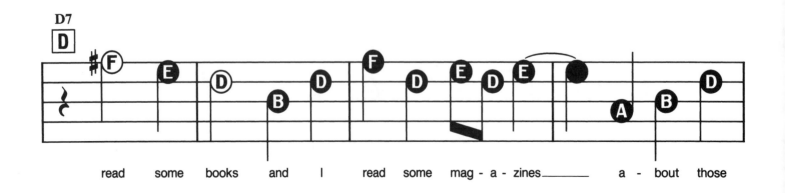

_____ from a bot - tle of wine._____ Well, I

D7

read some books and I read some mag - a - zines_____ a - bout those

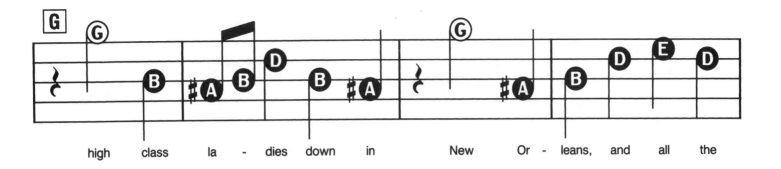

high class la - dies down in New Or - leans, and all the

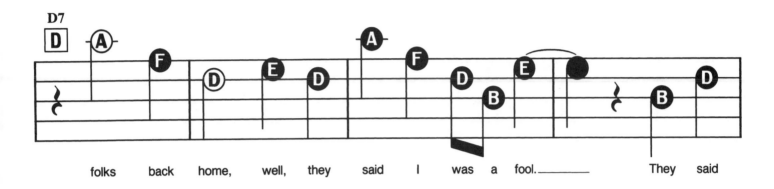

folks back home, well, they said I was a fool._____ They said

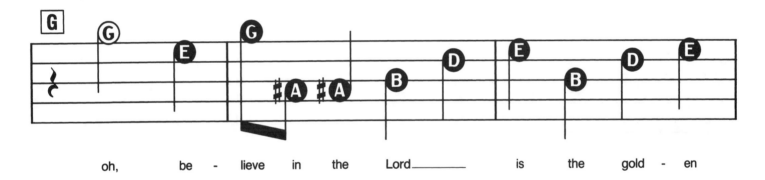

oh, be - lieve in the Lord_____ is the gold - en

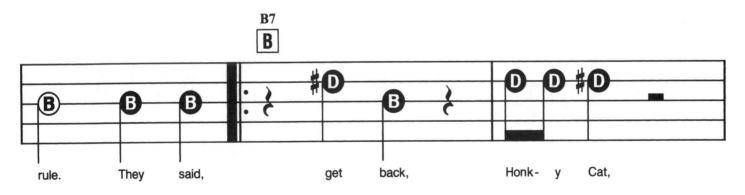

rule. They said, get back, Honk- y Cat,

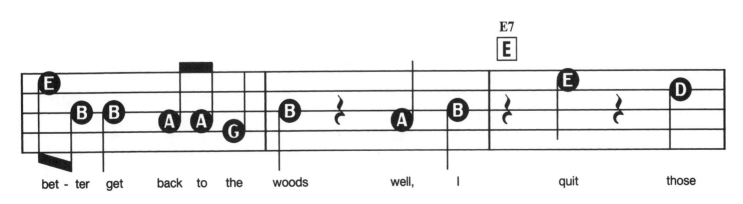

bet - ter get back to the woods well, I quit those

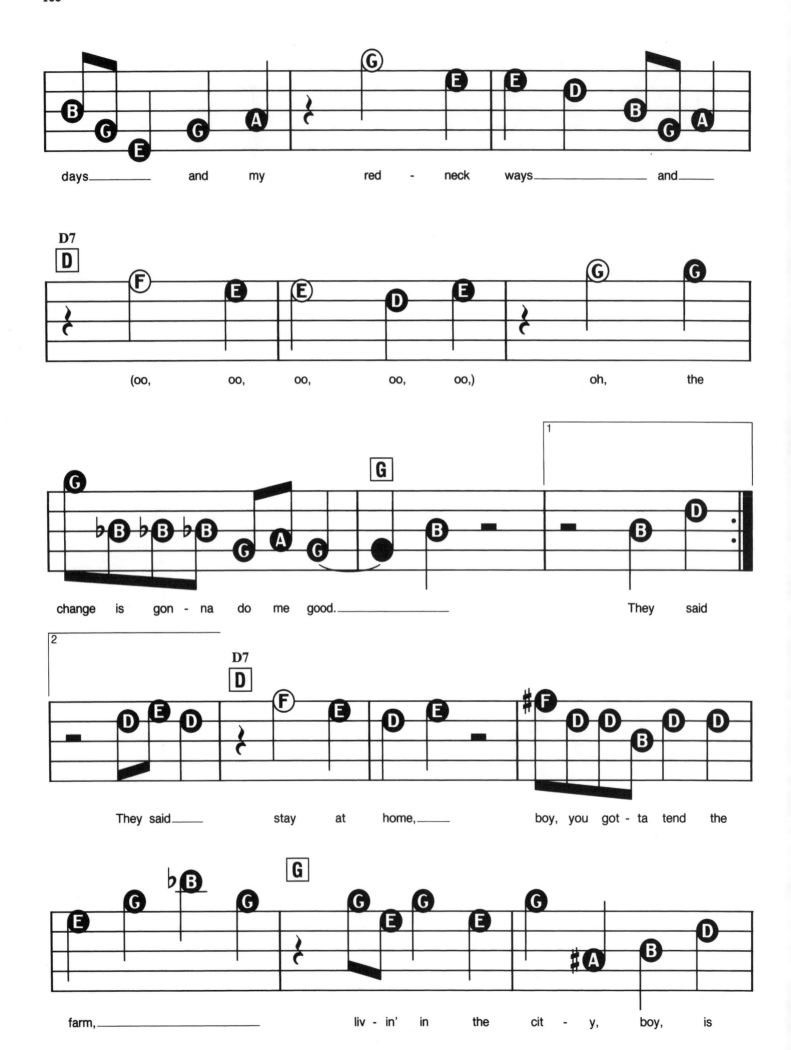

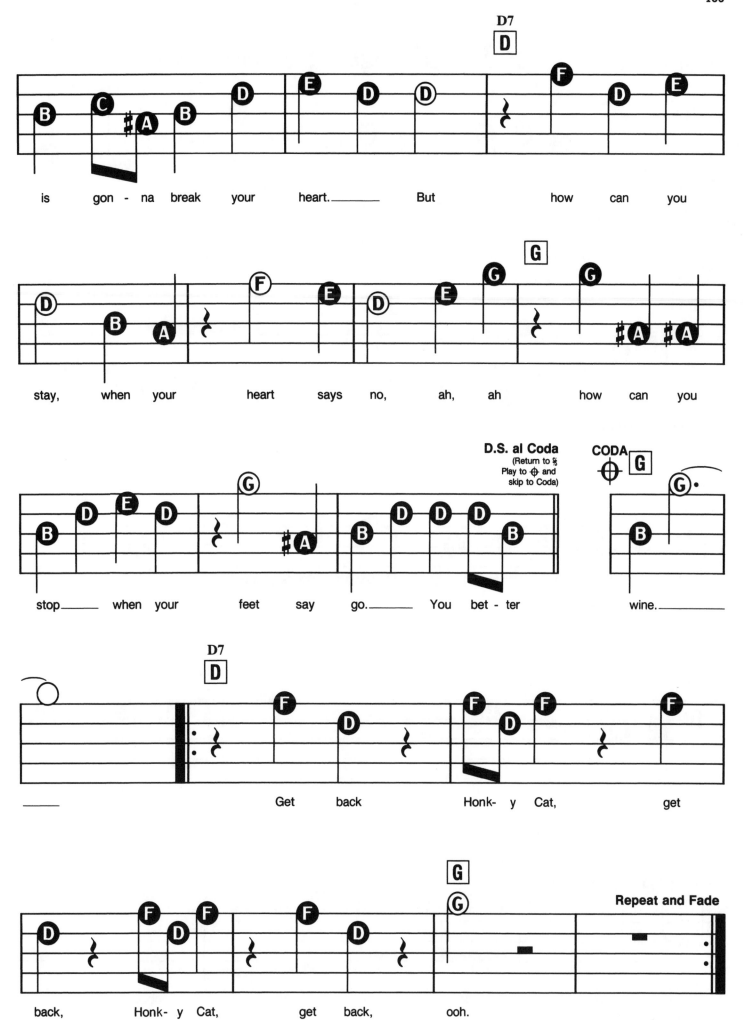

How Can You Mend a Broken Heart

Registration 5
Rhythm: Rock

Words and Music by Robin Gibb
and Barry Gibb

I can think of young - er days when liv - ing for my life was
I can still feel the breeze that rust - les through the trees and

ev - 'ry - thing a man could want to do. I could nev - er see to -
mis - ty mem - o - ries of days gone by. We could nev - er see to -

mor - row but I was nev - er told a -
mor - row, no one said a word a -

bout the sor - row. And how can you mend
bout the sor - row.

bro - ken heart? How can you stop the rain from fall - ing down?

171

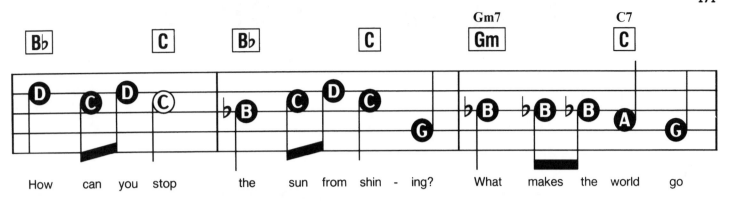

How can you stop the sun from shin - ing? What makes the world go

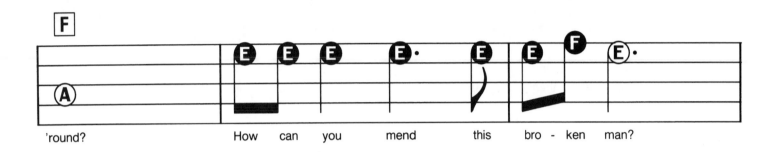

'round? How can you mend this bro - ken man?

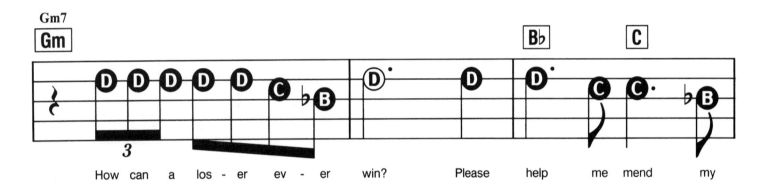

How can a los - er ev - er win? Please help me mend my

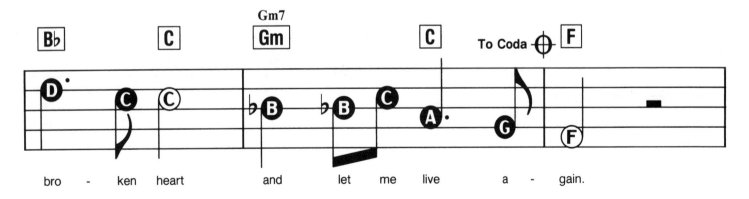

bro - ken heart and let me live a - gain.

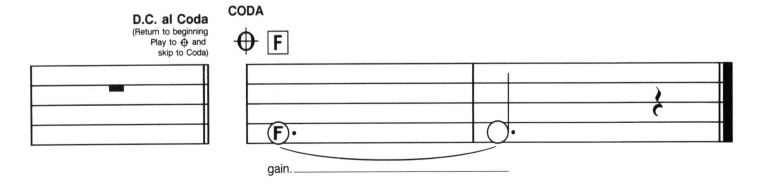

gain.

Hurting Each Other

Registration 8
Rhythm: Rock

Words by Peter Udell
Music by Gary Geld

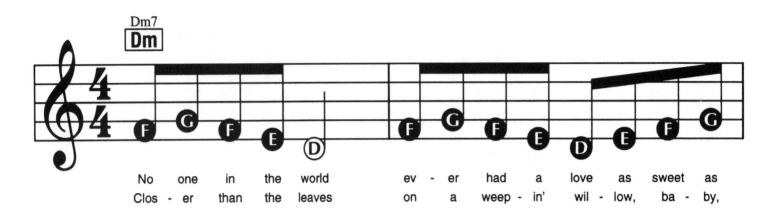

No one in the world ev - er had a love as sweet as
Clos - er than the leaves on a weep - in' wil - low, ba - by,

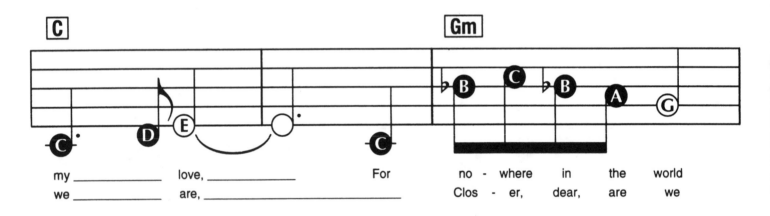

my love, For
we are, Clos - er, dear, are we

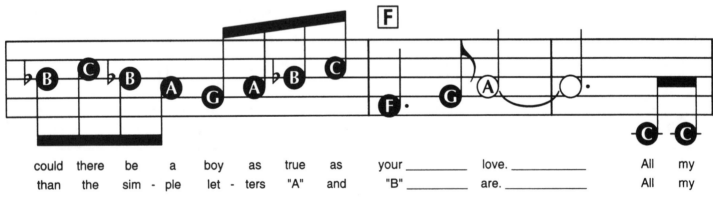

could there be a boy as true as your love.
than the sim - ple let - ters "A" and "B" are.
All my
All my

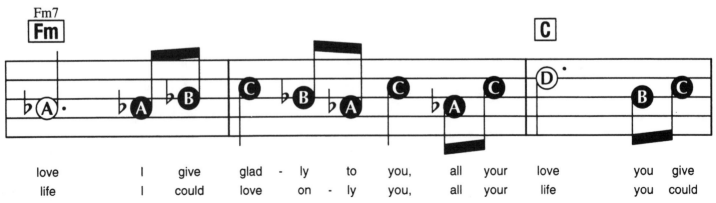

love I give glad - ly to you, all your love you give
life I could love on - ly you, all your life you could

173

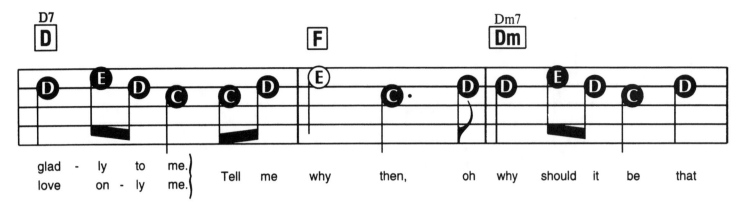

glad - ly to me.⎱ Tell me why then, oh why should it be that
love on - ly me.⎰

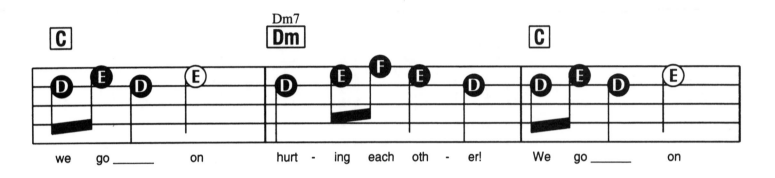

we go ____ on hurt - ing each oth - er! We go ____ on

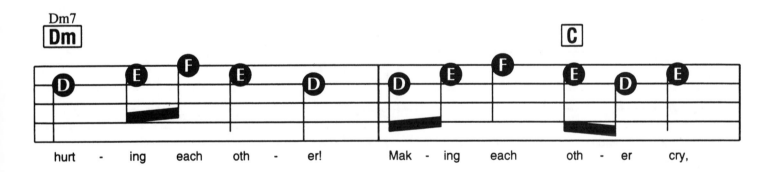

hurt - ing each oth - er! Mak - ing each oth - er cry,

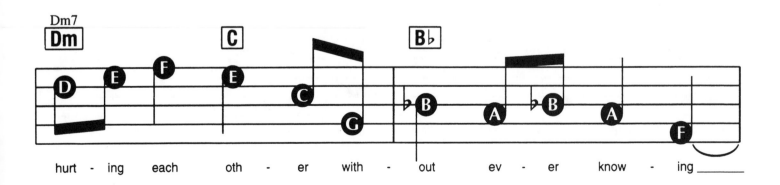

hurt - ing each oth - er with - out ev - er know - ing ____

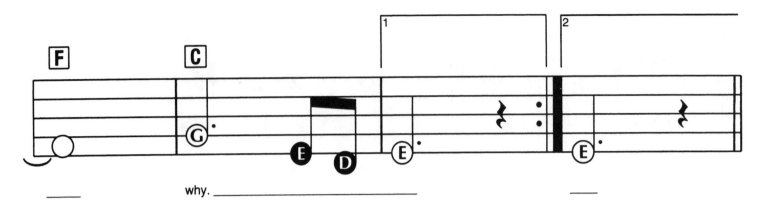

why.

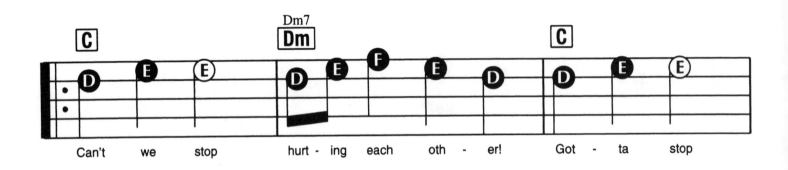

Can't we stop hurt - ing each oth - er! Got - ta stop

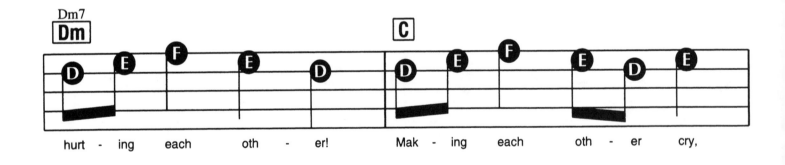

hurt - ing each oth - er! Mak - ing each oth - er cry,

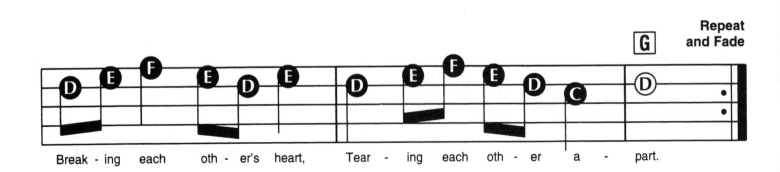

Break - ing each oth - er's heart, Tear - ing each oth - er a - part.

I Can Help

Registration 3
Rhythm: Country or Shuffle

Words and Music by
Billy Swan

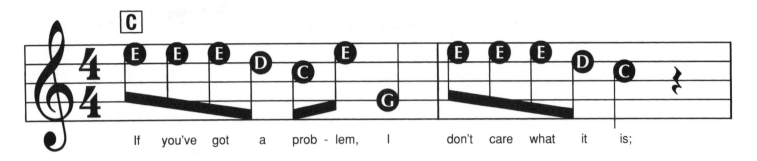

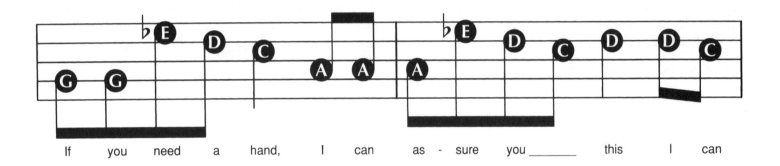

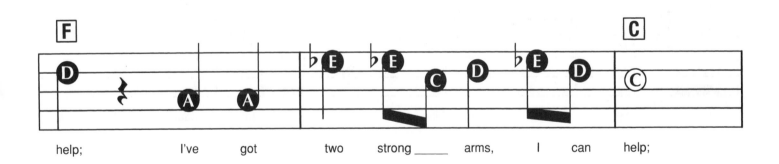

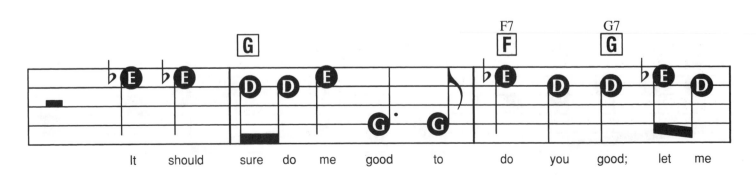

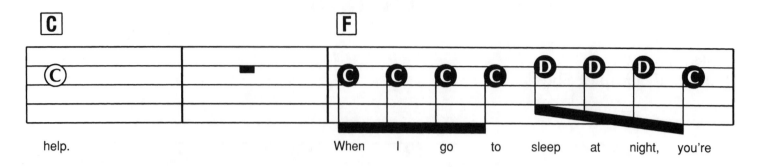

help. When I go to sleep at night, you're

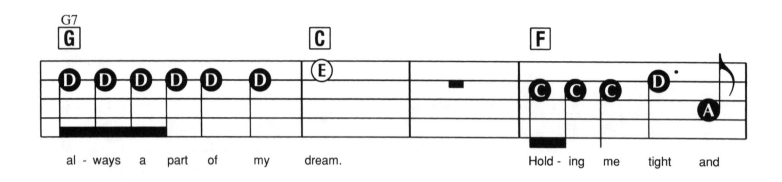

al - ways a part of my dream. Hold - ing me tight and

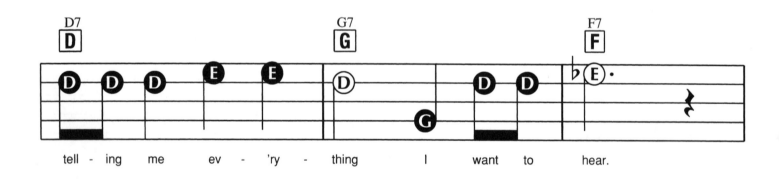

tell - ing me ev - 'ry - thing I want to hear.

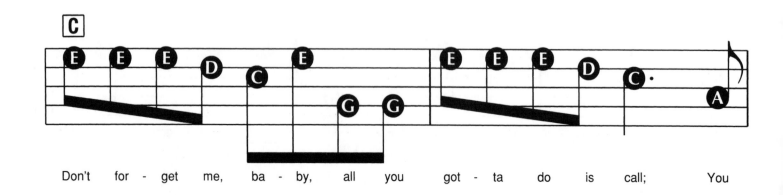

Don't for - get me, ba - by, all you got - ta do is call; You

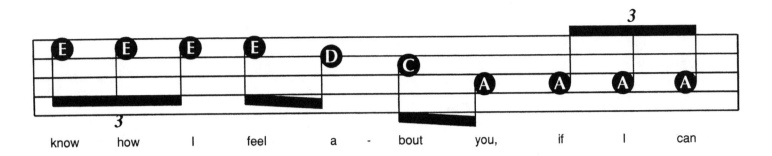

know how I feel a - bout you, if I can

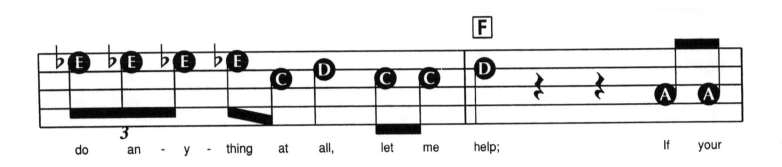

do an - y - thing at all, let me help; If your

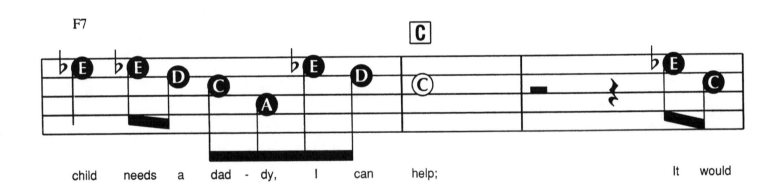

child needs a dad - dy, I can help; It would

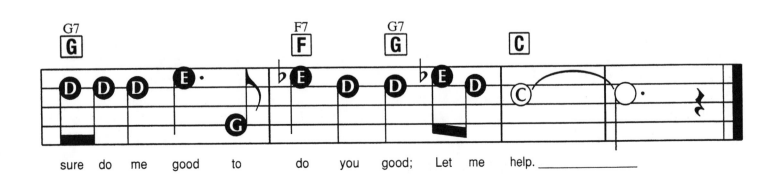

sure do me good to do you good; Let me help._____

I Feel the Earth Move

Registration 4
Rhythm: Rock

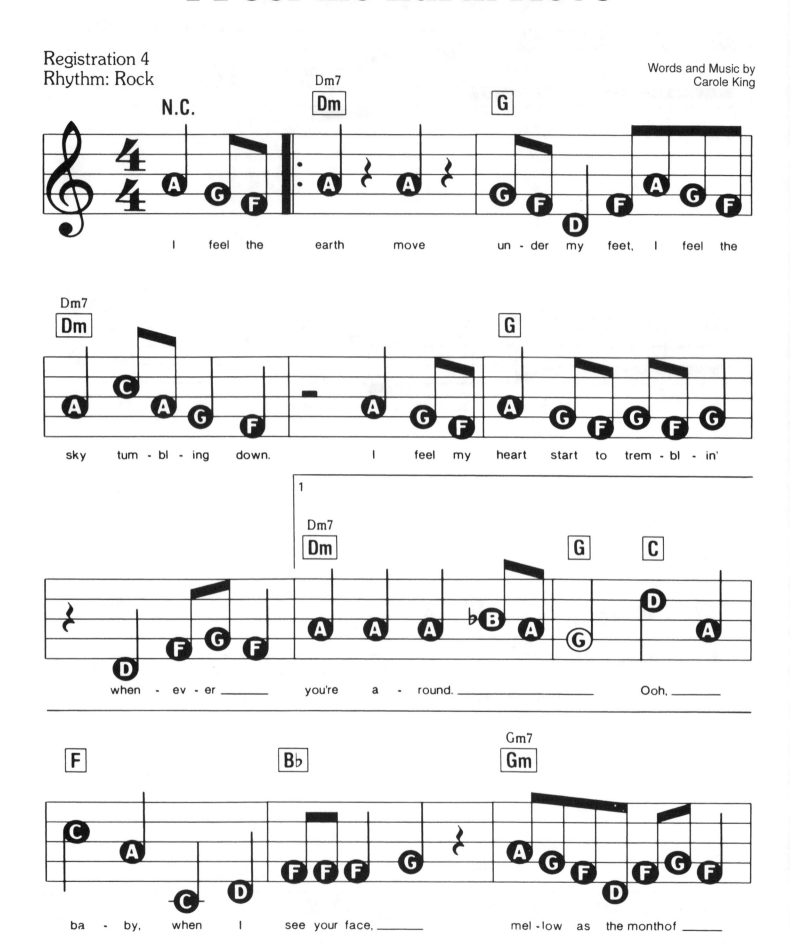

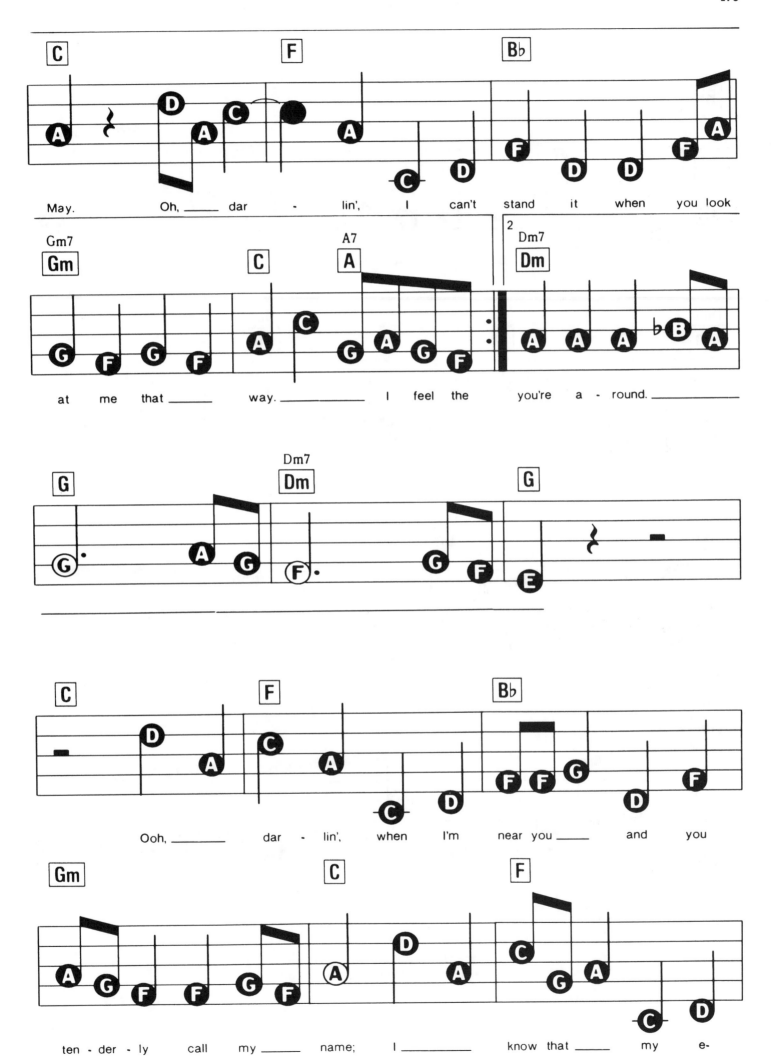

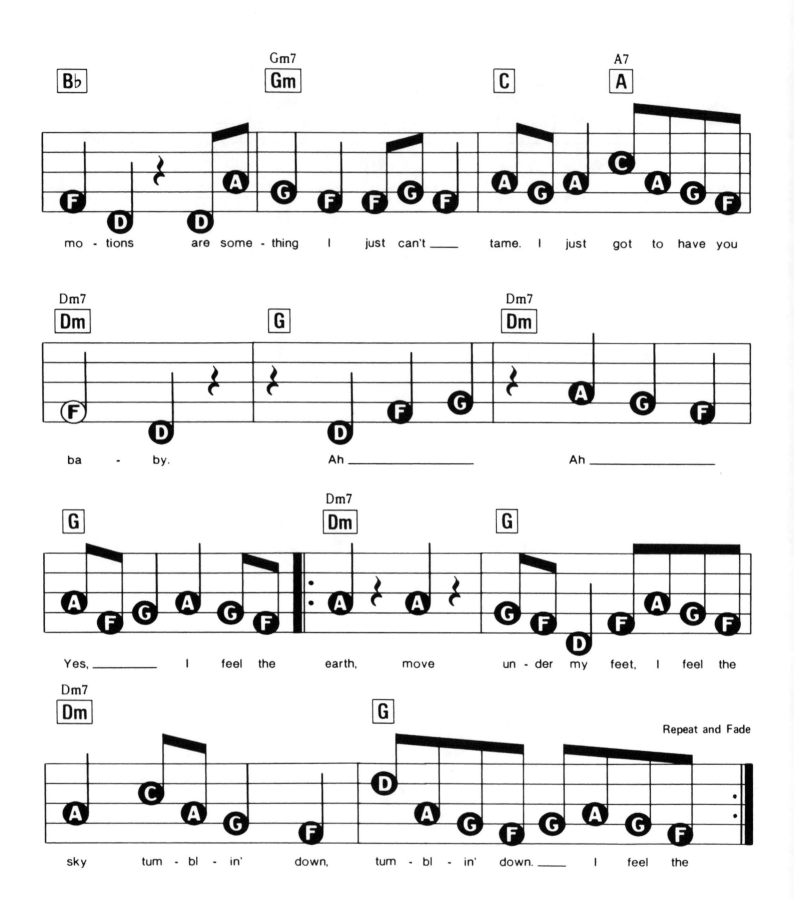

Additional Lyrics

I just lose control down to my very soul,
I get hot and cold all over, all over, all over.

It Never Rains
(In Southern California)

Registration 8
Rhythm: Rock

Words and Music by Albert Hammond
and Michael Hazelwood

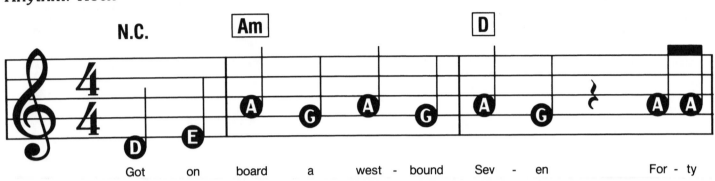

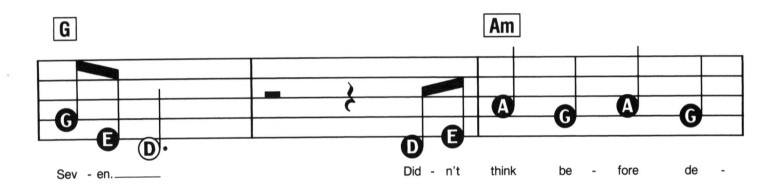

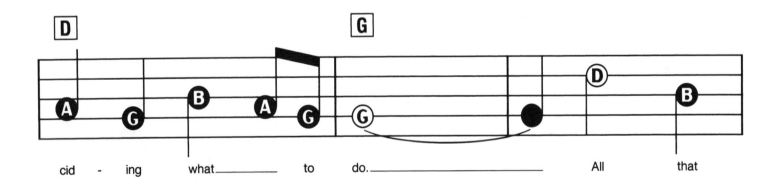

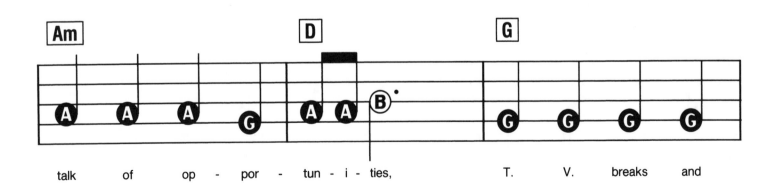

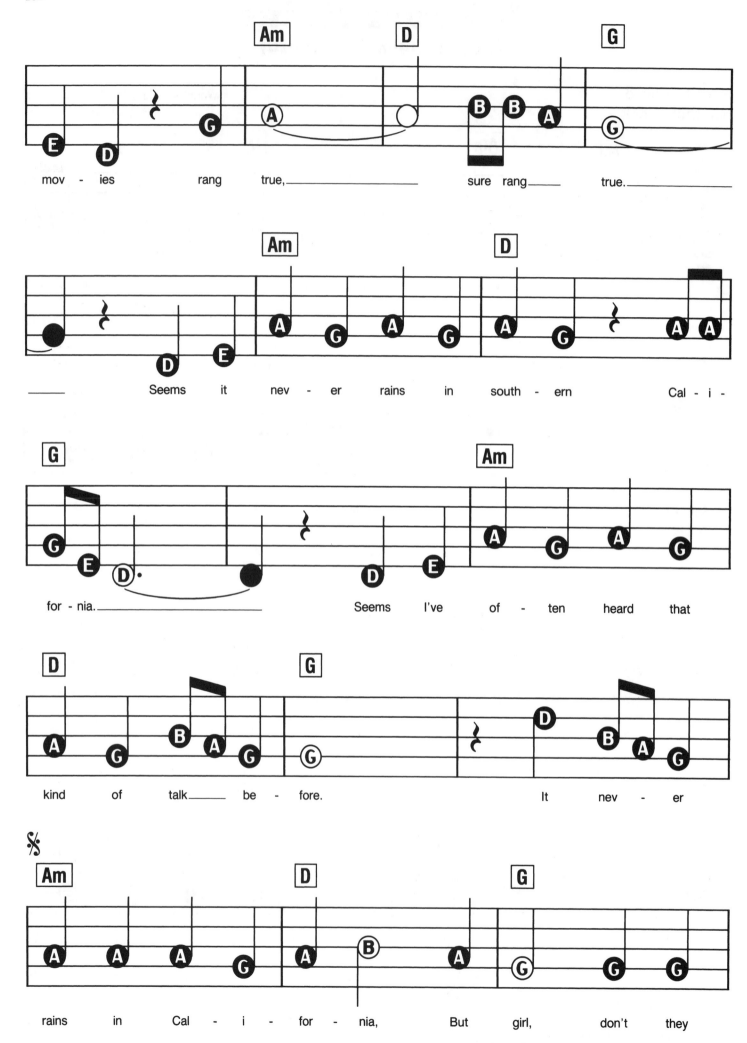

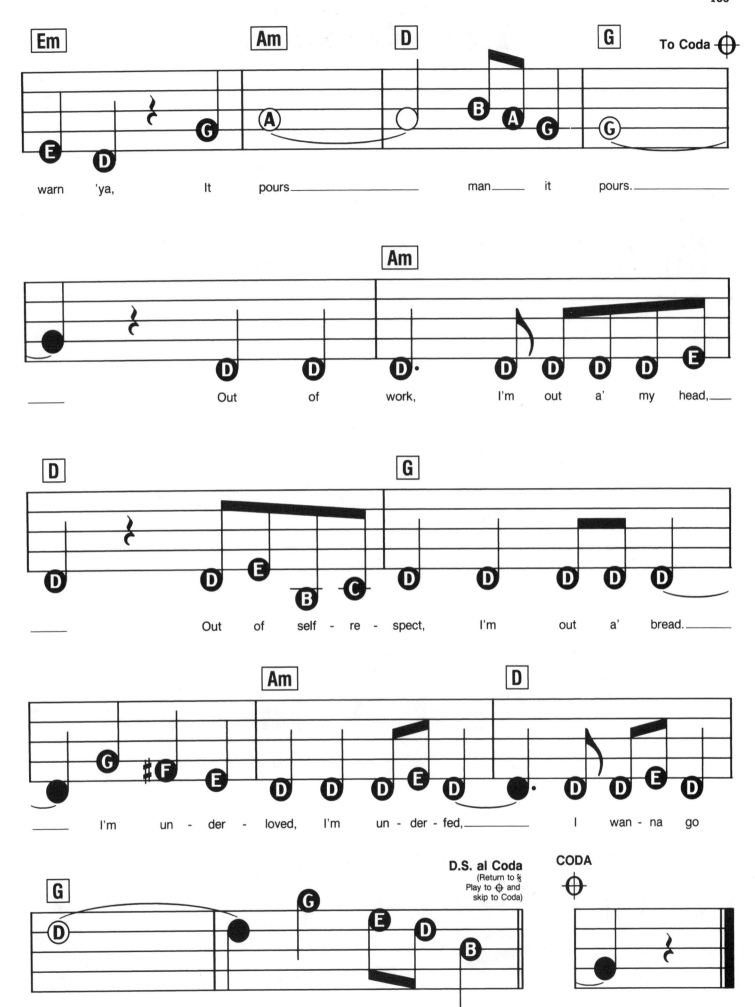

warn 'ya, It pours_____ man___ it pours._____

_____ Out of work, I'm out a' my head,_____

_____ Out of self - re - spect, I'm out a' bread._____

_____ I'm un - der - loved, I'm un - der - fed,_____ I wan - na go

home._____ It nev - er _____

(I Never Promised You A)
Rose Garden

Registration 4
Rhythm: Fox Trot

Words and Music by
Joe South

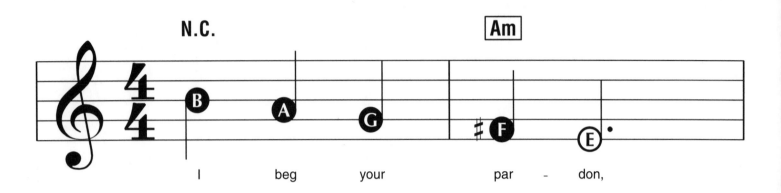

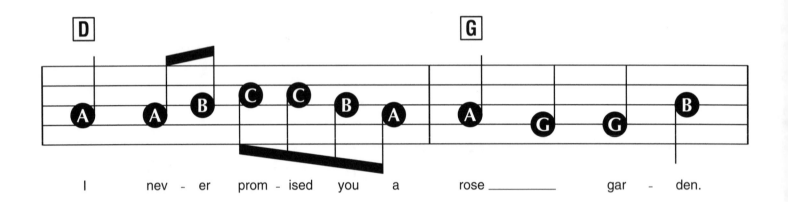

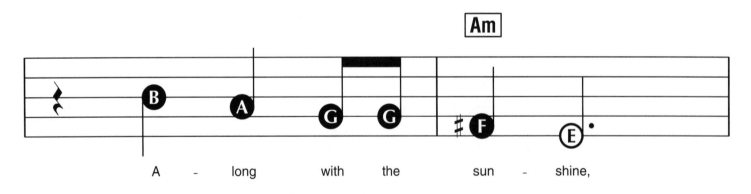

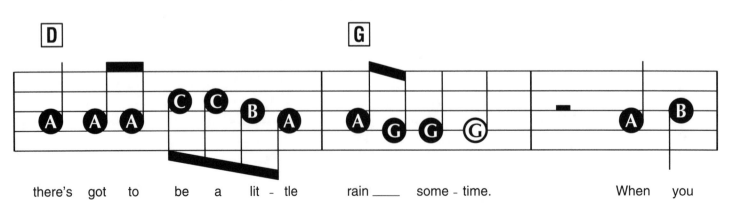

185

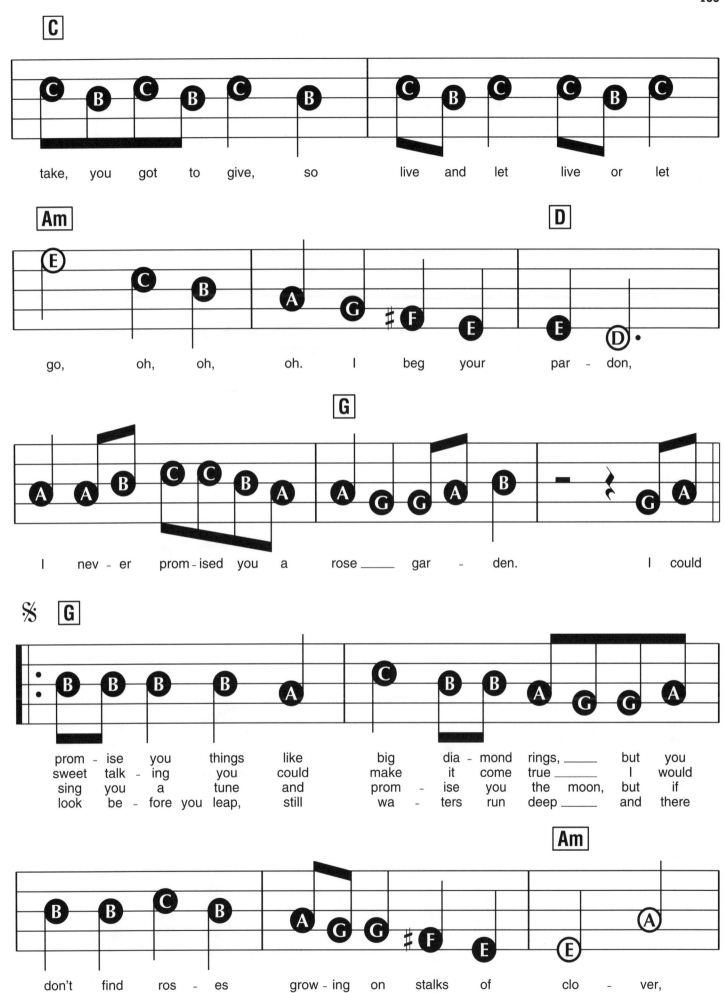

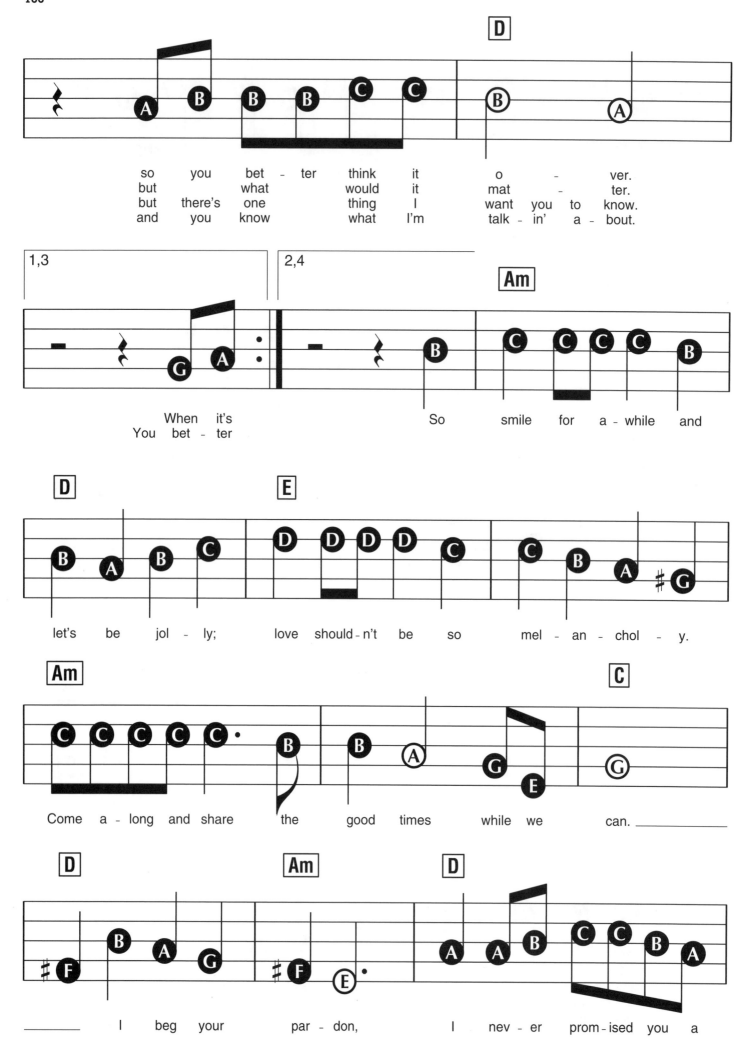

187

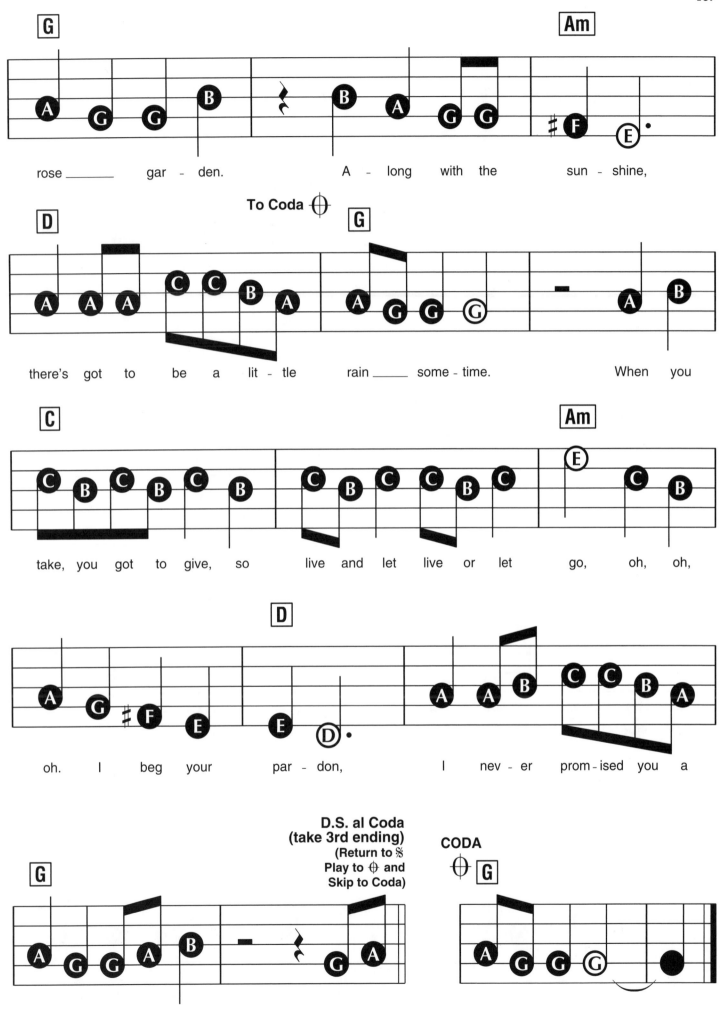

I Think I Love You

Registration 2
Rhythm: Rock or 8 Beat

Words and Music by
Tony Romeo

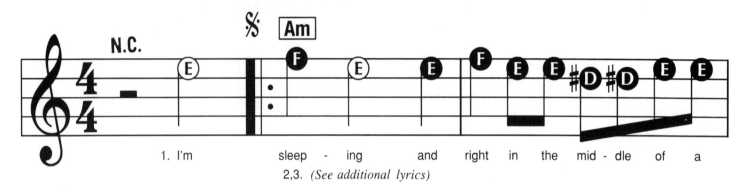

1. I'm sleep-ing and right in the mid-dle of a
2,3. *(See additional lyrics)*

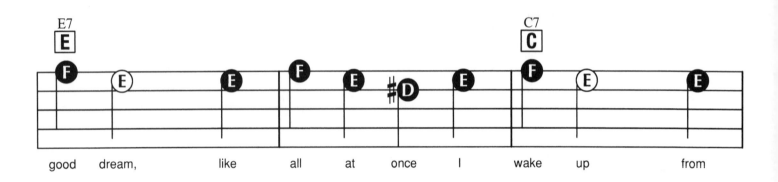

good dream, like all at once I wake up from

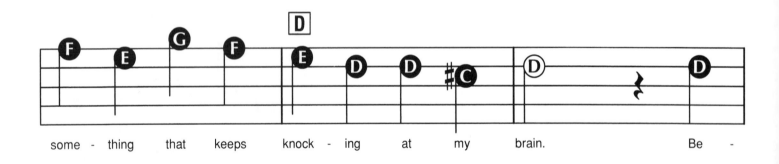

some-thing that keeps knock-ing at my brain. Be-

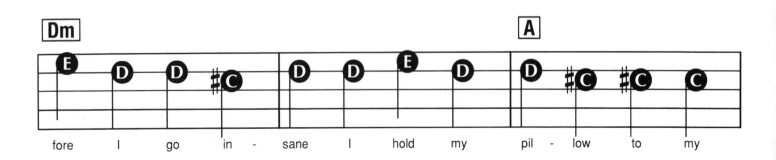

fore I go in-sane I hold my pil-low to my

189

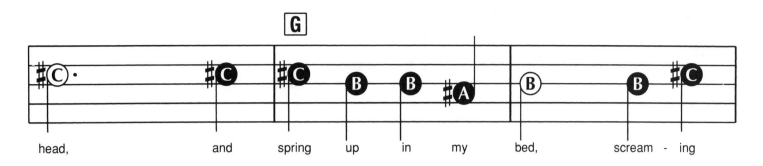

head, and spring up in my bed, scream - ing

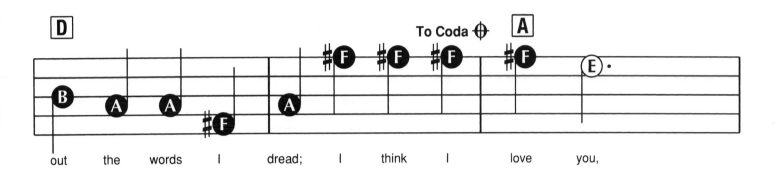

out the words I dread; I think I love you,

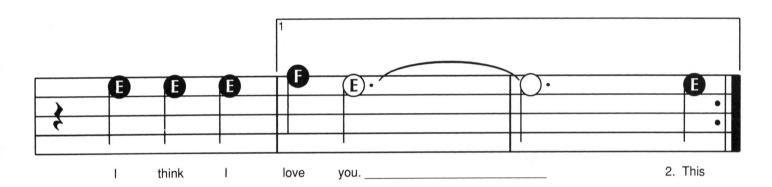

I think I love you. _____ 2. This

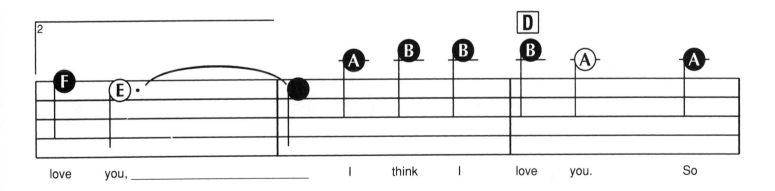

love you, _____ I think I love you. So

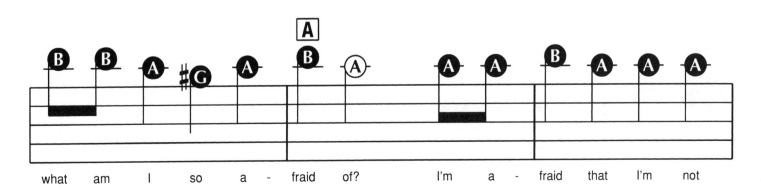

what am I so a - fraid of? I'm a - fraid that I'm not

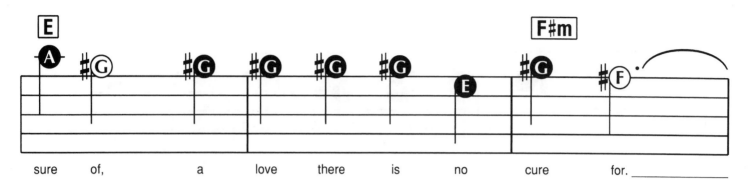

sure   of,   a   love   there   is   no   cure   for. _____

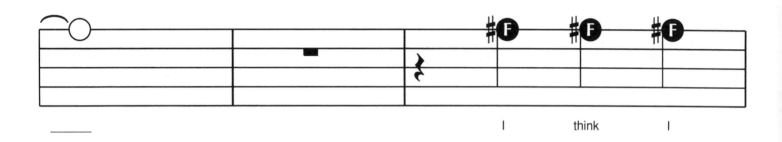

_____   I   think   I

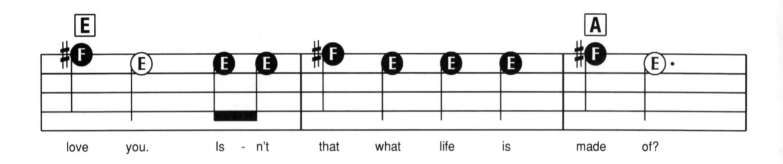

love you. Is - n't that what life is made of?

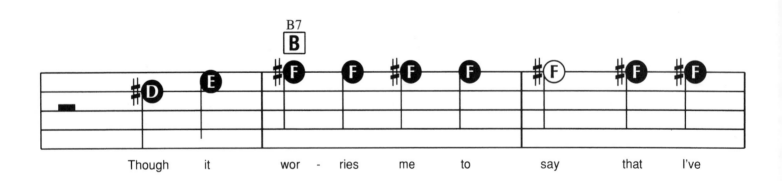

Though it wor - ries me to say that I've

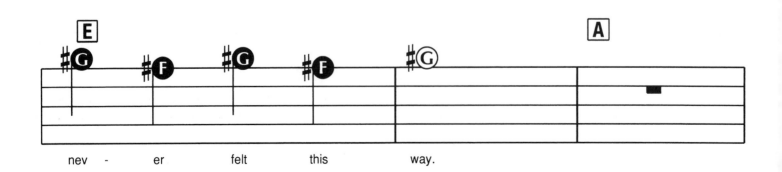

nev - er felt this way.

191

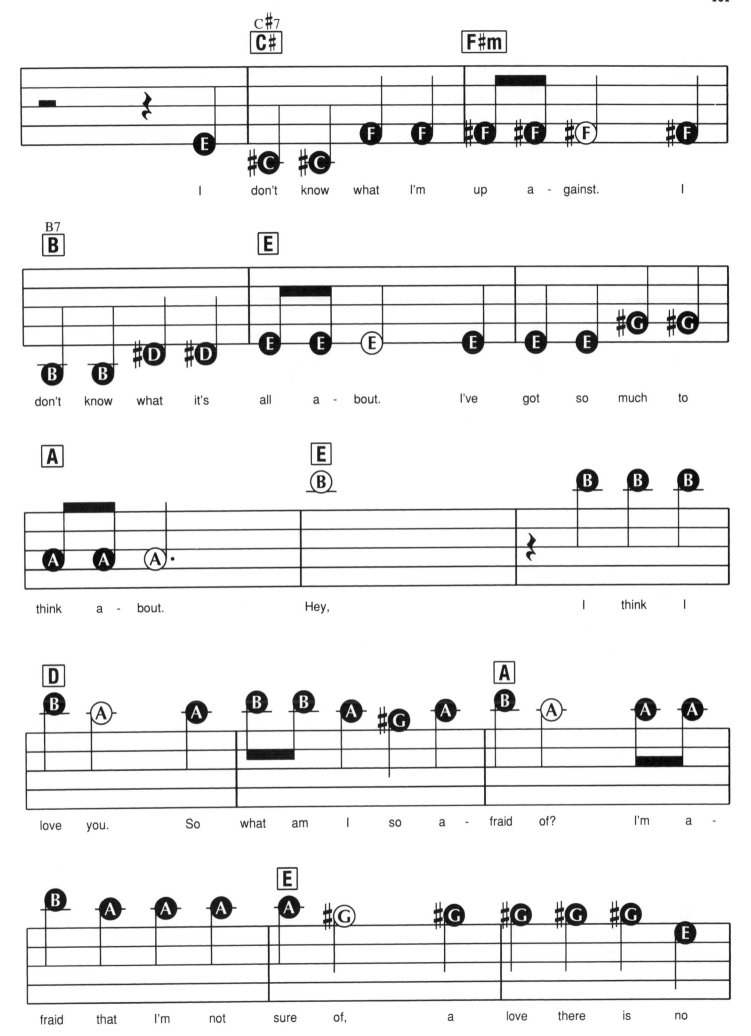

192

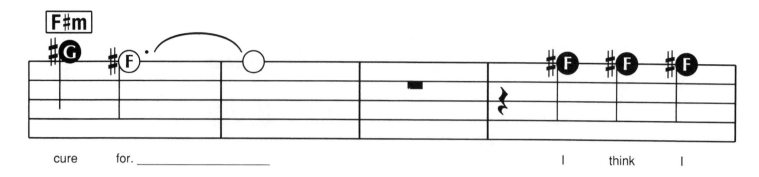

cure   for. _____   I   think   I

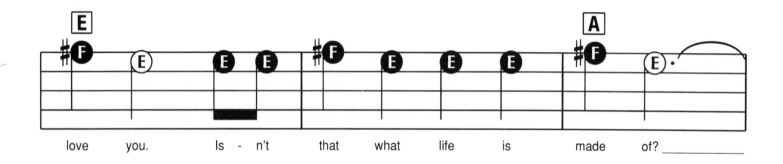

love   you.   Is - n't   that   what   life   is   made   of? _____

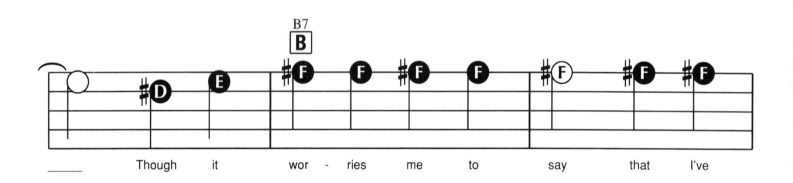

_____   Though   it   wor - ries   me   to   say   that   I've

D.S. al Coda
(Return to 𝄋
Play to ⊕
Skip to Coda)

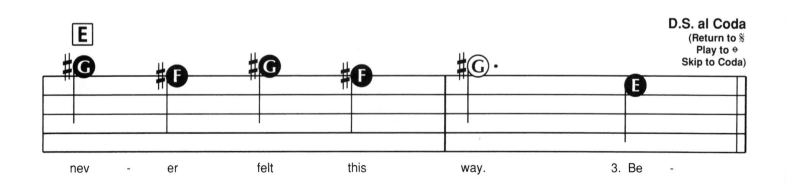

nev - er   felt   this   way.   3. Be -

193

CODA

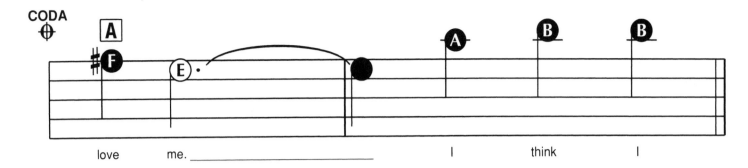

love me. _____ I think I

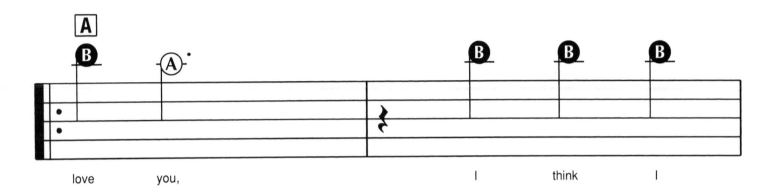

love you, I think I

Repeat and Fade

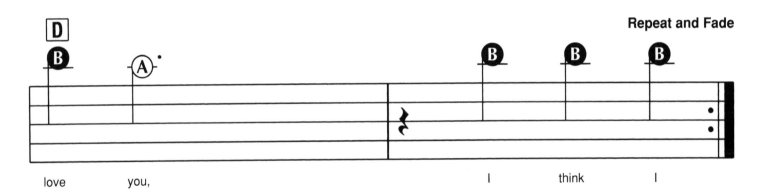

love you, I think I

Additional Lyrics

2. This morning I woke up with this feeling,
   I didn't know how to deal with.
   And so I just decided with myself,
   I'd hide it to myself.
   And never talk about it and didn't I go and shout it
   When you walked into the room:
   I think I love you. (etc.)

3. Believe me you really don't have to worry,
   I only want to make you happy.
   And if you say "Hey go away," I will.
   But I think better still.
   I'd better stay around and love you,
   Do you think I have a case? Let me ask you to your face.
   Do you think you love me?
   I think I love you! (etc.)

I Wish

Registration 9
Rhythm: Rock

Words and Music by
Stevie Wonder

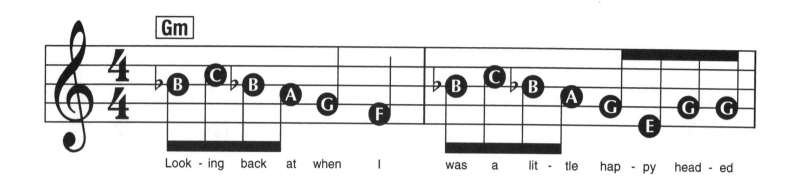

Look - ing back at when I was a lit - tle hap - py head - ed

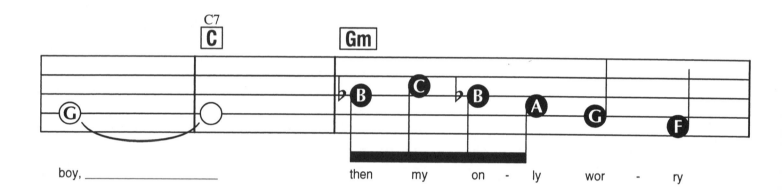

boy, _____ then my on - ly wor - ry

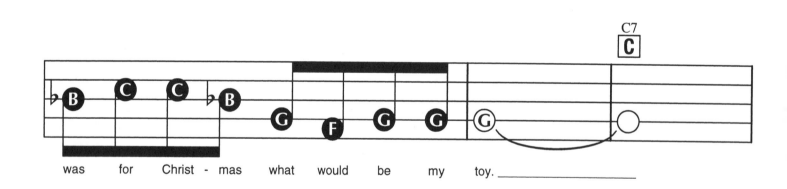

was for Christ - mas what would be my toy. _____

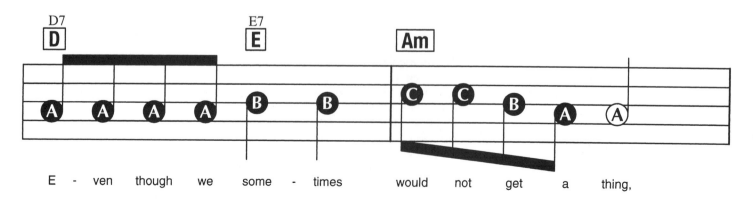

E - ven though we some - times would not get a thing,

195

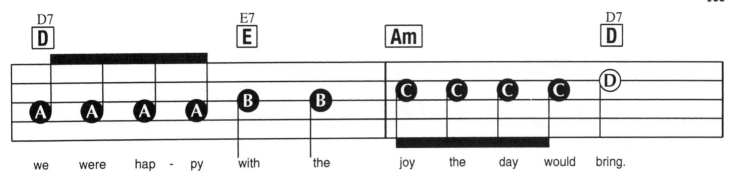

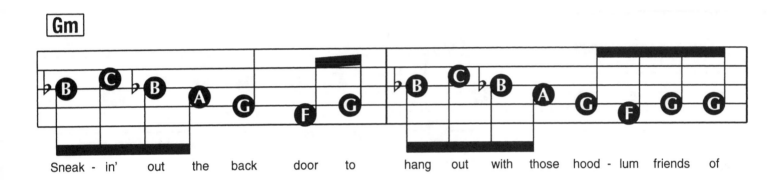

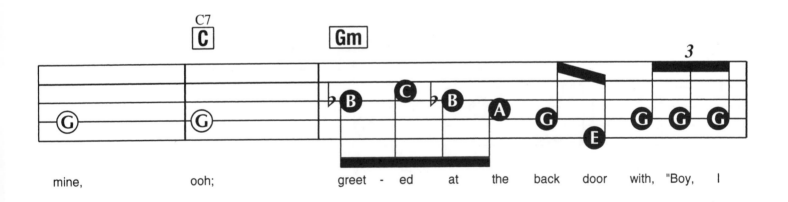

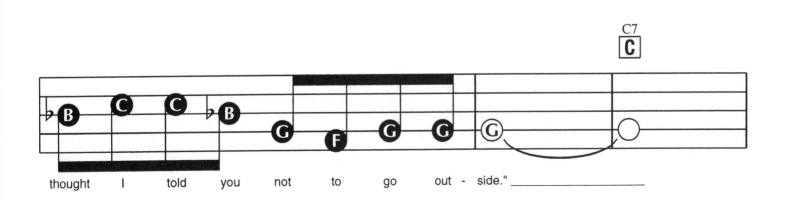

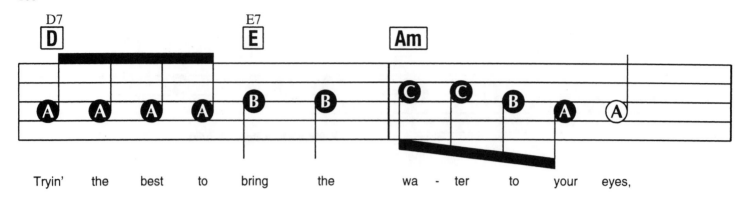

Tryin' the best to bring the wa - ter to your eyes,

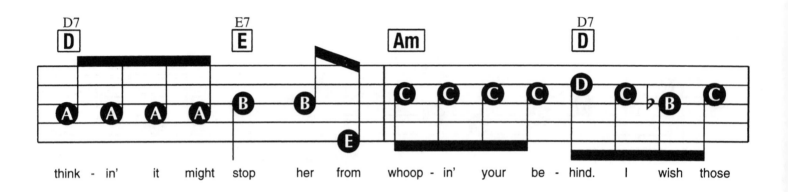

think - in' it might stop her from whoop - in' your be - hind. I wish those

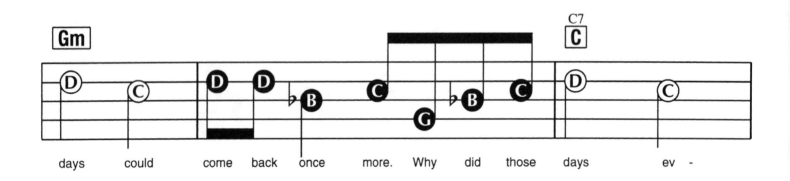

days could come back once more. Why did those days ev -

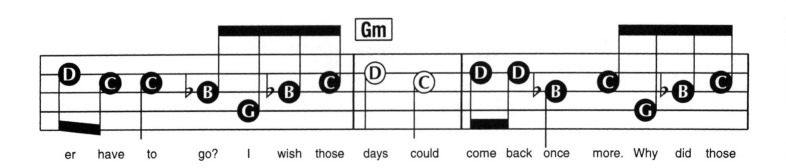

er have to go? I wish those days could come back once more. Why did those

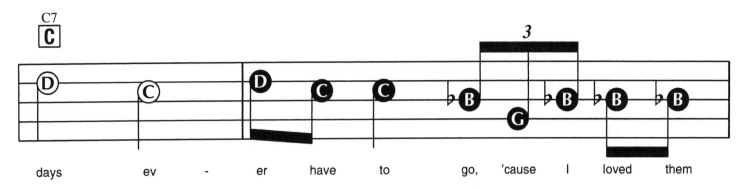

days ev - er have to go, 'cause I loved them

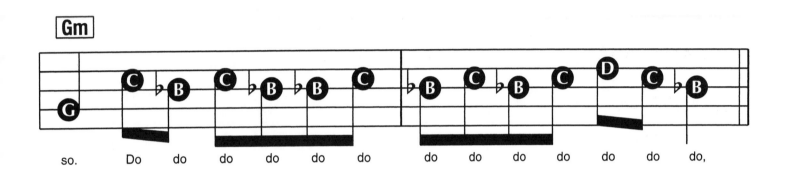

so. Do do do do do do do do do do do do do,

Repeat and Fade

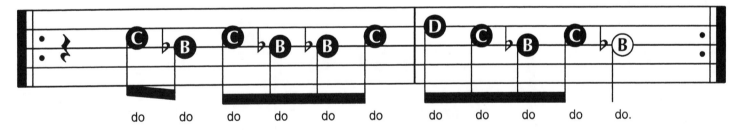

do do do do do do do do do do do.

Additional Lyrics

Brother says he's tellin'
'Bout you playin' doctor with that girl
Just don't tell, I'll give you
Anything you want in this whole wide world.
Mama gives you money for Sunday school;
You trade yours for candy after church is through.

Smokin' cigarettes and writing something nasty on the wall (you nasty boy);
Teacher sends you to the principal's office down the hall.
You grow up and learn that kinda thing ain't right,
But while you were doin' it - it sure felt outta sight.

I wish those days could come back once more.
Why did those days ever have to go?
I wish those days could come back once more.
Why did those days ever have to go?

I'll Be There

Registration 8
Rhythm: Rock or 8 Beat

Words and Music by Berry Gordy, Hal Davis,
Willie Hutch and Bob West

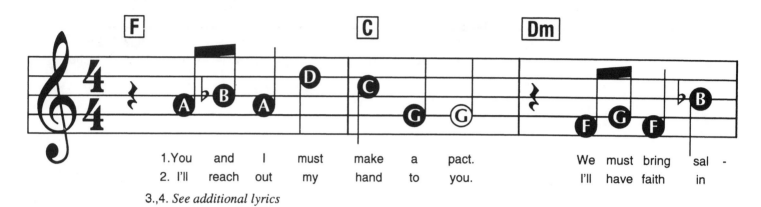

1. You and I must make a pact.
2. I'll reach out my hand to you.

We must bring sal-
I'll have faith in

3., 4. *See additional lyrics*

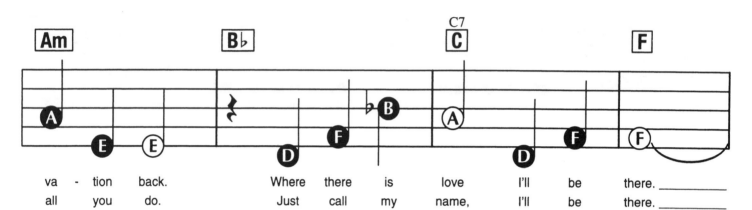

va - tion back.
all you do.

Where there is love
Just call my name,

I'll be there. _____
I'll be there. _____

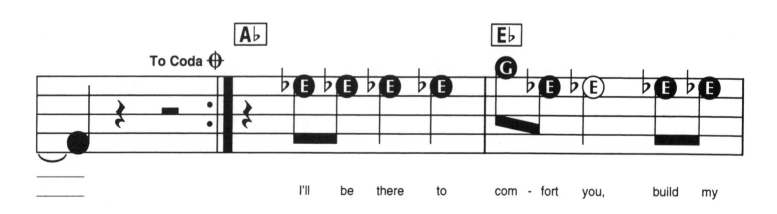

To Coda ⊕

_____

I'll be there to com - fort you, build my

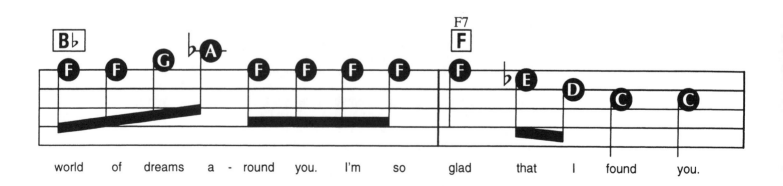

world of dreams a - round you. I'm so glad that I found you.

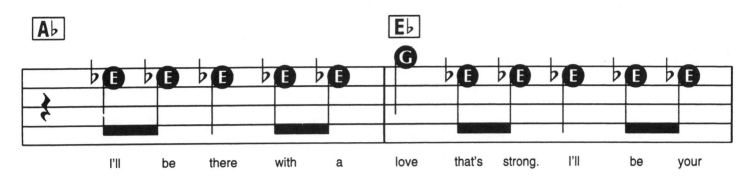

I'll be there with a love that's strong. I'll be your

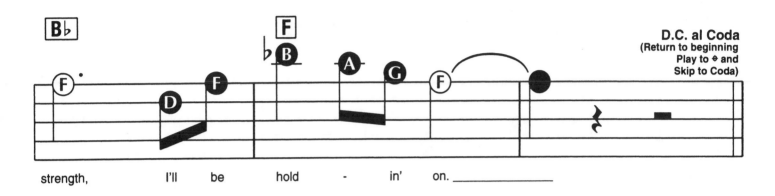

strength, I'll be hold - in' on. _____

D.C. al Coda
(Return to beginning
Play to ✛ and
Skip to Coda)

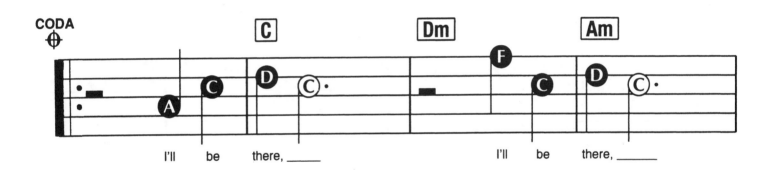

I'll be there, _____ I'll be there, _____

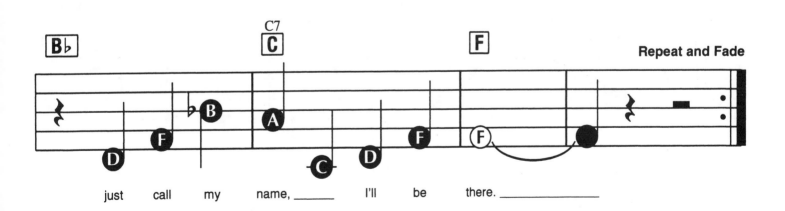

just call my name, _____ I'll be there. _____

Repeat and Fade

Additional Lyrics

3. Let me fill your heart with joy and laughter.
Togetherness, girl, is all I'm after.
Whenever you need me, I'll be there.

4. I'll be there to protect you
With unselfish love that respects you.
Just call my name, I'll be there.

If

Registration 2
Rhythm: Slow Rock or Ballad

Words and Music by
David Gates

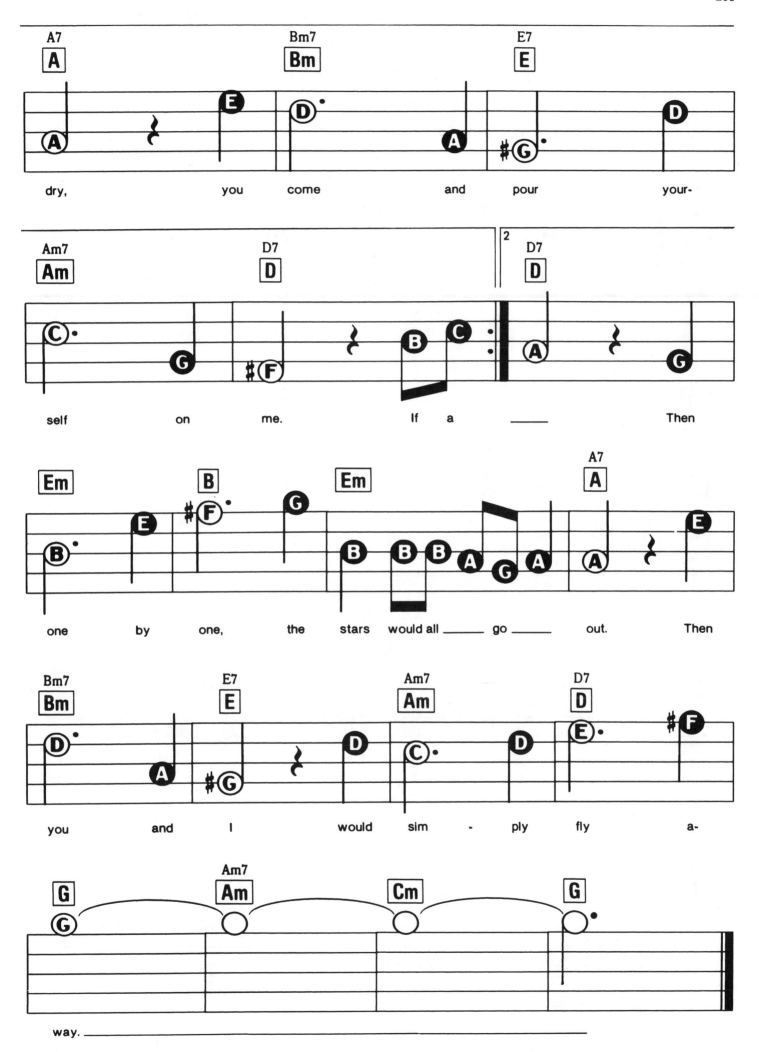

If You Leave Me Now

Words and Music by
Peter Cetera

Registration 1
Rhythm: 8 Beat, Pops or Bossa Nova

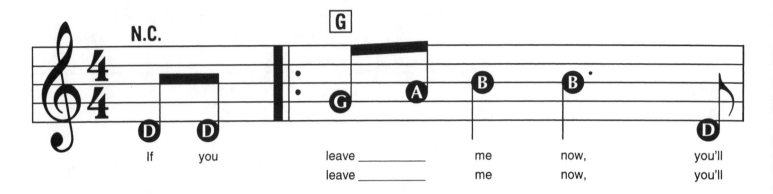

If you leave _____ me now, you'll
leave _____ me now, you'll

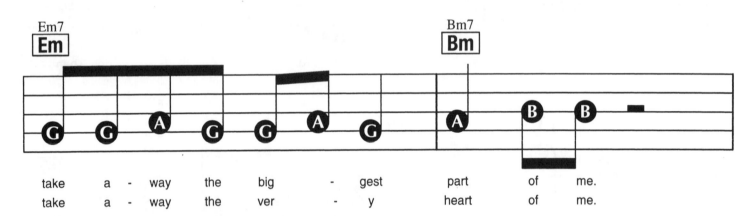

take a - way the big - gest part of me.
take a - way the ver - y heart of me.

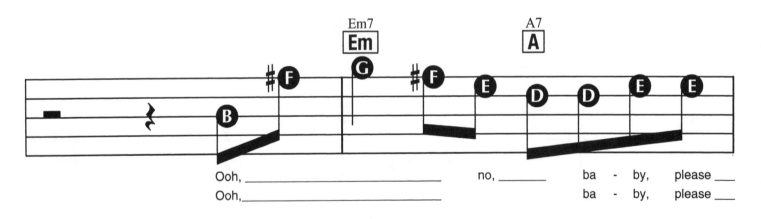

Ooh, _____ no, _____ ba - by, please ____
Ooh, _____ ba - by, please ____

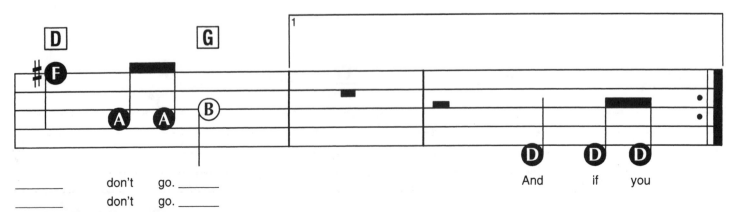

_____ don't go. _____
_____ don't go. _____

And if you

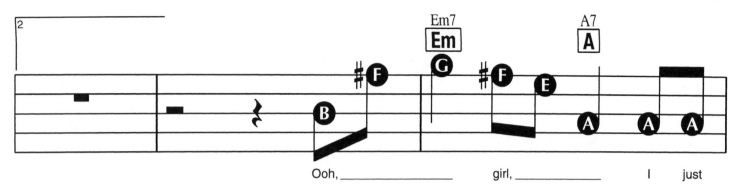

Ooh, _____ girl, _____ I just

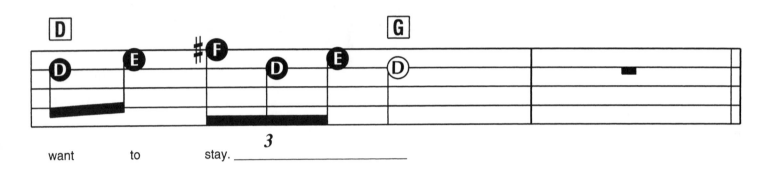

want to stay. _____

3

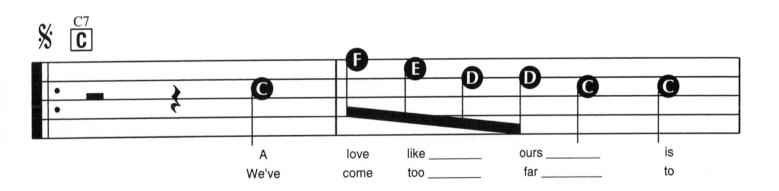

A love like _____ ours _____ is
We've come too _____ far _____ to

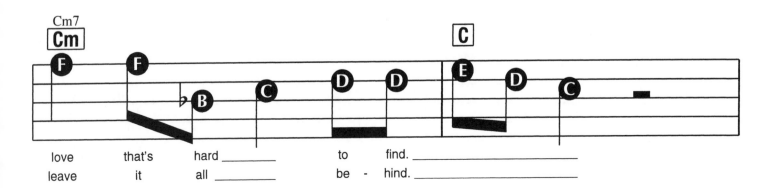

love that's hard _____ to find. _____
leave it all _____ be - hind. _____

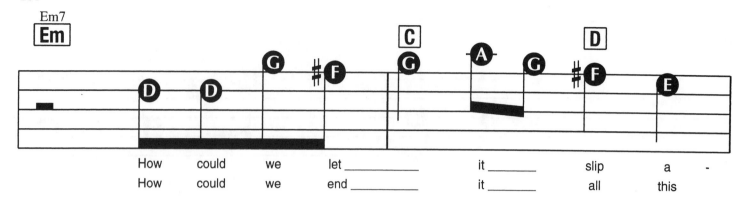

How could we let _____ it _____ slip a -
How could we end _____ it _____ all this

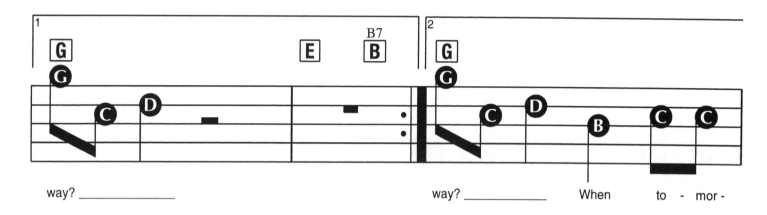

way? _____   way? _____ When to - mor -

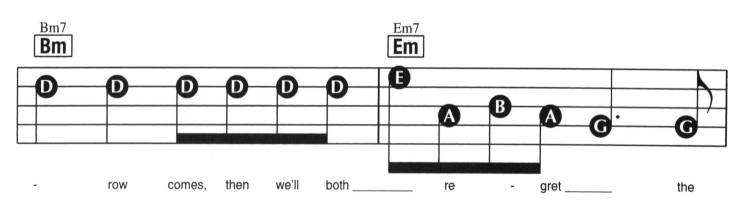

- row comes, then we'll both _____ re - gret _____ the

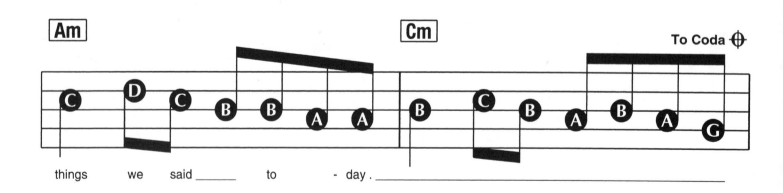

things we said _____ to - day. _____

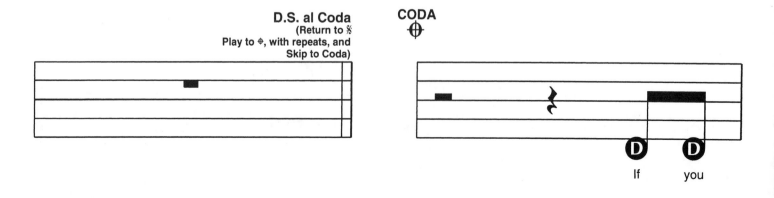

If you

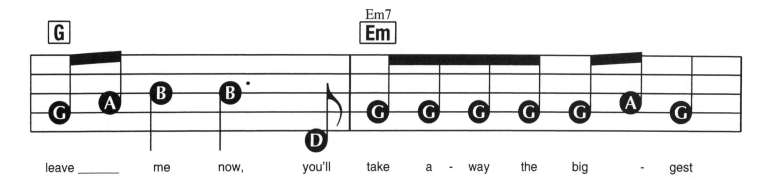

leave _____ me now, you'll take a - way the big - gest

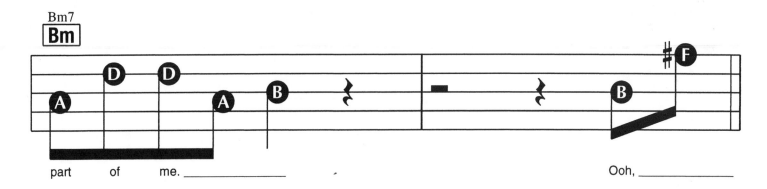

part of me. _____ Ooh, _____

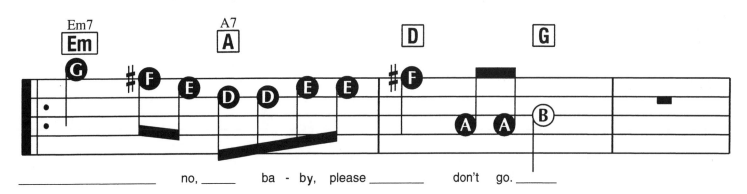

_____ no, _____ ba - by, please _____ don't go. _____

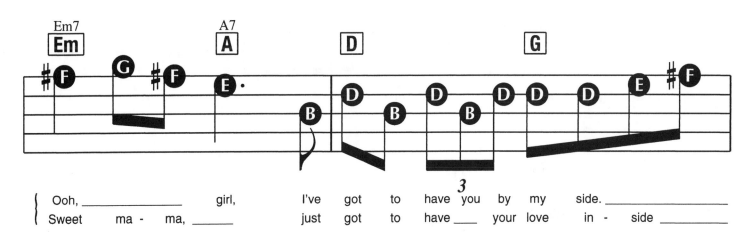

3

Repeat and Fade

Ooh, _____ girl, I've got to have you by my side. _____
Sweet ma - ma, _____ just got to have ___ your love in - side _____

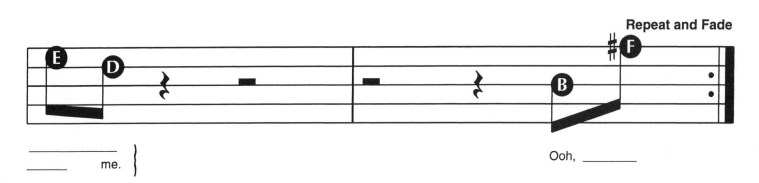

_____ me. Ooh, _____

It's So Easy

Registration 2
Rhythm: Rock

Words and Music by Buddy Holly
and Norman Petty

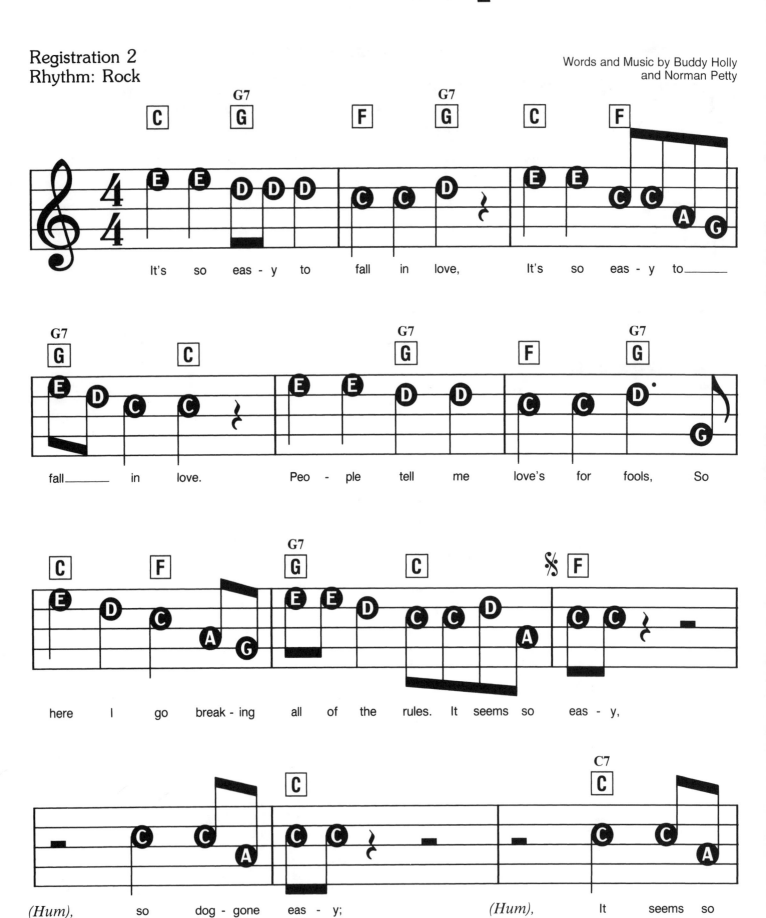

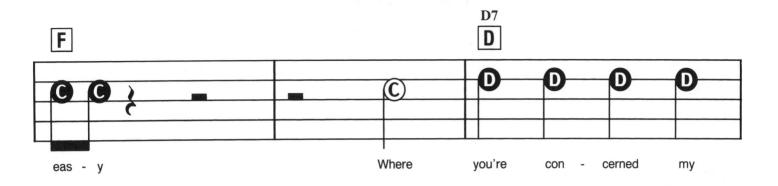

eas - y　　　　　　　　　Where you're con - cerned my

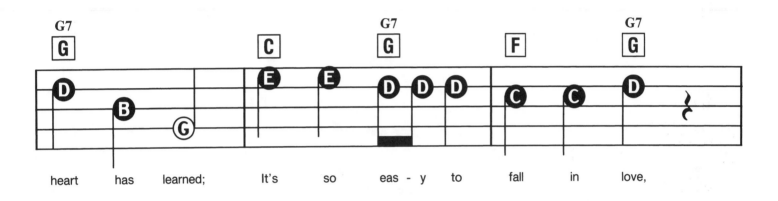

heart has learned;　It's so eas - y to fall in love,

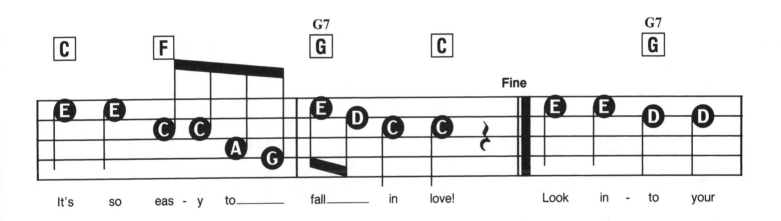

It's so eas - y to＿＿ fall＿＿ in love!　Look in - to your

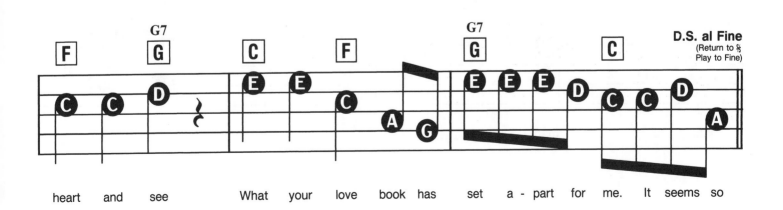

heart and see　What your love book has set a - part for me. It seems so

Jazzman

Registration 7
Rhythm: Rock

Words and Music by Carole King
and David Palmer

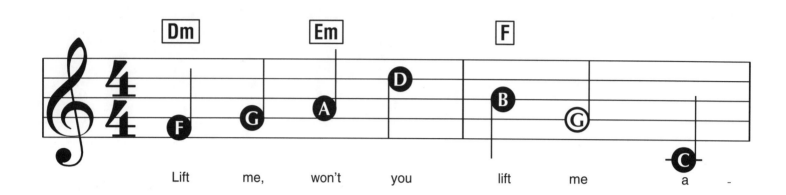

Lift me, won't you lift me a-

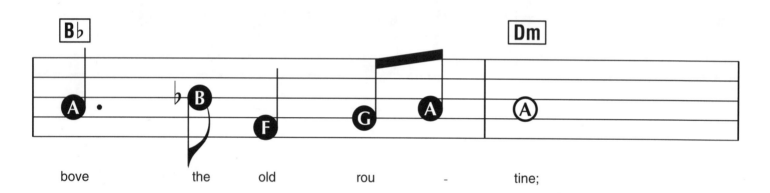

bove the old rou - tine;

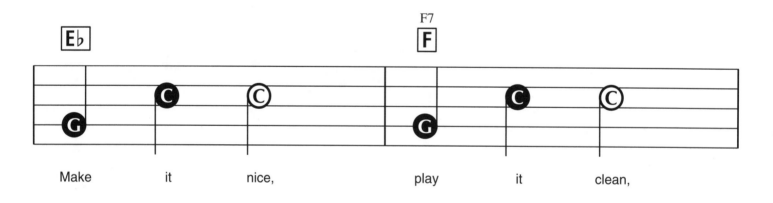

Make it nice, play it clean,

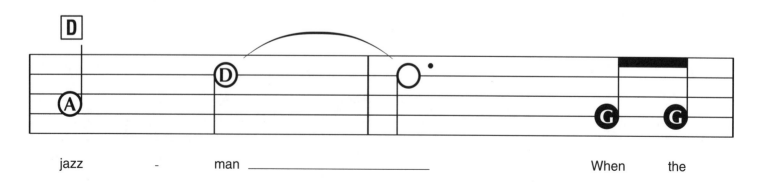

jazz - man _____ When the

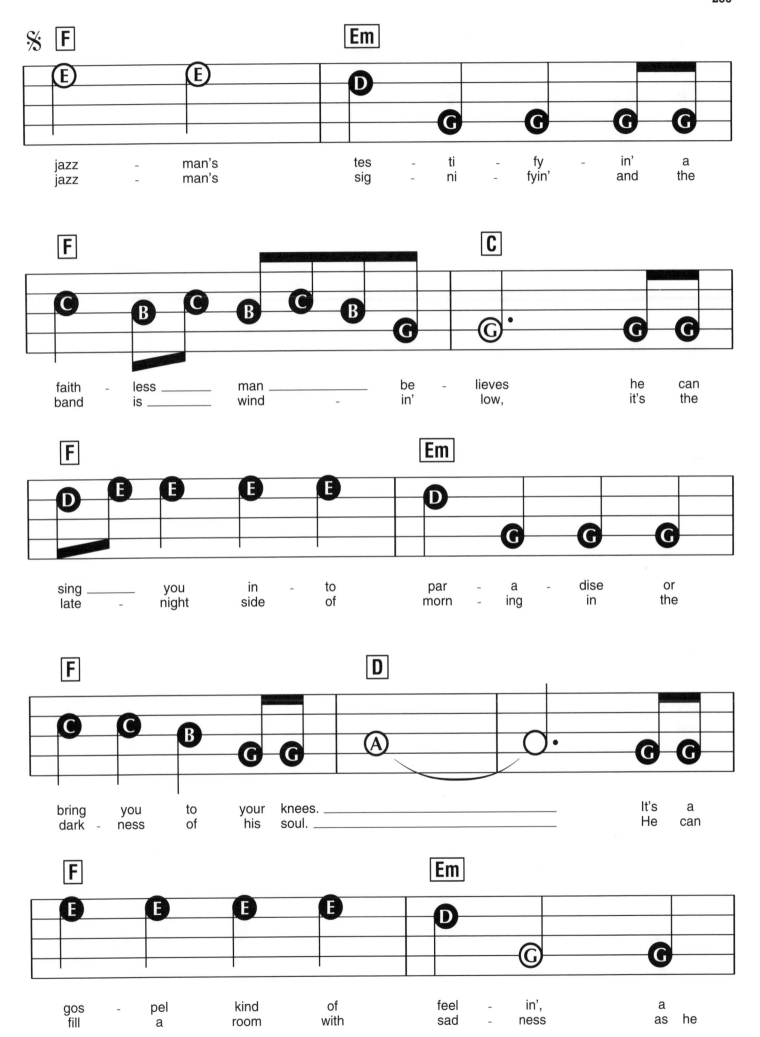

209

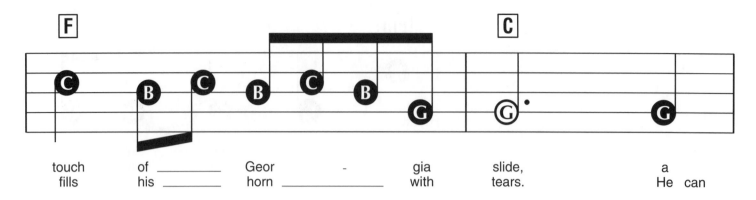

touch of _____ Geor - gia slide, a
fills his _____ horn _____ with tears. He can

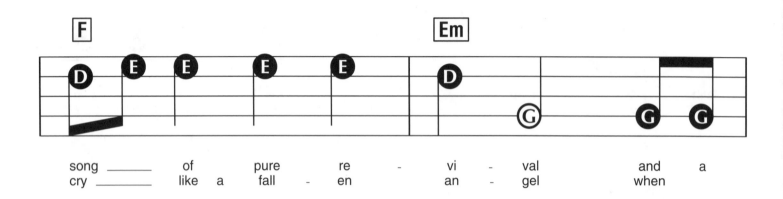

song _____ of pure re - vi - val and a
cry _____ like a fall - en an - gel when

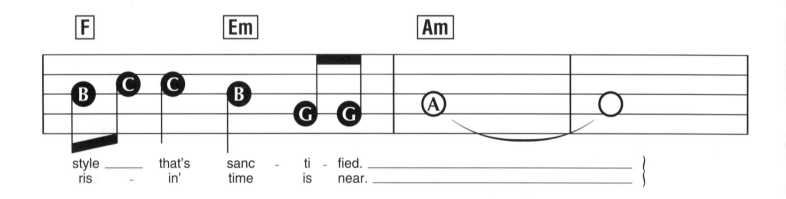

style _____ that's sanc - ti - fied. _____
ris - in' time is near. _____

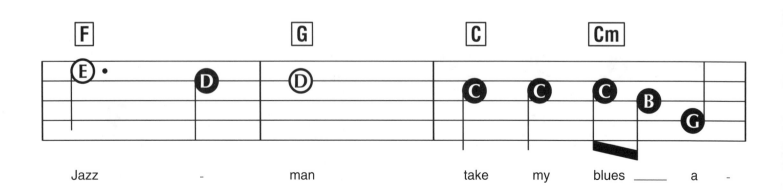

Jazz - man take my blues _____ a -

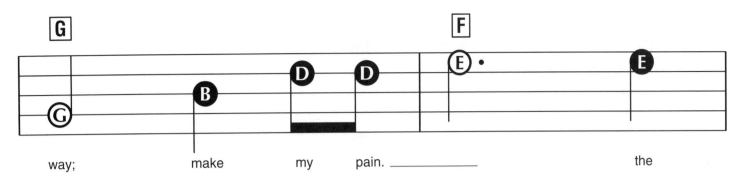

way; make my pain. _____ the

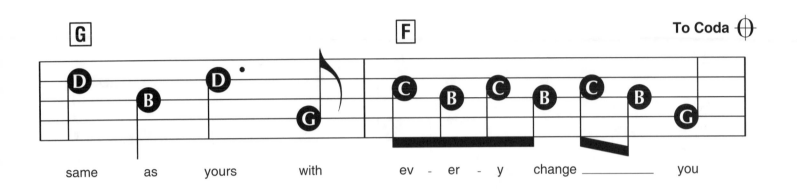

To Coda ⊕

same as yours with ev - er - y change _____ you

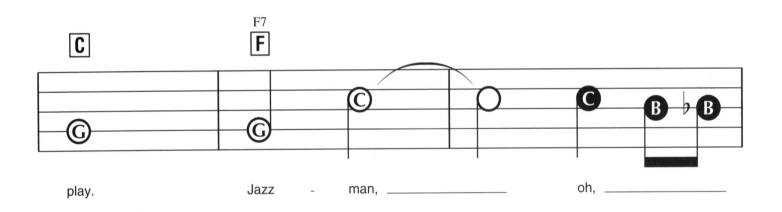

play. Jazz - man, _____ oh, _____

D.S. al Coda
(Return to 𝄋
Play to ⊕ and
Skip to Coda)

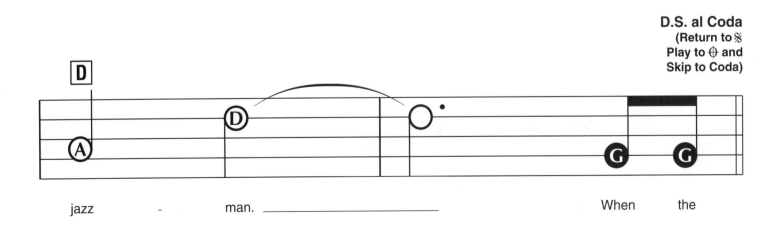

jazz - man. _____ When the

CODA

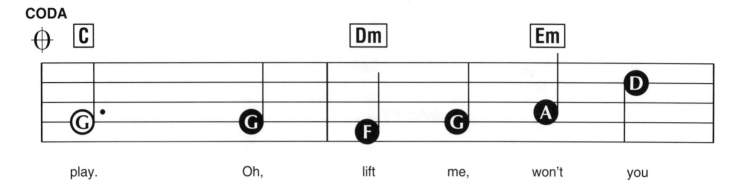

play.   Oh,   lift   me,   won't   you

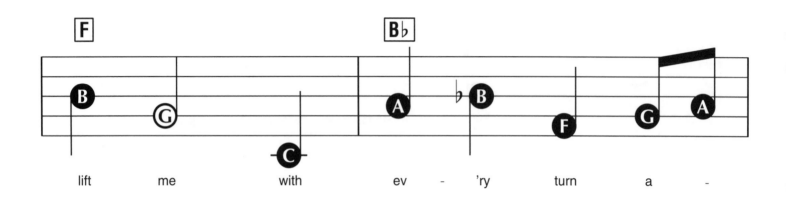

lift   me   with   ev - 'ry   turn   a -

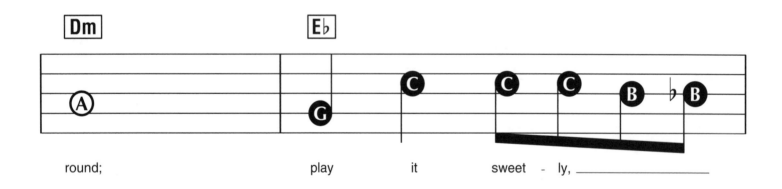

round;   play   it   sweet - ly, _____

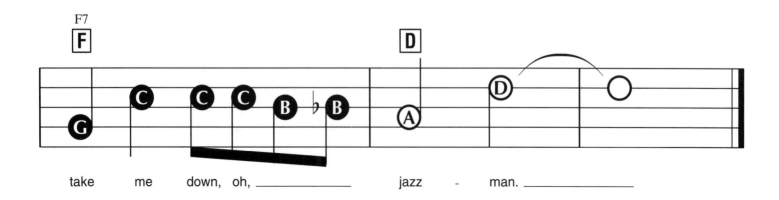

take   me   down,   oh, _____   jazz - man. _____

The Joker

Registration 7
Rhythm: Swing, Slow Rock

Words and Music by Steve Miller,
Eddie Curtis and Ahmet Ertegun

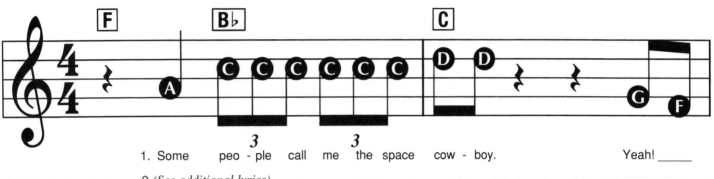

1. Some peo - ple call me the space cow - boy.   Yeah! _____

2. (See additional lyrics)

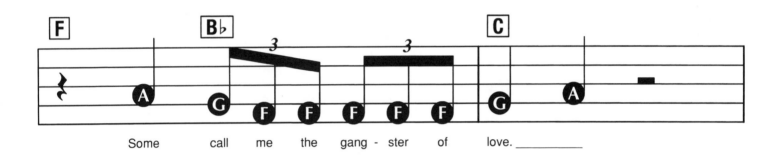

Some call me the gang - ster of love. _____

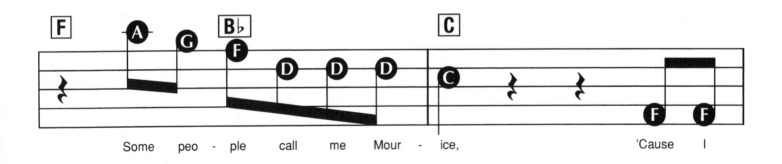

Some peo - ple call me Mour - ice,   'Cause I

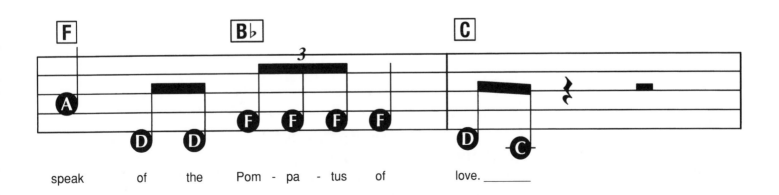

speak of the Pom - pa - tus of love. _____

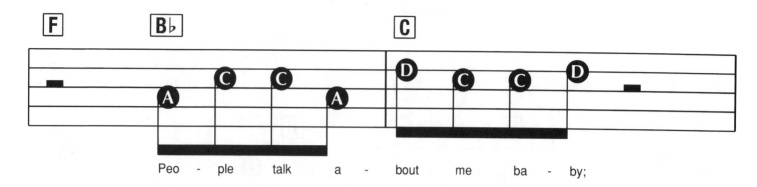

Peo - ple talk a - bout me ba - by;

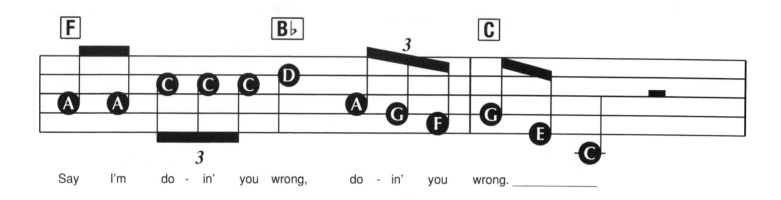

Say I'm do - in' you wrong, do - in' you wrong.

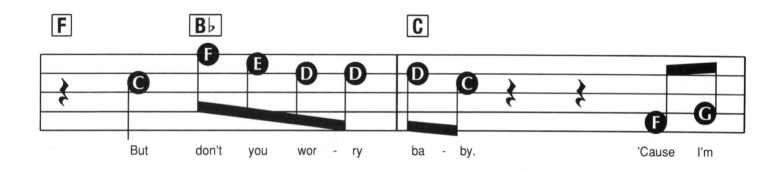

But don't you wor - ry ba - by. 'Cause I'm

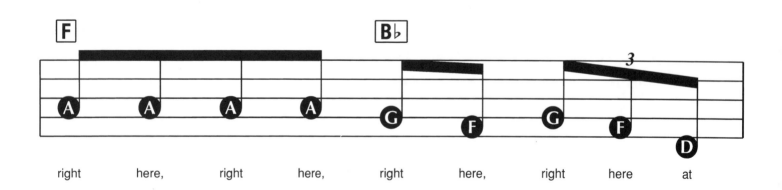

right here, right here, right here, right here at

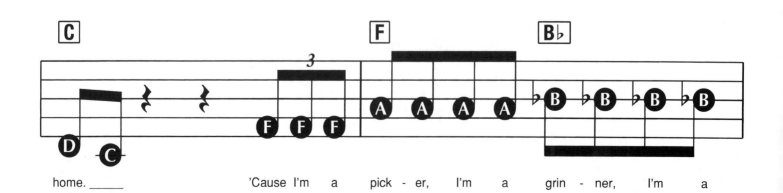

home. 'Cause I'm a pick - er, I'm a grin - ner, I'm a

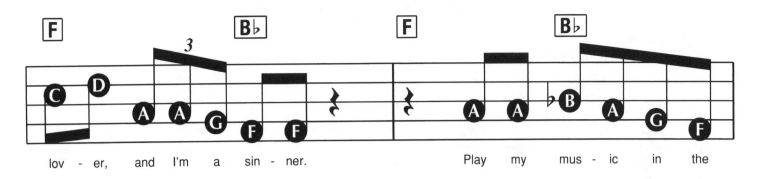

lov - er, and I'm a sin - ner. Play my mus - ic in the

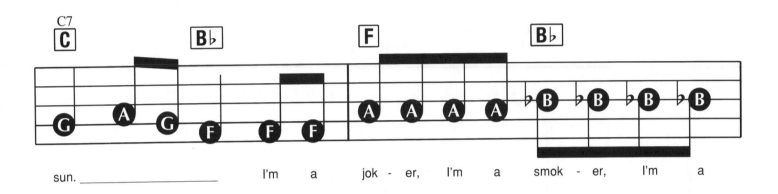

sun. _____ I'm a jok - er, I'm a smok - er, I'm a

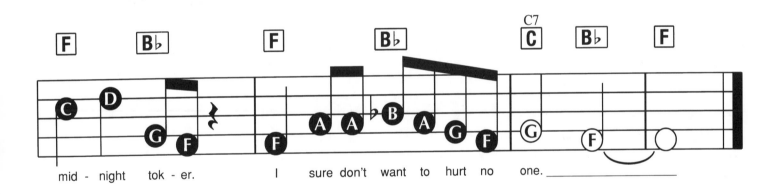

mid - night tok - er. I sure don't want to hurt no one. _____

Additional Lyrics

2. You're the cutest thing that I ever did see;
   I really love your peaches, want to shake your tree.
   Lovey dovey, lovey dovey, lovey dovey all the time;
   Come on baby I'll show you a real good time.

Just the Way You Are

Registration 4
Rhythm: Rock or Jazz Rock

Words and Music by
Billy Joel

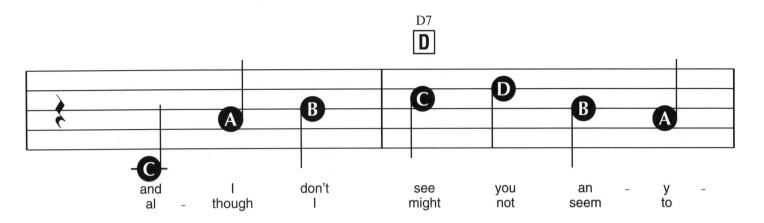

and   I   don't   see   you   an - y -
al - though   I   might   not   seem   to

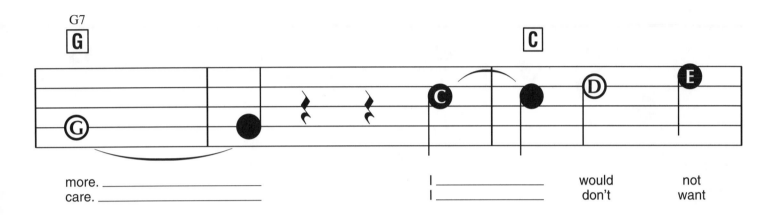

more. _____   I _____ would   not
care. _____   I _____ don't   want

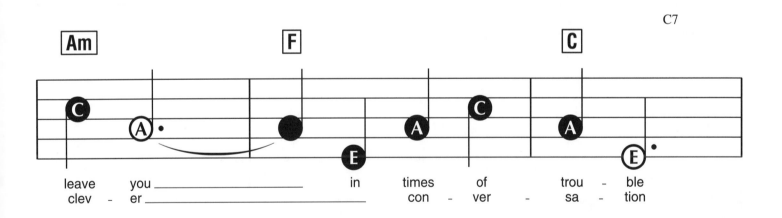

leave   you _____   in   times   of   trou - ble
clev - er _____   con - ver - sa - tion

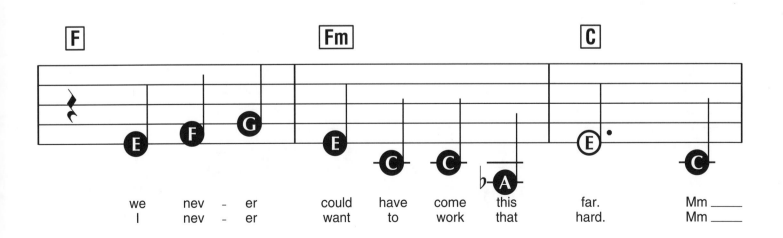

we   nev - er   could   have   come   this   far.   Mm ____
I   nev - er   want   to   work   that   hard.   Mm ____

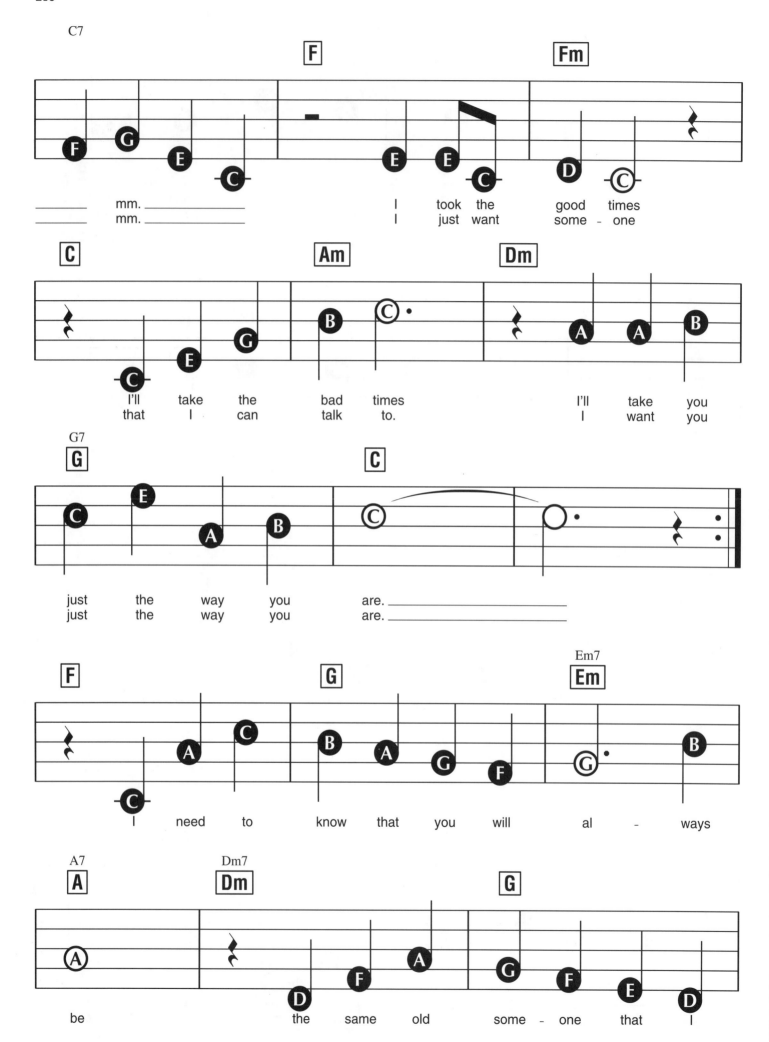

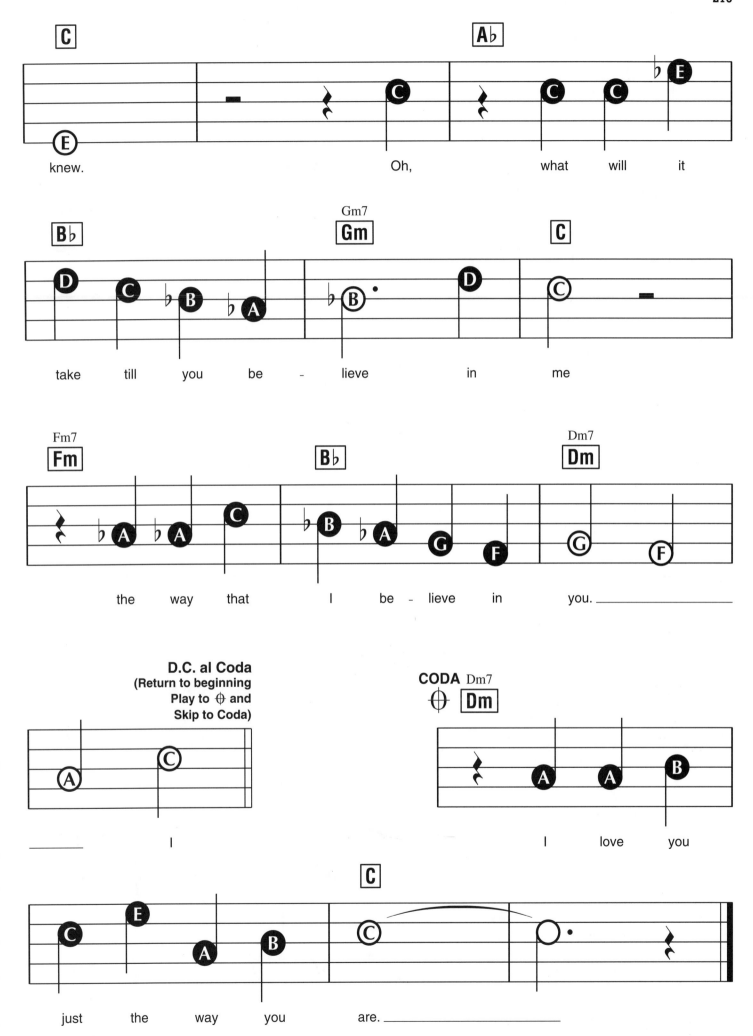

Knock Three Times

Registration 4
Rhythm: Rock

Words and Music by Irwin Levine
and L. Russell Brown

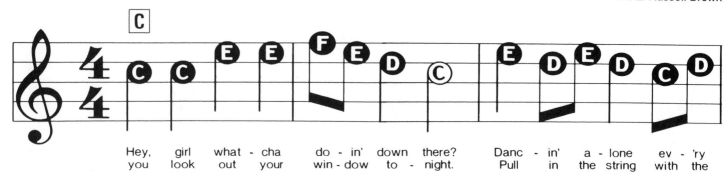

Hey, girl what - cha do - in' down there?
you look out your win - dow to - night.

Danc - in' a - lone ev - 'ry
Pull in the string with the

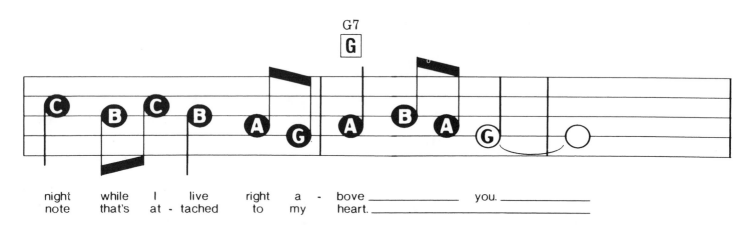

night while I live right a - bove _____ you. _____
note that's at - tached to my heart. _____

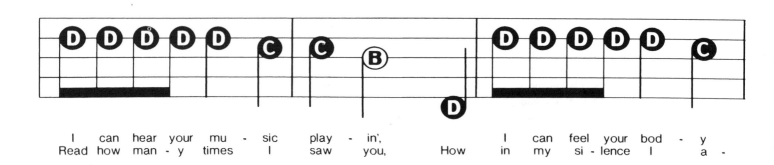

I can hear your mu - sic play - in',
Read how man - y times I saw you,

I can feel your bod - y
How in my si - lence I a -

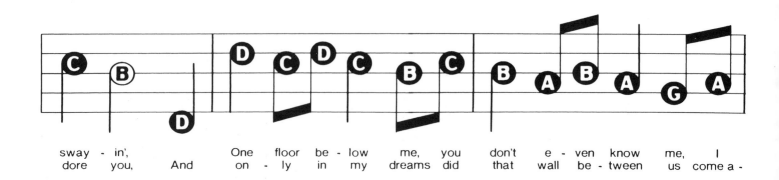

sway - in',
dore you,

And

One floor be - low me, you
on - ly in my dreams did

don't e - ven know me, I
that wall be - tween us come a -

221

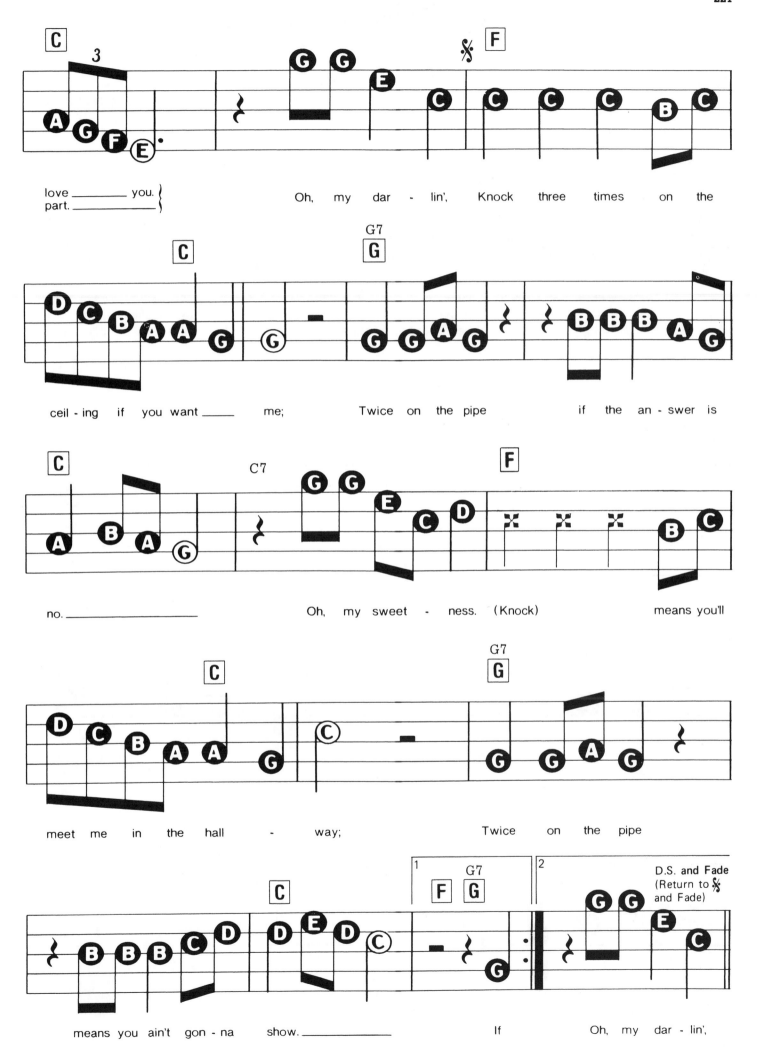

Lay Down Sally

Registration 9
Rhythm: Rock or 8 Beat

Words and Music by Eric Clapton,
Marcy Levy and George Terry

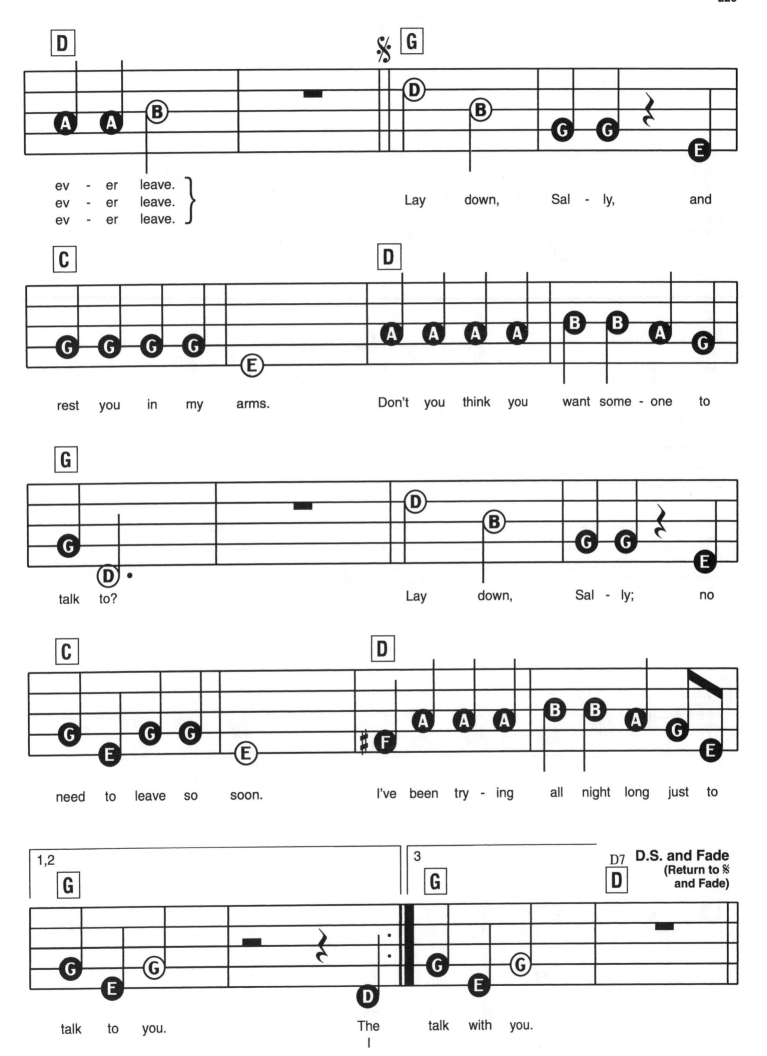

Let It Be

Registration 3
Rhythm: Rock or Pops

Words and Music by John Lennon
and Paul McCartney

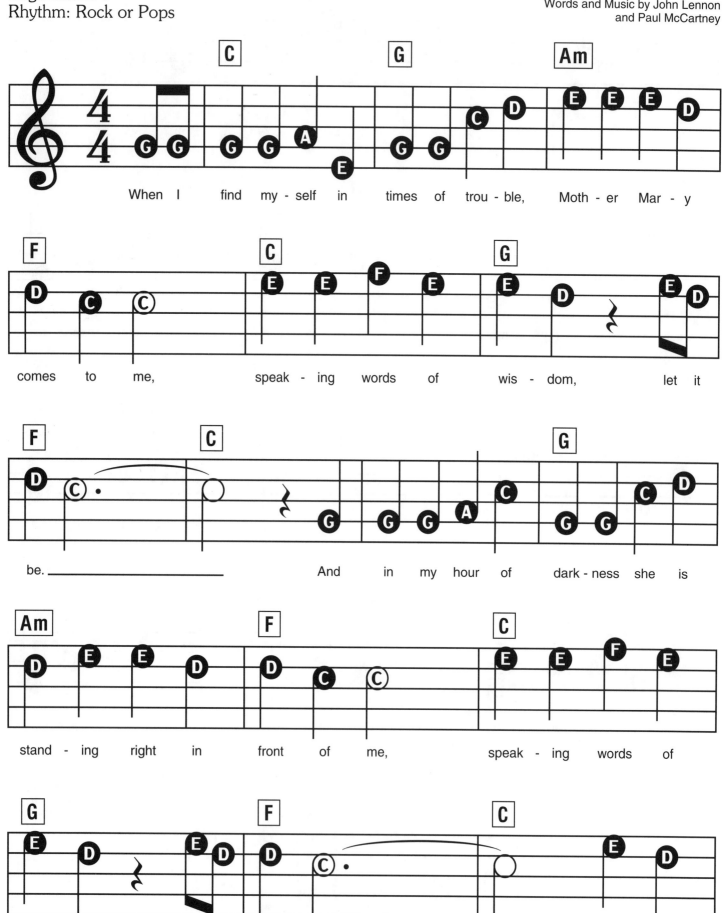

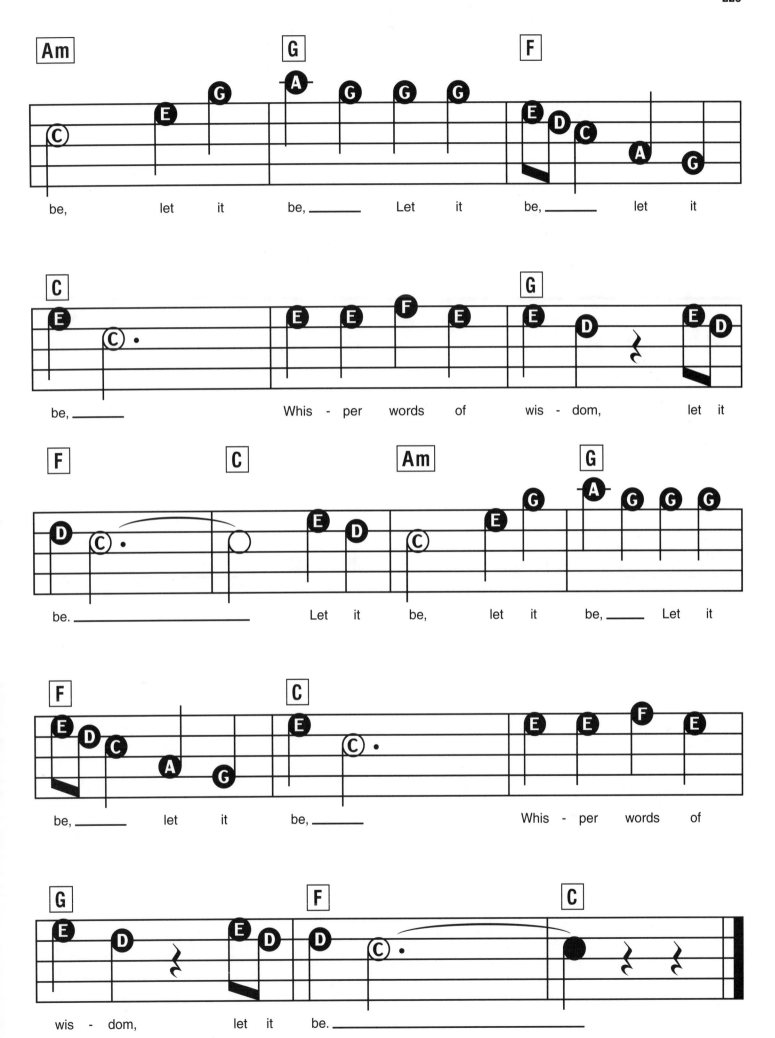

The Logical Song

Registration 4
Rhythm: 8 Beat or Rock

Words and Music by Rick Davies
and Roger Hodgson

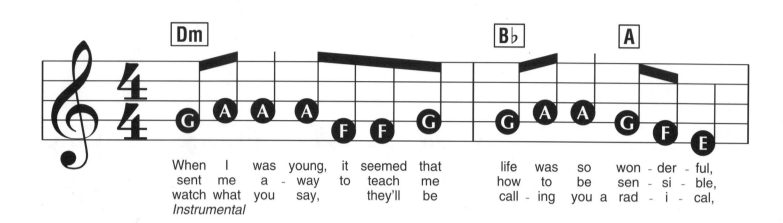

When I was young, it seemed that life was so won-der-ful,
sent me a-way to teach me how to be sen-si-ble,
watch what you say, they'll be call-ing you a rad-i-cal,
Instrumental

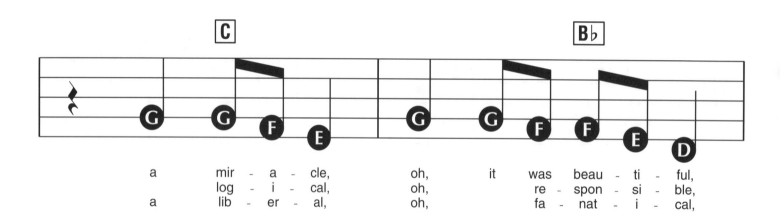

a mir-a-cle, oh, it was beau-ti-ful,
log-i-cal, oh, re-spon-si-ble,
a lib-er-al, oh, fa-nat-i-cal,

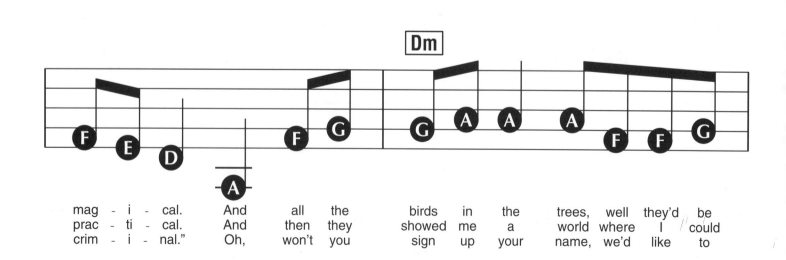

mag-i-cal. And all the birds in the trees, well they'd be
prac-ti-cal. And then they showed me a world where I could
crim-i-nal." Oh, won't you sign up your name, we'd like to

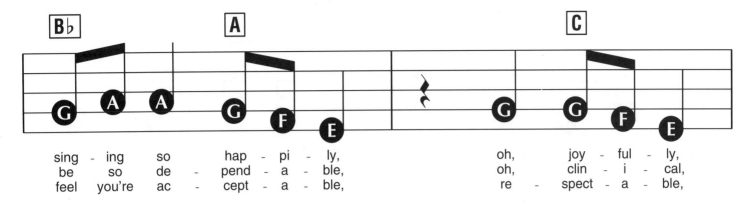

singing so hap - pi - ly,
be so de - pend - a - ble,
feel you're ac - cept - a - ble,

oh, joy - ful - ly,
oh, clin - i - cal,
re - spect - a - ble,

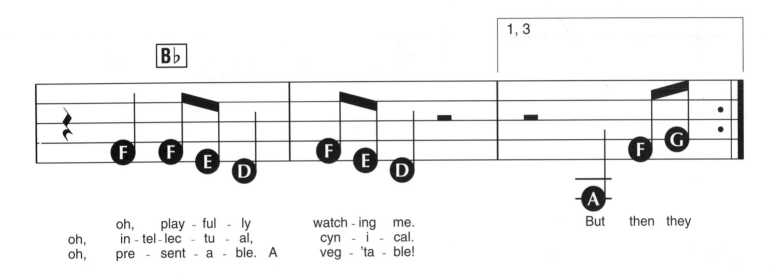

oh, play - ful - ly
oh, in - tel - lec - tu - al,
oh, pre - sent - a - ble. A

watch - ing me.
cyn - i - cal.
veg - 'ta - ble!

But then they

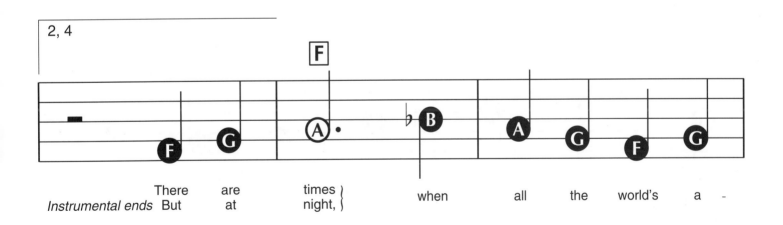

There are times
Instrumental ends But at night,

when all the world's a -

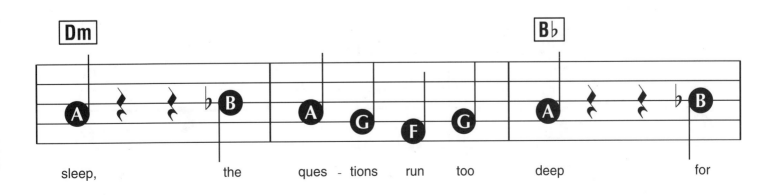

sleep, the ques - tions run too deep for

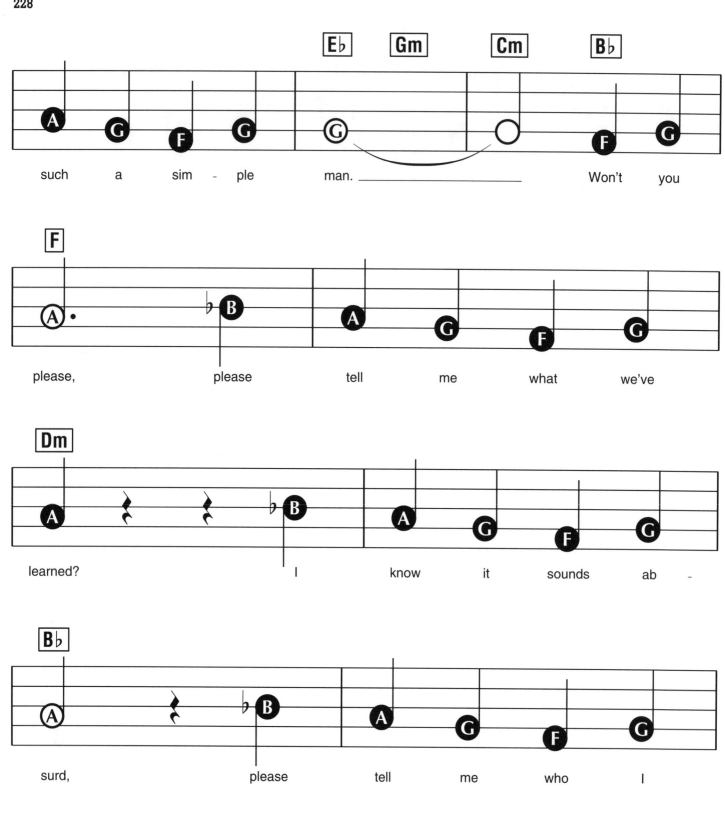

such a sim - ple man. _____ Won't you

please, please tell me what we've

learned? I know it sounds ab -

surd, please tell me who I

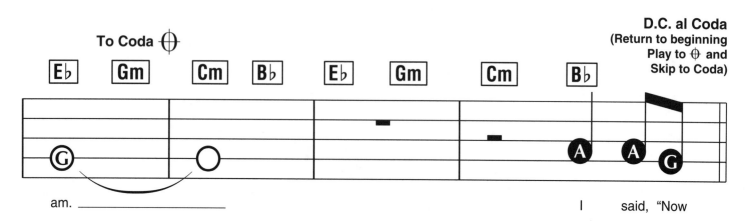

To Coda ⊕

D.C. al Coda
(Return to beginning
Play to ⊕ and
Skip to Coda)

am. _____ I said, "Now

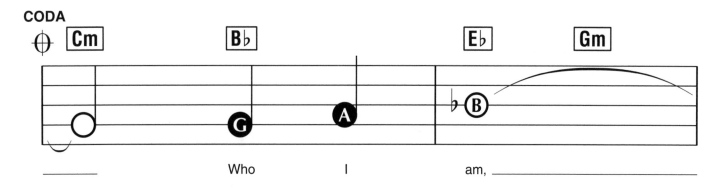

CODA

Who I am,

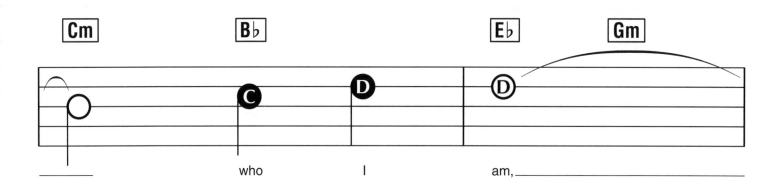

who I am,

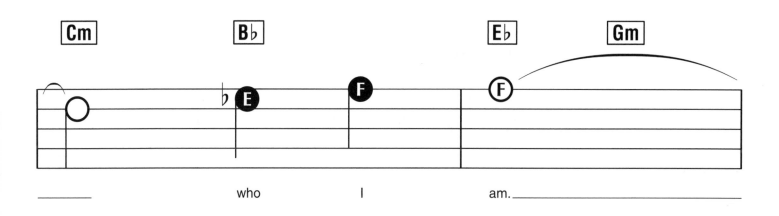

who I am.

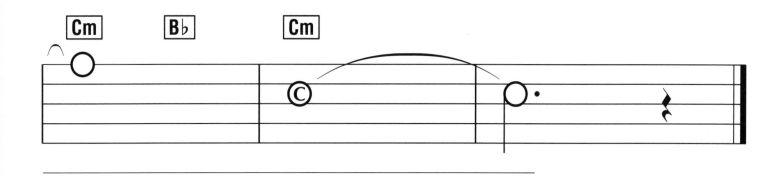

Looks Like We Made It

Registration 4
Rhythm: Rock

Words and Music by Richard Kerr
and Will Jennings

There you are, look-in' just the same as you
Love's so strange, play-ing hide and seek with _____

did last time I touched you. _____
hearts and al - ways hurt - ing. _____

And here I
And we're the

am, close to get - tin' tan - gled up in - side the
fools, stand - ing close e - nough to touch those burn - ing

thought of you. _____ Do you love him as
mem - o - ries. _____ And if I _____ hold you for the

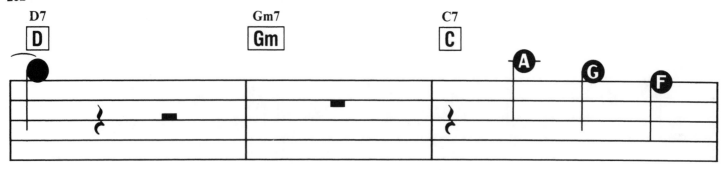

Looks like we

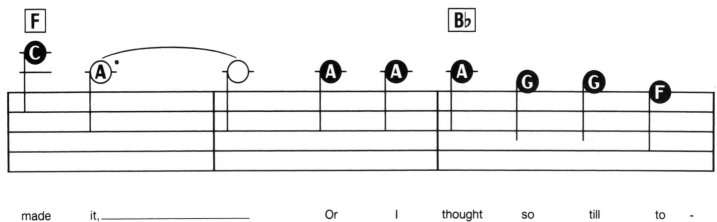

made it,_____ Or I thought so till to -

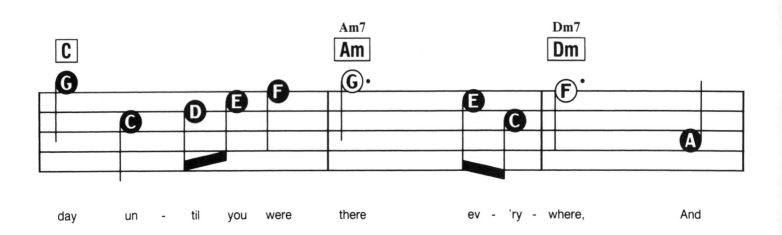

day un - til you were there ev - 'ry - where, And

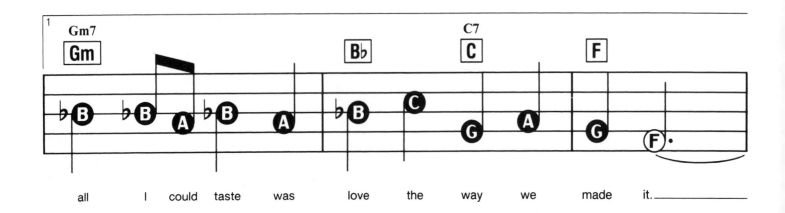

all I could taste was love the way we made it._____

233

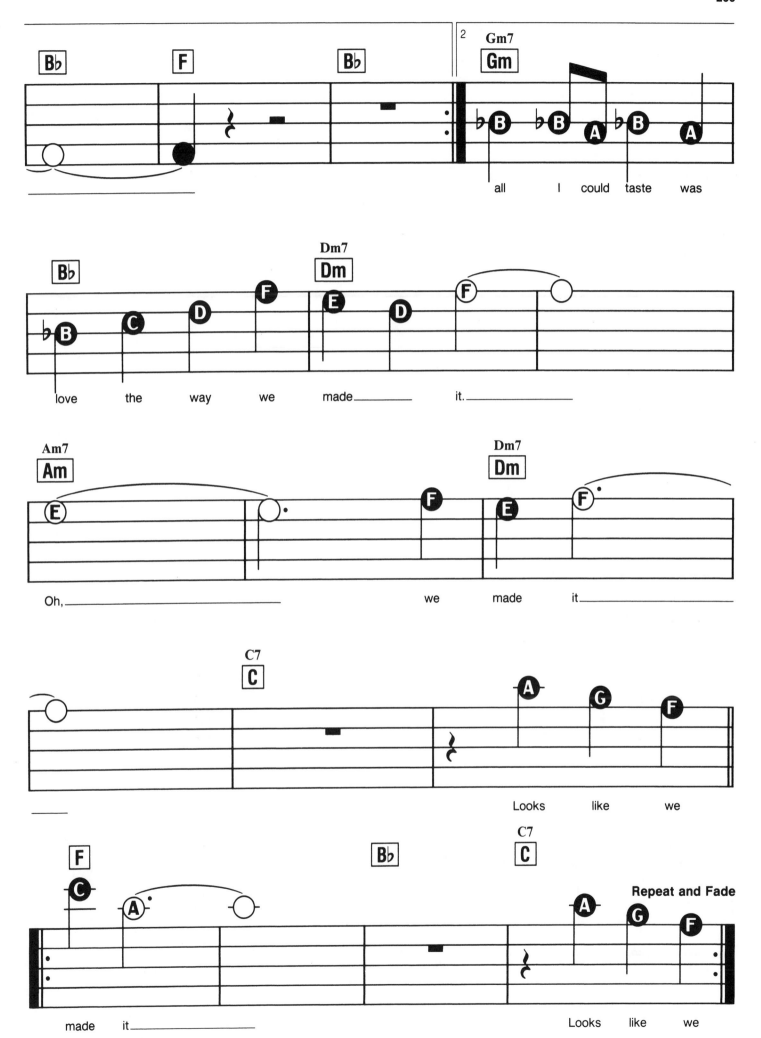

Make It with You

Registration 1
Rhythm: Ballad

Words and Music by
David Gates

235

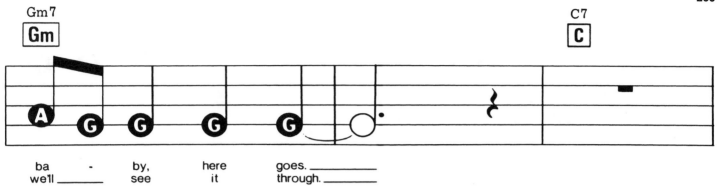

ba - by, here goes. _____
we'll _____ see it through. _____

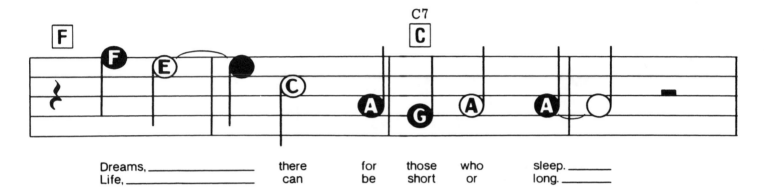

Dreams, _____ there for those who sleep. _____
Life, _____ can be short or long. _____

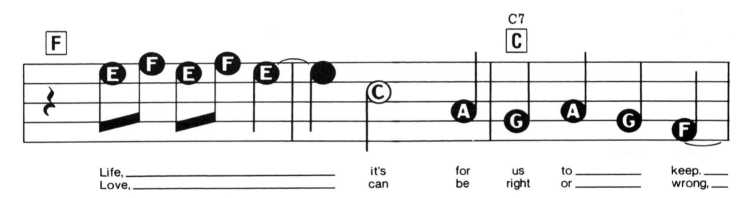

Life, _____ it's for us to _____ keep. ___
Love, _____ can be right or _____ wrong, ___

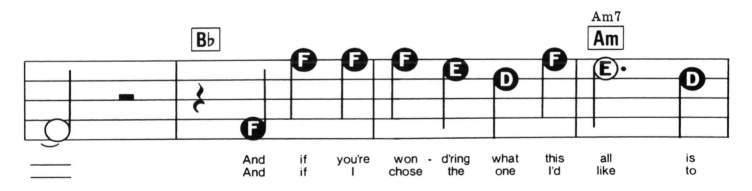

_____ And if you're won - d'ring what this all is
_____ And if I chose the one I'd like to

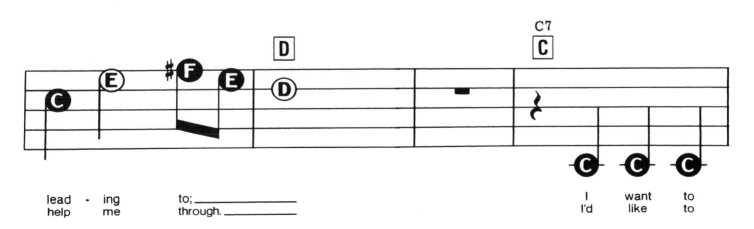

lead - ing to; _____ I want to
help me through. _____ I'd like to

236

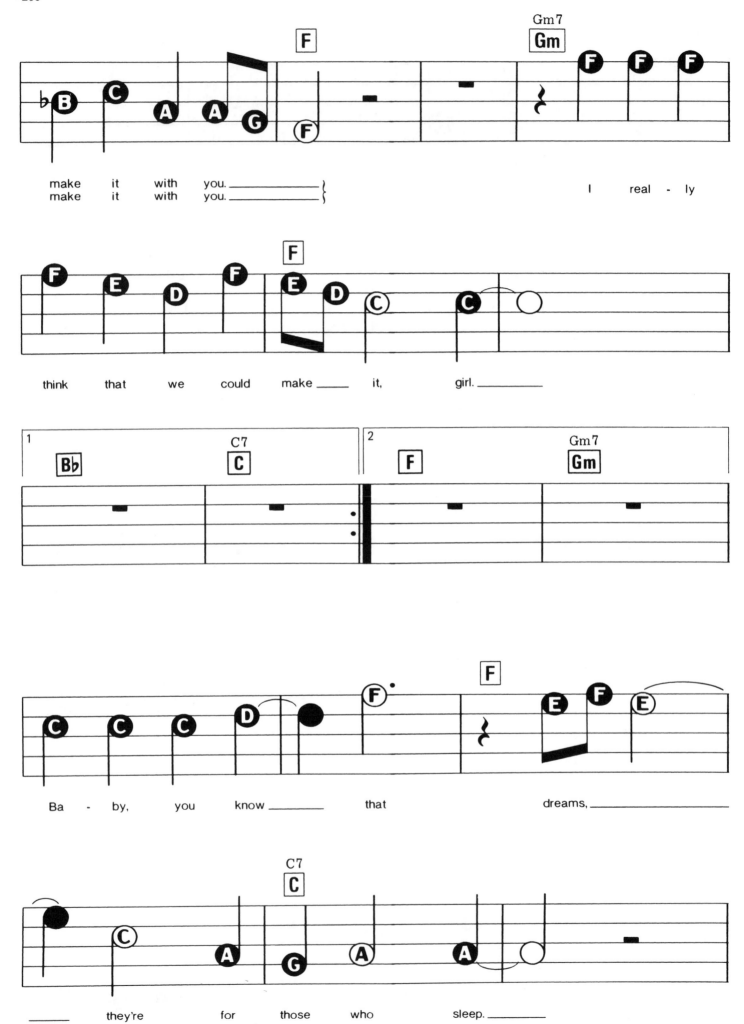

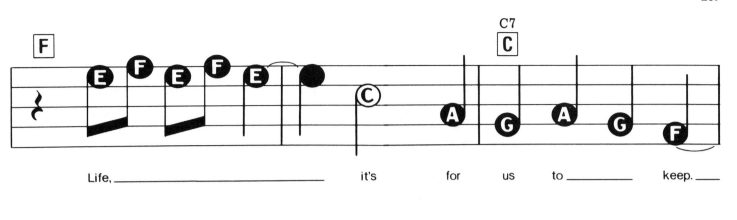

Life, _____ it's for us to _____ keep. ___

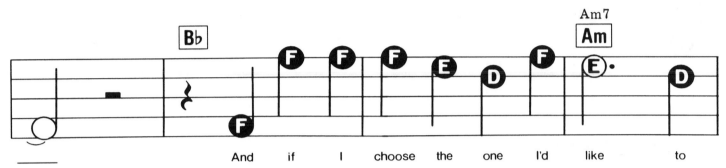

___ And if I choose the one I'd like to

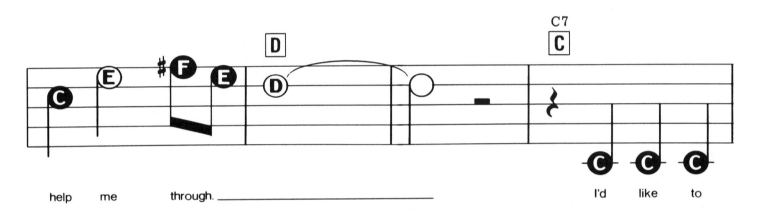

help me through. _____ I'd like to

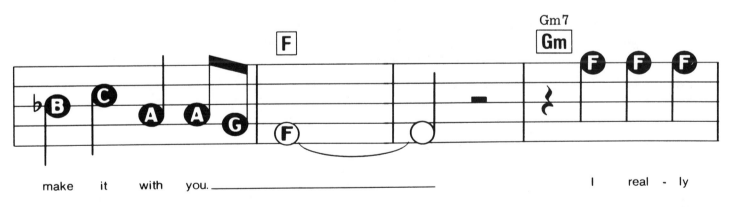

make it with you. _____ I real - ly

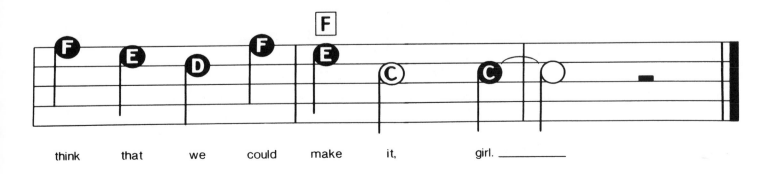

think that we could make it, girl. _____

Mandy

Registration 1
Rhythm: Rock

Words and Music by Scott English
and Richard Kerr

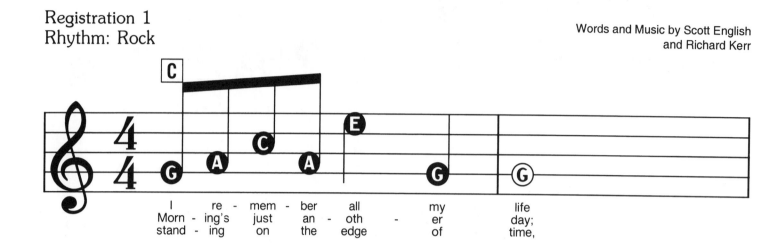

I re - mem - ber all my life
Morn - ing's just an - oth - er day;
stand - ing on the edge of time,

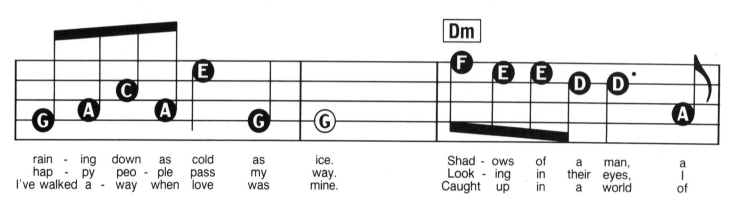

rain - ing down as cold as ice.
hap - py peo - ple pass as my way.
I've walked a - way when love was mine.

Shad - ows of a man, a
Look - ing in their eyes, a I
Caught up in a world of

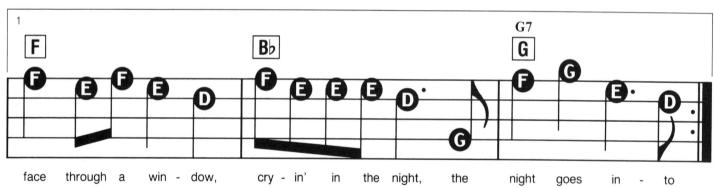

face through a win - dow, cry - in' in the night, the night goes in - to

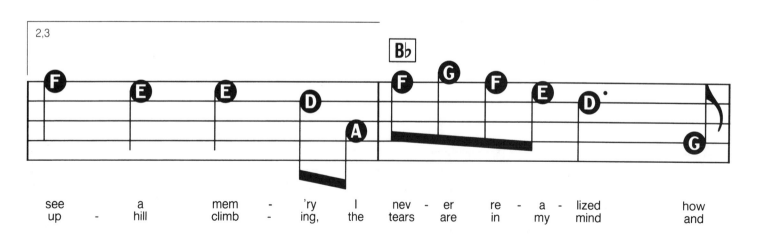

see a mem - 'ry I nev - er re - a - lized how
up - hill climb - ing, the tears are in my mind and

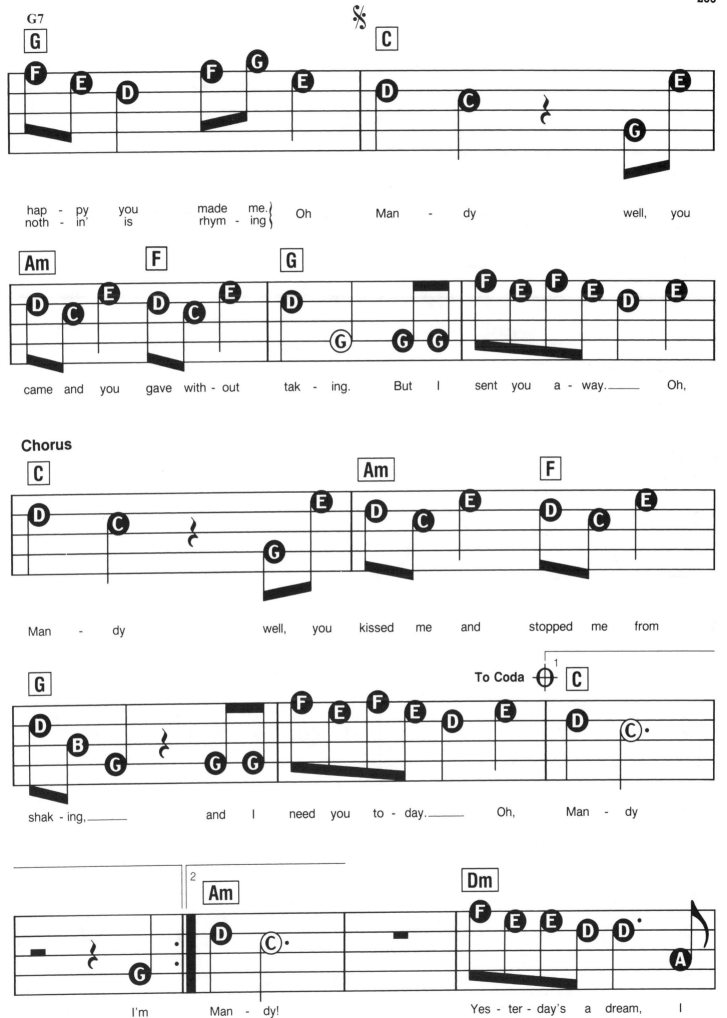

240

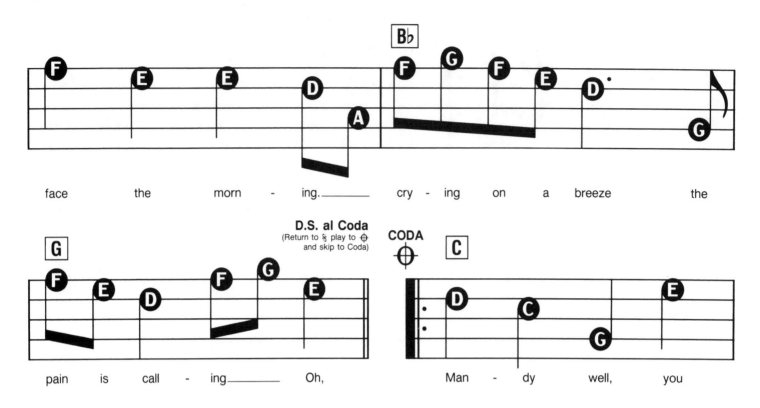

face the morn - ing._____ cry - ing on a breeze the

D.S. al Coda
(Return to % play to ⊕ and skip to Coda)

CODA

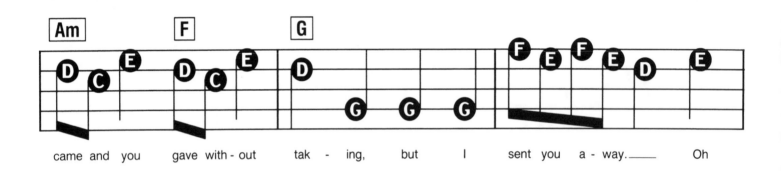

pain is call - ing_____ Oh,   Man - dy well, you

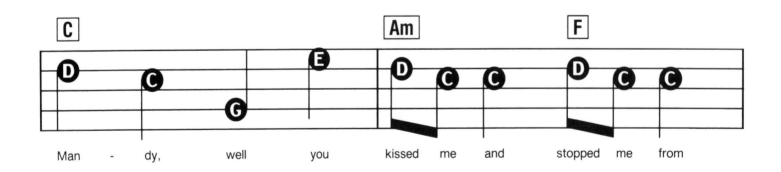

came and you gave with - out tak - ing, but I sent you a - way._____ Oh

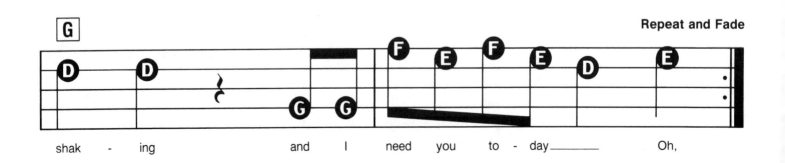

Man - dy, well you kissed me and stopped me from

shak - ing   and I need you to - day_____ Oh,

Repeat and Fade

Me and You and a Dog Named Boo

Registration 1
Rhythm: Rock, March or Polka

Words and Music by
Lobo

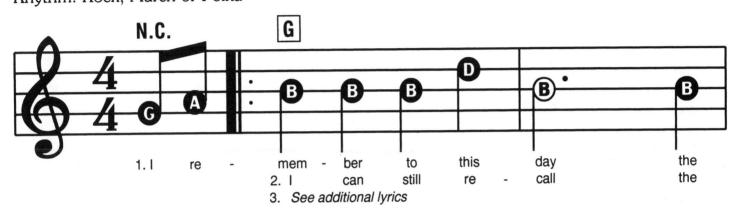

1. I re - mem - ber to this day the
2. I can still re - call the
3. *See additional lyrics*

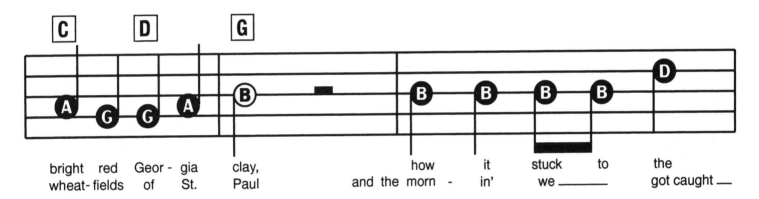

bright red Geor - gia clay, how it stuck to the
wheat- fields of St. Paul and the morn - in' we _____ got caught _____

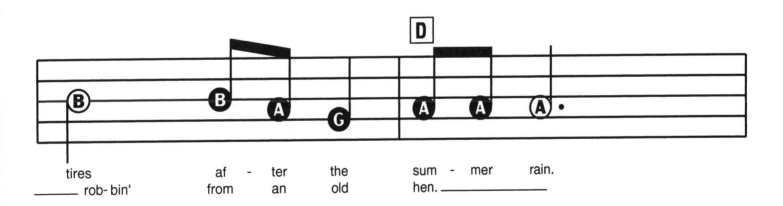

tires af - ter the sum - mer rain.
_____ rob- bin' from an old hen. _____

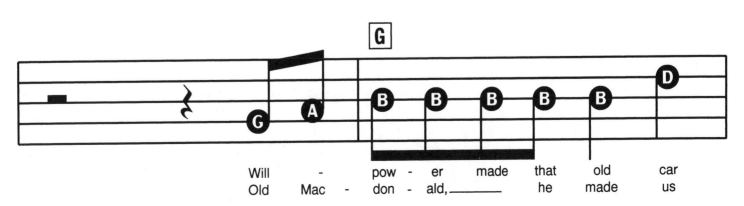

Will - pow - er made that old car
Old Mac - don - ald, _____ he made us

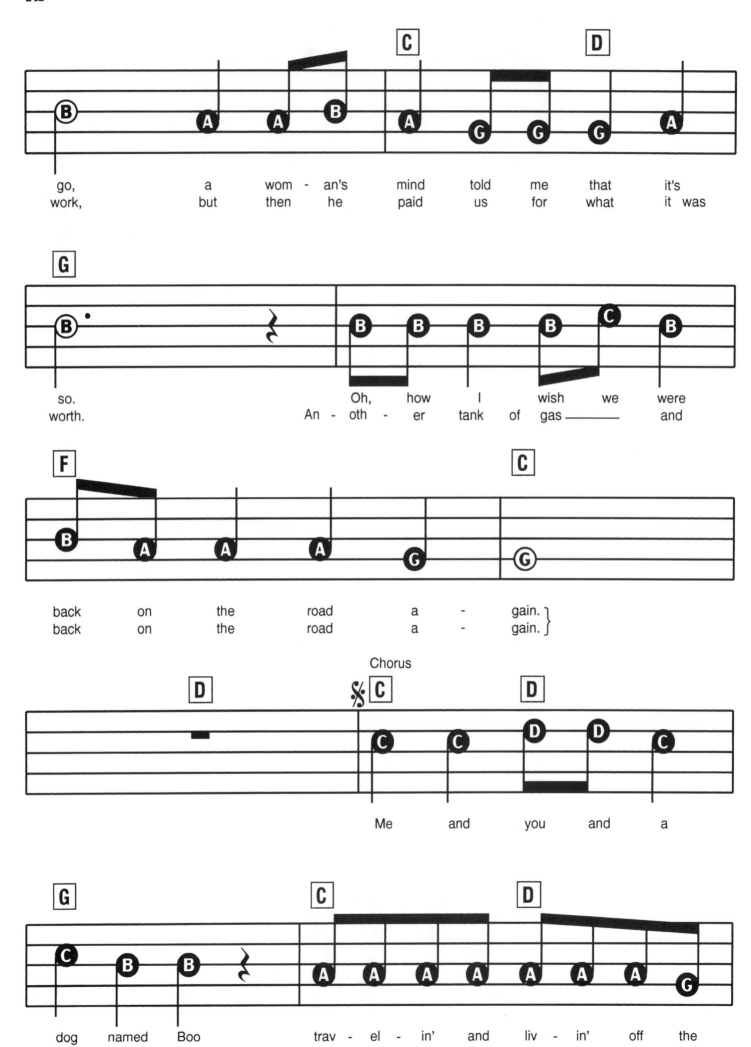

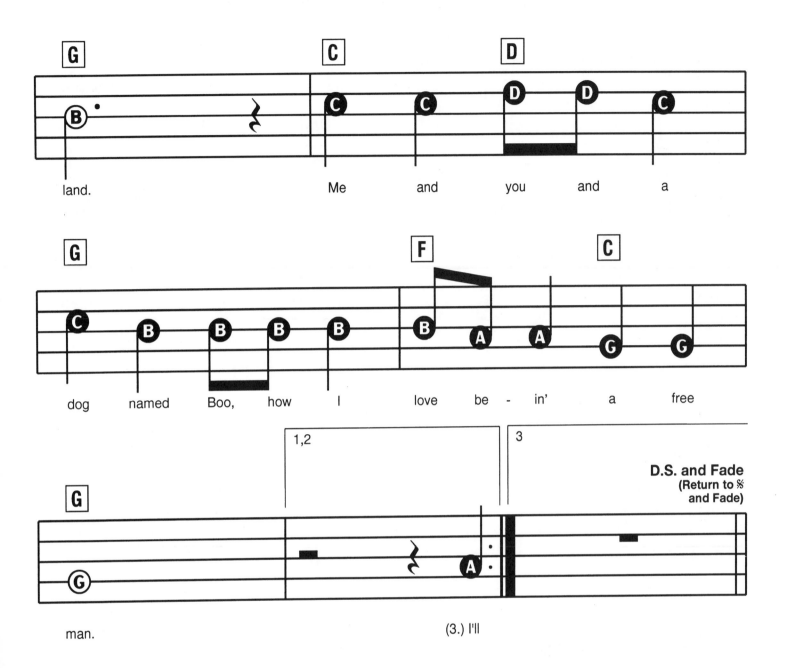

Additional Lyrics

3. I'll never forget that day,
   We motored stately into L.A.
   The lights of the city put setttlin' down in my brain.
   Though it's only been a month or so,
   That old car's buggin' us to go.
   You gotta get away and get back on the road again.
   To Chorus:

Morning Has Broken

Registration 10
Rhythm: Waltz

Musical Arrangement by Cat Stevens
Words by Eleanor Farjeon

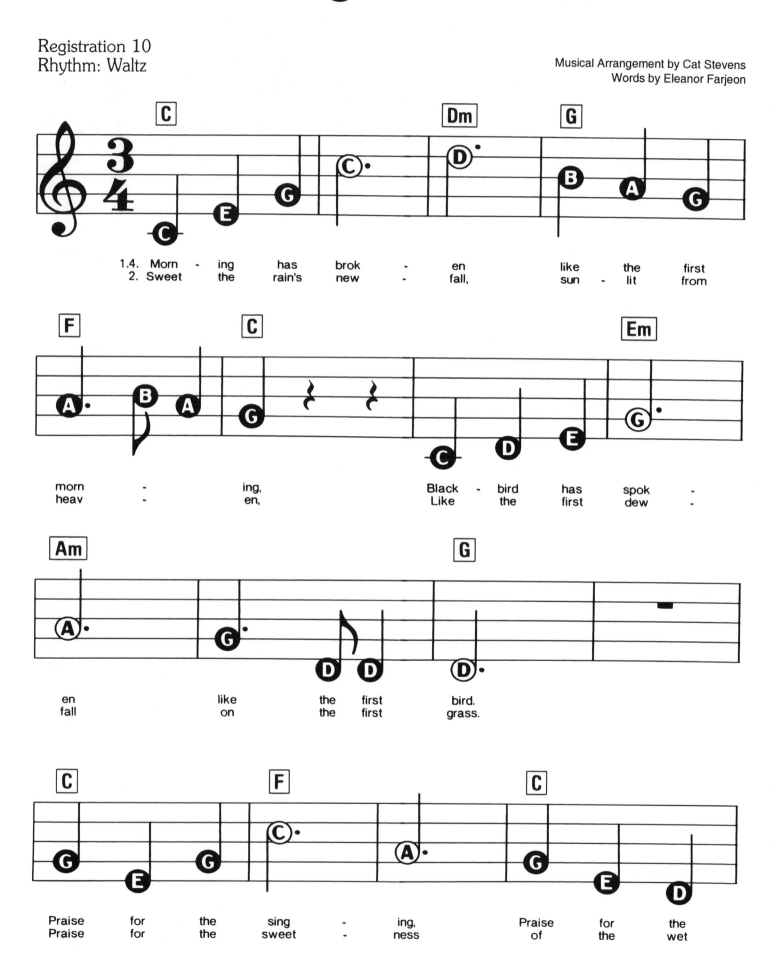

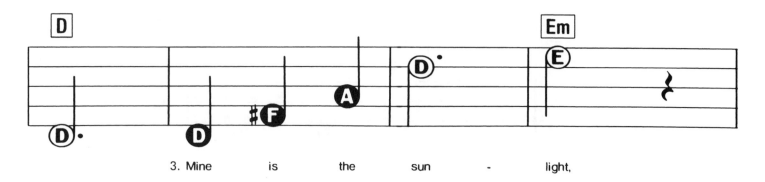

3. Mine is the sun - light,

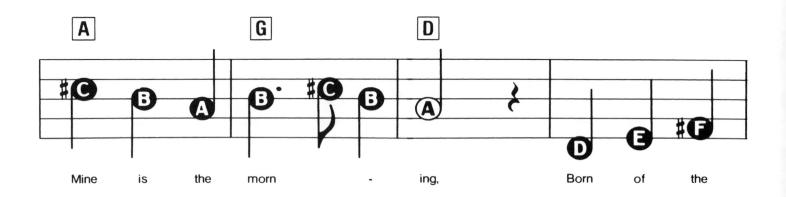

Mine is the morn - ing, Born of the

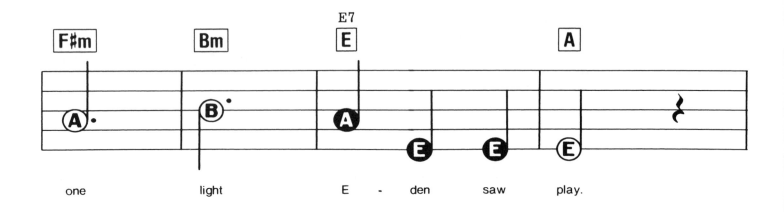

one light E - den saw play.

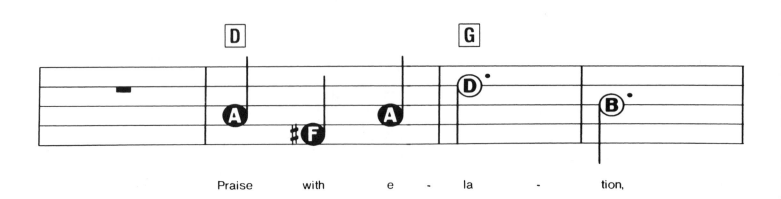

Praise with e - la - tion,

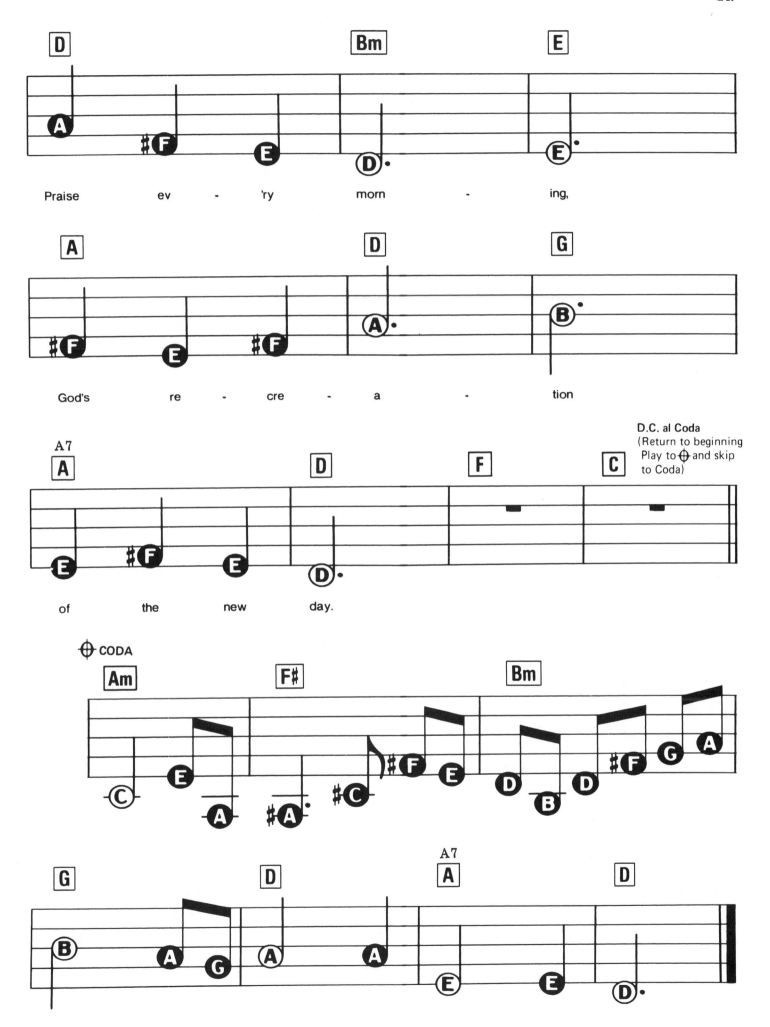

My Love

Registration 10
Rhythm: Ballad

Words and Music by
Paul and Linda McCartney

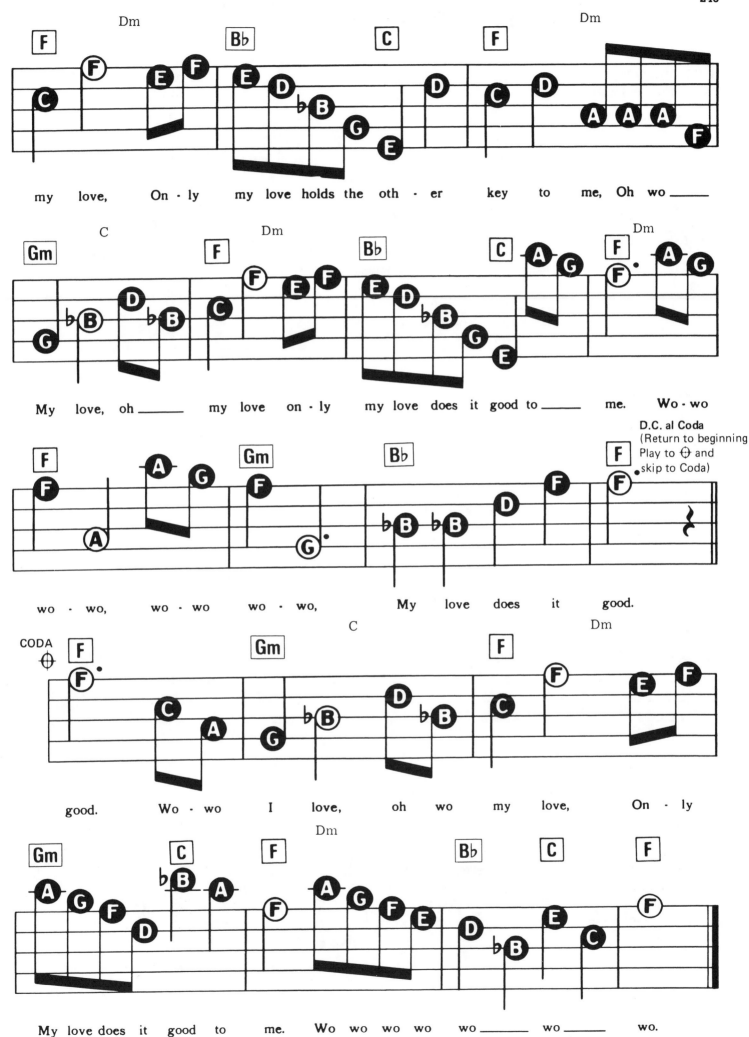

Nothing from Nothing

Registration 1
Rhythm: 8 Beat or Rock

Words and Music by Billy Preston
and Bruce Fisher

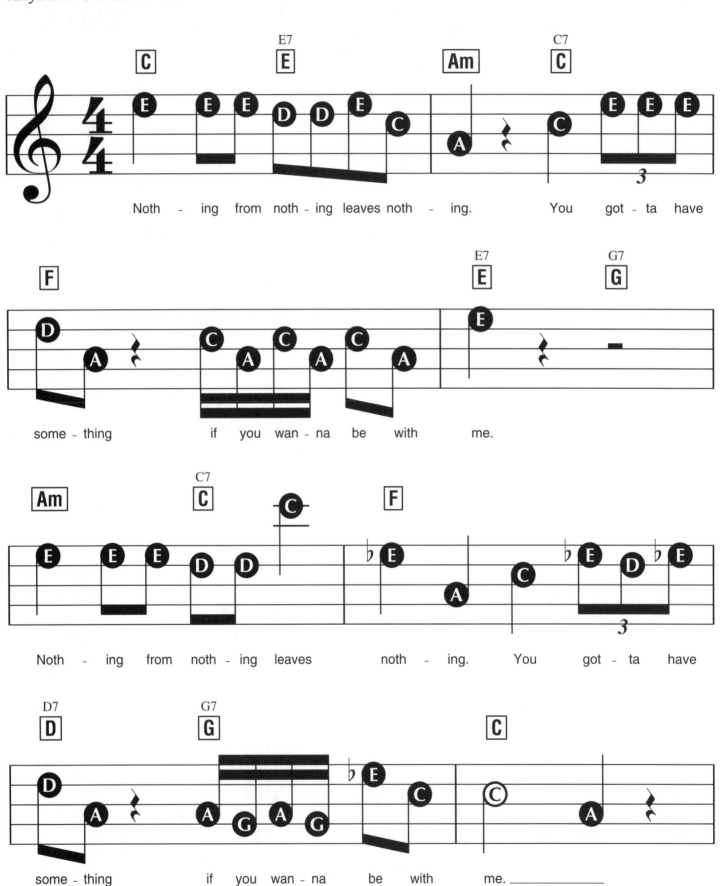

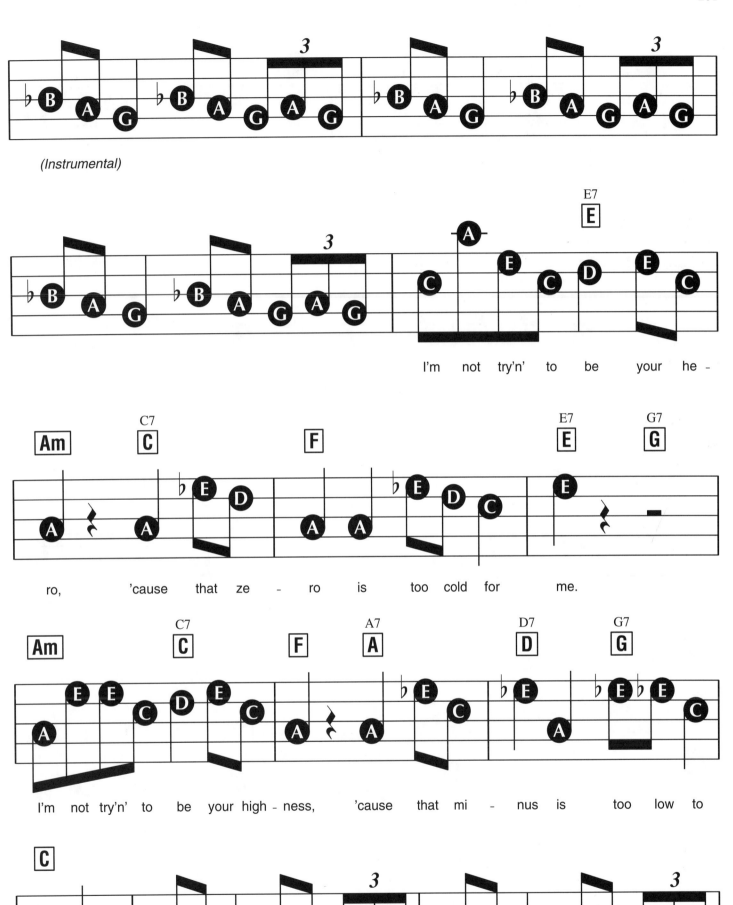

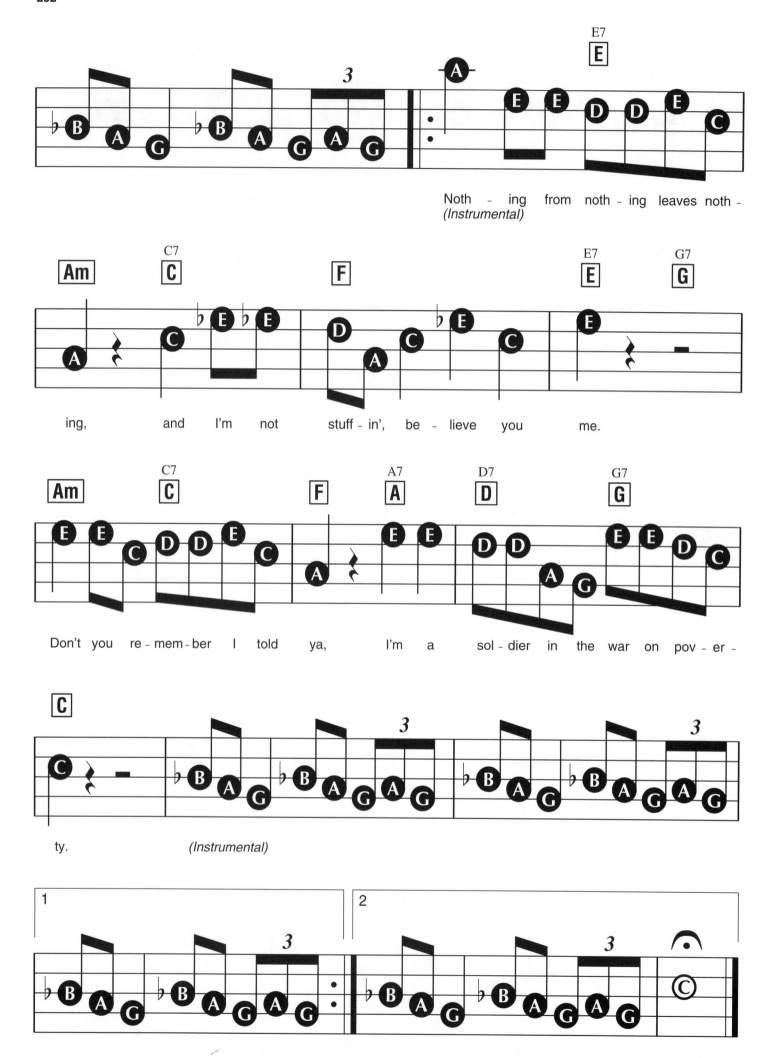

Noth – ing from noth – ing leaves noth –
(Instrumental)

ing, and I'm not stuff – in', be – lieve you me.

Don't you re – mem – ber I told ya, I'm a sol – dier in the war on pov – er –

ty. *(Instrumental)*

Precious and Few

Registration 7
Rhythm: Pop Rock or 8 Beat

Words and Music by
Walter D. Nims

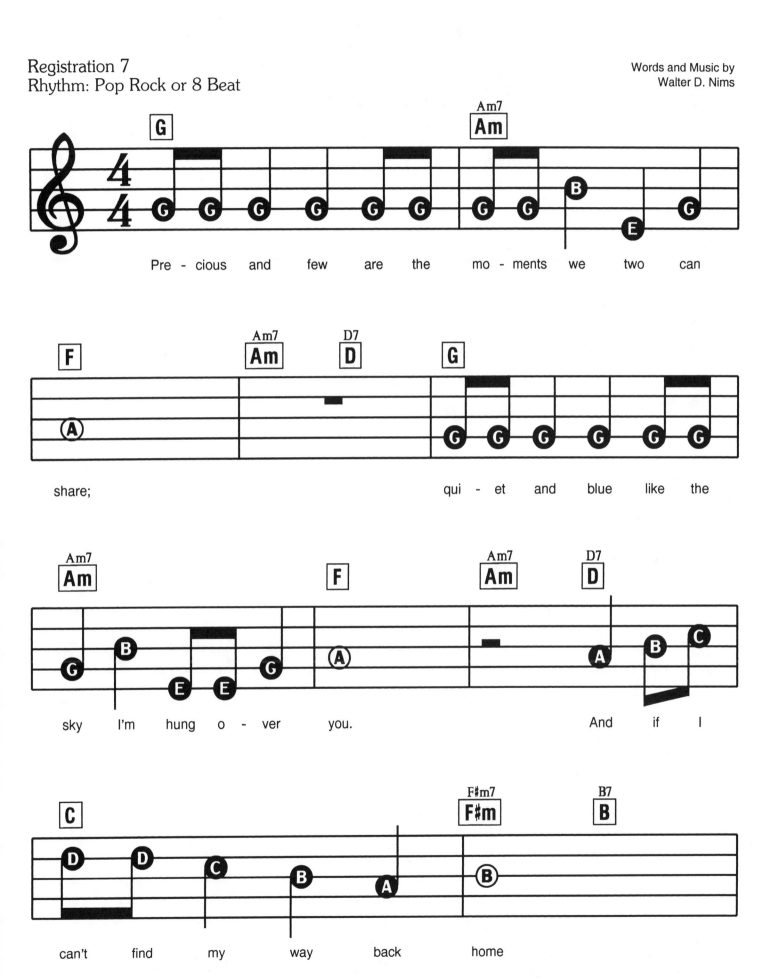

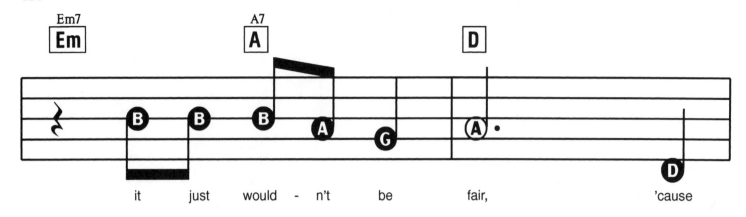

it just would - n't be fair, 'cause

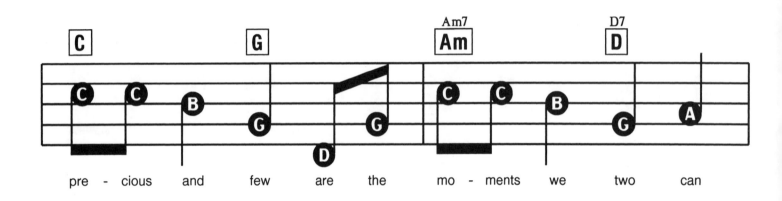

pre - cious and few are the mo - ments we two can

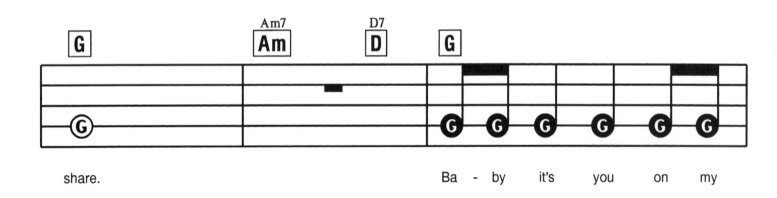

share. Ba - by it's you on my

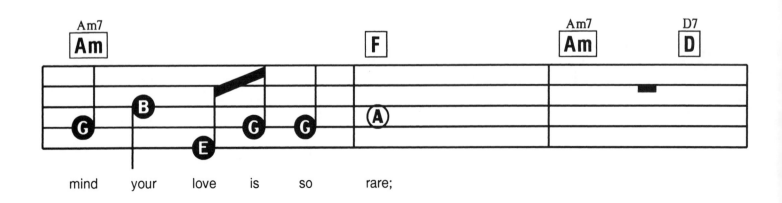

mind your love is so rare;

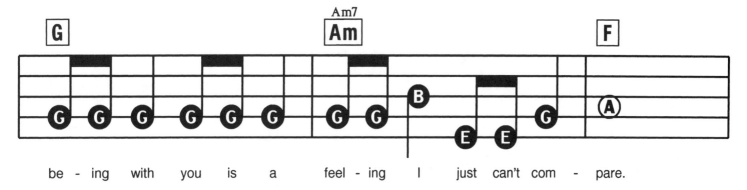

be - ing with you is a feel - ing I just can't com - pare.

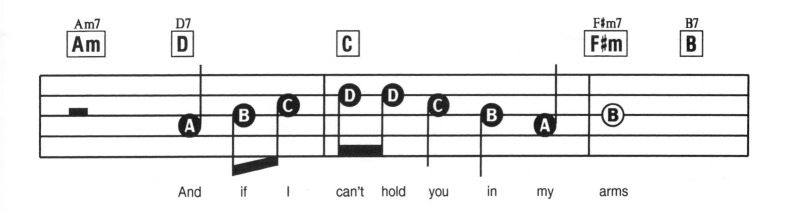

And if I can't hold you in my arms

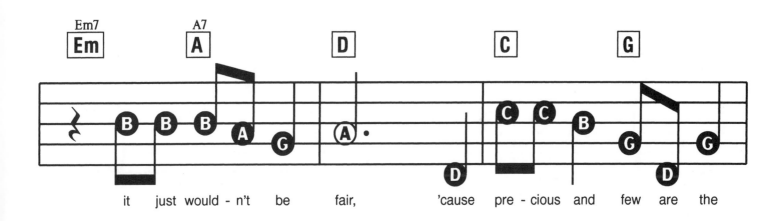

it just would - n't be fair, 'cause pre - cious and few are the

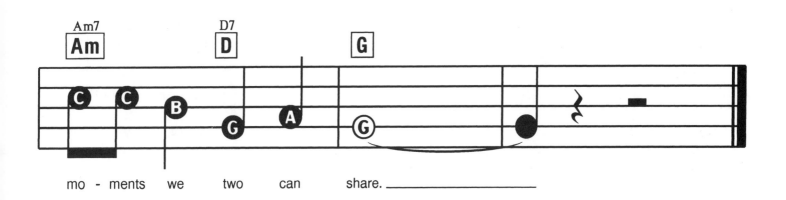

mo - ments we two can share. _____

Peg

Registration 7
Rhythm: Rock or 8 Beat

Words and Music by Walter Becker
and Donald Fagen

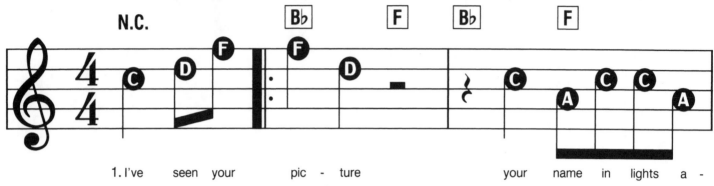

1. I've seen your pic - ture   your name in lights a -
2. *(See additional lyrics)*

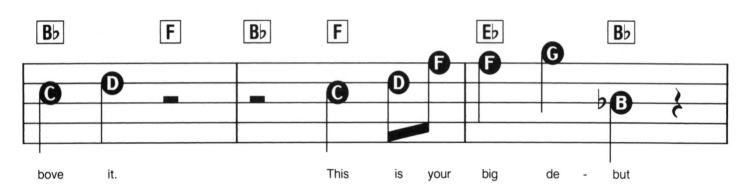

bove it.   This is your big de - but

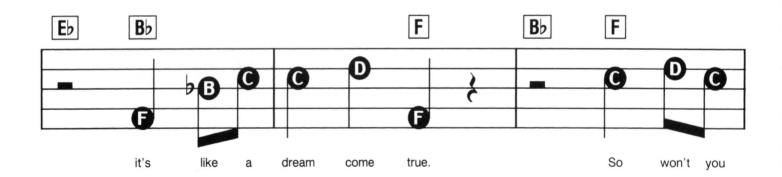

it's like a dream come true.   So won't you

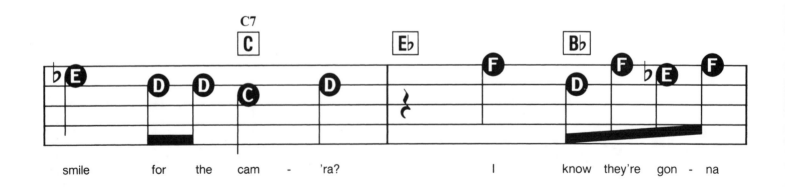

smile for the cam - 'ra?   I know they're gon - na

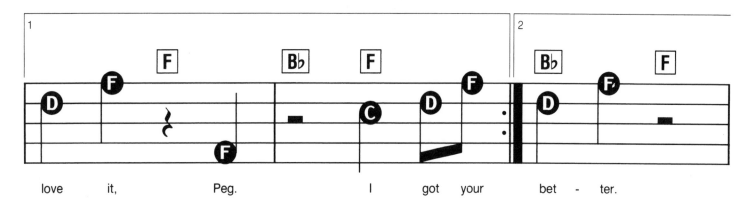

love it, Peg. I got your bet - ter.

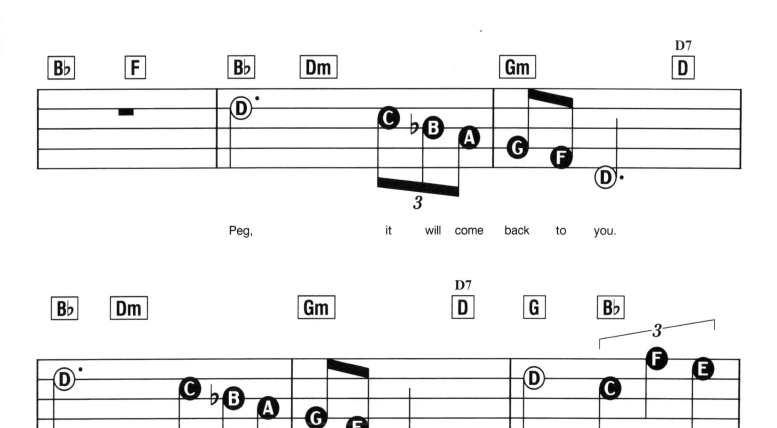

Peg, it will come back to you.

Peg, it will come back to you. Then the shut - ter

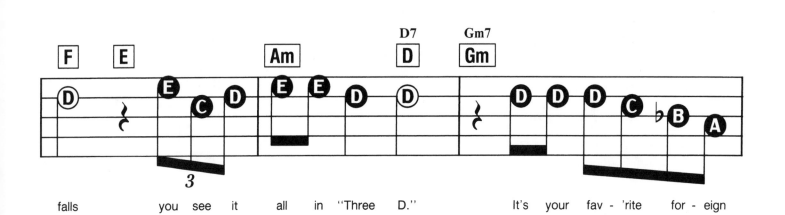

falls you see it all in ''Three D.'' It's your fav - 'rite for - eign

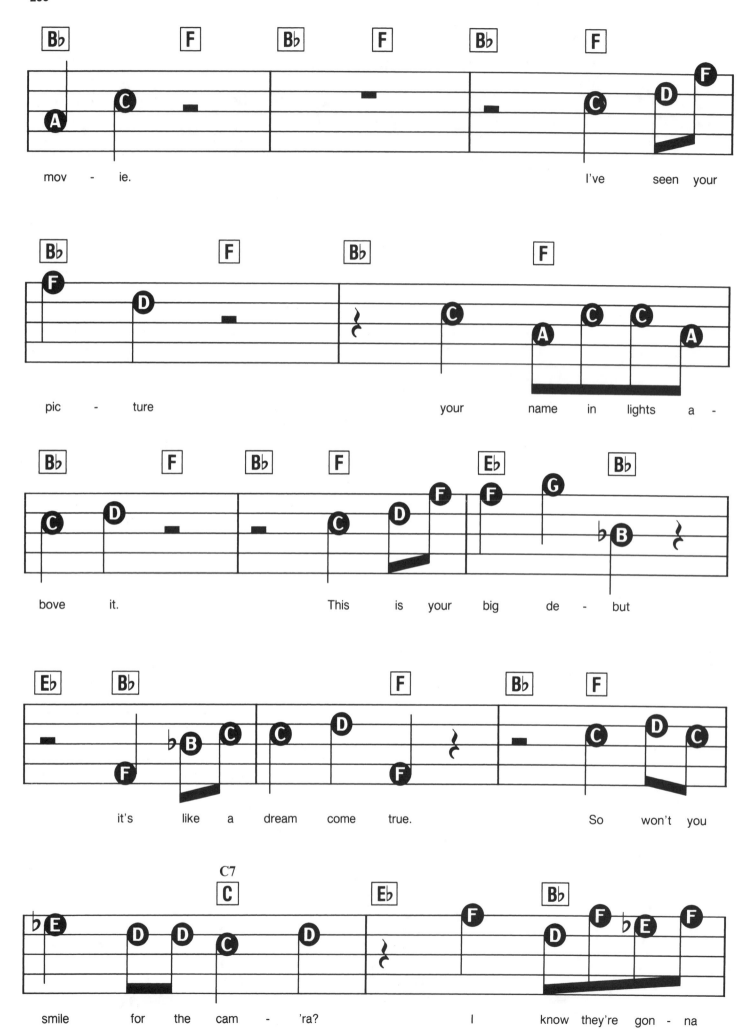

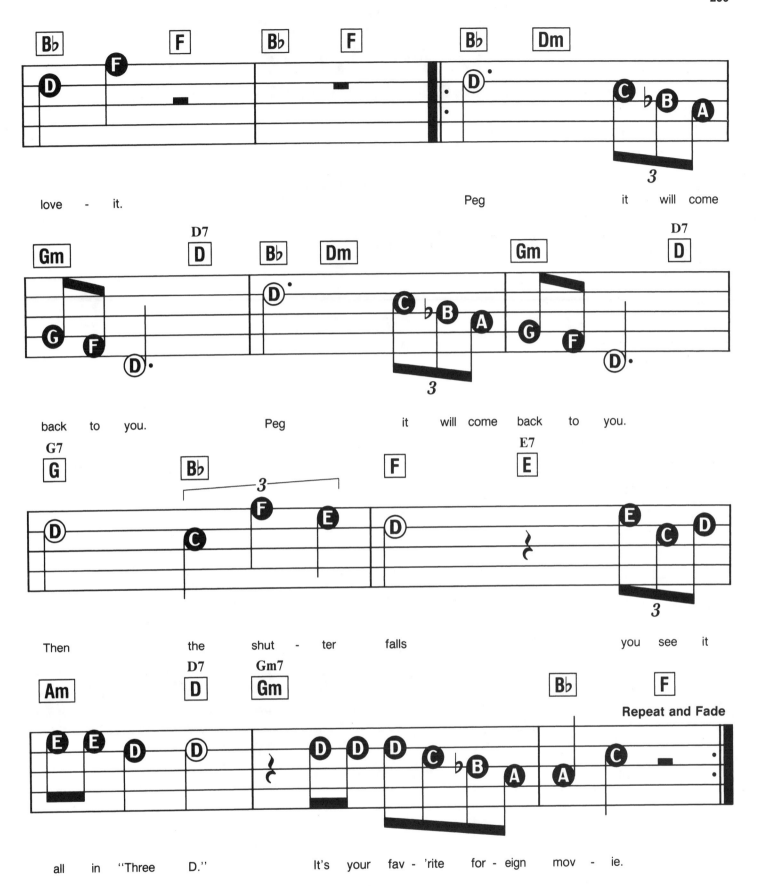

love - it.   Peg   it   will   come

back   to   you.   Peg   it   will   come   back   to   you.

Then   the   shut - ter   falls   you   see   it

all   in "Three D."   It's   your   fav - 'rite   for - eign   mov - ie.

Additional Lyrics

2. I got your pin shot
   I keep it with your letter
   Done up in a blueprint blue,
   It sure looks good on you.
   So won't you smile for the camera,
   I know I'll love you better.

Raindrops Keep Fallin' on My Head
from BUTCH CASSIDY AND THE SUNDANCE KID

Registration 5
Rhythm: Swing or Shuffle

Lyric by Hal David
Music by Burt Bacharach

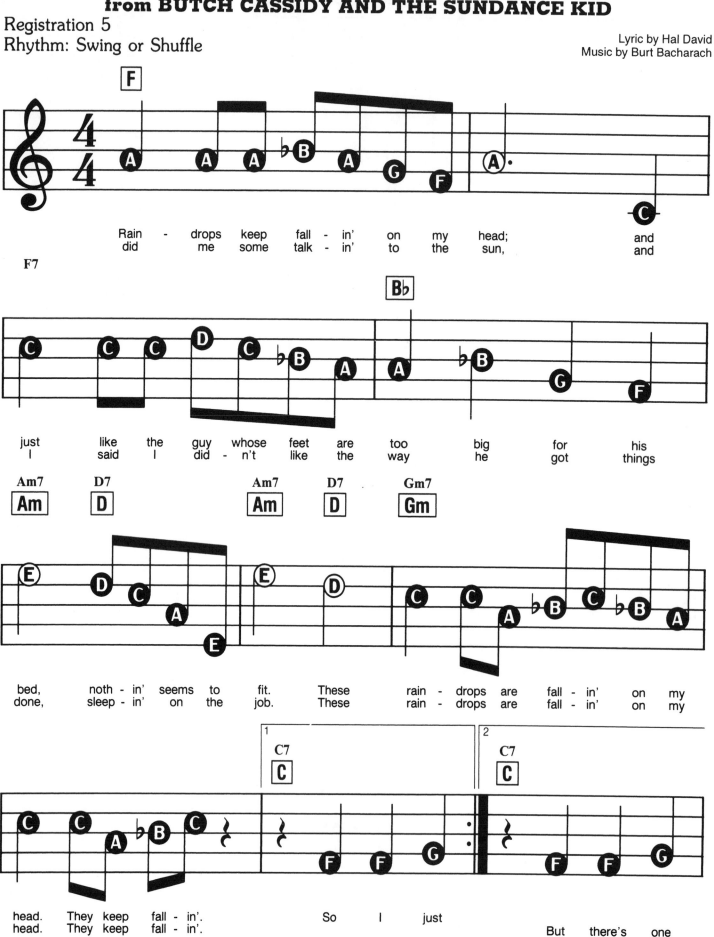

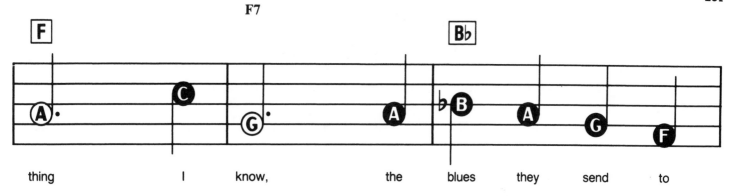

thing I know, the blues they send to

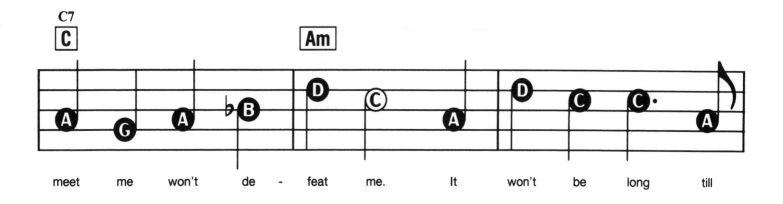

meet me won't de - feat me. It won't be long till

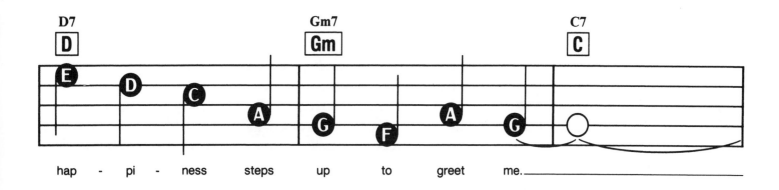

hap - pi - ness steps up to greet me.____

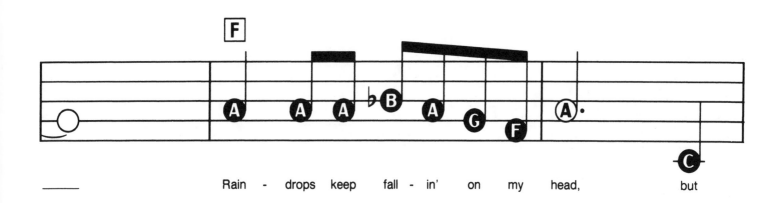

____ Rain - drops keep fall - in' on my head, but

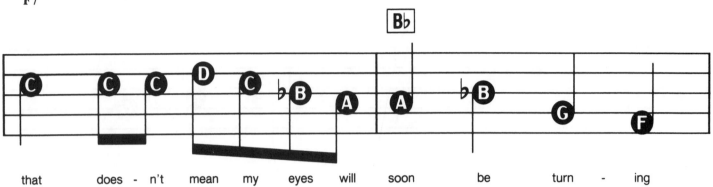

that   does - n't   mean   my   eyes   will   soon   be   turn - ing

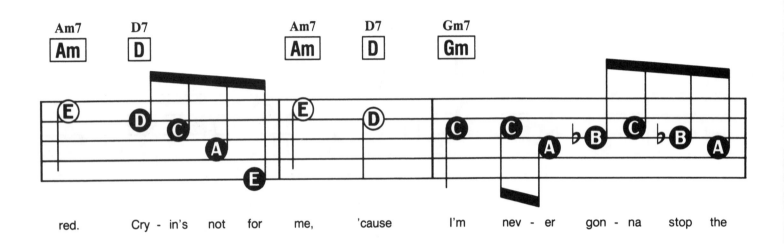

red.   Cry - in's   not   for   me,   'cause   I'm   nev - er   gon - na   stop   the

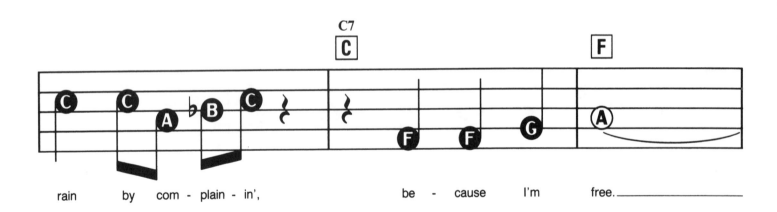

rain   by   com - plain - in',   be - cause   I'm   free._____

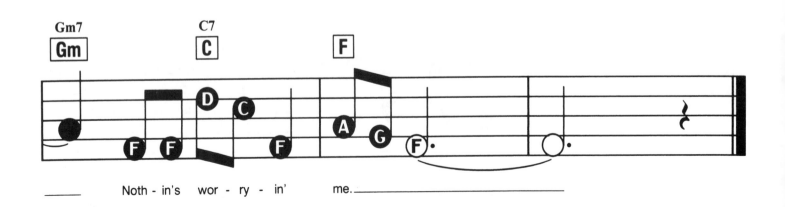

_____   Noth - in's   wor - ry - in'   me._____

Sara Smile

Registration 3
Rhythm: Rock

Words and Music by Daryl Hall
and John Oates

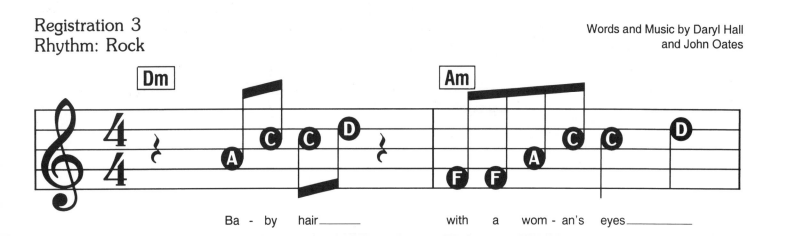

Ba - by hair____ with a wom - an's eyes____

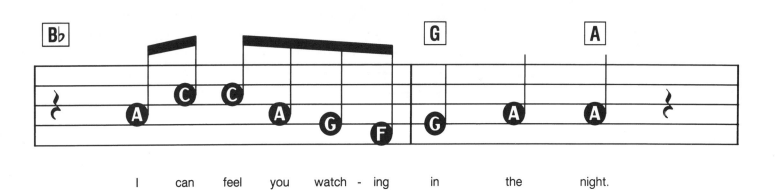

I can feel you watch - ing in the night.

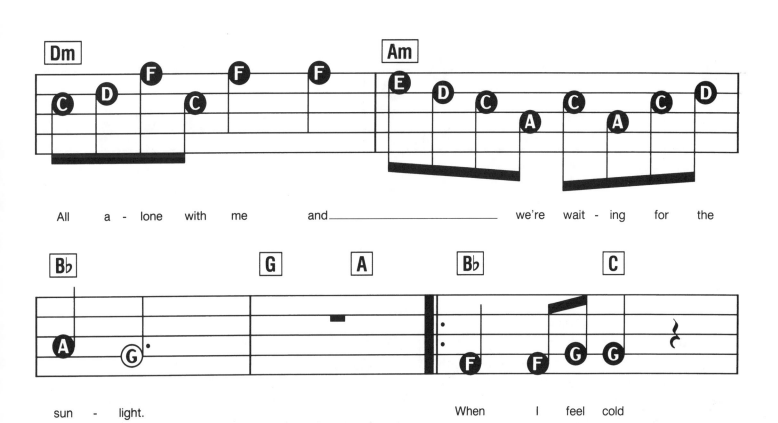

All a - lone with me and_____ we're wait - ing for the

sun - light.

When I feel cold

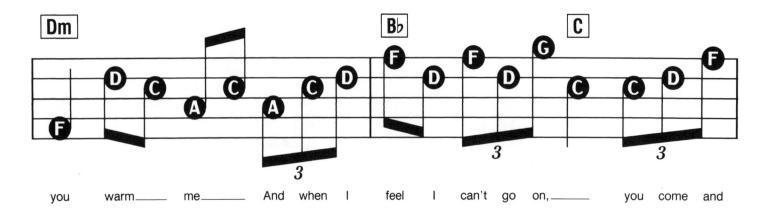

you warm___ me___ And when I feel I can't go on,___ you come and

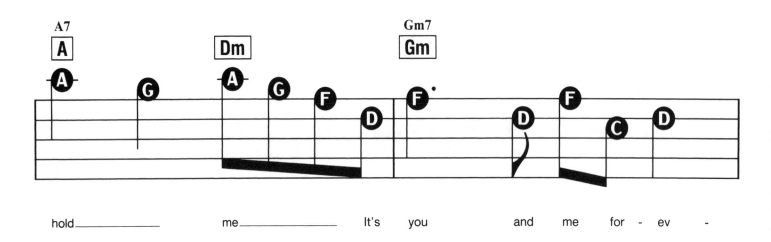

hold___ me___ It's you and me for - ev -

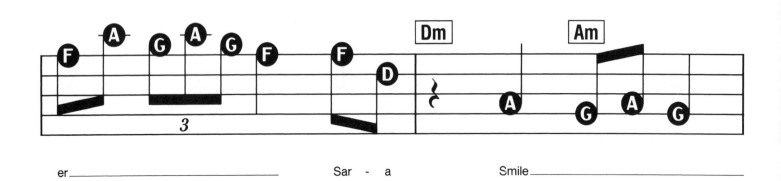

er___ Sar - a Smile___

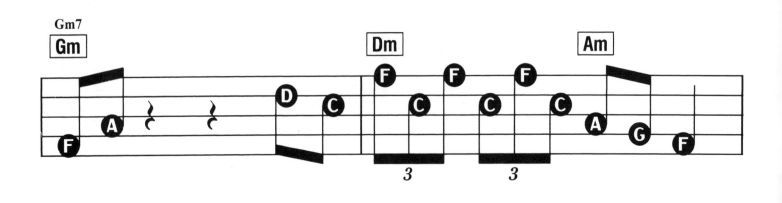

___ Won't you smile a while for me___ Sar - a___

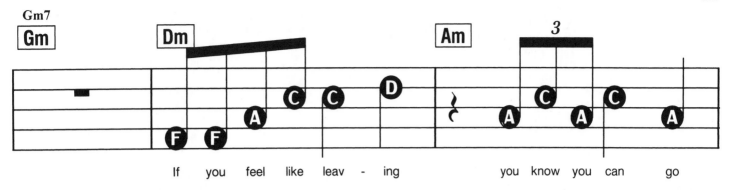

If you feel like leav - ing you know you can go

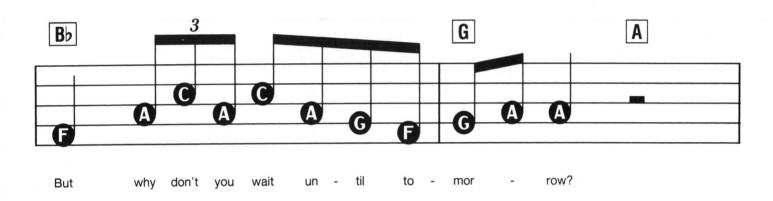

But why don't you wait un - til to - mor - row?

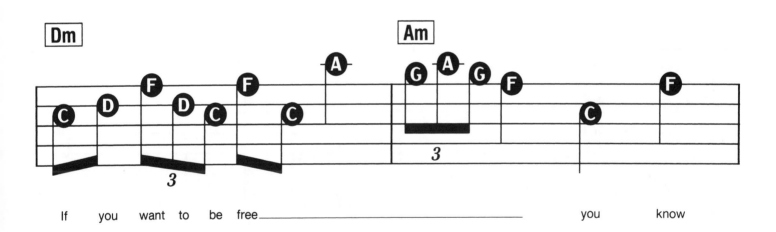

If you want to be free_____ you know

Repeat and Fade

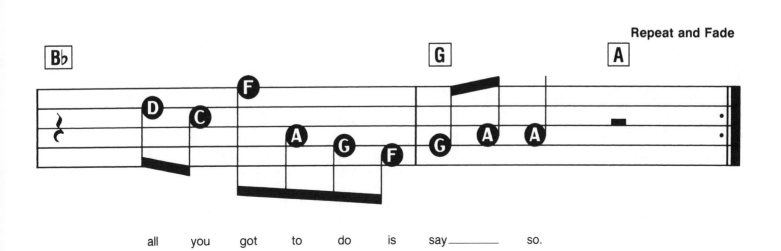

all you got to do is say_____ so.

A Rainy Night in Georgia

Registration 5
Rhythm: Ballad or Fox Trot

Words and Music by
Tony Joe White

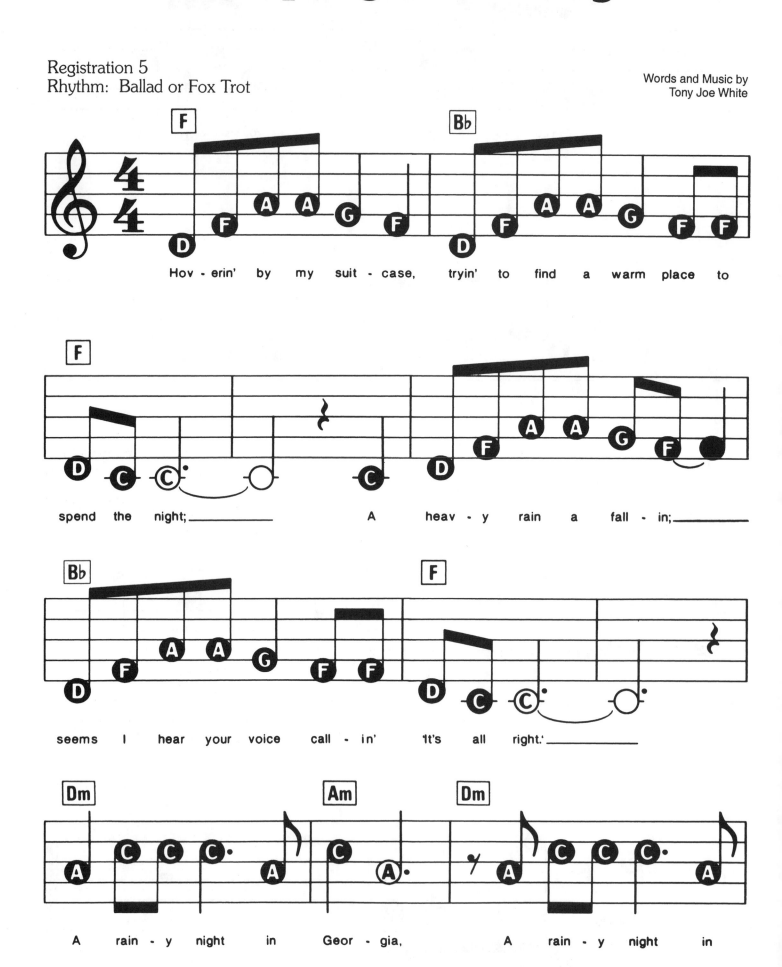

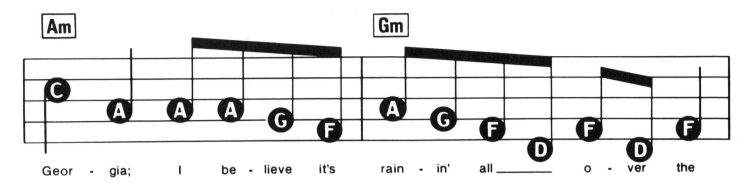

Geor - gia; I be - lieve it's rain - in' all _____ o - ver the

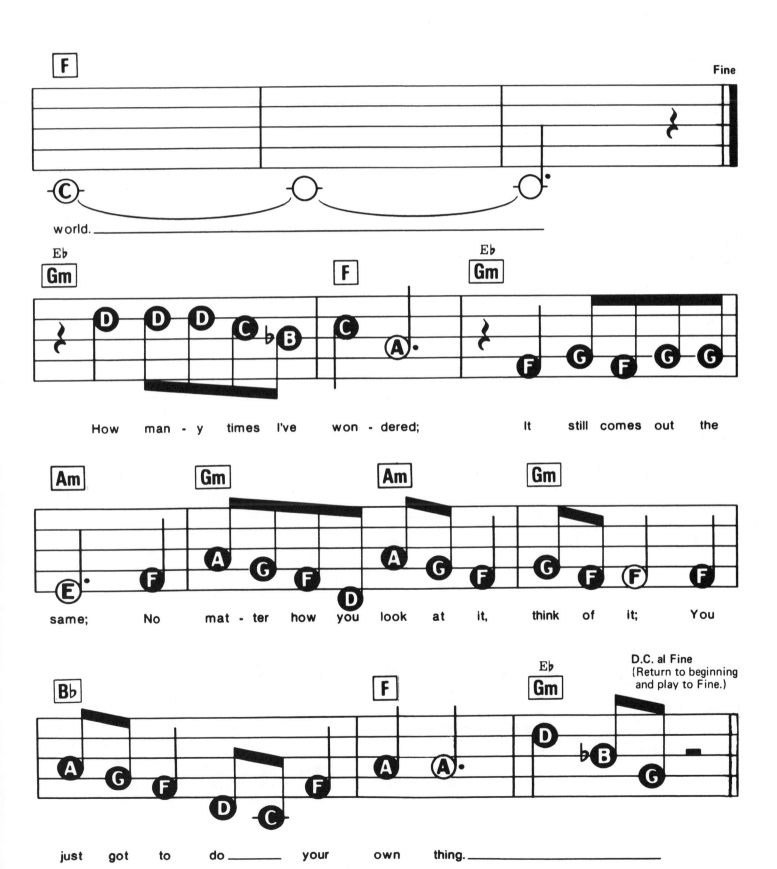

world. _____

How man - y times I've won - dered; It still comes out the

same; No mat - ter how you look at it, think of it; You

D.C. al Fine
(Return to beginning
and play to Fine.)

just got to do _____ your own thing. _____

Rikki Don't Lose That Number

Registration 7
Rhythm: Rock 'n' Roll

Words and Music by Walter Becker
and Donald Fagen

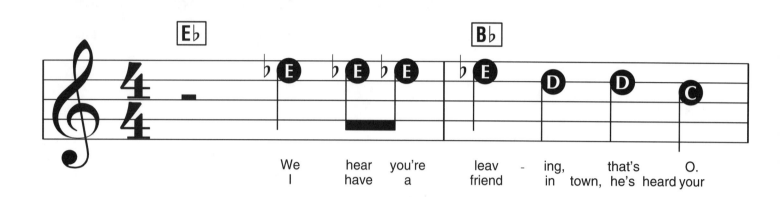

We hear you're leav - ing, that's O.
I have a friend in town, he's heard your

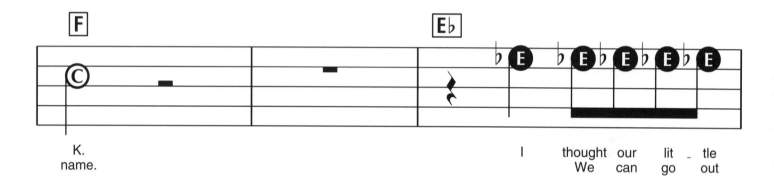

K.
name.

I thought our lit - tle
We can go out

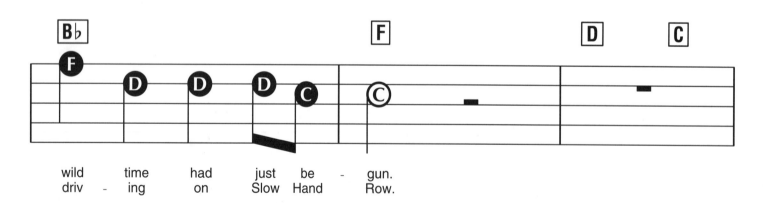

wild time had just be - gun.
driv - ing on Slow Hand Row.

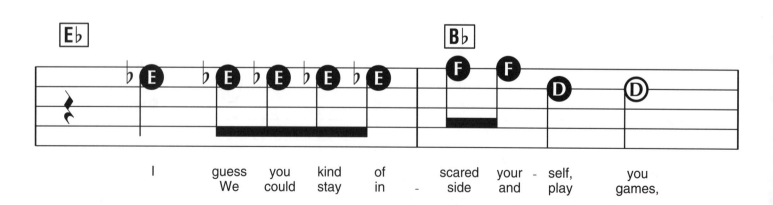

I guess you kind of scared your - self, you
We could stay in - side and play you games,

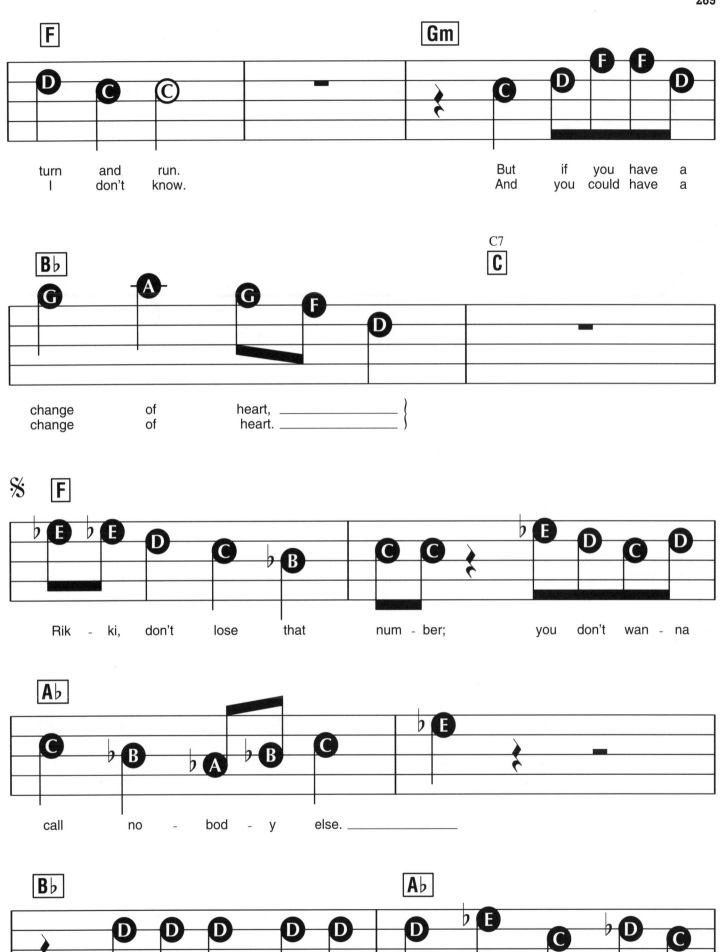

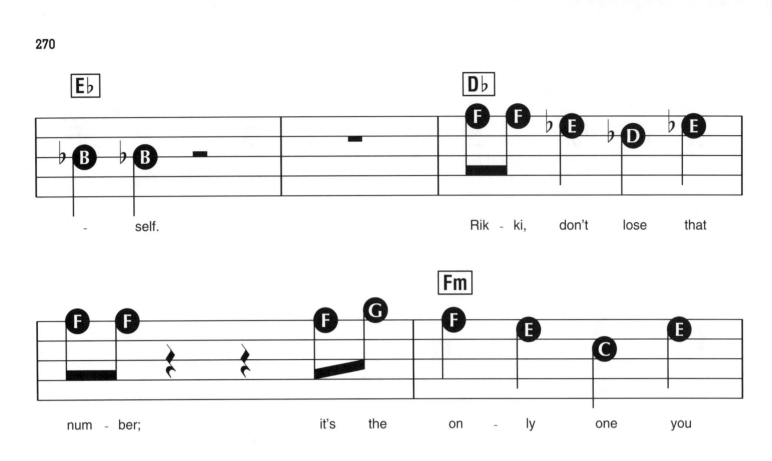

-self.   Rik - ki,   don't   lose   that

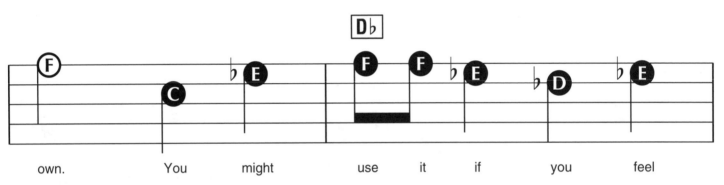

num - ber;   it's   the   on - ly   one   you

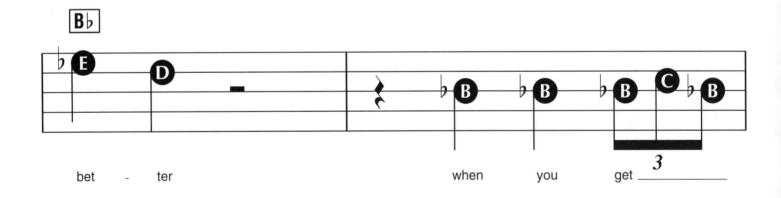

own.   You   might   use   it   if   you   feel

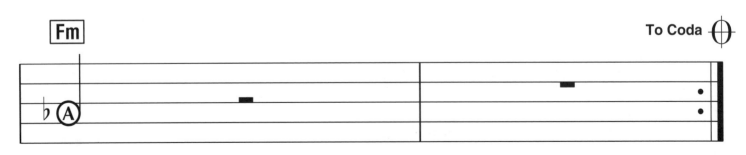

bet - ter   when   you   get _____

home.

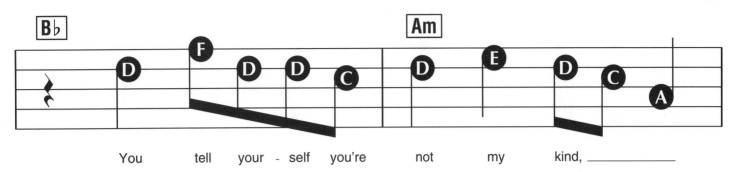

You tell your - self you're not my kind, _____

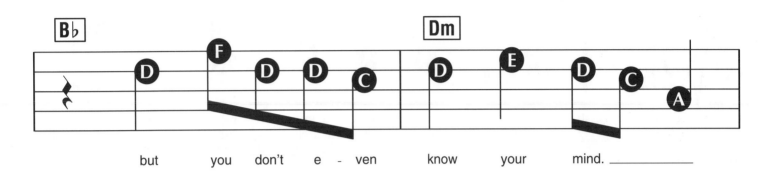

but you don't e - ven know your mind. _____

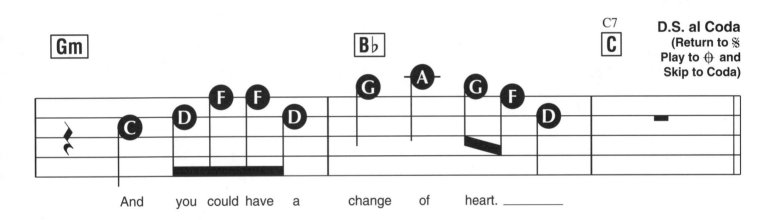

And you could have a change of heart. _____

D.S. al Coda
(Return to 𝄋
Play to ⊕ and
Skip to Coda)

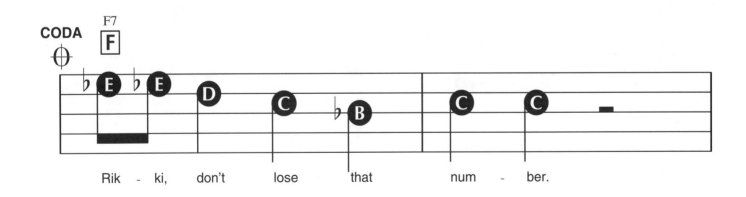

CODA

Rik - ki, don't lose that num - ber.

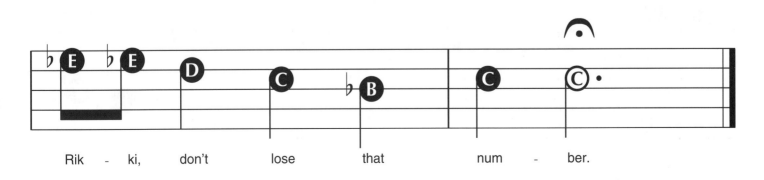

Rik - ki, don't lose that num - ber.

Shambala

Registration 7
Rhythm: 8 Beat or Rock

Words and Music by
Daniel Moore

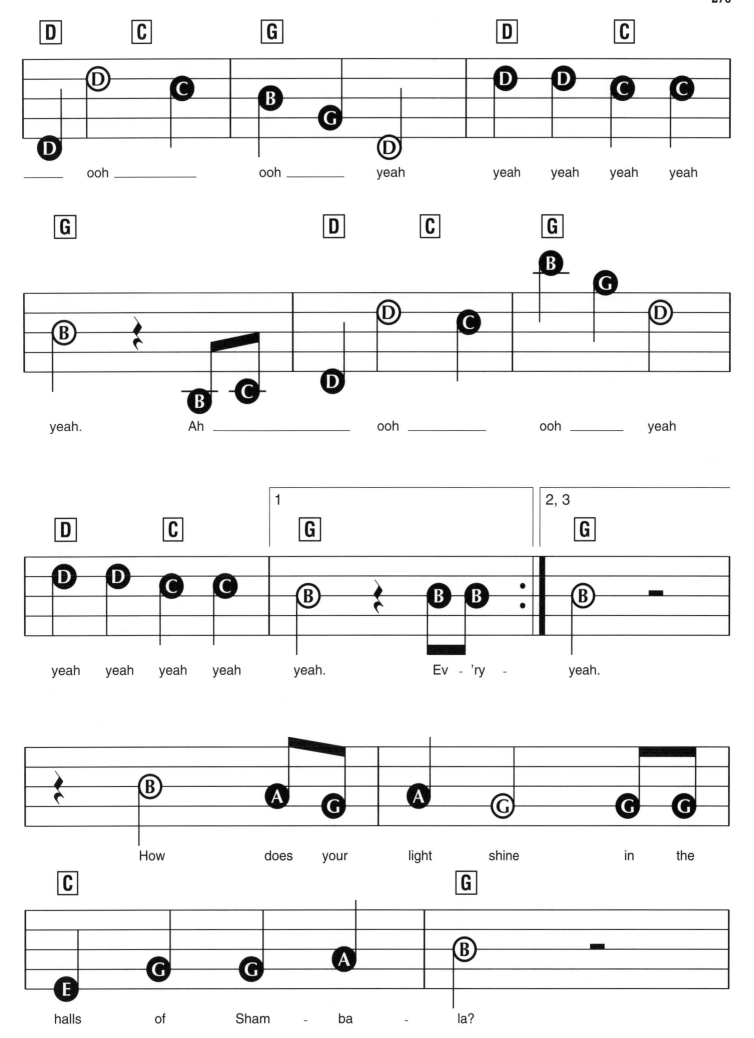

274

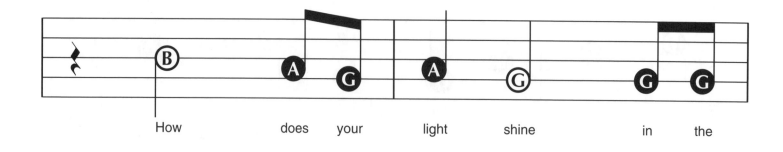

How does your light shine in the

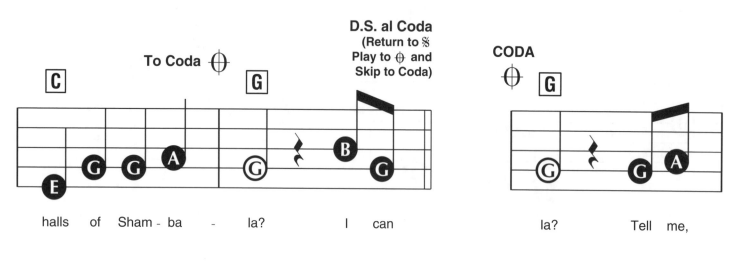

halls of Sham - ba - la? I can

la? Tell me,

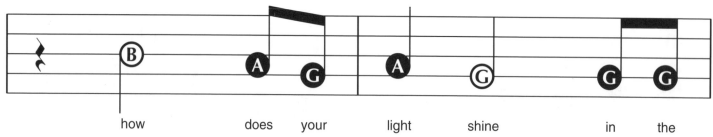

how does your light shine in the

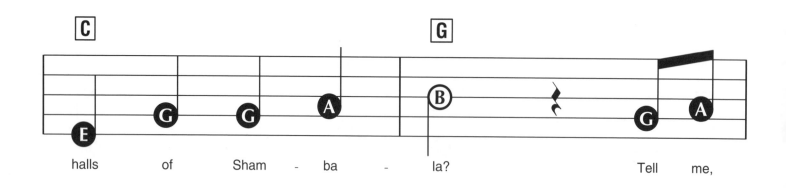

halls of Sham - ba - la? Tell me,

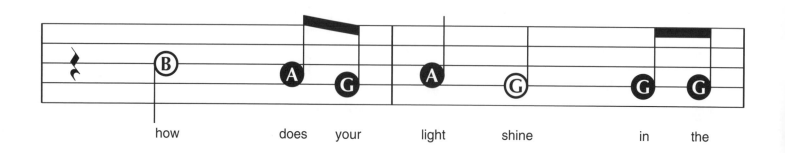

how does your light shine in the

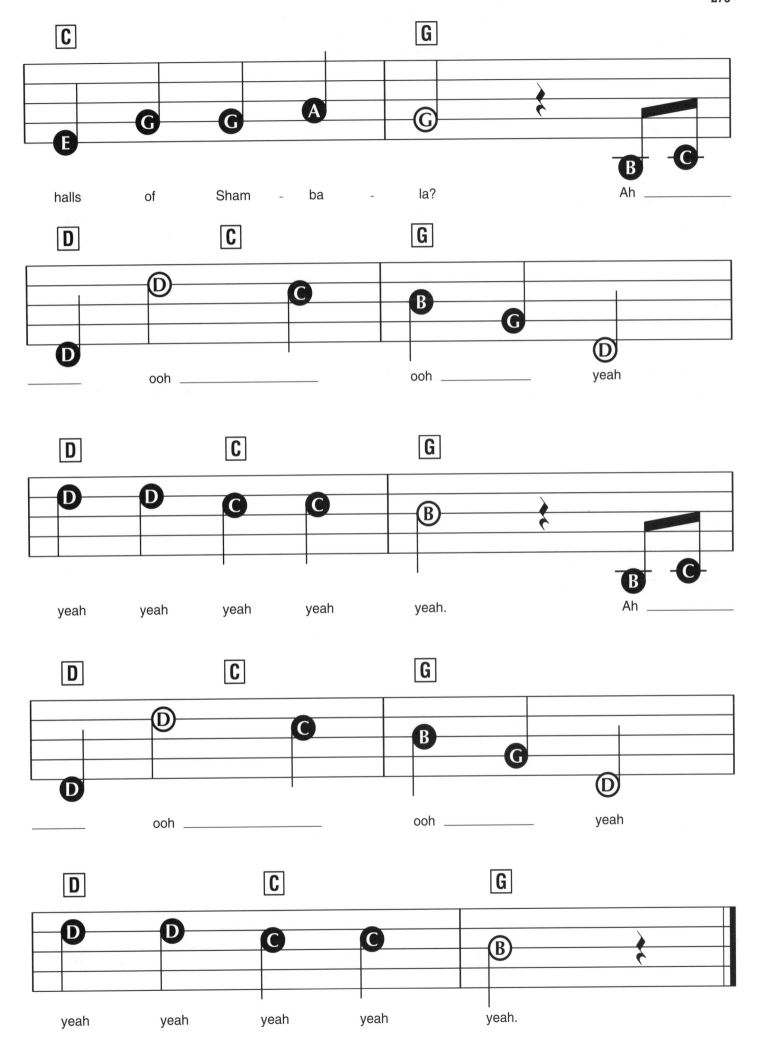

Sing
from SESAME STREET

Registration 8
Rhythm: Rock or 8 Beat

Words and Music by
Joe Raposo

C

Dm

E   E G   F   F A

Sing! ____ Sing a song. ____ Sing out

C

G   G C ♭B

loud, ____ sing out strong. ____

F

C

A A A C E G

Sing of good things, not bad. ____

D D7

G G7

C C C E D F

Sing of hap - py, not sad. ____

C

Dm

E   E G F   F A

Sing! ____ Sing a song. ____ Make it

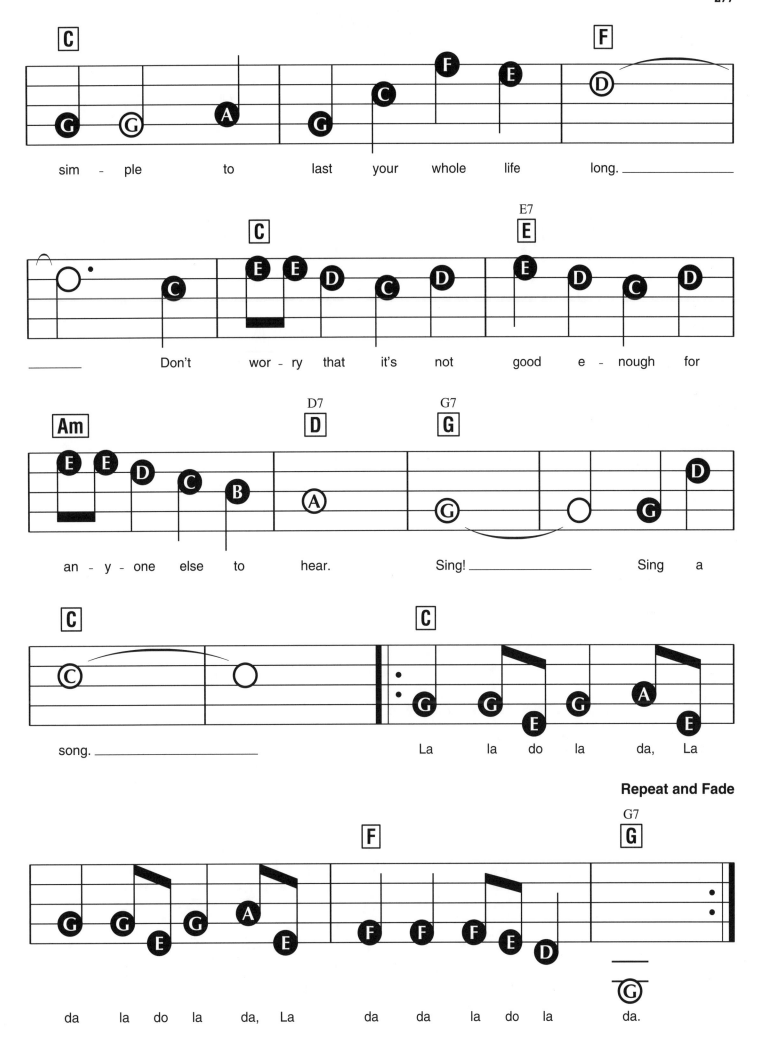

Smoke on the Water

Registration 2
Rhythm: 8 Beat or Rock

Words and Music by Ritchie Blackmore,
Ian Gillan, Roger Glover,
Jon Lord and Ian Paice

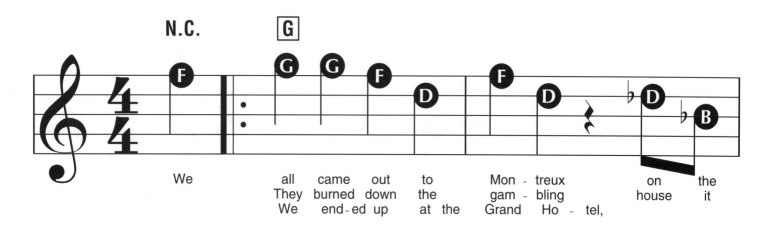

We all came out to the Mon - treux on the
They burned down the gam - bling house it
We end-ed up at the Grand Ho - tel,

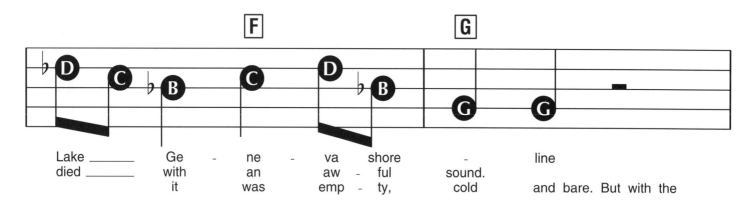

Lake _____ Ge - ne - va shore - line
died _____ with an aw - ful sound.
it was emp - ty, cold and bare. But with the

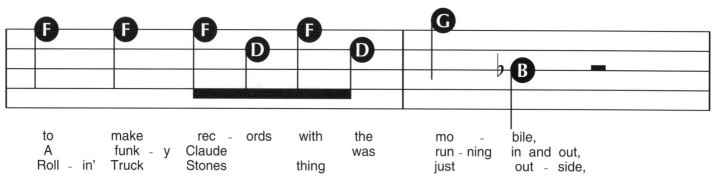

to make rec - ords with the mo - bile,
A funk - y Claude Stones thing was run - ning in and out,
Roll - in' Truck Stones thing just out - side,

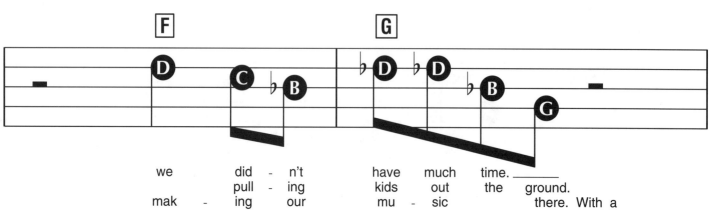

we did - n't have much time. _____
pull - ing kids out the ground.
mak - ing our mu - sic there. With a

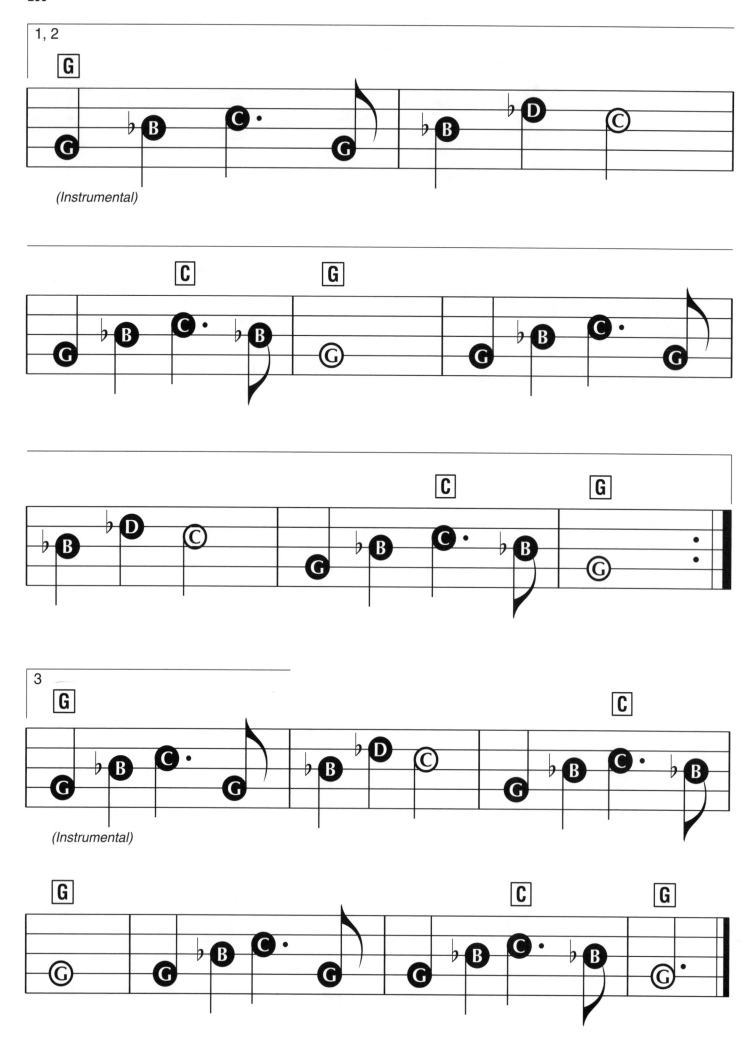

Stayin' Alive
from the Motion Picture SATURDAY NIGHT FEVER

Registration 7
Rhythm: Disco or Rock

Words and Music by Robin Gibb,
Maurice Gibb and Barry Gibb

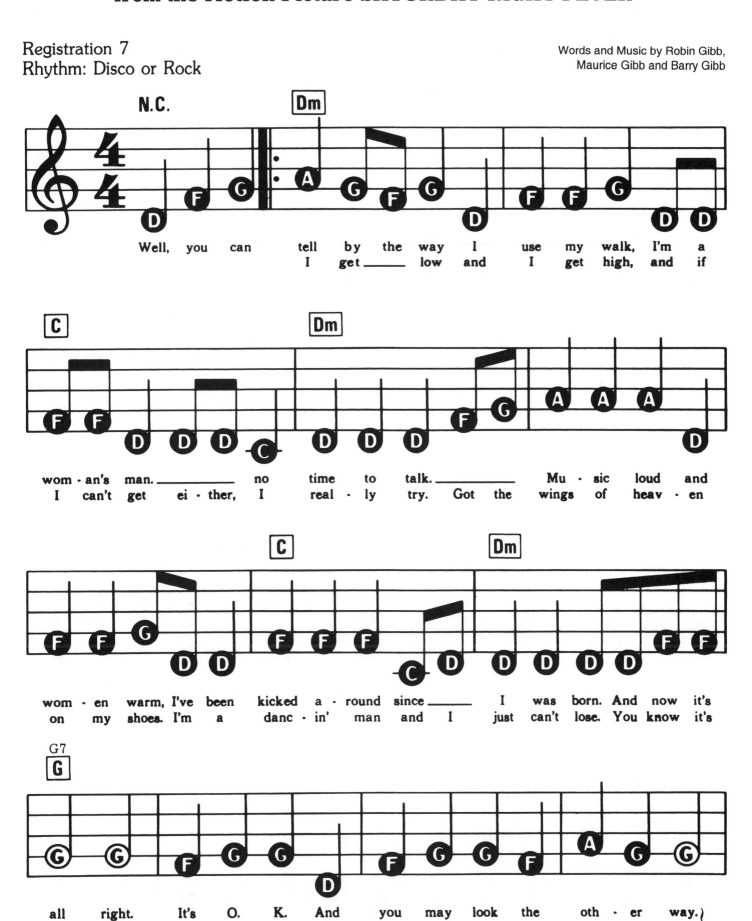

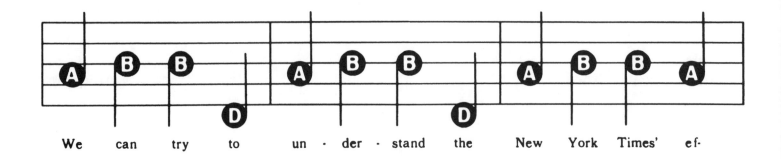

We can try to un-der-stand the New York Times' ef-

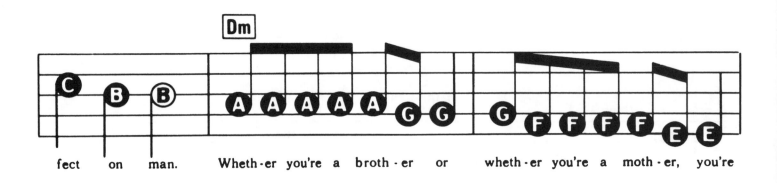

fect on man. Wheth-er you're a broth-er or wheth-er you're a moth-er, you're

stay-in' a-live, stay-in' a-live. Feel the cit-y break-in' and

ev-'ry-bod-y shak-in', and we're stay-in' a-live, stay-in' a-live.

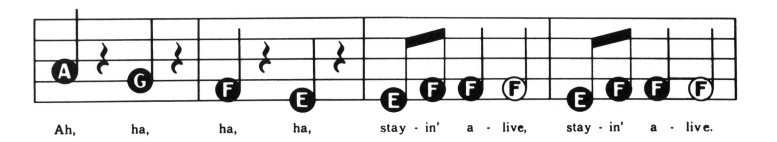

Ah, ha, ha, ha, stay-in' a-live, stay-in' a-live.

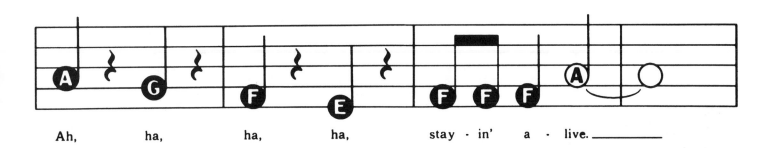

Ah, ha, ha, ha, stay-in' a-live. _____

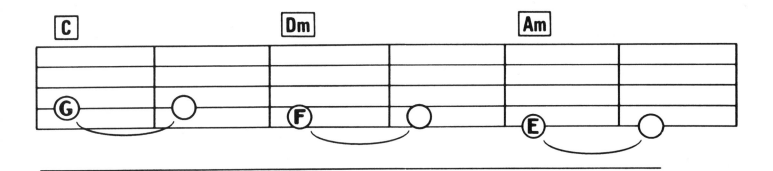

C   Dm   Am

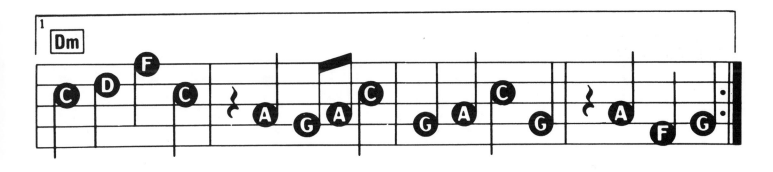

1 Dm

Well now

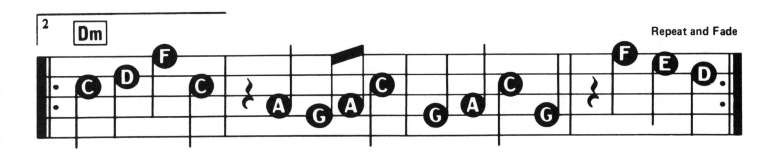

2 Dm   Repeat and Fade

Summer Breeze

Registration 7
Rhythm: Moderate Rock Ballad

Words and Music by James Seals
and Dash Crofts

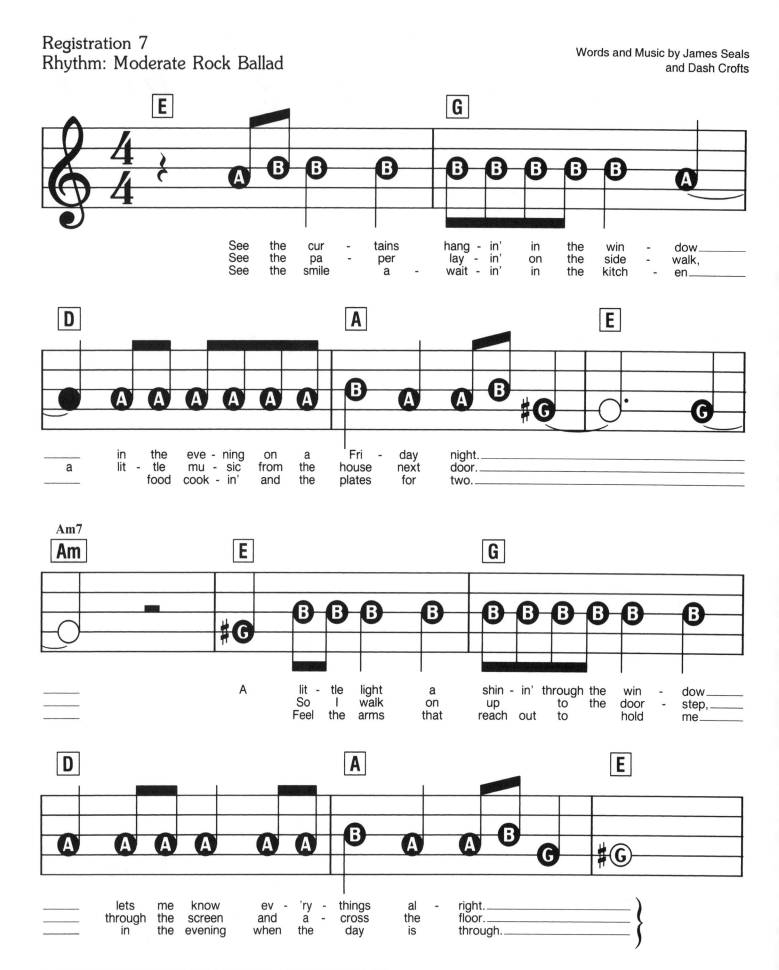

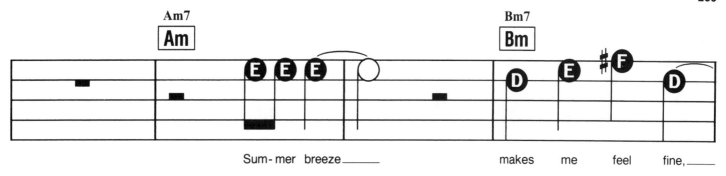

Sum- mer breeze_____ makes me feel fine,_____

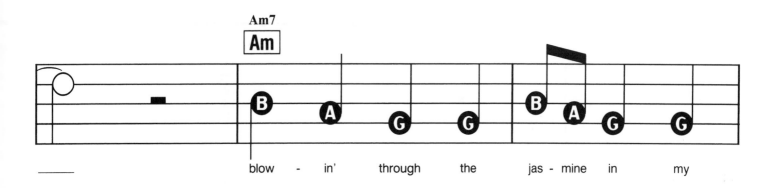

_____ blow - in' through the jas - mine in my

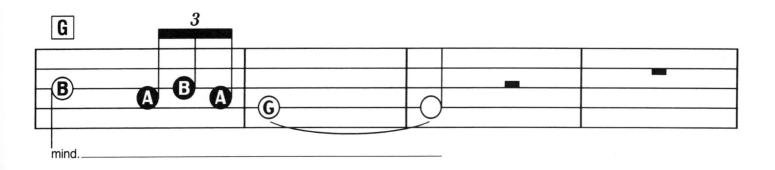

mind._____

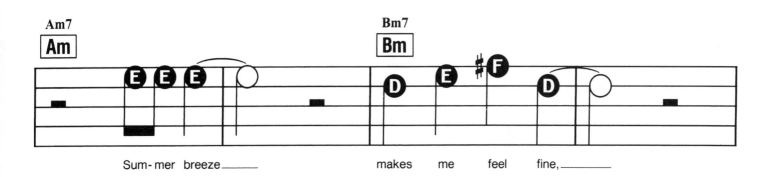

Sum- mer breeze_____ makes me feel fine,_____

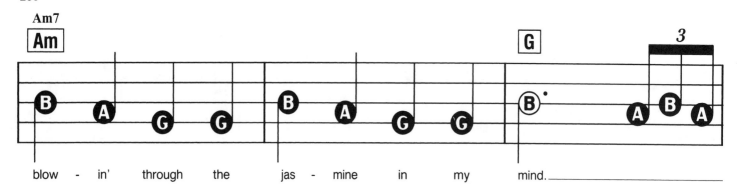

blow - in' through the jas - mine in my mind.

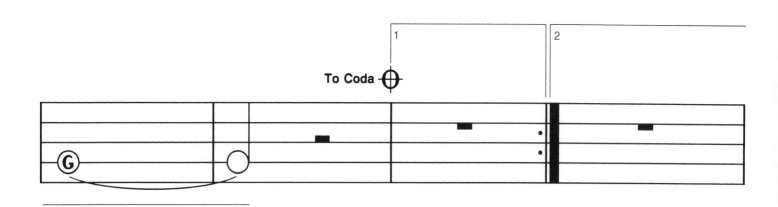

To Coda

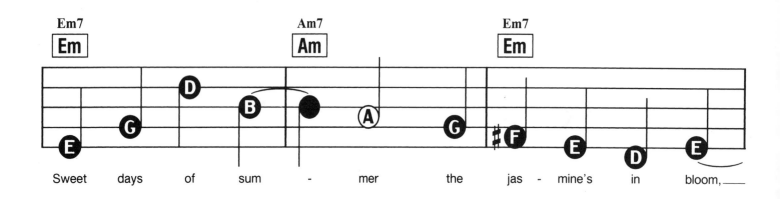

Sweet days of sum - mer the jas - mine's in bloom,

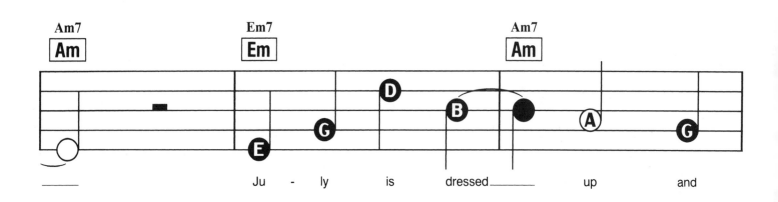

Ju - ly is dressed up and

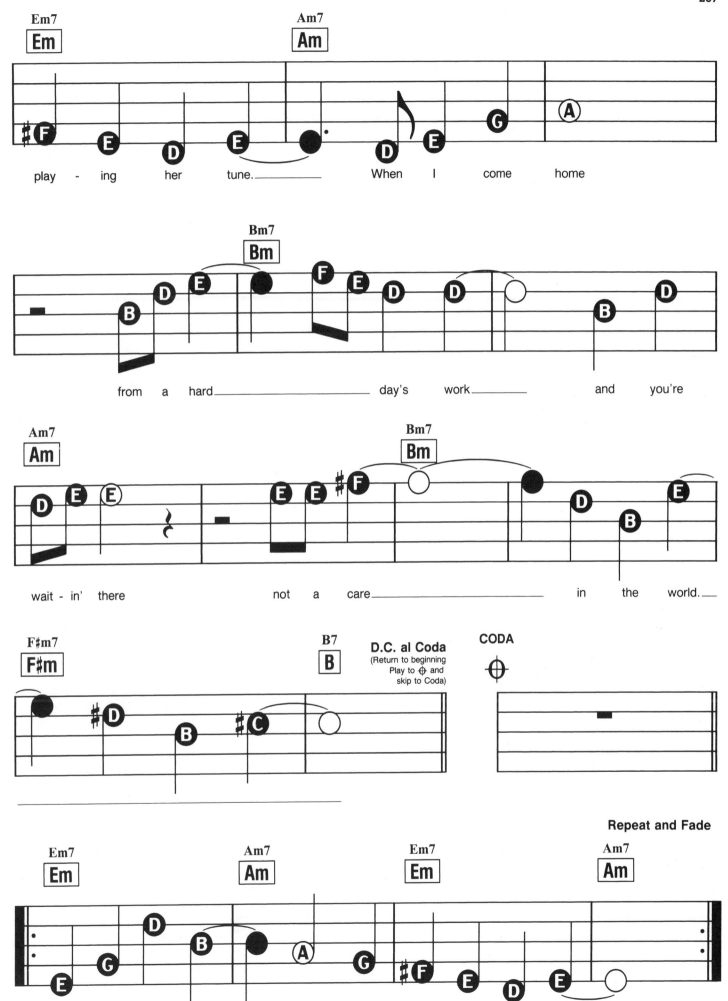

play - ing her tune._____ When I come home

from a hard_____ day's work_____ and you're

wait - in' there   not a care_____ in the world.__

D.C. al Coda
(Return to beginning
Play to ⊕ and
skip to Coda)

CODA

Repeat and Fade

Superstition

Registration 5
Rhythm: Rock or Disco

Words and Music by
Stevie Wonder

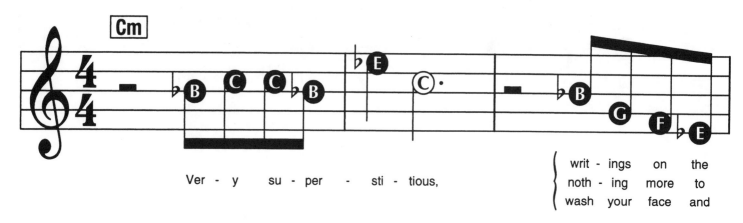

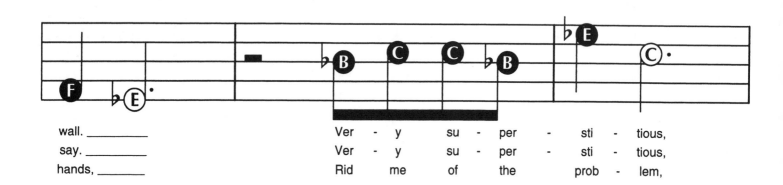

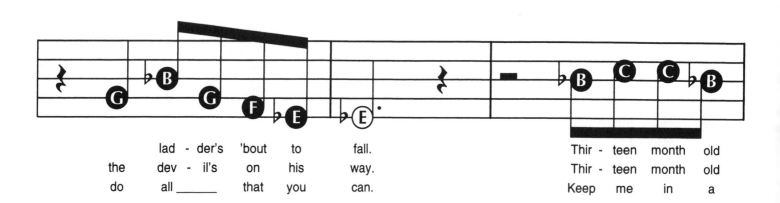

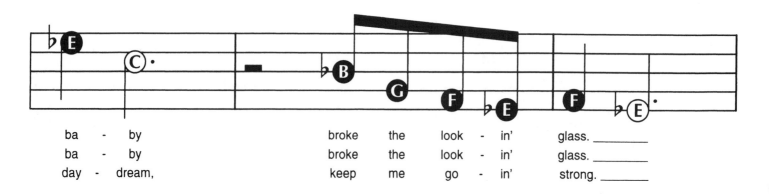

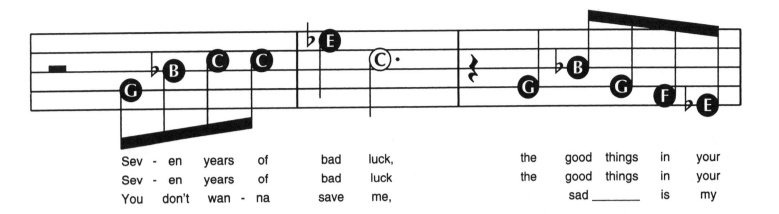

Sev - en years of bad luck, the good things in your
Sev - en years of bad luck the good things in your
You don't wan - na save me, sad _____ is my

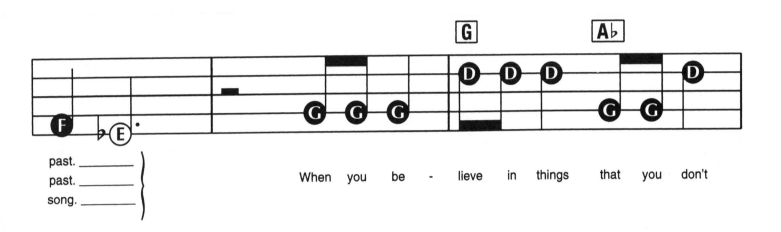

past. _____
past. _____
song. _____

When you be - lieve in things that you don't

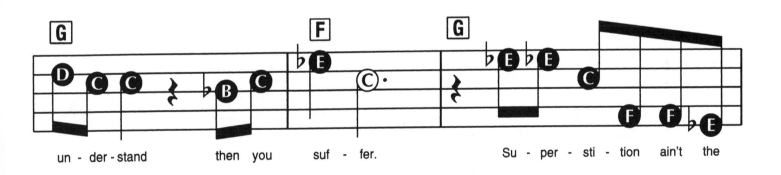

un - der - stand then you suf - fer. Su - per - sti - tion ain't the

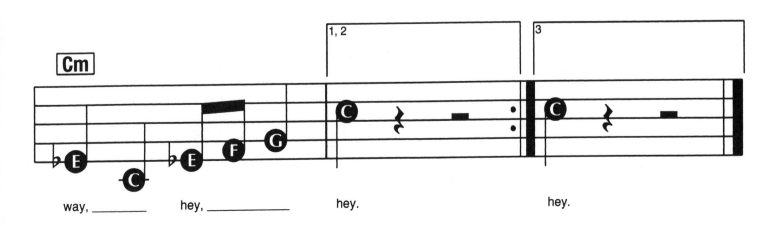

way, _____ hey, _____ hey. hey.

Take a Chance on Me

Registration 1
Rhythm: Rock

Words and Music by Benny Andersson
and Bjorn Ulvaeus

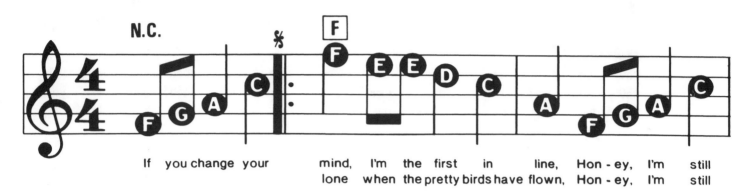
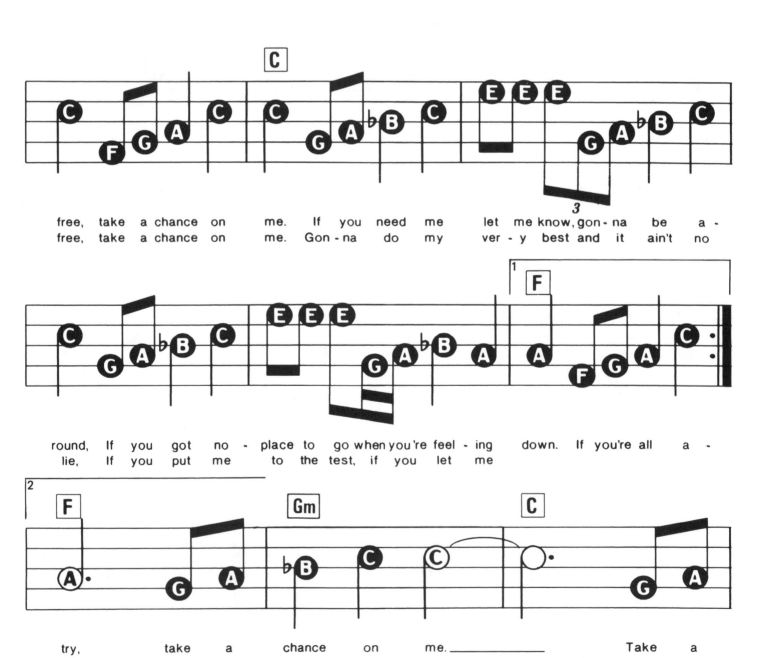

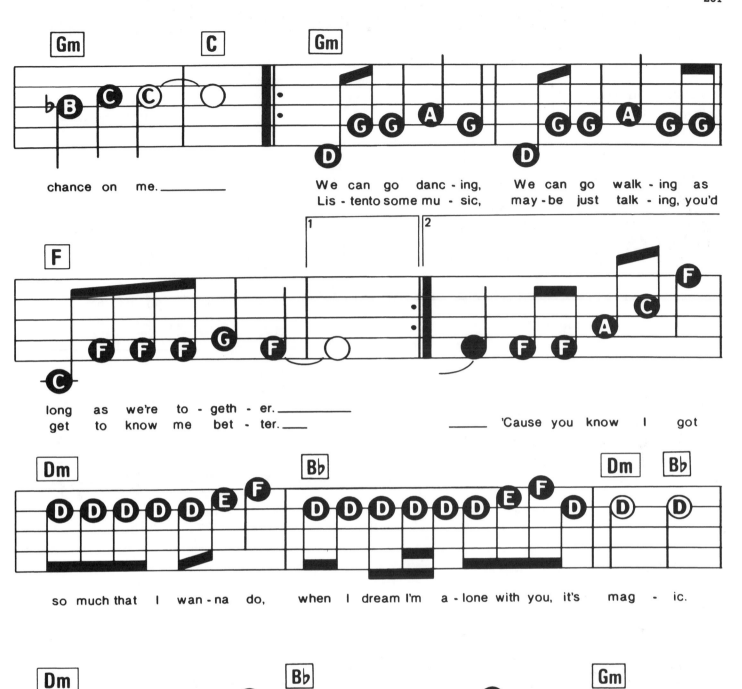

chance on me.＿＿＿＿

We can go danc - ing,
Lis - ten to some mu - sic,

We can go walk - ing as
may - be just talk - ing, you'd

long as we're to - geth - er.＿＿＿＿＿
get to know me bet - ter.＿＿

＿＿＿ 'Cause you know I got

so much that I wan - na do, when I dream I'm a - lone with you, it's mag - ic.

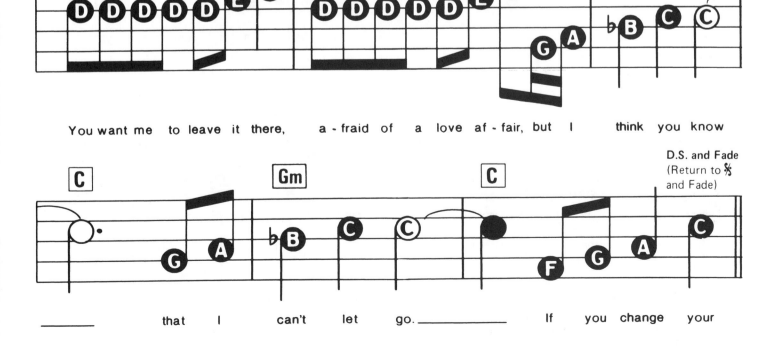

You want me to leave it there, a - fraid of a love af - fair, but I think you know

D.S. and Fade
(Return to 𝄋
and Fade)

＿＿＿ that I can't let go.＿＿＿＿ If you change your

Take Me Home, Country Roads

Registration 10
Rhythm: Country

Words and Music by John Denver,
Bill Danoff and Taffy Nivert

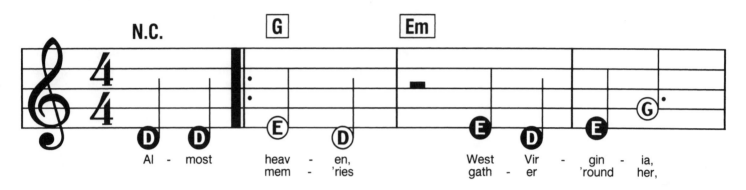

Al - most heav - en, West Vir - gin - ia,
mem - 'ries gath - er 'round her,

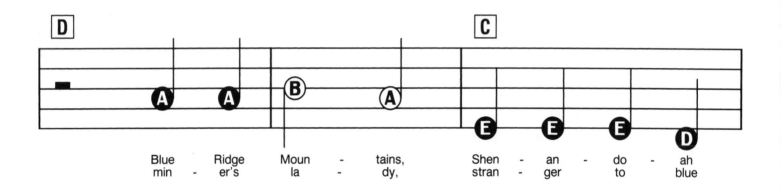

Blue Ridge Moun - tains, Shen - an - do - ah
min - er's la - dy, stran - ger to blue

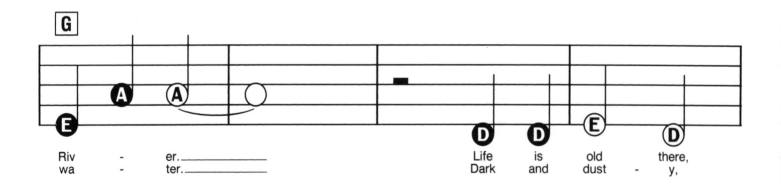

Riv - er. Life is old there,
wa - ter. Dark and dust - y,

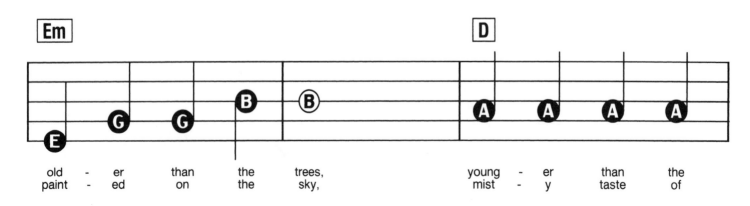

old - er than the trees, young - er than the
paint - ed on the sky, mist - y taste of

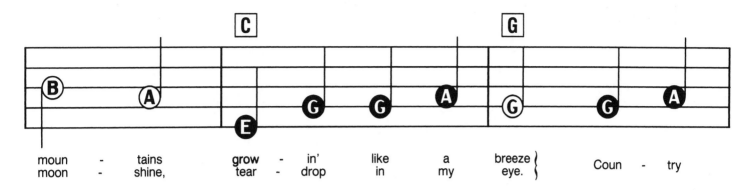

moun - tains grow - in' like a breeze }
moon - shine, tear - drop in my eye. } Coun - try

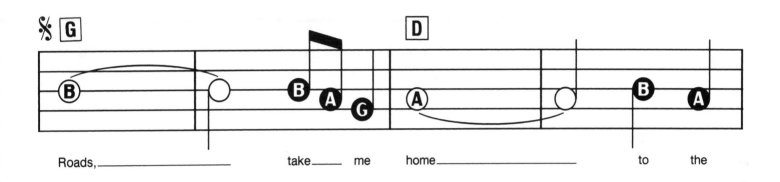

Roads,_____ take____ me home_____ to the

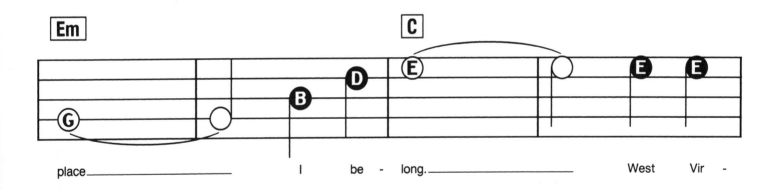

place_____ I be - long._____ West Vir -

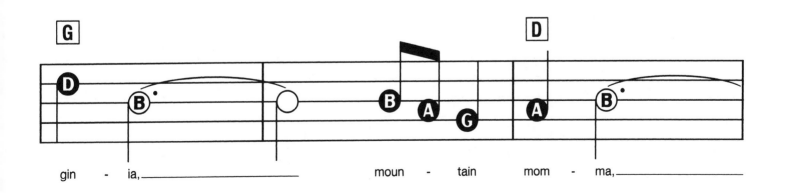

gin - ia,_____ moun - tain mom - ma,_____

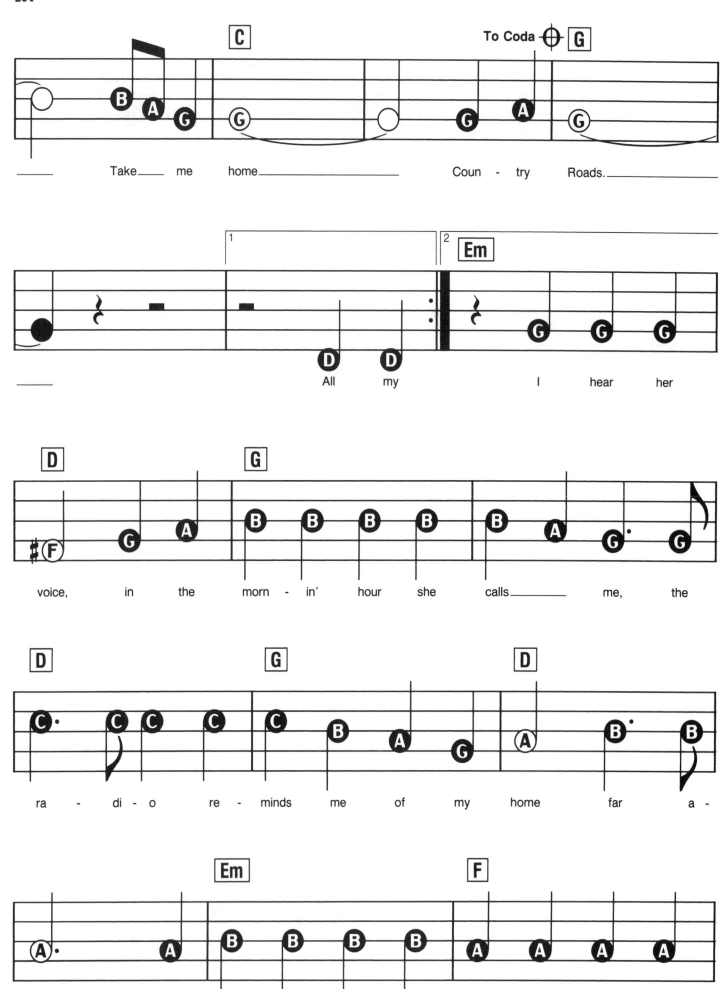

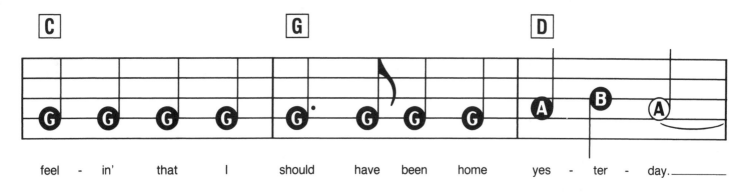

feel - in' that I should have been home yes - ter - day.

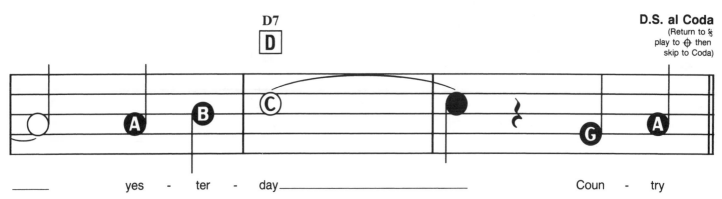

_____ yes - ter - day_____ Coun - try

CODA

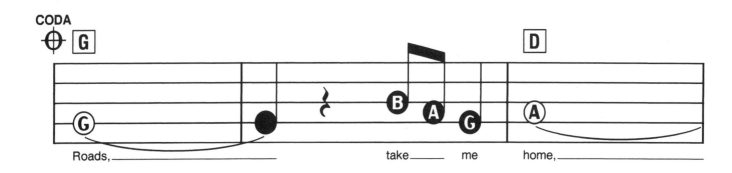

Roads,_____ take_____ me home,_____

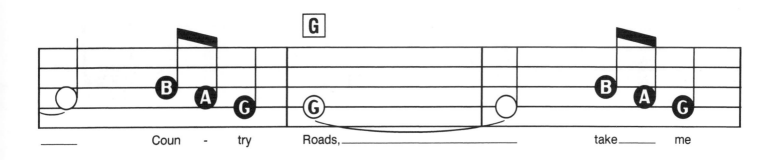

_____ Coun - try Roads,_____ take_____ me

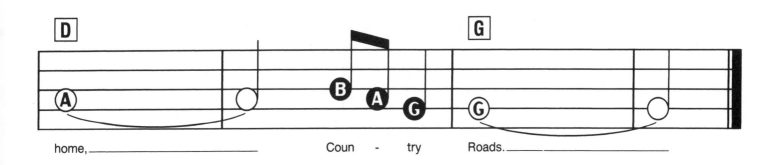

home,_____ Coun - try Roads._____

Three Times a Lady

Registration 1
Rhythm: Waltz

Words and Music by
Lionel Richie

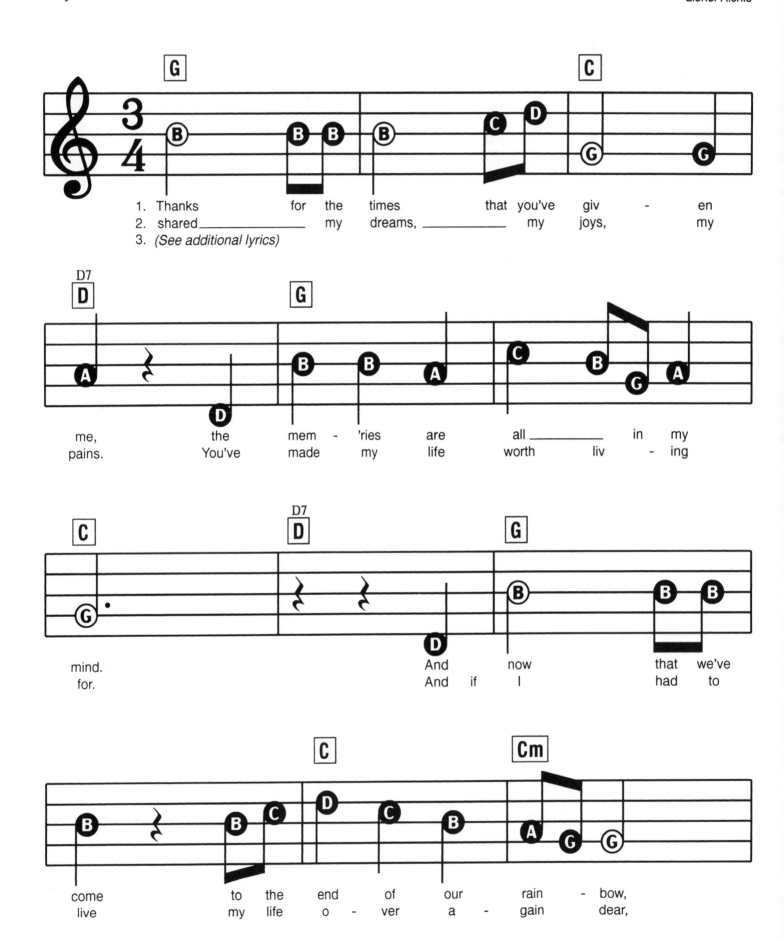

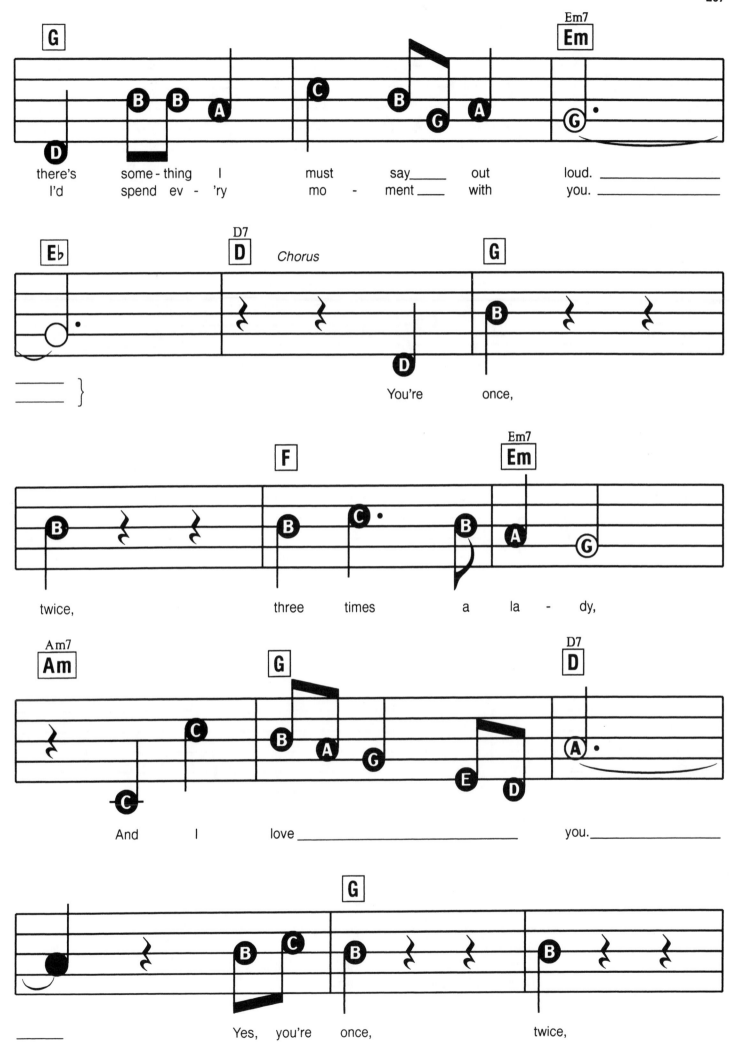

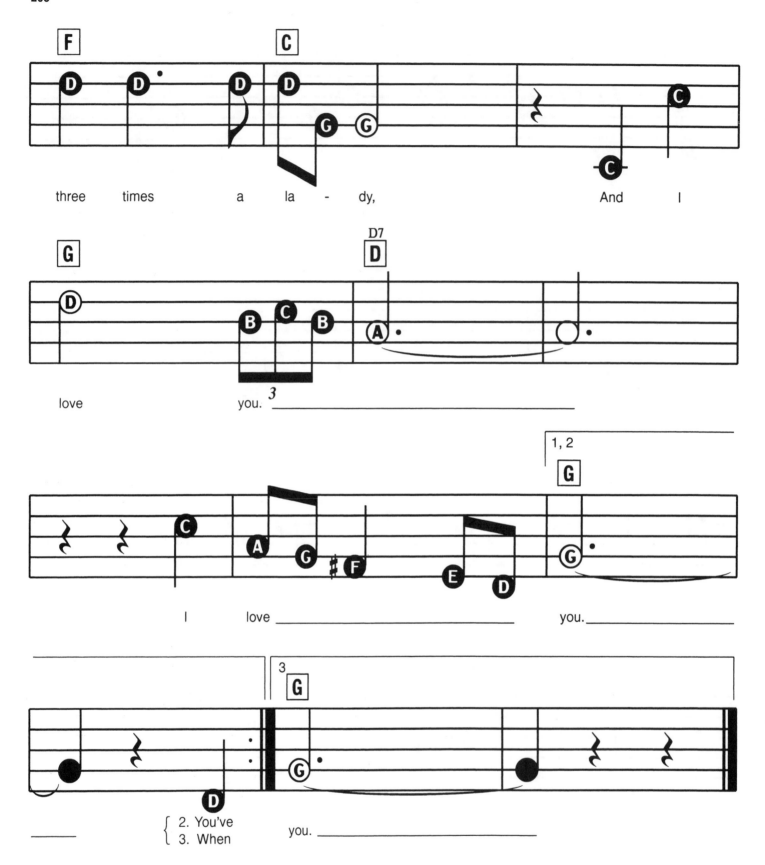

three   times   a   la - dy,   And   I

love   you.

I   love   you.

2. You've
3. When   you.

Additional Lyrics

3. When we are together the moments I cherish
   With ev'ry beat of my heart.
   To touch you, to hold you, to feel you, to need you.
   There's nothing to keep us apart.
   Chorus

You Light Up My Life

Registration 7
Rhythm: Waltz

Words and Music by
Joseph Brooks

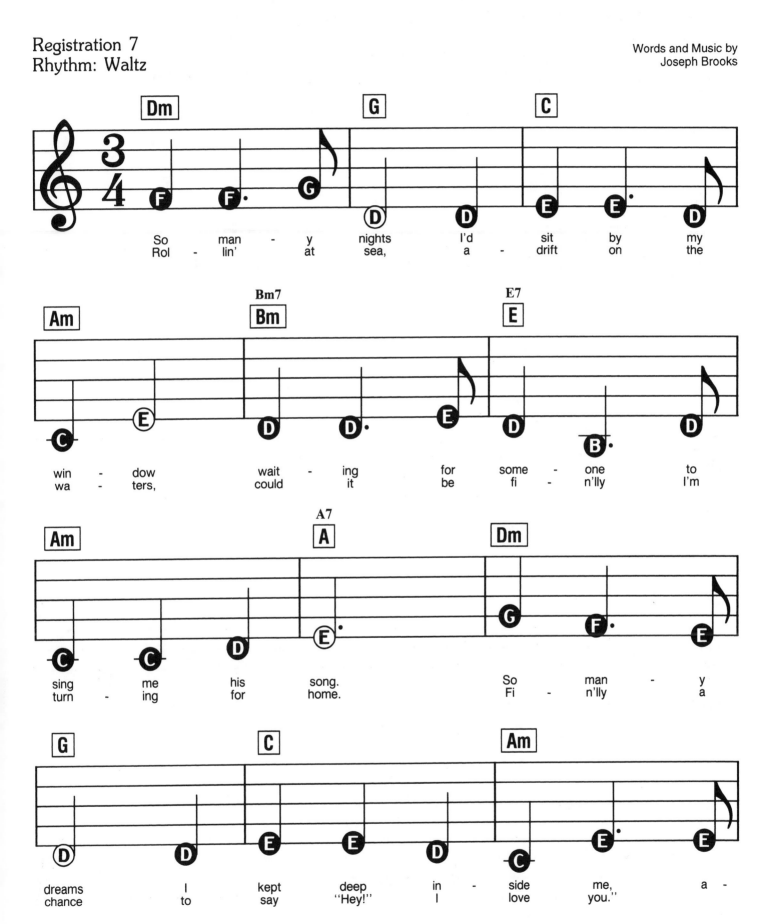

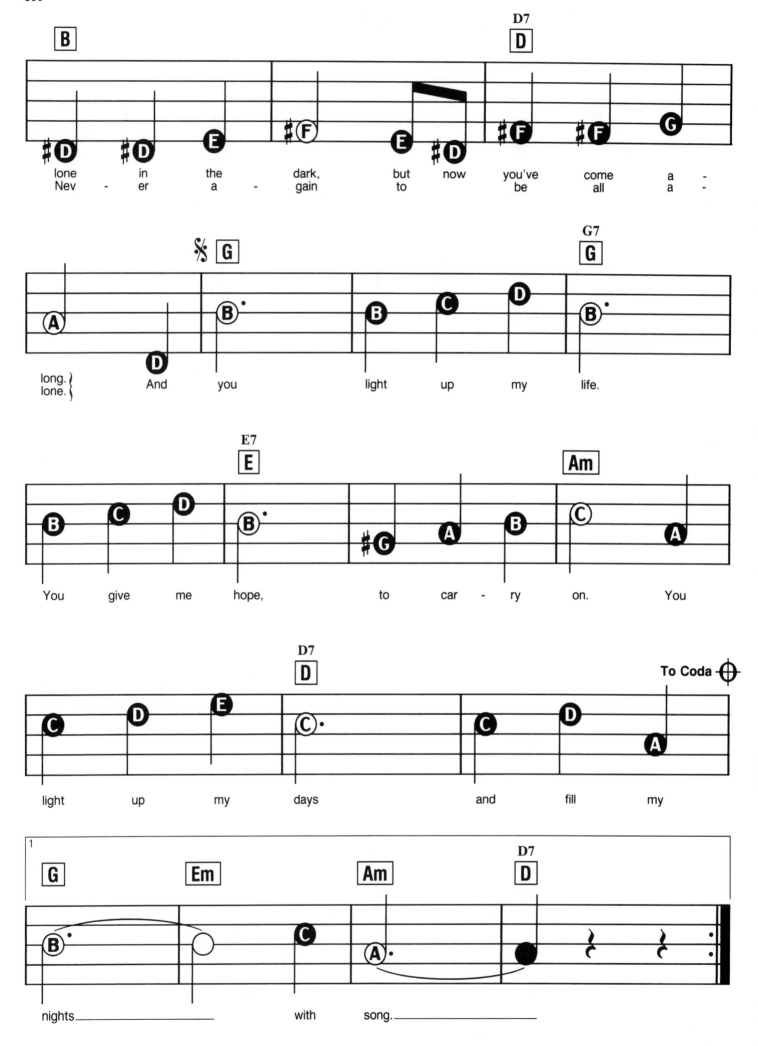

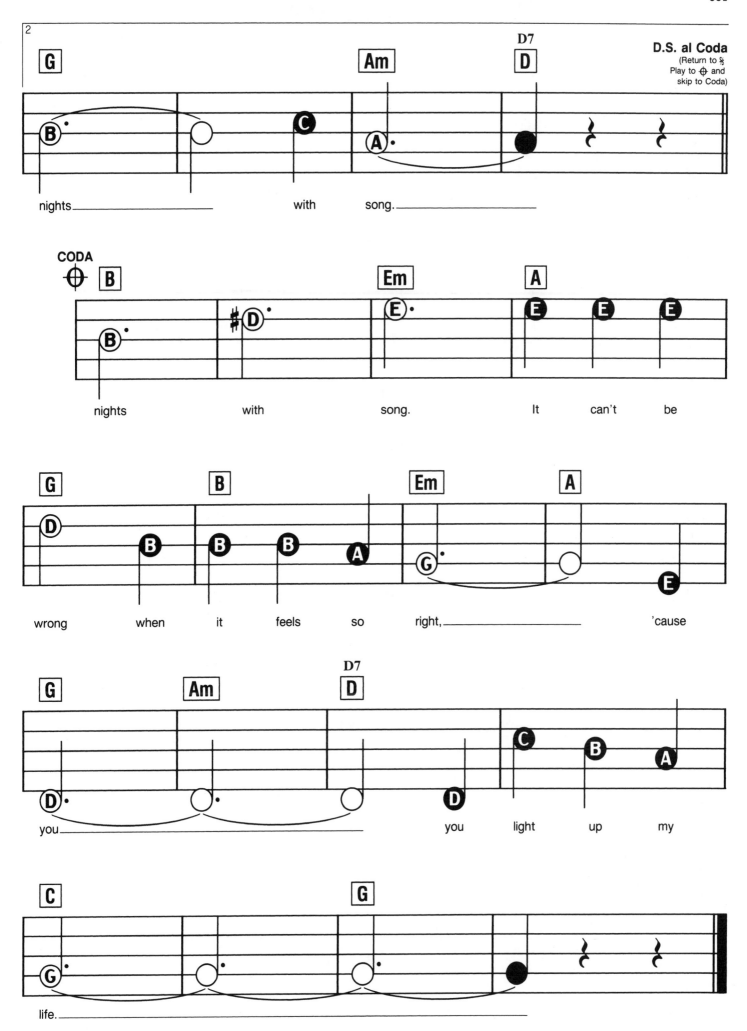

Time in a Bottle

Registration 8
Rhythm: Waltz

Words and Music by
Jim Croce

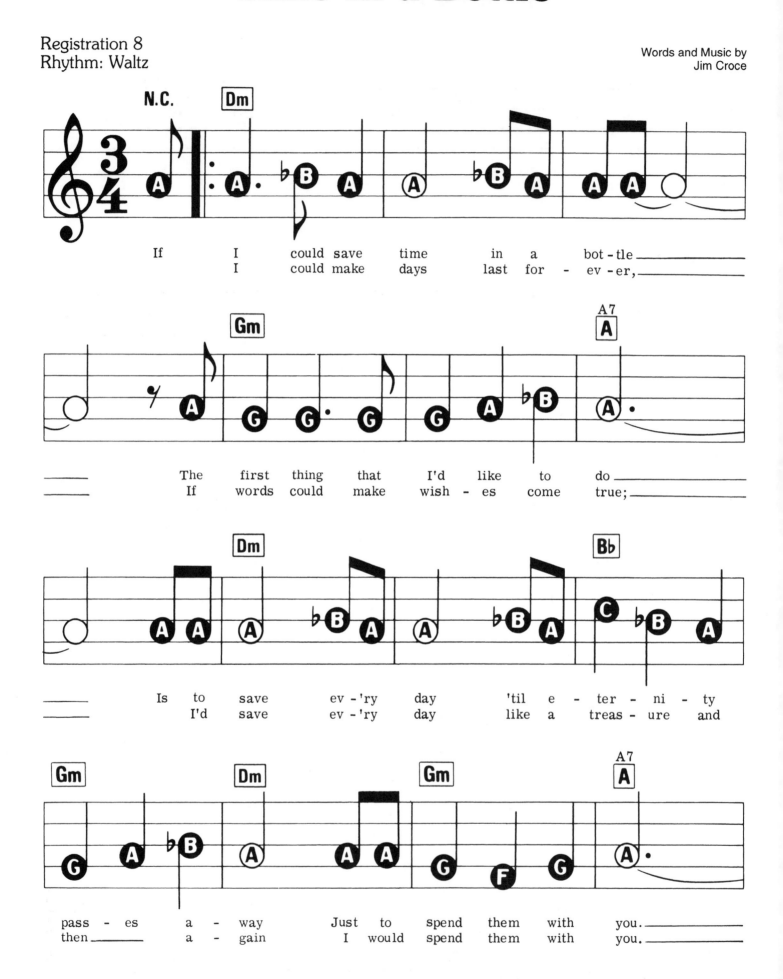

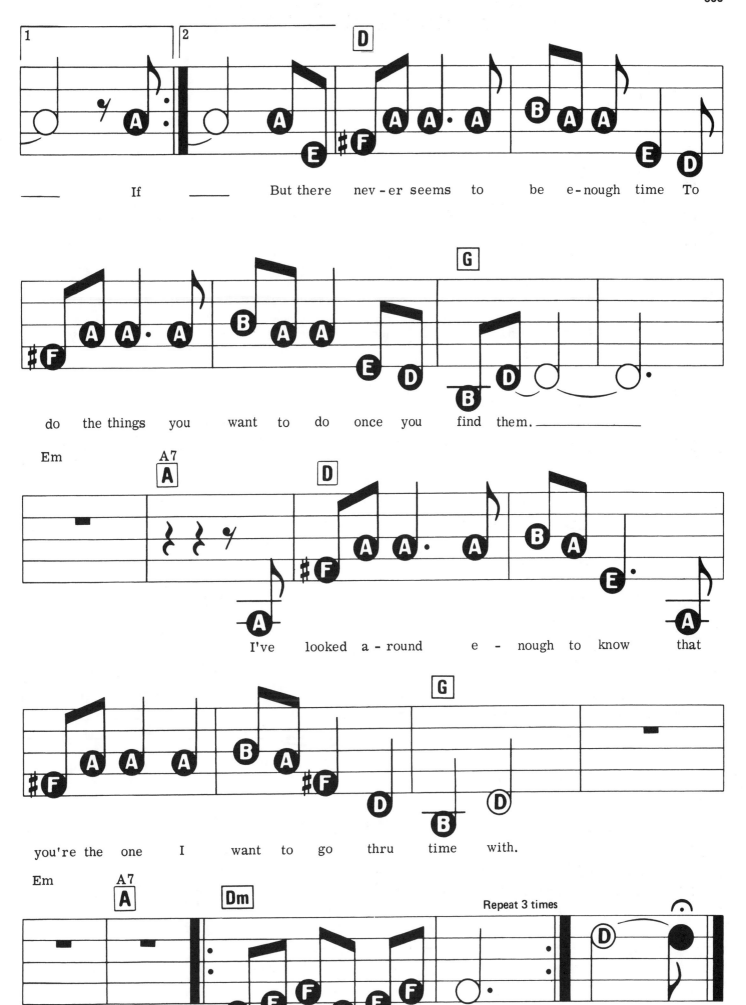

Top of the World

Registration 2
Rhythm: Fox Trot

Words and Music by John Bettis
and Richard Carpenter

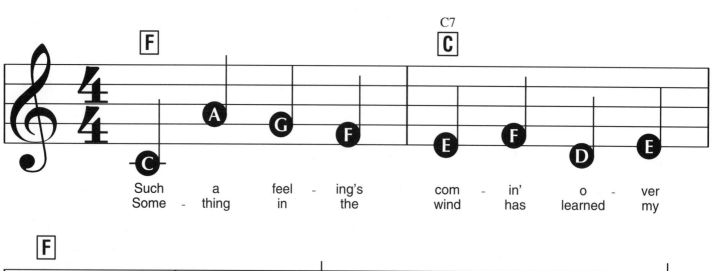

Such a feel - ing's com - in' o - ver
Some - thing in the wind has learned my

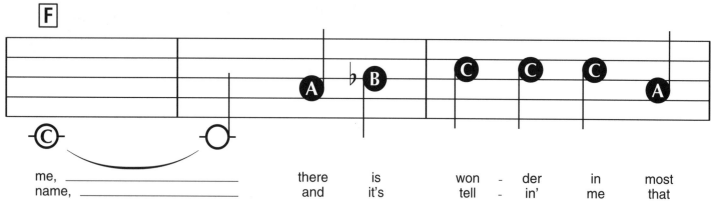

me, _____ there is won - der in most
name, _____ and it's tell - in' me that

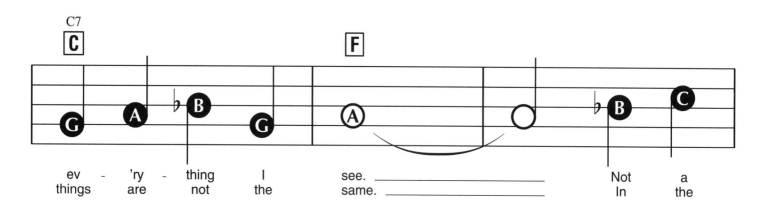

ev - 'ry - thing I see. _____ Not a
things are not the same. _____ In the

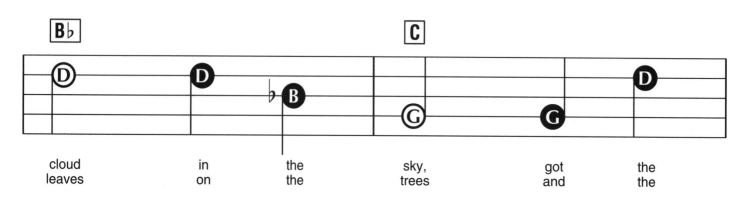

cloud in the sky, got the
leaves on the trees and the

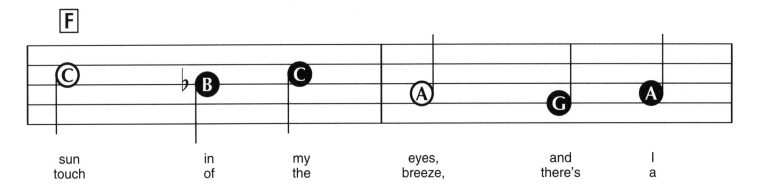

sun in my eyes, and I
touch of the breeze, there's a

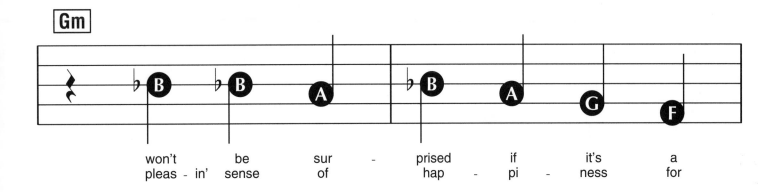

won't be sur - prised if it's a
pleas - in' sense of hap - pi - ness a for

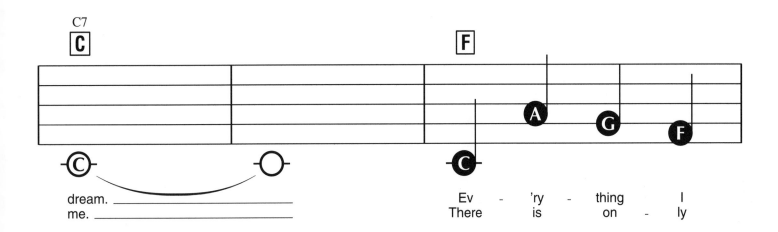

dream. _____
me. _____
Ev - 'ry - thing I
There is on - ly

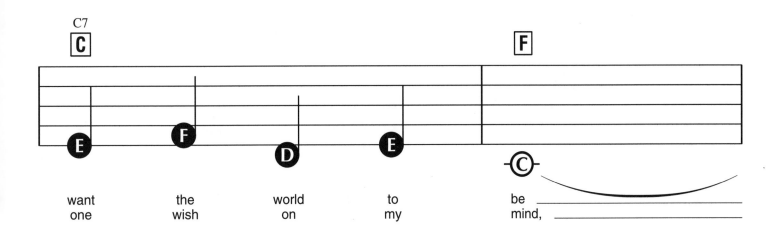

want the world to be _____
one wish on my mind, _____

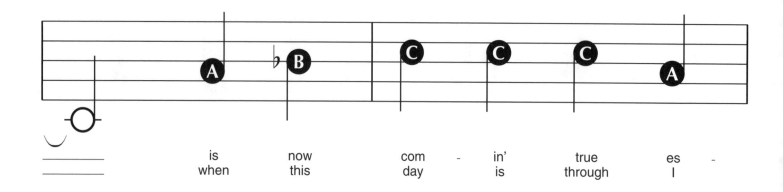

is   now   com   -   in'   true   es   -
when   this   day   is   through   I

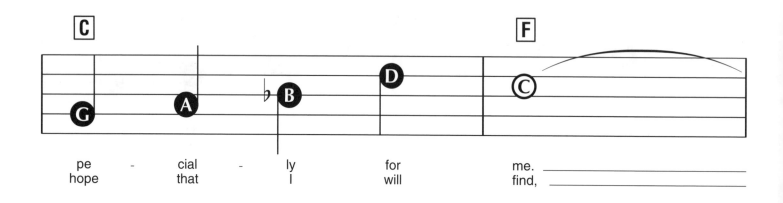

pe   -   cial   -   ly   for   me. _____
hope   that   I   will   find, _____

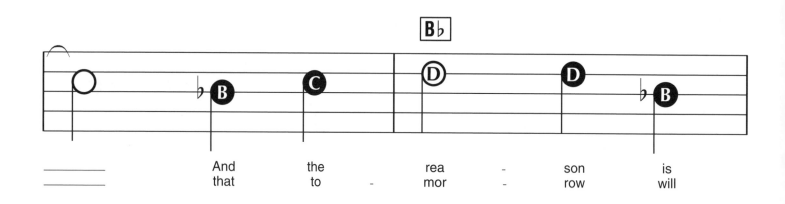

And   the   rea   -   son   is
that   the   to -   mor   -   row   will

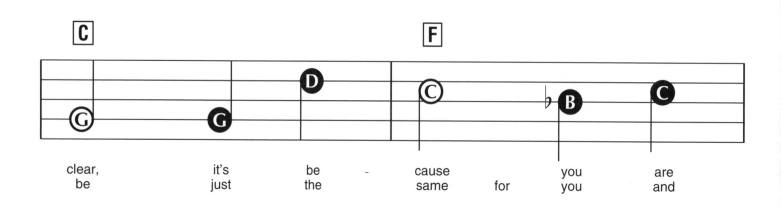

clear,   it's   be   -   cause   you   are
be   just   the   same   for you   and

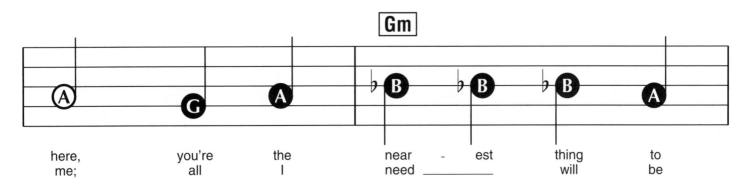

here,   you're   the   near - est   thing   to
me;   all   I   need ____   will   be

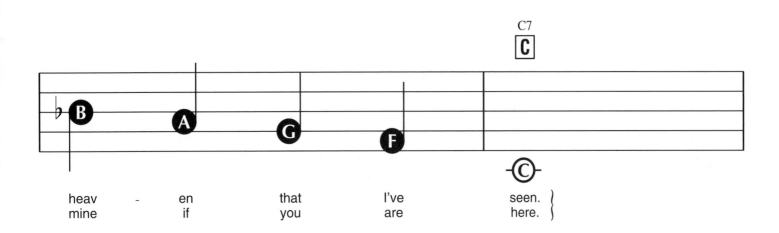

heav - en   that   I've   seen.
mine   if   you   are   here.

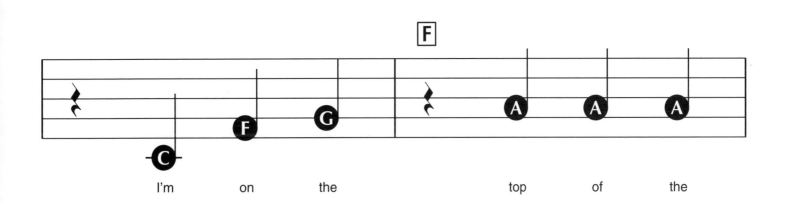

I'm   on   the   top   of   the

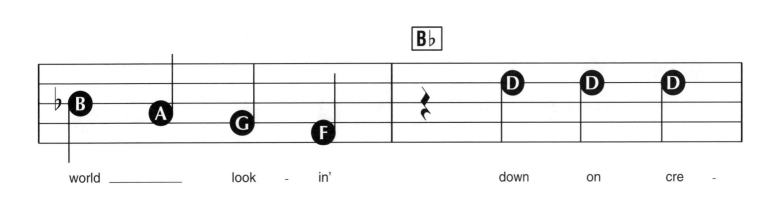

world ____   look - in'   down   on   cre -

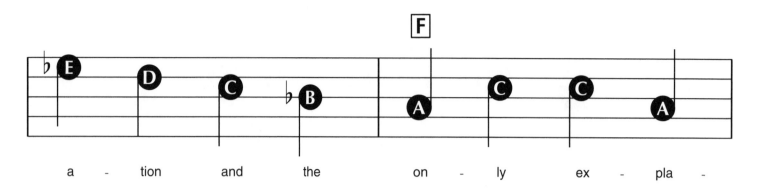

a - tion and the on - ly ex - pla -

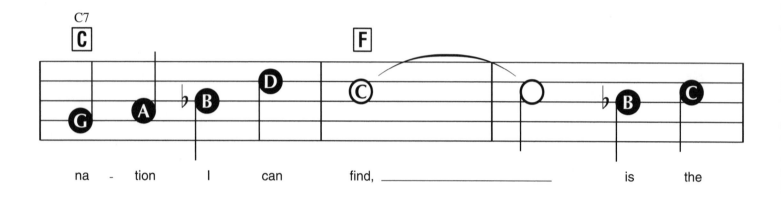

na - tion I can find, _____ is the

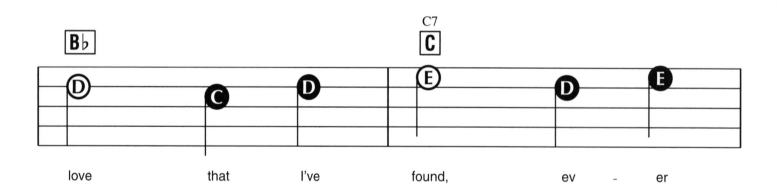

love that I've found, ev - er

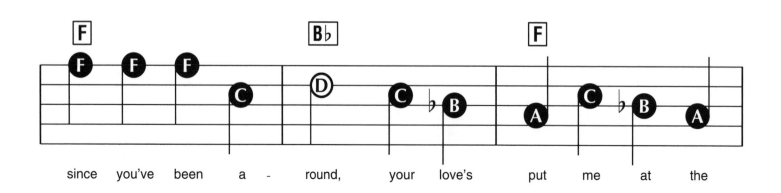

since you've been a - round, your love's put me at the

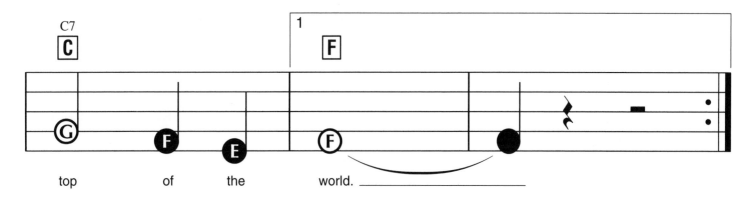

top   of   the   world. _____

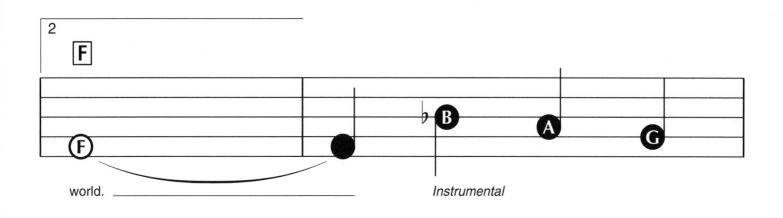

world. _____   *Instrumental*

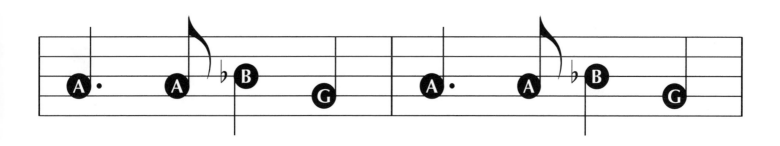

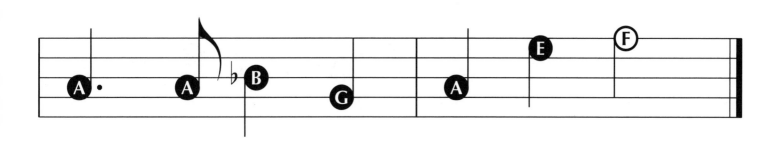

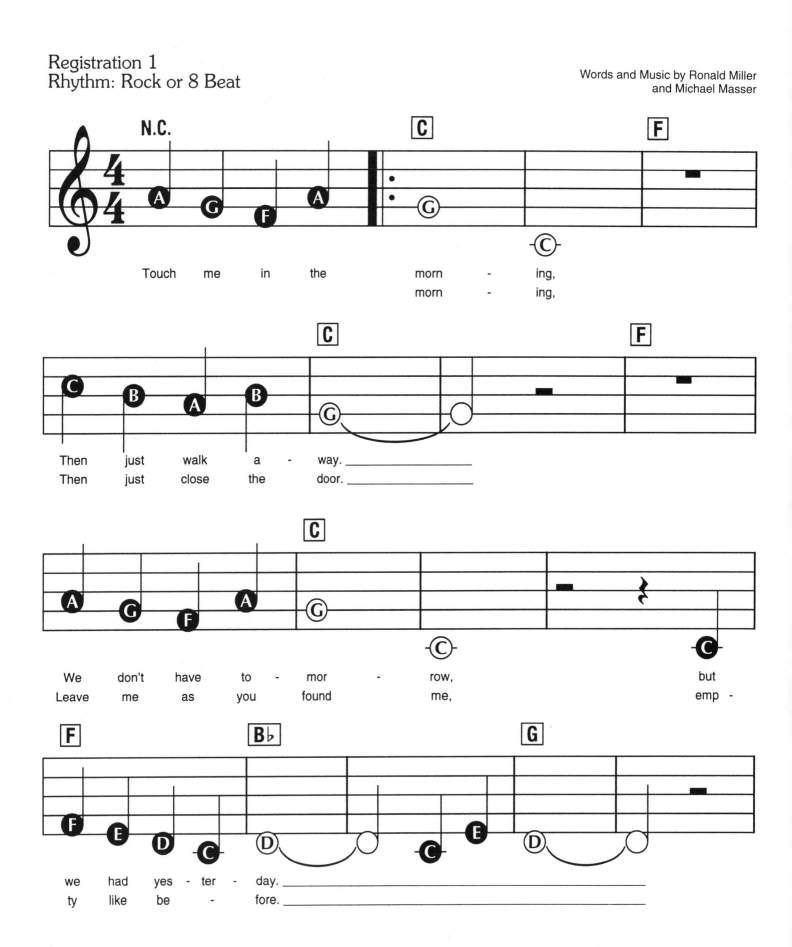

Touch Me in the Morning

310

Registration 1
Rhythm: Rock or 8 Beat

Words and Music by Ronald Miller
and Michael Masser

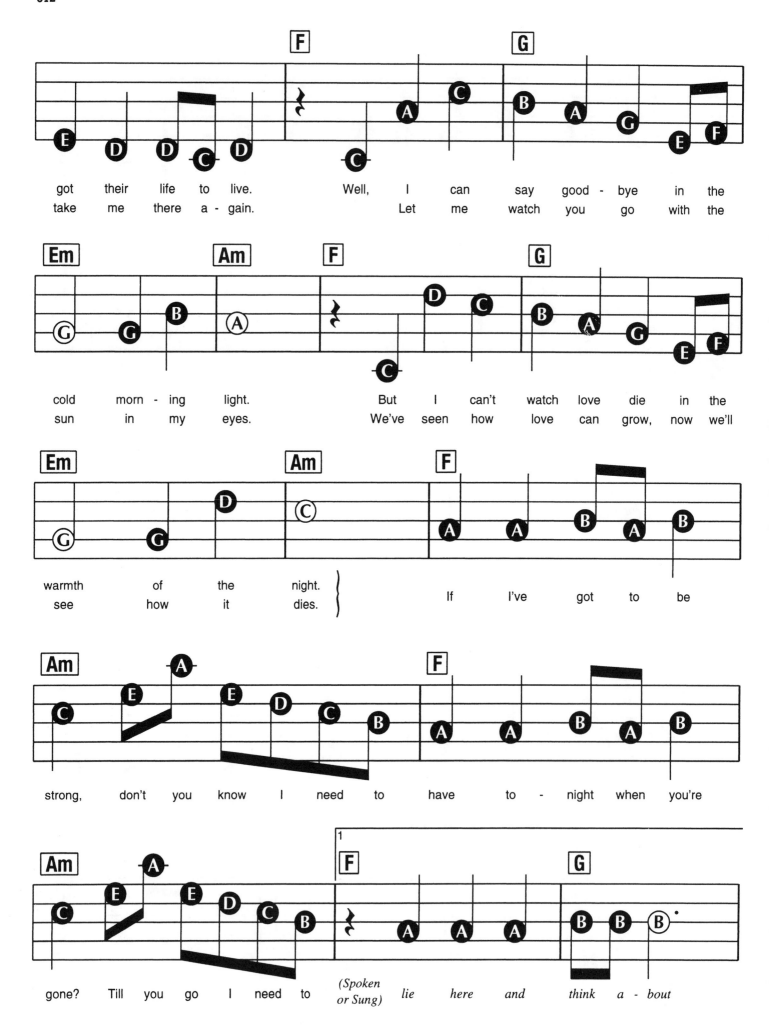

313

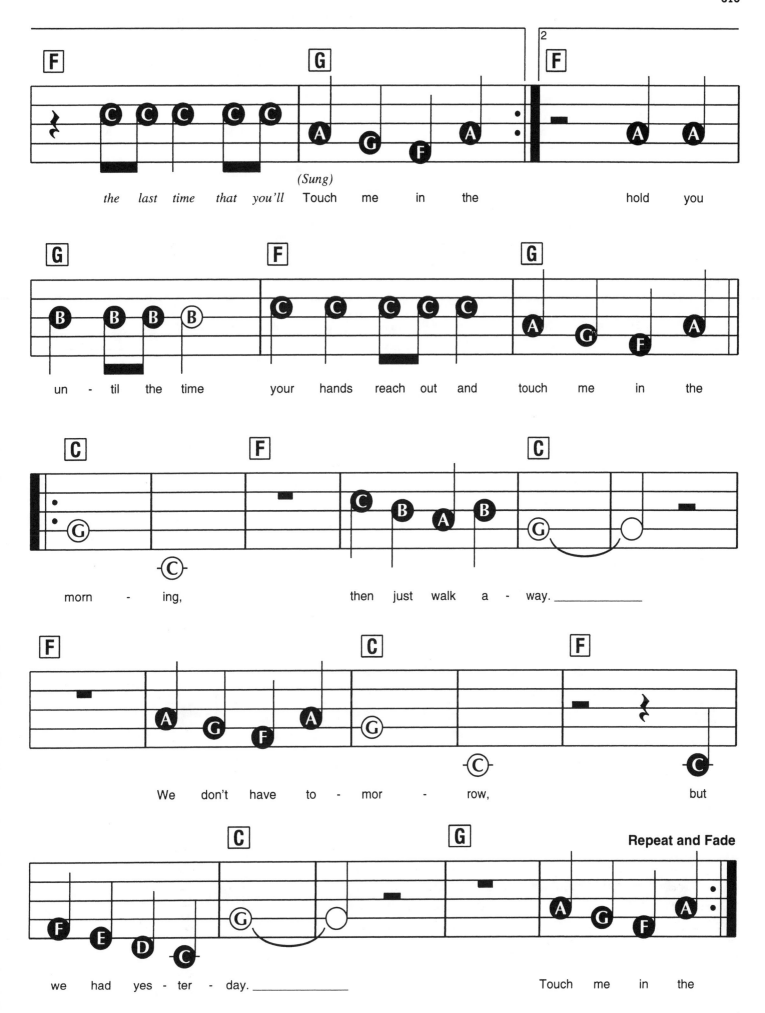

The Way We Were
from the Motion Picture THE WAY WE WERE

Registration 8
Rhythm: Pops or Rock

Words by Alan and Marilyn Bergman
Music by Marvin Hamlisch

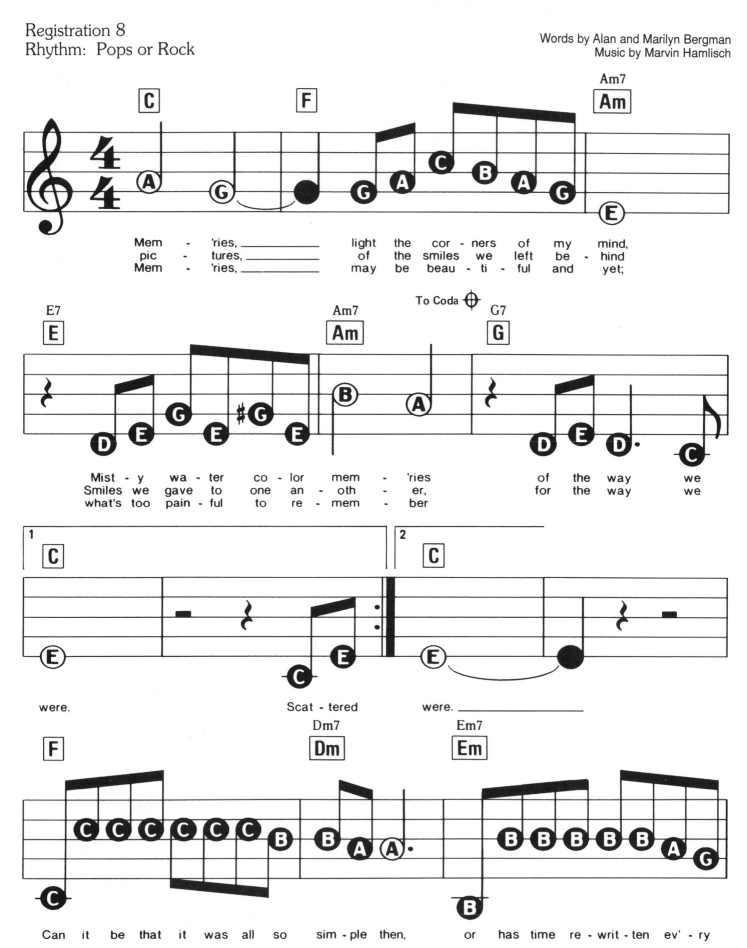

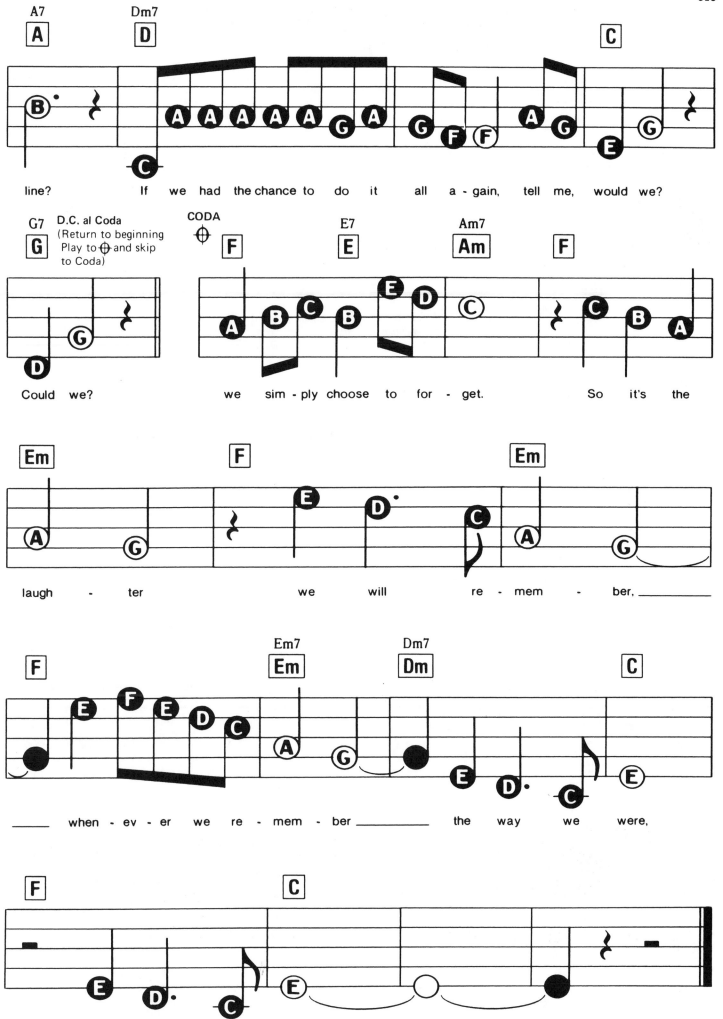

We Are the Champions

Registration 1
Rhythm: Waltz

Words and Music by
Freddie Mercury

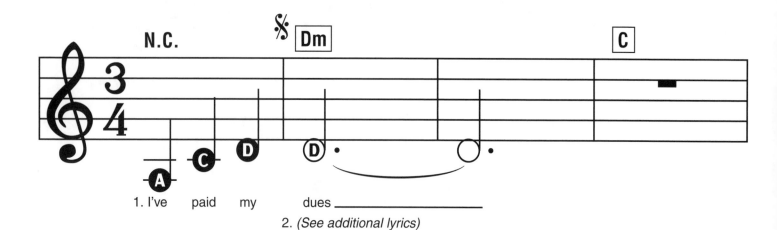

1. I've paid my dues _____

2. *(See additional lyrics)*

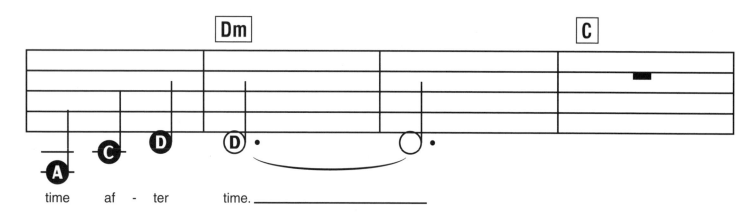

time af - ter time. _____

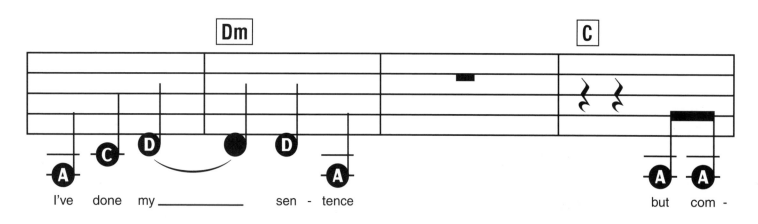

I've done my _____ sen - tence but com -

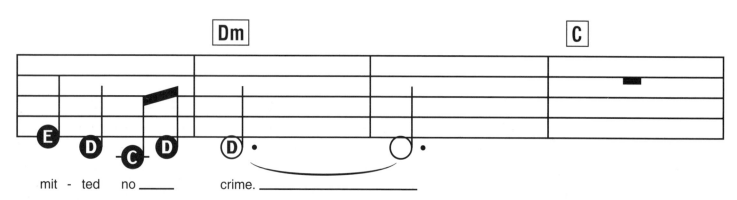

mit - ted no _____ crime. _____

317

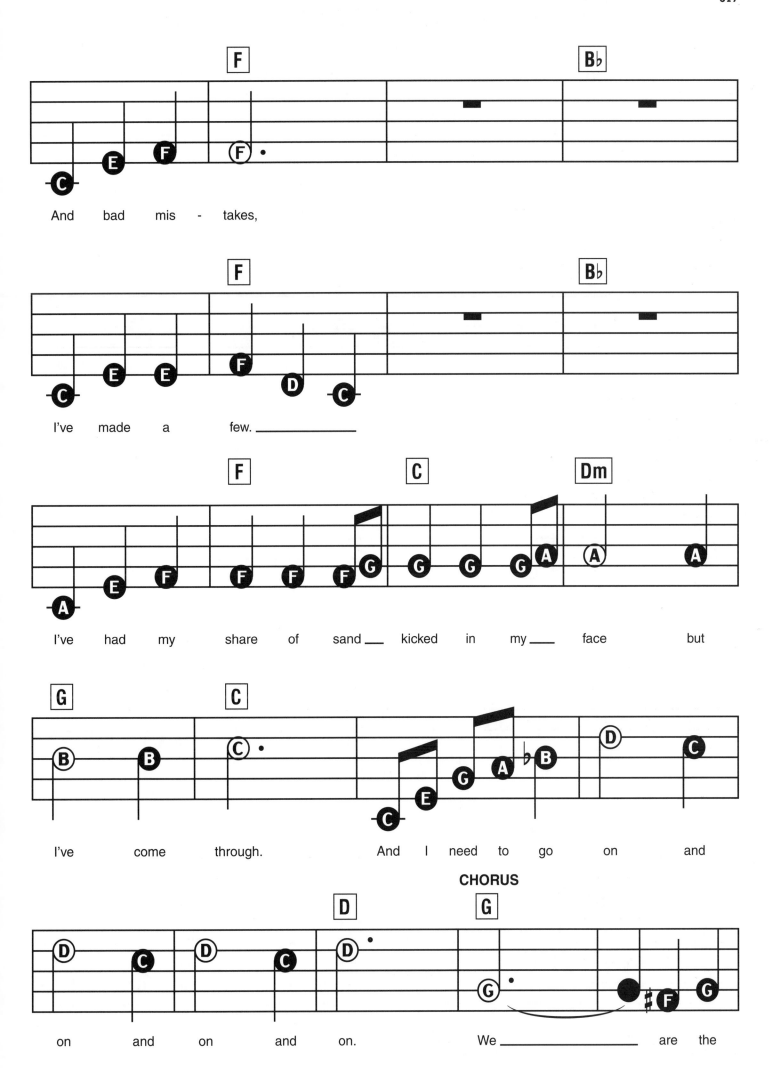

318

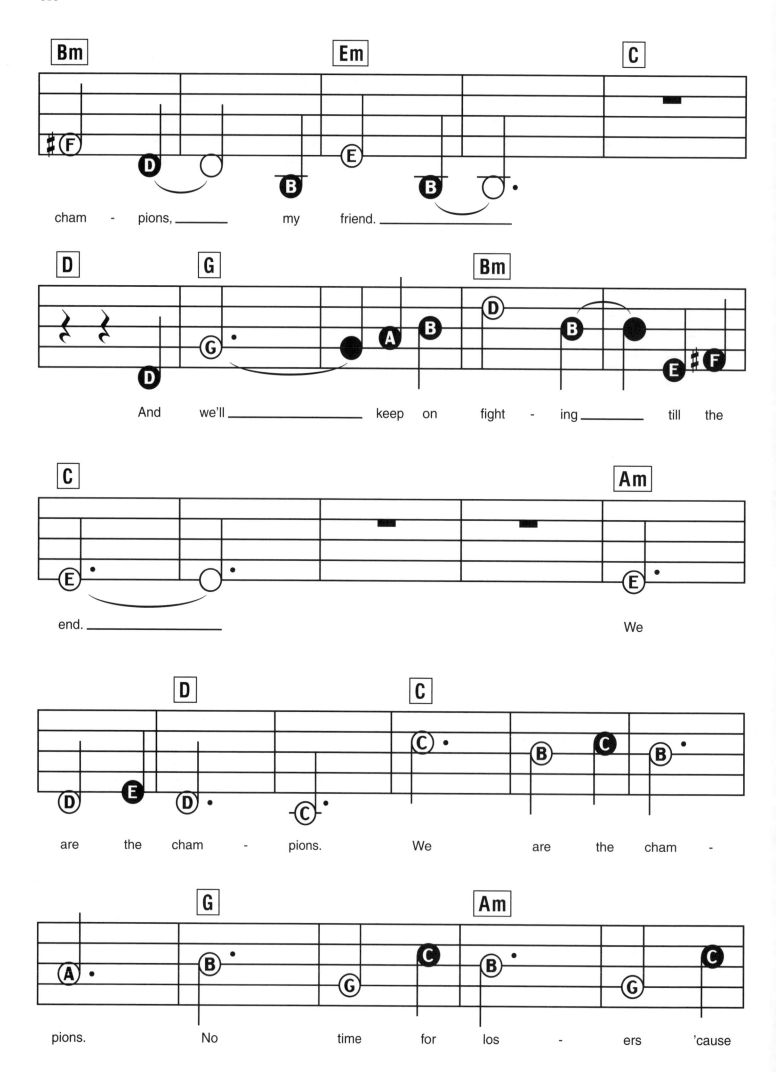

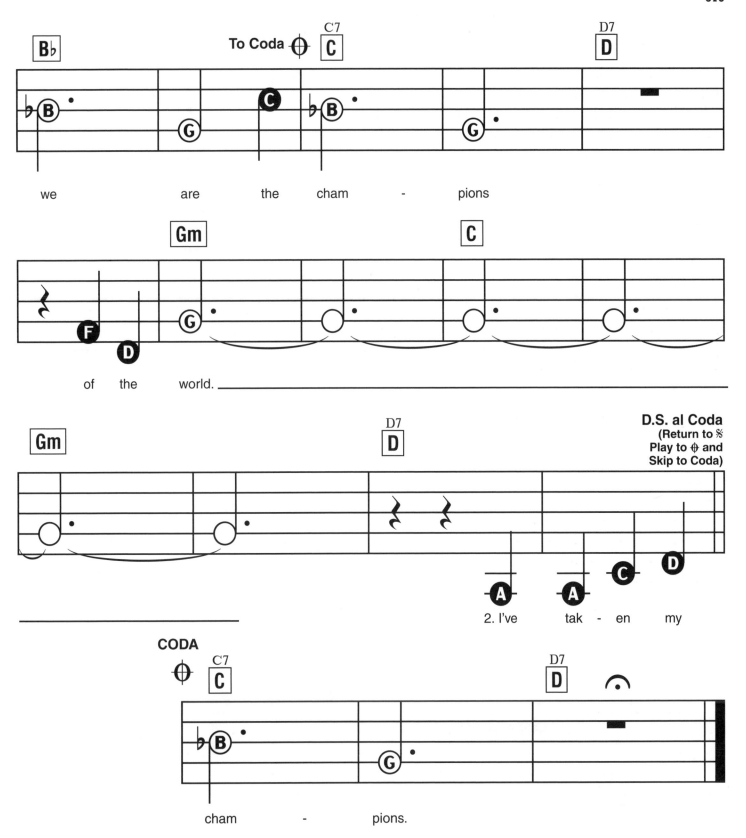

Additional Lyrics

2. I've taken my bows
   And my curtain calls.
   You brought me fame and fortune
   And everything that goes with it.
   I thank you all,
   But it's been no bed of roses,
   No pleasure cruise.
   I consider it a challenge before the whole human race
   And I ain't gonna lose.
   Chorus

What's Going On

Registration 7
Rhythm: Rock or 16 - Beat

Words and Music by Marvin Gaye,
Al Cleveland and Renaldo Benson

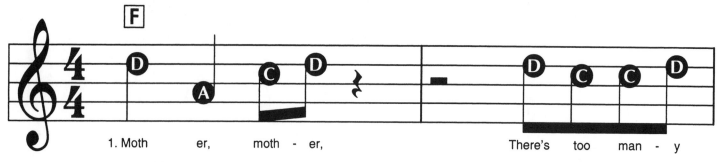

1. Moth - er, moth - er,   There's too man - y

2., 3. *See additional lyrics*

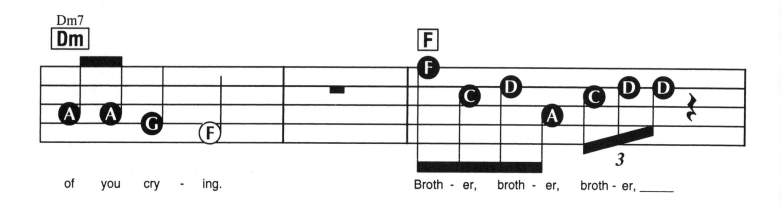

of you cry - ing.   Broth - er, broth - er, broth - er, _____

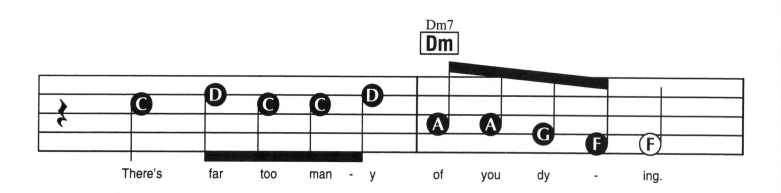

There's   far   too   man - y   of   you   dy - ing.

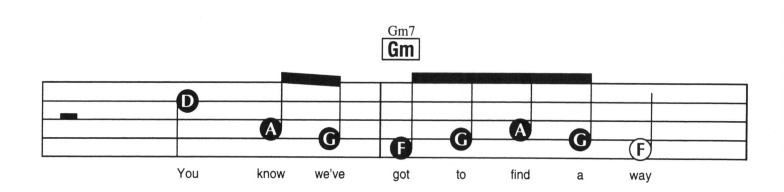

You   know   we've   got   to   find   a   way

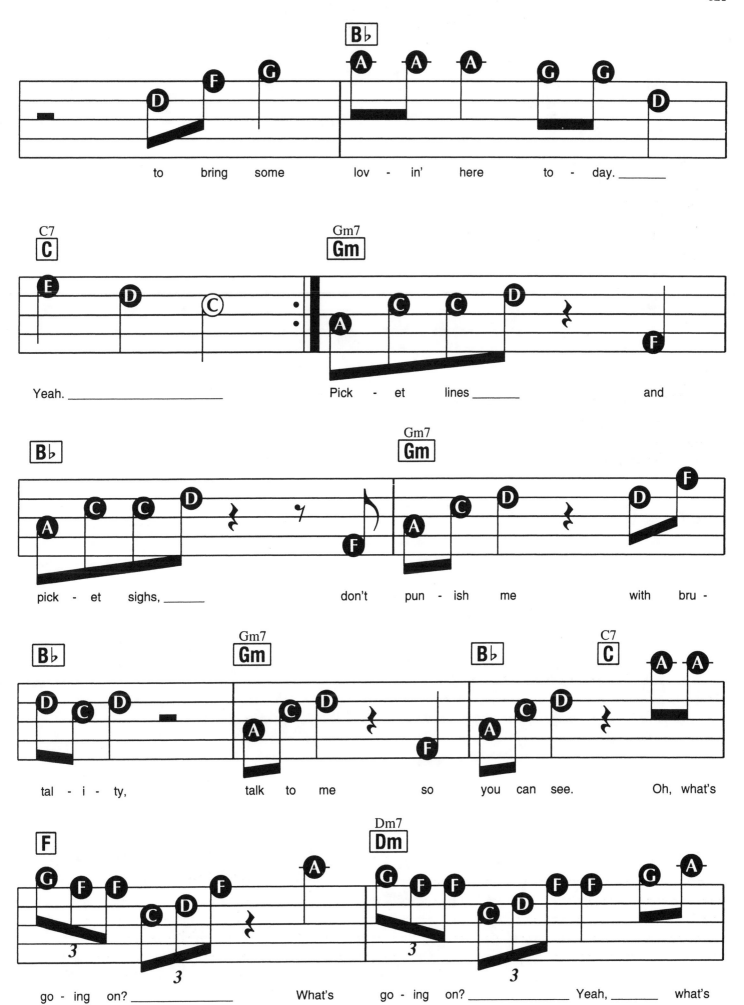

322

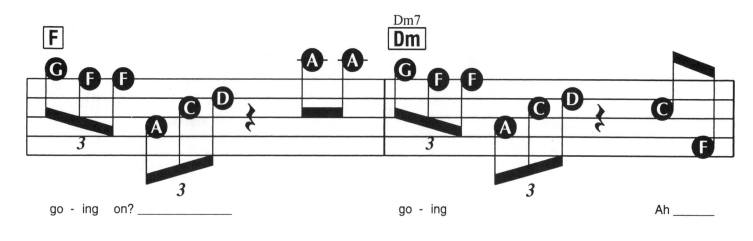

go - ing on? _____ go - ing Ah _____

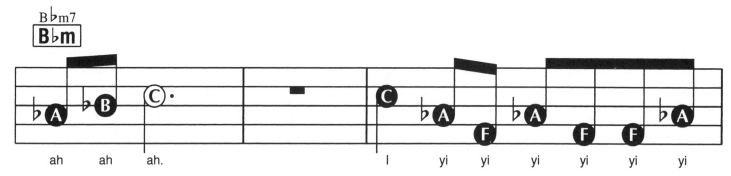

ah ah ah. I yi yi yi yi yi yi

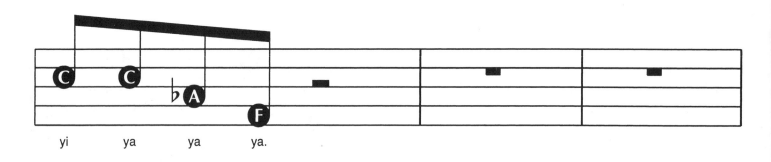

yi ya ya ya.

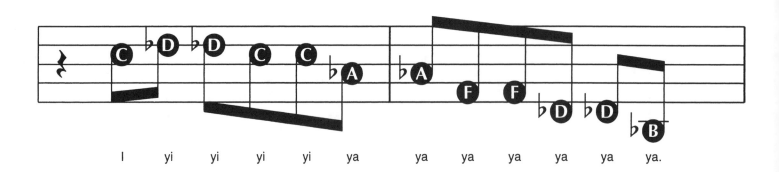

I yi yi yi yi ya ya ya ya ya ya ya.

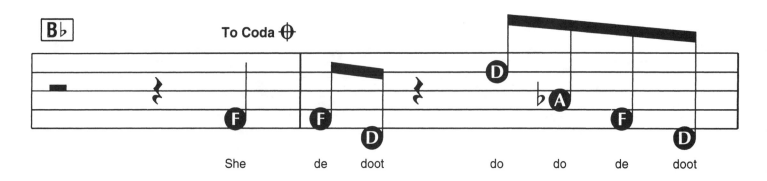

She de doot do do de doot

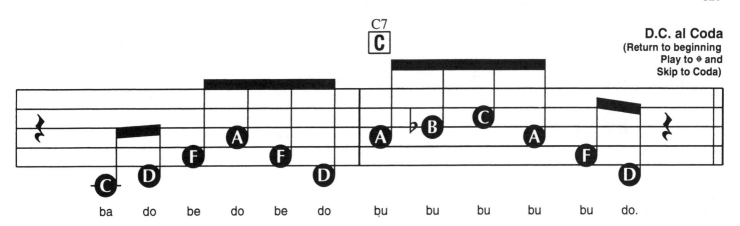

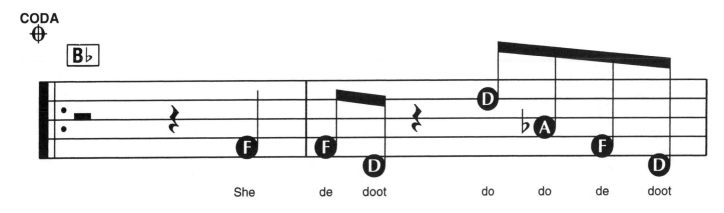

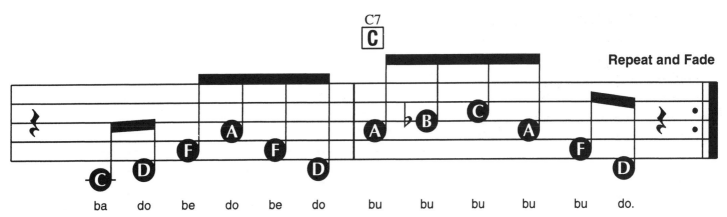

Additional Lyrics

2. Father, father, we don't need to escalate,
You see, war is not the answer, for only love can conquer hate.
You know we've got to find a way to bring some lovin' here today. *(Chorus)*

3. Father, father, everybody thinks we're wrong.
Oh but, who are they to judge us simply because our hair is long?
Oh, you know we've got to find a way bring some understanding here today. *(Chorus)*

When I Need You

Registration 9
Rhythm: Waltz

Words by Carole Bayer Sager
Music by Albert Hammond

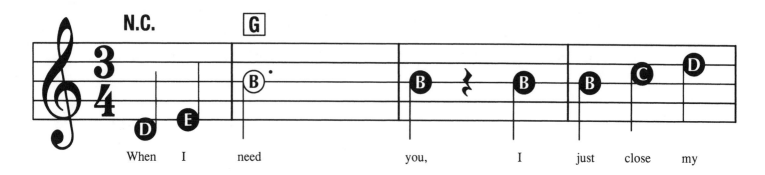

When I need you, I just close my

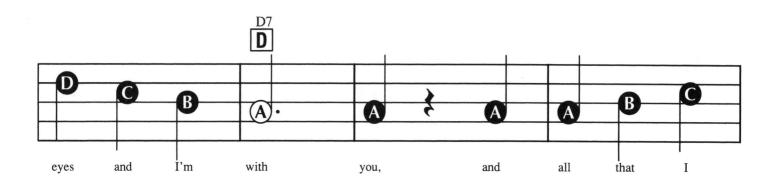

eyes and I'm with you, and all that I

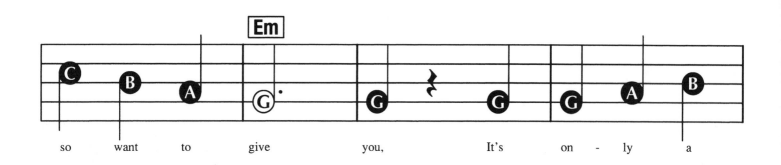

so want to give you, It's on - ly a

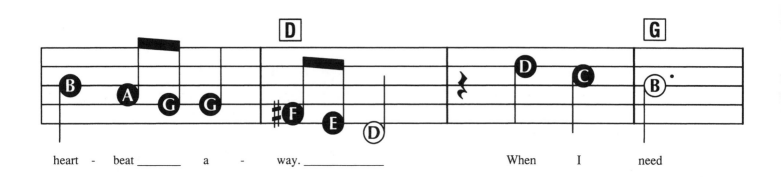

heart - beat _____ a - way. _____ When I need

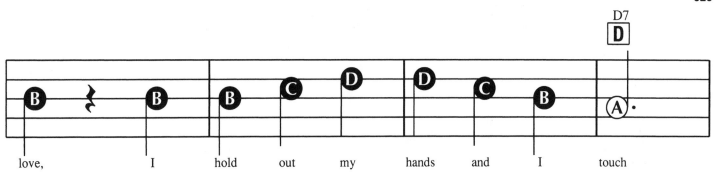

love,   I   hold   out   my   hands   and   I   touch

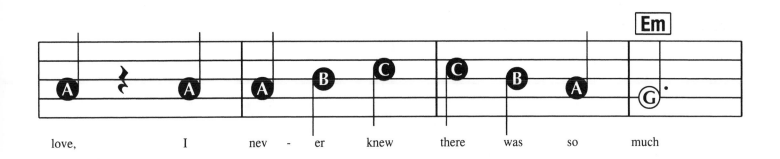

love,   I   nev - er   knew   there   was   so   much

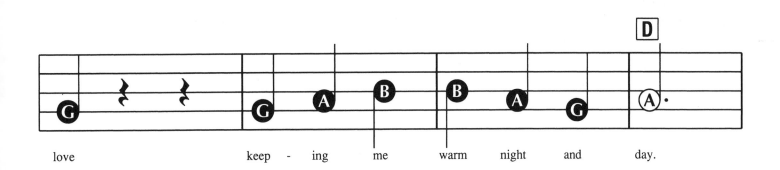

love   keep - ing   me   warm   night   and   day.

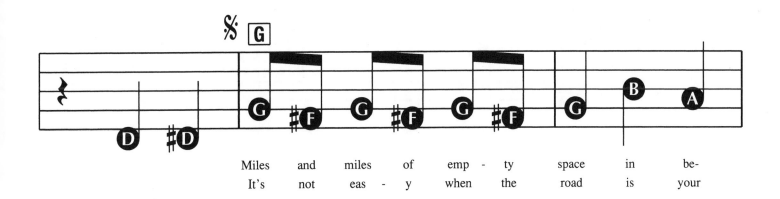

Miles   and   miles   of   emp - ty   space   in   be-you
It's   not   eas - y   when   the   space   road   is   your

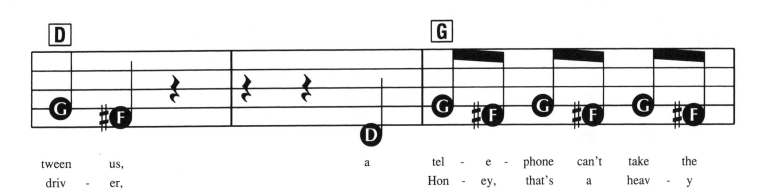

tween   us,   a   tel - e - phone can't   take   the
driv - er,   Hon - ey,   that's   a   heav - y

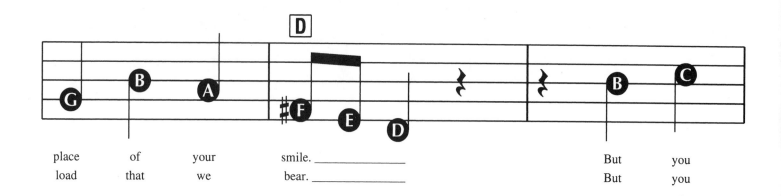

place   of   your   smile. _____   But   you
load   that   we   bear. _____   But   you

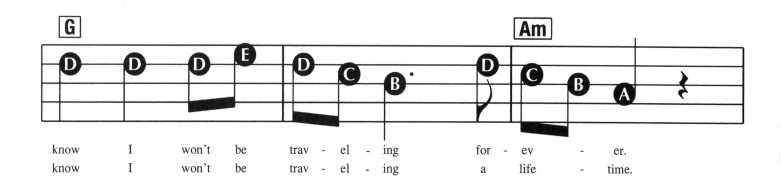

know   I   won't   be   trav - el - ing   for - ev - er.
know   I   won't   be   trav - el - ing   a   life - time.

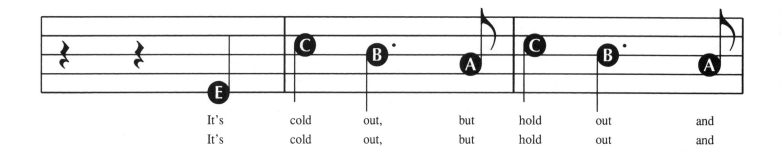

It's   cold   out,   but   hold   out   and
It's   cold   out,   but   hold   out   and

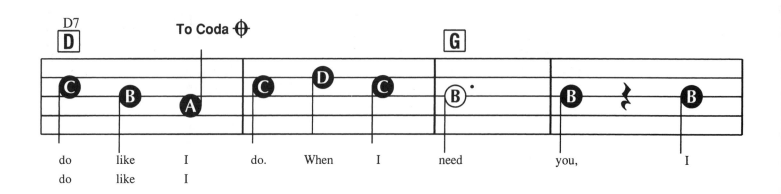

do   like   I   do.   When   I   need   you,   I
do   like   I

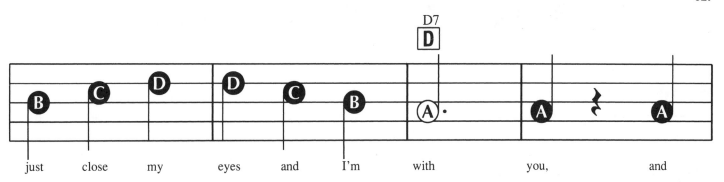

just close my eyes and I'm with you, and

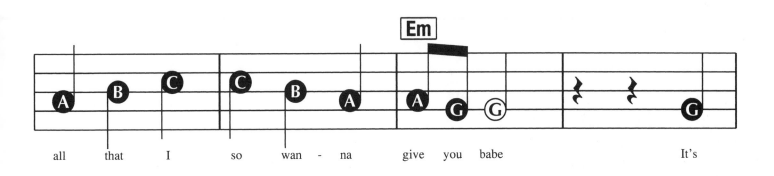

all that I so wan - na give you babe It's

D.S. al Coda
(Return to %
Play to ⊕ and
Skip to Coda)

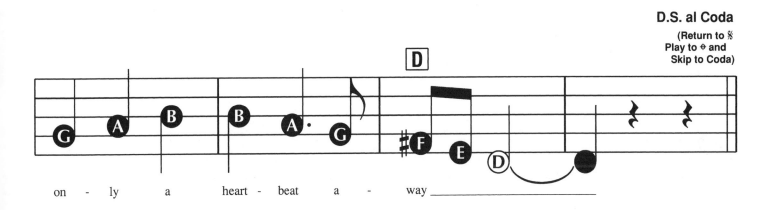

on - ly a heart - beat a - way _____

CODA

Repeat and Fade

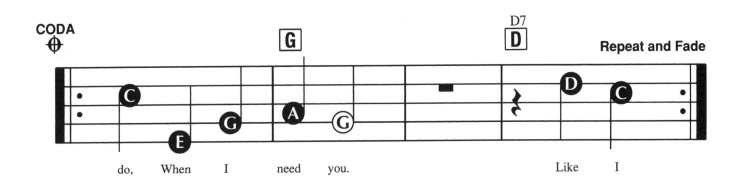

do, When I need you. Like I

Yesterday Once More

Registration 1
Rhythm: Pop or Rock

Words and Music by John Bettis
and Richard Carpenter

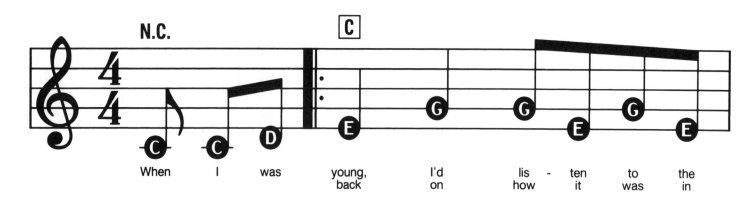

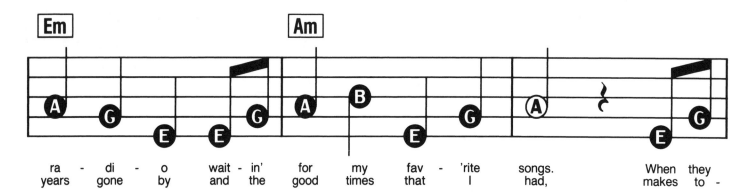

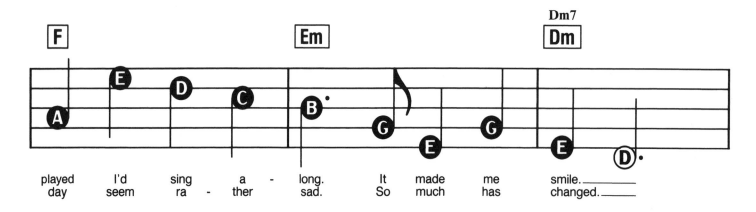

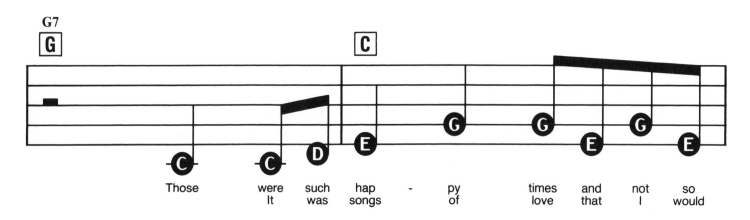

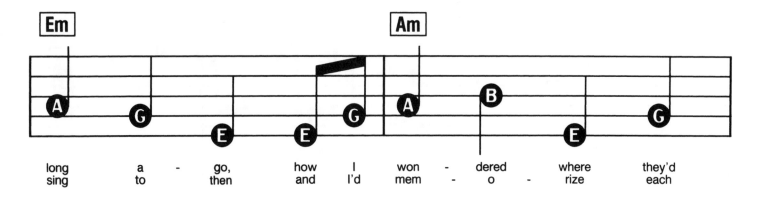

long a - go, how I won - dered where they'd
sing to then and I'd mem - o - rize each

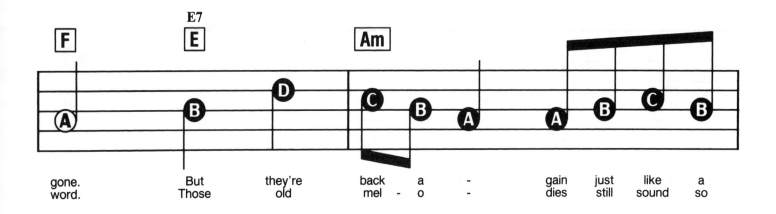

gone. But they're back a - gain just like a
word. Those old mel - o - dies still sound so

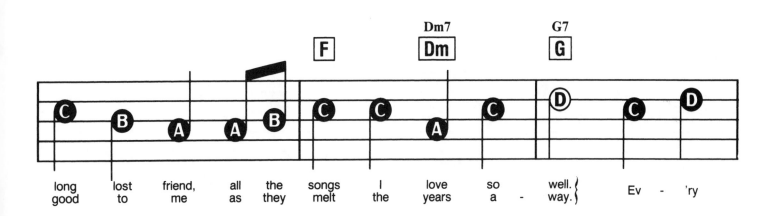

long lost friend, all the songs I love so well. Ev - 'ry
good to me, as they melt the years a - way.

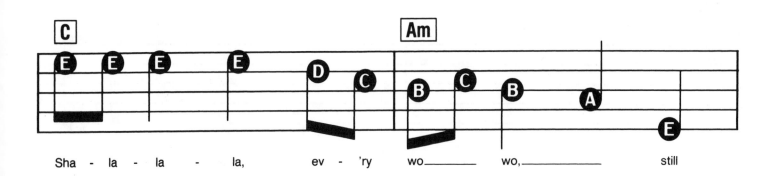

Sha - la - la - la, ev - 'ry wo_____ wo,_____ still

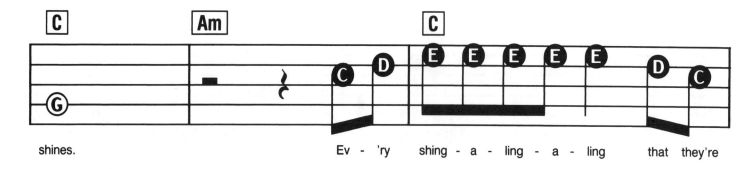

shines.   Ev - 'ry shing - a - ling - a - ling   that they're

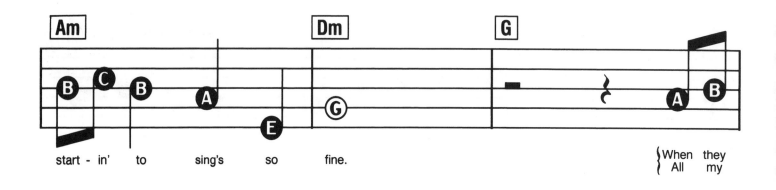

start - in' to sing's so fine.   { When they
                                                       { All   my

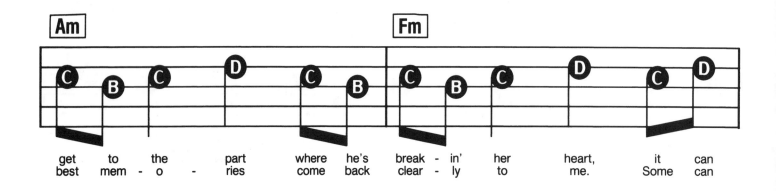

get   to the   part   where he's break - in' her   heart,   it can
best mem - o -   ries   come back clear - ly   to   me.   Some can

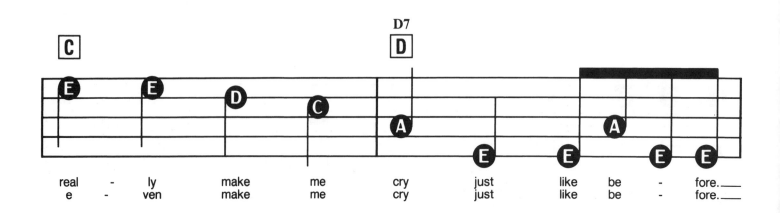

real - ly   make me   cry   just   like be - fore.___
e - ven   make me   cry   just   like be - fore.___

You Are the Sunshine of My Life

Registration 7
Rhythm: 8 Beat or Bossa Nova

Words and Music by
Stevie Wonder

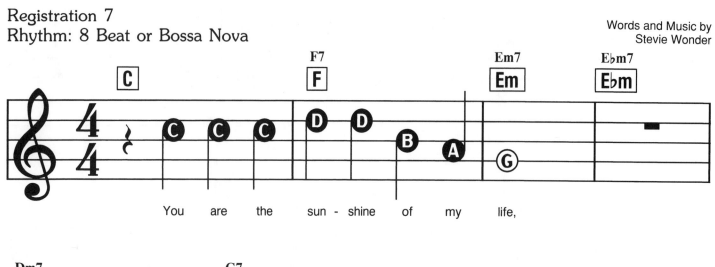

You are the sun - shine of my life,

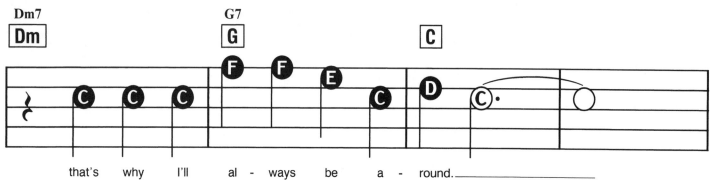

that's why I'll al - ways be a - round.____

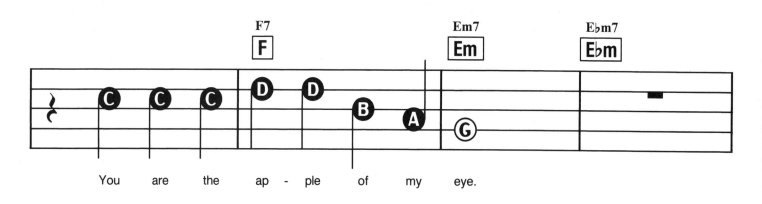

You are the ap - ple of my eye.

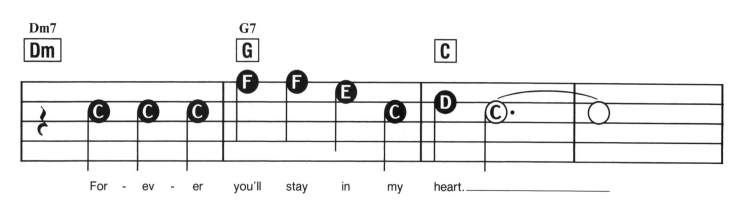

For - ev - er you'll stay in my heart.____

333

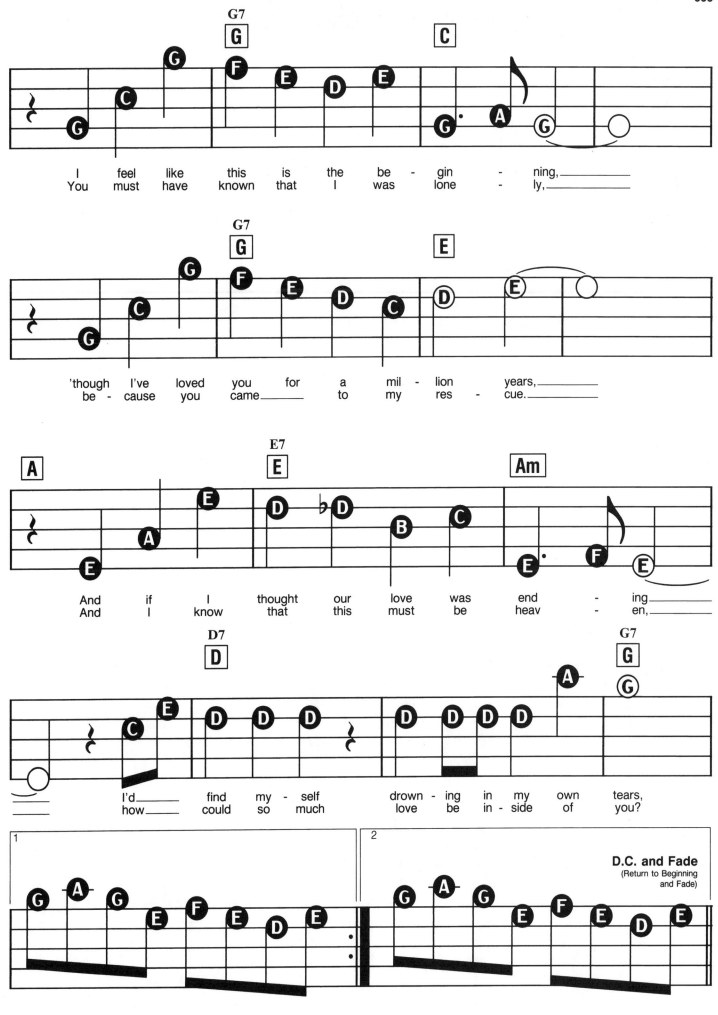

You're So Vain

Registration 2
Rhythm: Rock or 8 Beat

Words and Music by
Carly Simon

335

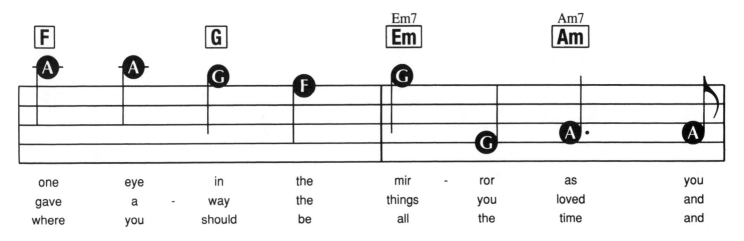

one eye in the mir - ror as you
gave a - way the things you loved and
where you should be all the time and

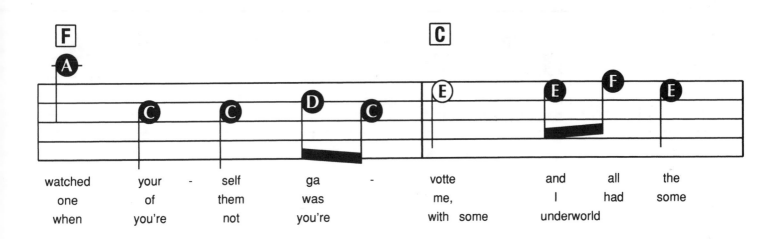

watched your - self ga - votte and all the
one of them was me, I had the some
when you're not you're with some underworld

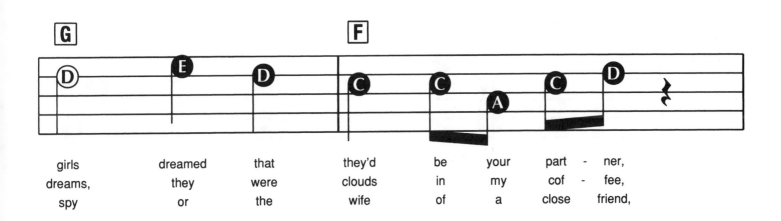

girls dreamed that they'd be your part - ner,
dreams, they were clouds in my cof - fee,
spy or the wife of a close friend,

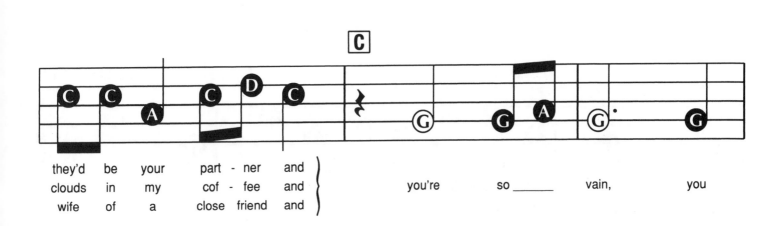

they'd be your part - ner and
clouds in my cof - fee and
wife of a close friend and

you're so ____ vain, you

336

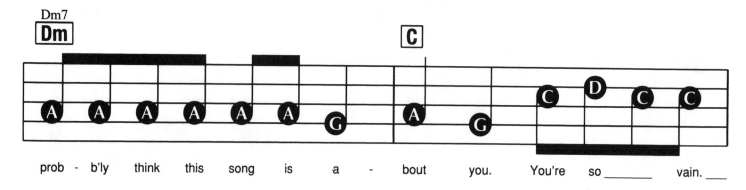

prob - b'ly think this song is a - bout you. You're so _____ vain. ___

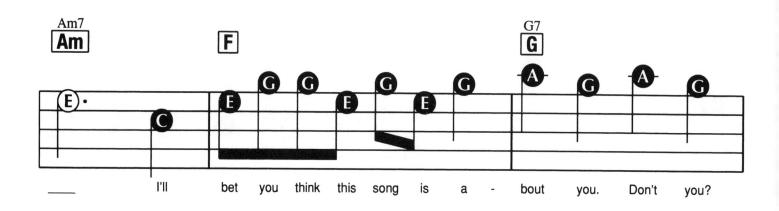

___ I'll bet you think this song is a - bout you. Don't you?

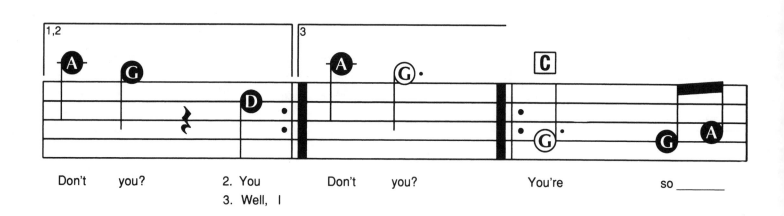

Don't you? 2. You Don't you? You're so _____
3. Well, I

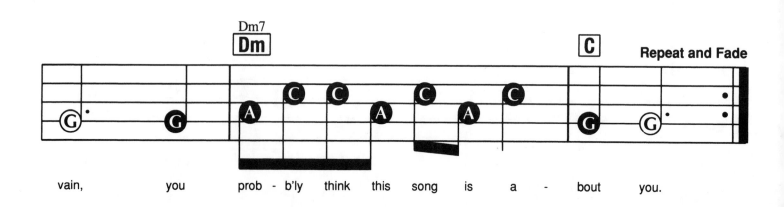

vain, you prob - b'ly think this song is a - bout you.

You've Got a Friend

Registration 3
Rhythm: Slow Rock or Ballad

Words and Music by
Carole King

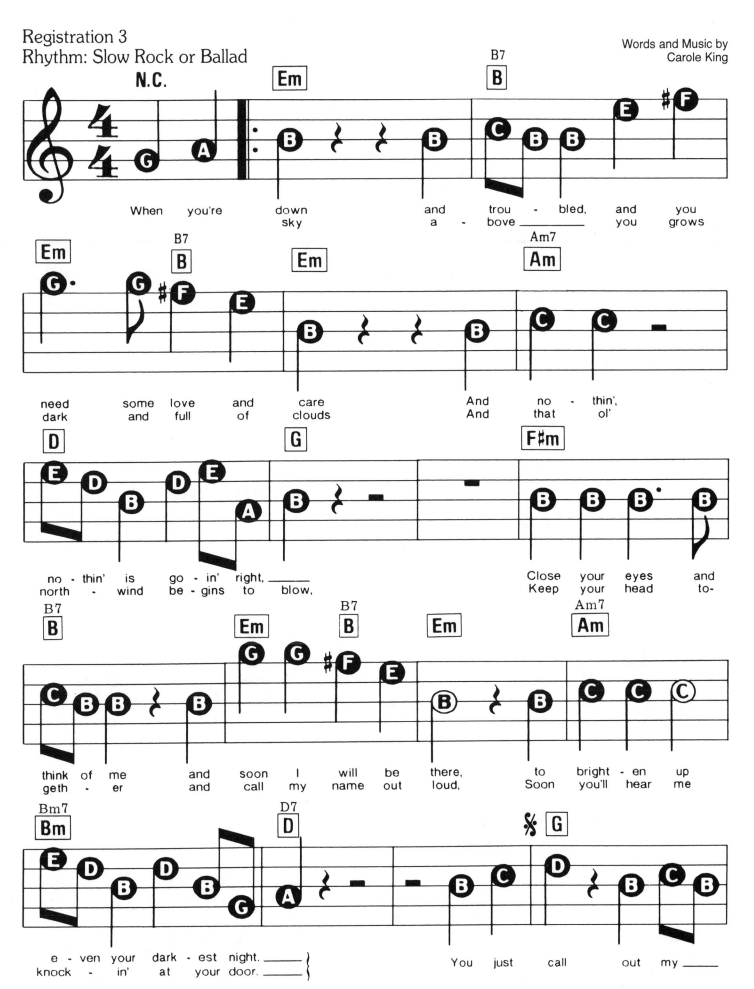

338

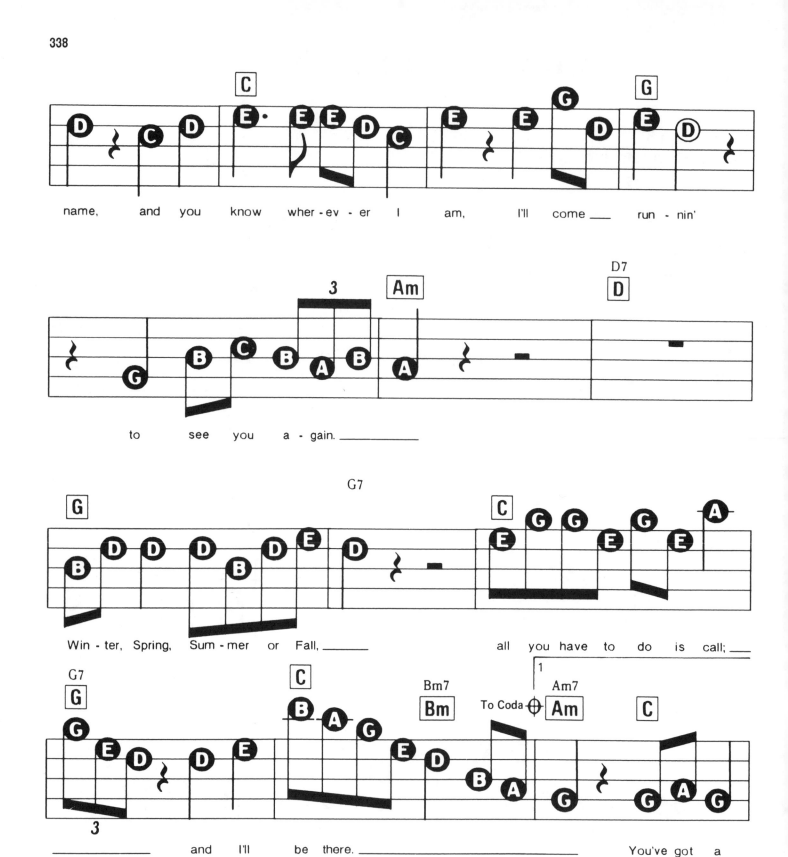

name, and you know wher-ev-er I am, I'll come ___ run-nin'

to see you a-gain. ___

Win-ter, Spring, Sum-mer or Fall, ___ all you have to do is call; ___

___ and I'll be there. ___ You've got a

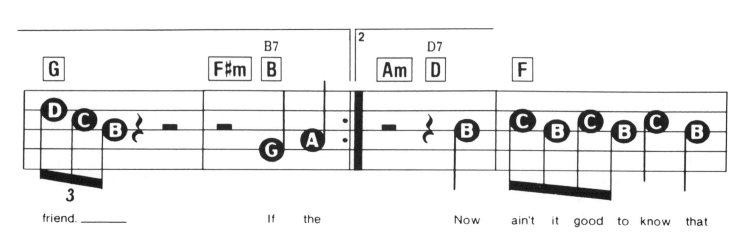

friend. ___ If the Now ain't it good to know that

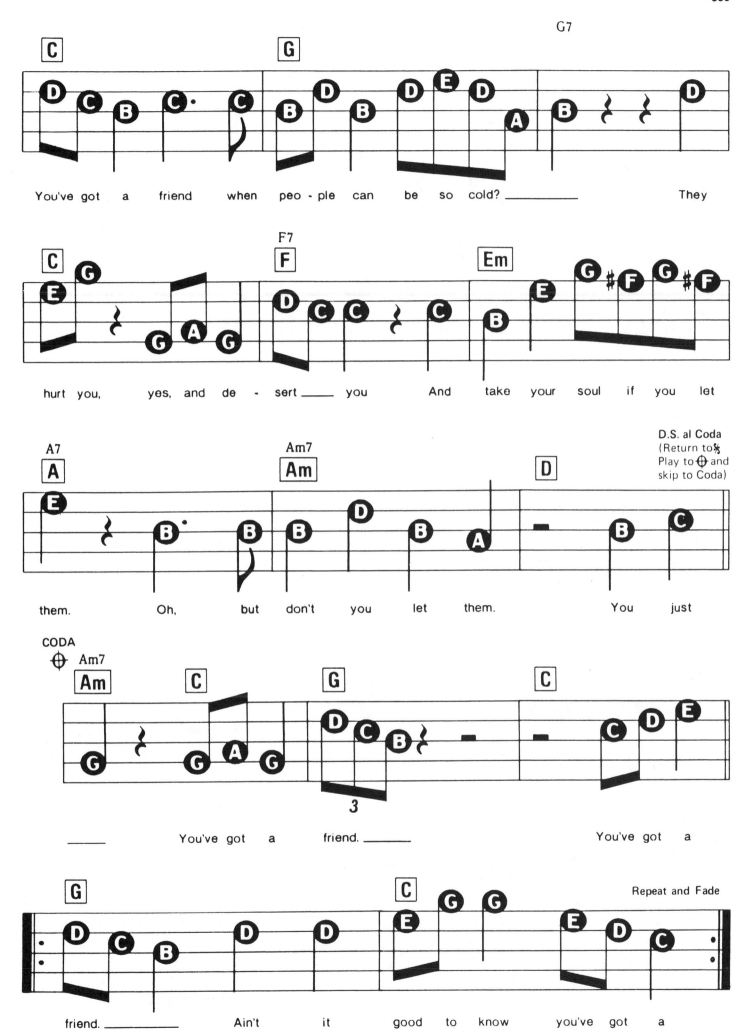

Your Song

Registration 3
Rhythm: Rock or Jazz Rock

Words and Music by Elton John
and Bernie Taupin

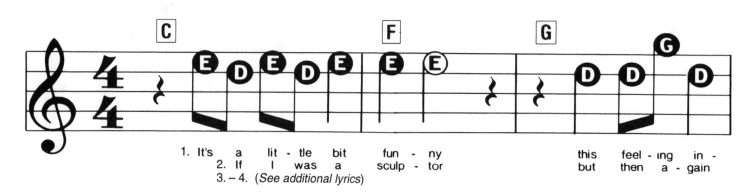

1. It's a lit - tle bit fun - ny   this feel - ing in -
2. If I was a sculp - tor   but then a - gain
3. - 4. (See additional lyrics)

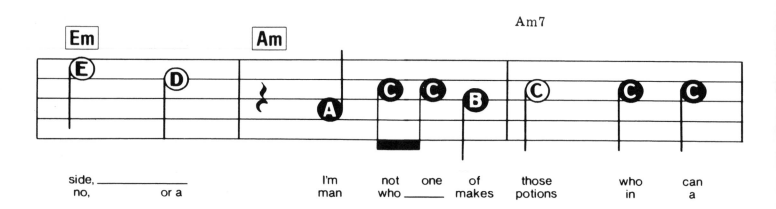

side, _____   I'm not one of those who can
no, _____ or a   man who _____ of makes potions who in a

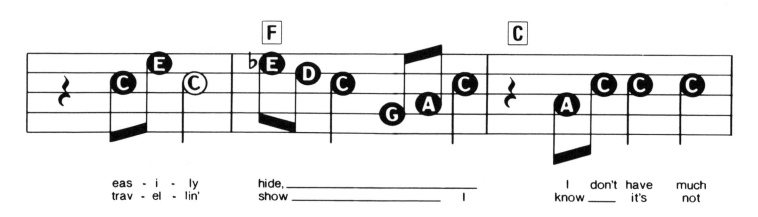

eas - i - ly hide, _____   I don't have much
trav - el - lin' show _____ I   know ____ it's not

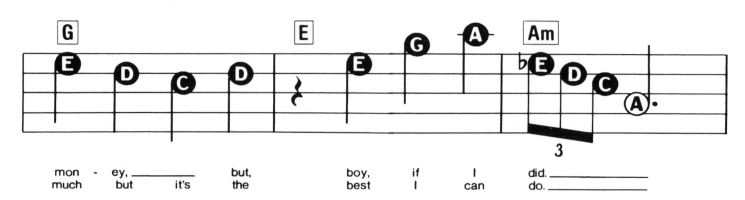

mon - ey, _____ but,   boy, if I did. _____
much but it's the   best I can do. _____

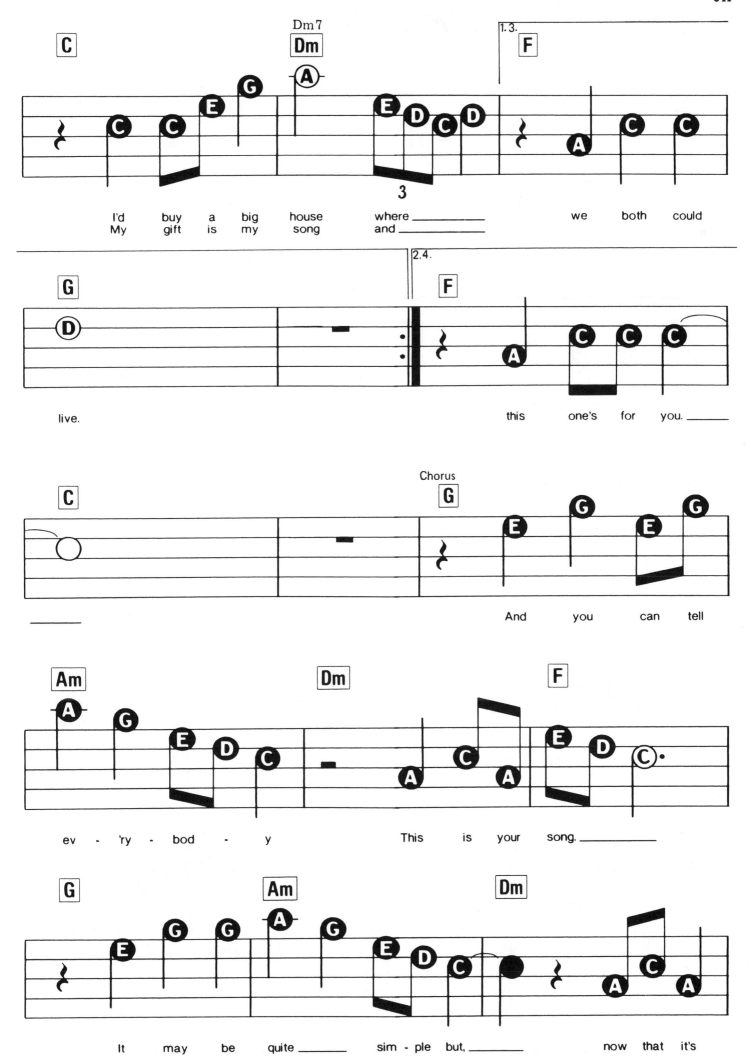

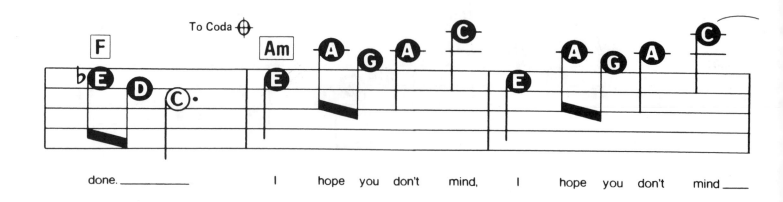

done._____ I hope you don't mind, I hope you don't mind ____

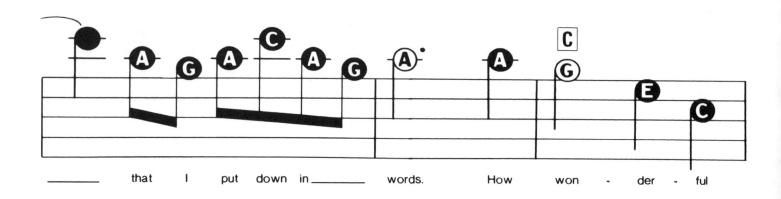

_____ that I put down in _____ words. How won - der - ful

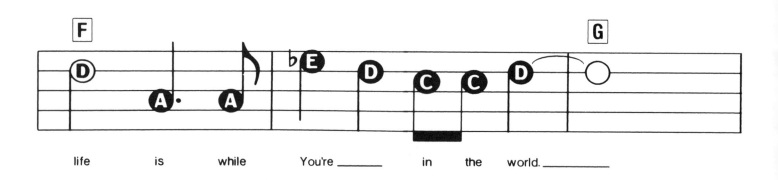

life is while You're _____ in the world. _____

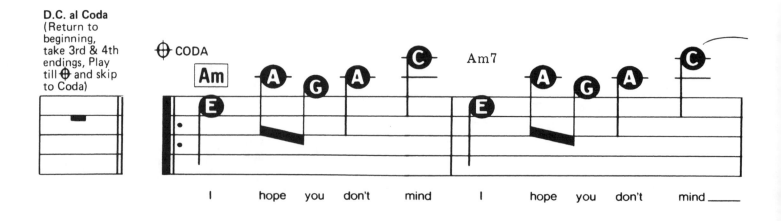

I hope you don't mind I hope you don't mind ____

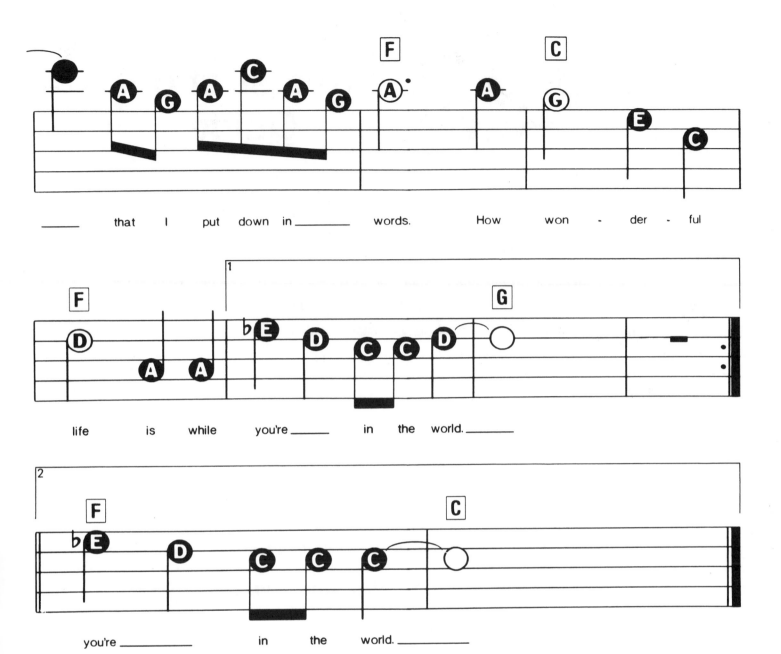

_____ that I put down in _____ words. How won - der - ful

life is while you're _____ in the world. _____

you're _____ in the world. _____

Additional Lyrics

3. I sat on the roof and kicked off the moss.
   well a few of the verses, well they've got me quite cross,
   But the sun's been quite kind while I wrote this song,
   It's for people like you that keep it turned on.

4. So excuse me forgetting but these things I do
   You see I've forgotten if they're green or they're blue,
   Anyway the thing is what I really mean
   Yours are the sweetest eyes I've ever seen.

Registration Guide

- Match the Registration number on the song to the corresponding numbered category below. Select and activate an instrumental sound available on your instrument.

- Choose an automatic rhythm appropriate to the mood and style of the song. (Consult your Owner's Guide for proper operation of automatic rhythm features.)

- Adjust the tempo and volume controls to comfortable settings.

Registration

1	Mellow	Flutes, Clarinet, Oboe, Flugel Horn, Trombone, French Horn, Organ Flutes
2	Ensemble	Brass Section, Sax Section, Wind Ensemble, Full Organ, Theater Organ
3	Strings	Violin, Viola, Cello, Fiddle, String Ensemble, Pizzicato, Organ Strings
4	Guitars	Acoustic/Electric Guitars, Banjo, Mandolin, Dulcimer, Ukulele, Hawaiian Guitar
5	Mallets	Vibraphone, Marimba, Xylophone, Steel Drums, Bells, Celesta, Chimes
6	Liturgical	Pipe Organ, Hand Bells, Vocal Ensemble, Choir, Organ Flutes
7	Bright	Saxophones, Trumpet, Mute Trumpet, Synth Leads, Jazz/Gospel Organs
8	Piano	Piano, Electric Piano, Honky Tonk Piano, Harpsichord, Clavi
9	Novelty	Melodic Percussion, Wah Trumpet, Synth, Whistle, Kazoo, Perc. Organ
10	Bellows	Accordion, French Accordion, Mussette, Harmonica, Pump Organ, Bagpipes